The Kingdom of Insignificance

The Kingdom of Insignificance

MIRON BIAŁOSZEWSKI AND THE QUOTIDIAN, THE QUEER, AND THE TRAUMATIC

Joanna Niżyńska

NORTHWESTERN UNIVERSITY PRESS / EVANSTON, ILLINOIS

Northwestern University Press
www.nupress.northwestern.edu

This book has been published with the support of the Andrew W. Mellon Foundation.

Printed in the United States of America

10 9 8 7 6 5 4 3 2 1

Library of Congress Cataloging-in-Publication Data

Niżyńska, Joanna.
The kingdom of insignificance : Miron Białoszewski and the quotidian, the queer, and the traumatic / Joanna Niżyńska.
p. cm.
Includes bibliographical references.
ISBN 978-0-8101-2846-0 (cloth : alk. paper)
1. Białoszewski, Miron—Criticism and interpretation. 2. Psychic trauma in literature. 3. Homosexuality in literature. I. Title.
PG7161.I2Z78 2012
891.858703—dc23

2012022495

♾ The paper used in this publication meets the minimum requirements of the American National Standard for Information Sciences—Permanence of Paper for Printed Library Materials, ANSI Z39.48-1992.

Rodzicom i Dziadkom

Contents

Acknowledgments

Writing a book takes a village, and I owe thanks to many people on both sides of the Atlantic.

My colleagues in the Department of Slavic Languages and Literatures at Harvard have supported me academically, institutionally, and otherwise, and I would like to thank all of them here: Jonathan Bolton, Svetlana Boym, Julie Buckler, Michael Flier, George Grabowicz, John Malmstad, Stephanie Sandler, William Mills Todd III, and Justin Weir. Judy Klasson and Stuart Robbins-Butcher have offered superb administrative assistance. I am also thankful to the institutions at Harvard for their financial support during my sabbatical leaves, particularly a John F. Cogan Junior Faculty Leave Grant from the Davis Center for Russian and Eurasian Studies and the Dean's Fund for Faculty Research.

Joanna Epstein, a bibliographer responsible for the Polish collection at Harvard's Widener Library, has been patiently responding to my bibliographic requests. Anna Sobolewska and Justyna Sobolewska years ago in Warsaw gave me copies of their private sound recordings of Białoszewski and showed me the Białoszewski memorabilia on Hoża Street. I thank them for their hospitality and for creating for me a meaningful encounter with Białoszewski's world early in my explorations.

I owe thanks to my advisors at the University of California, Los Angeles. Their teaching has remained a source of inspiration throughout the years. I am particularly grateful to Roman Koropeckyj for his stimulating perspective on Polish literature, which he conveyed with his inimitable wit; to Kenneth Reinhard, whose "theory" seminars and the Lacanian "links" and his generosity as a teacher have influenced me in more ways than he will ever know; to Samuel Weber, for his fascinating take on cultural criticism and philosophy and his attentiveness to every question asked; and to Stephen Yenser, who introduced me to American poetry and in turn influenced the way I read Polish works. Last, but not least, I owe a debt of gratitude to Katherine King and Ross Shideler. They were my unfailing supporters in academic and life matters. Without them, I would not be where I am.

Different parts and various drafts of this book found magnanimous readers in Bożena Shallcross, of the University of Chicago, who supported this project from its inception; Bożena Karwowska, of the University of British Columbia, who dedicated many hours to discussing its theoretical framework; and Ryszard Nycz, of the Jagiellonian University, whose endorsement of my approach to Białoszewski provided much-needed encouragement. Two anonymous reviewers for Northwestern University Press offered extensive and insightful comments on the manuscript. I am immensely grateful to Stephanie Sandler and Jonathan Bolton for their patient and precise criticism, and for their continuous support throughout the long process of writing and revising this book.

I thank Mike Levine of Northwestern University Press, for having faith in this project, and Gianna Mosser, for her diligence in getting the manuscript ready. Throughout my work, I relied on William Myers and Kristen Ebert-Wagner, whose editorial skills and dedication went a great deal beyond fixing deficiencies of my non-native English. I also would like to acknowledge Peter Schertz, who was a careful editor in the earliest stage of my work.

I greatly appreciate the assistance of Philip Redko, a doctoral student at Harvard's Slavic Department, with fine-tuning the translations of Białoszewski's passages incorporated in this book to better convey the colloquial flair of the original. Phil's poetic ear and sensitivity to Białoszewski's diction has been invaluable especially in the case of my own literal renderings of Białoszewski's unique language.

I have been fortunate to have brilliant interlocutors. Whether in academic settings or around kitchen tables, I have had a chance to discuss my work with Tamara Trojanowska, Przemysław Czapliński and Ewa Guderian-Czaplińska, Bożena Keff, Tomasz Bilczewski, Błażej Warkocki, Hanna Gosk, Marek Zaleski, William Martin, and many others. I cannot list them all here, but I hope that they all know the depth of my gratitude.

My graduate students from the seminar "Białoszewski: The Art of Private Life" made me wish I had had a chance to teach them when I first started to work on Białoszewski. For all of them, *Pamiętnik z powstania warszawskiego* was the first book they read in Polish from cover to cover, and accompanying them on their challenging but passionate journey through the idiosyncrasies of Białoszewski's language generated a welcome burst of energy for the conclusion of the project.

My friends in greater Boston provided me with hot meals when I had no time to cook, child care when I had to delegate my maternal duties, and psychological support as often as it was needed. I am grateful to Liiz Rahman and her family, Cecil Adderley, Joy and Justin Weir, Mike Flier and David Trueblood, Serge Roy and Ania Śmietanko, Alex Luis, Lori Jackson, Maria

Bradley, Stasia Wojewodzic, Campbell Ellsworth and Natalia Bard, Gray Fisher, Anu Nanda, and Olga Friedman. Kristin Kopp, my academic collaborator on other projects and a sounding board in all matters, has always been just a phone call away. I cannot imagine my work without her friendship.

Finally, this book would not be possible without the unwavering love and support of my family. My daughter, Sophia, proves that a generous spirit and a sense of empathy do not require two digits in age. My sister, Maria Niżyńska, and my parents have always been willing to fly across the ocean to provide relief whenever I raised the white flag. My close and extended family in Poland (Poznań, Gdańsk, Lwów, Szczecin . . .) does not share my everyday, but witnesses my life nevertheless. They know what their presence means to me. This book is dedicated to my parents, Aleksandra and Zdzisław Niżyńscy, and to the memory of my maternal and paternal grandparents. Their lives have inspired my work.

Fragments of chapter 2 appeared as "The Something More of 'Almost Nothing': Miron Białoszewski's Kairotic Everyday," in *New Perspectives on Polish Culture: Private Encounters, Public Affairs*, ed. Tamara Trojanowska, Artur Płaczkiewicz, Agnieszka Polakowska, and Olga Ponichtera (New York: PIASA, 2012), 130–42.

Passages from chapter 3 were published in "Traumatyczny, codzienny, queer: 'Znaleziony list' Mirona Białoszewskiego," in *(Nie)obecność: Pominięcia i przemilczenia w narracjach XX wieku* (*Non-Presence: Gaps and Silences in 20th Century Polish Narrations*), ed. Hanna Gosk and Bożena Karwowska, Seria prac zakładu literatury polskiej XX wieku Instytutu Literatury Polskiej Uniwersytetu Warszawskiego (Warsaw: Dom wydawniczy Elipsa, 2008), 272–91.

Author's Note

Page numbers following Polish quotations of Miron Białoszewski's work refer to the multivolume edition of his collected works (*Utwory Zebrane* [Warsaw: Państwowy Instytut Wydawniczy, 1987–]). My abbreviations of titles refer to Białoszewski's individual works contained in this edition rather than to the group titles of the volumes. In my discussion of *Pamiętnik z powstania warszawskiego*, I quote Madeline Levine's translation (*A Memoir of the Warsaw Uprising*, 1977), which has been modified (with Philip Redko's help) for the purposes of my analysis. Białoszewski's early poetry is quoted from Andrzej Busza and Bogdan Czaykowski's translations (*The Revolution of Things: Selected Poems*, 1974). All other translations are mine.

The Kingdom of Insignificance

Introduction

Playing Out Life in the Everyday: The Quotidian, the Queer, and the Traumatic

> Ważne są wszystkie szczególiki, bo inaczej
> nie będzie to nasycone . . . Bez tego jest tylko
> literatura, aforyzm, brak człowieka.
>
> Every little detail is important otherwise
> the writing's not saturated . . . Without this
> saturation there is only literature, aphorism,
> absence of the human.
> —Miron Białoszewski, "Szacunek dla każdego
> drobiazgu," interview (1971)

WHEN IMAGINING THE TASK of explaining what makes Miron Białoszewski a great poet, Michał Głowiński playfully lays out the main challenges of Białoszewski's work:

> Białoszewski is a fascinating phenomenon because of his paradoxical nature. I can imagine talking to a foreigner who never read anything by Białoszewski and telling him or her that Białoszewski was a great poet. But if you skip his early poems such as "Merry-Go-Round with Madonnas" ("Karuzela z madonnami")[1] or *A Memoir of the Warsaw Uprising* (*Pamiętnik z powstania warszawskiego*), which is a separate thing, what was this Białoszewski really writing about? That Malina came over and that Ania said this and Agnieszka said that, and that he went to Garwolin, and that he bought something . . . Those who don't know his writing and rely only on a summary would think that he's like, I'm not sure, like Wiech?[2] In any case, he could be taken for someone who simply describes everyday life, for some columnist for an ordinary paper. And it is a bit like this. Białoszewski was a writer who, at some point of his career, did not go beyond the everyday, beyond the prosaic life, which is not worth describing. A respected writer should reject it in a Romantic gesture. But such is the paradox of Białoszewski—in his work this everyday doesn't stop being the everyday, but it simultaneously becomes something more. He plays out life in this everyday.[3]

Głowiński's assessment is correct: there is something suspiciously simple in Białoszewski's writing. It is saturated with scenes of daily life: conversations overheard on the street, recollections of dreams, descriptions of flowers bought at the market, musings on the bus, observations of his favorite tree in front of his window, remarks on friends' visits, and myriad insignificant happenings. All this simplicity and yet, almost three decades since the writer's death in 1983, Białoszewski's voice resonates in Polish culture stronger than ever, still fresh and unmistakably his own.

Miron Białoszewski (1922–1983) wrote poetry, prose, and theatrical plays. Often, he invented his own poetico-prosaic genres whose playful names were to suggest that they emerge from specific situations and observations, such as his cycles of "mini-trances" ("transiki"), "hums" ("szumy"), and "walking diaries" ("spacerowniki"). The majority of Białoszewski's works are written in a language that reenacts colloquial speech, the most recognizable feature of his aesthetics. He was interested in orality from the time of his acclaimed poetry debut, the volume *Obroty rzeczy* (*The Revolution of Things*) in 1956, and he continued to explore the colloquial through his subsequent poetry volumes, from *Rachunek zachciankowy* (1959; *Calculus of Whims*) and *Mylne wzruszenia* (1961; *Misdirected Sentiments*) up until his most radical *Było and było* (1965; *There Was and There Was*), a volume in which the traditional determinants of poetic diction disappear in the mimicry of speech articulation. *Było and było* was a failure in the eyes of the critics, but Białoszewski redeemed himself with *Pamiętnik z powstania warszawskiego* (1970; *A Memoir of the Warsaw Uprising*), the work that brought him critical recognition and a popular readership. In the *Memoir*, in which he recounts the Warsaw Uprising of 1944, Białoszewski showcased all his poetic devices, but this time a historical referent was clear, and Białoszewski's linguistic idiosyncrasies were cast in a new light even for an uninitiated reader. The performative aspect of the *Memoir* owed a great deal to Białoszewski's theatrical experience; throughout the 1950s and early 1960s, he wrote avant-garde plays and acted in them, although his collective theatrical works were not published until 1971 under the title *Teatr Osobny: 1955–1963* (*The Separate Theater: 1955–1963*).

After the *Memoir* and until his death, Białoszewski wrote the "small narrations," also known as "life-writing," a series of works in which he represents a narrator who bears the name of his author and surrounds himself with a supporting cast of characters bearing the names of Białoszewski's own friends and family members. The dozen-some volumes of the small narrations—from the opening volume, *Donosy rzeczywistości* (1973; *Reporting Reality*) to the recently published *Chamowo* (2009; *Chamowo*)—have the form of diary-like entries, in which Białoszewski presents an autobiographical narrator and stresses the sense of "here and now." As Białoszewski returned to writing poetry at the end of the 1970s, some volumes of the small narrations contain poetic cycles, including his "cabaret" cycle, *Kabaret Kici-Koci* (*The Cabaret of Kicia-Kocia*).

It has been a matter of critical contention whether all of Białoszewski's post-*Memoir* works can be subsumed under the category of the small narrations; their combination of the poetic and the prosaic prevents a definite categorization of genre; they also differ significantly in length, from short vignettes to a several-page-long story. All of them are preoccupied with the representation of experience from the leveling perspective of the everyday; no particular event changes the style of narration: for Białoszewski's narrator, traveling to Garwolin (a small town in the suburbs of Warsaw) is as stimulating as his journey to New York.

The philosopher Stanley Cavell wrote that Thoreau's *Walden* "means in every word it says" and "is fully sensible of its mysteries and fully open about them."[4] Białoszewski's everyday turns this openness into a paradox of accessibility and elusiveness. Resilient to critical attempts to define its puzzling quality, Białoszewski's life-writing, too, means every word it says and offers the promise of full exposure; nevertheless, it resists our efforts to formulate questions and to identify the source of its revelatory quality. Some critics have associated this revelatory quality with an epiphanic tradition—the notion that the inexpressible manifests itself in the banality of everyday experience.[5] Others, like Głowiński, localized the striking quality of Białoszewski's writing in his commitment to the reenactment of colloquial orality; as Głowiński put it, "the everyday for [Białoszewski] is a form of speech."[6] This reenactment may have been aided by Białoszewski's performances of his writing; whether he shared his works with a circle of close friends or read his work in public, Białoszewski's acting skills allowed him to emphasize the theatricality of his writing. In the 1970s his creative process often involved reading his works into a recording device and listening to himself read before revising the text for publication. Close to the elemental force of spoken language, life-writing presents a literature that is constituted by jotted-down notes "on the go," meant to be received as unfinished, rough, and outside of any genre norms. No other writer in postwar Polish literature equals Białoszewski in his consistent vision of literature as *energeia*—an open-ended process of creation—rather than *ergon*, a self-contained work.

Due largely to problems involving translation rights after the writer's death, Białoszewski has been known to English-speaking aficionados of Eastern European (or Central European) literature only from translations that were published during his life. Madeline Levine's 1977 translation of *A Memoir of the Warsaw Uprising* and Andrzej Busza and Bogdan Czaykowski's small anthology of Białoszewski's early poems, *The Revolution of Things*, published in 1974, give only a taste of Białoszewski's idiom.[7] The recent and long-awaited release of the rights by the writer's executor, and the interest of leading translators from Polish in Białoszewski's work, should soon bear fruit and finally introduce English-speaking audiences to a writer who represents an alternative to mainstream Polish literature.

I focus mainly on *A Memoir of the Warsaw Uprising* and on these small narrations, which convey the first-person perspective and contain many biographical details reminiscent of Białoszewski's life. These works, I believe, are emblematic of his construction of the everyday—the sphere that in its repeatability resists thematization—as a domain of the fullness of life. Yet, this life is full of paradoxes. It encompasses the sphere of the traumatic, but the traumatic of a peculiar quality, in which even the extreme reality—as that of the Warsaw Uprising—is represented as quotidian. At the same time, it is through the subtle, most often non-thematized, presence of traumatic memories that Białoszewski's writing of the everyday acquires its own eventfulness. To add to this, the life-writing takes place in alternative families, in which gender roles and relations are destabilized and yet which evade critical labels proposed by gay and queer studies.

In Polish culture, whose preoccupation with history diminished the receptivity to the everyday, Białoszewski's life-writing remains a puzzling phenomenon: it is both a self-contained work that also stands at the very center of new possibilities for Polish literature. Białoszewski has been enjoying a great posthumous career in post-Communist Poland. During his lifetime, he was a cult writer, albeit an acquired taste, for a steady following of loyal readers and critics. He gained a wider recognition after the *Memoir* was published, but his image was always of someone withdrawn into his own niche (about which more in a moment). A steady upsurge of interest in Białoszewski suggests that his work is playing a vital role in the search for new languages and identities in the post-1989 period. It is often claimed, and rightfully so, that Białoszewski "privatized" the Polish language through his consistent transposition of the qualities of colloquial speech into a set of stylistic devices that defy the traditional binaries of "high/low," "spoken/written," "colloquial/literary." Their linguistic singularities and flair are unmistakably "Białoszewskian," and some of the best writers of the young generation prove themselves as careful readers of Białoszewski's idiom. Their works, in turn, open up new horizions for the reception of Białoszewski. A great stimulus for the critics of Białoszewski was, for instance, the publication in 2005 of Michał Witkowski's best-selling queer novel *Lubiewo* (*Lovetown*), whose incorporation of an extensive passage from Białoszewski's small narrations generated a new set of questions about the ways Białoszewski's representation of homosexuality can be contextualized (and intertextualized) in contemporary Polish culture. The long-awaited publication of Białoszewski's private diaries in February 2012 has created another path to explore the phenomenon of Białoszewski's writing and its still-underexamined potential.

But, Białoszewski will also be a striking addition to what might be called the transatlantic canon of Polish literature. By "transatlantic canon," I mean the corpus of literary works that circulates in the North American cultural sphere and is considered by the English-speaking audience to be representative of Polish literature.[8] This canon is subject to political and economic considerations that drive the market for translations, changes in the educational curriculum that render some authors more desirable than others, and, ultimately, a cultural tendency to reinforce rather than challenge the familiar understandings of foreign literatures. Białoszewski challenges such understandings as he resists being incorporated into the categories of Polish writers who have gained recognition with an English-speaking audience. He does not belong to the group of well-known writers of the war and the Holocaust (such as Jerzy Kosiński, Tadeusz Borowski, Hanna Krall, and Henryk Grynberg), although his *Memoir* is a fascinating testimony of a survivor. He also cannot be aligned with the most popular Cold War category of Polish literature known as the "poetry of witness," meditating on history, particularly on the entanglement of the individual in political regimes. The theme of poetry witnessing dramatic historical moments, the elevated position of the writer struggling between an ethical imperative of solidarity with humankind and an individual desire for solitude, has long been associated with Polish authors such as Zbigniew Herbert, Tadeusz Różewicz, Tadeusz Konwicki, Sławomir Mrożek, Adam Zagajewski, and, most of all, the towering figure of Czesław Miłosz.[9] The wide spectrum of artistic pursuits and formal qualities of these poets, playwrights, and novelists should complicate this dominant perception; nevertheless, the image of the entire region of Central Europe as, in Milan Kundera's famous formulation, "the kidnapped conscience of the West," has weighed greatly on Polish literature's ability to diversify its portfolio in the eyes of a foreign audience. It remains to be seen whether the new generation of post-Communist writers who entered the international literary scene in English translation in the 1990s and 2000s will affect the status quo.

Białoszewski was an uncloseted homosexual writer who spent his entire life in Communist, homophobic Poland, and who for much of his career remained on the margins of the culture. If some form of dissent was necessarily a condition of his life, this dissent challenges what we usually associate with ideas of political and ethical resistance. Białoszewski's life-writing from the 1970s and early 1980s portrays the private and domestic spheres as if they could exist outside of political determinations. History and politics cross the threshold of what is constructed in life-writing as the domestic circle, but they do so lightly and surreptitiously, as if the author did not wish for his reader to notice their presence. It is perhaps for this reason that Białoszewski is frequently described as the "most private" author of Polish literature. Although privacy is never a purely private affair, least of all for writers, it is important to receive Białoszewski's legacy on its own terms. His work reflects neither the Western gaze on Polish literature nor Poland's self-image. It stands apart from the canon on both sides of the Atlantic.

It is worth emphasizing that the transatlantic canon that organizes Polish literature under a broad label of "ethics and poetics"[10] is, in some sense, a distilled version of what Poles have considered to be their culture's driving force for some two centuries. Poland's national paradigm—its metanarrative, in the Lyotardian sense of a narrative that organizes communal imagination and reinforces its self-image—has been overwhelmingly Romantic. The Romantic tradition's enduring career was launched by the loss of independence in 1795, and from the early eighteenth century until today, Romanticism has continued to influence Poles' collective imagination. It overrode earlier cultural formations (to mention only the Sarmatian tradition) and became formative for Poland's understanding of its national identity. Literature was to be the "conscience of the nation," probing and symbolically compensating collective wounds. Often its main task was to alleviate unquantifiable losses—of population, territory, heritage—and to transform them into a sense of communal identity.

Poland's misfortunes were, indeed, numerous. The loss of political sovereignty in 1795 followed by 123 years of domination by foreign powers, punctuated by two bloody uprisings in 1831 and 1863, finally led to independence at the end of World War I. The twenty-year period of independence and rebuilding was interrupted by the outbreak of World War II and followed by the horrors of the Nazi and Soviet division of Poland in 1939, the Holocaust, bloodbaths in the country's ethnically mixed borderlands, and, finally, by the post-Yalta territorial surgeries which moved one third of the Polish territory westward. This was accompanied by another loss of sovereignty, this time to the Soviet Union, which bargained with the Allies to keep Poland as its "satellite country." Polish literature and its place in the life of Polish society emerge from such history, and the cultural transmission and posthumous life of the Romantic paradigm are inextricably linked to it.

I use the expression "posthumous life" because, to a great extent, the Romantic paradigm has been detached from the complexities and richness of the Romantic period (in Polish literature falling roughly between 1822 and 1863) from which it originally sprang. The Romantic paradigm organized Polish literary and public language as a set of communally recognizable topoi, and it served as a compensatory mechanism for political failures and historical traumas. In its most simplistic, albeit most persistent form, it fetishized suffering, elevated Polish fate to the status of martyrology, and often promoted self-congratulatory patriotism. Its force as a meta-narrative manifested itself in moments of social effervescence; a century after it was over as a cultural period, it continued to shape Polish history. Thus, the Warsaw Uprising of 1944 and the Solidarity Movement of 1980 were both understood in relation to nineteenth-century Romantic uprisings against the partitioning powers. The Romantic paradigm owed its longevity to its flexibility. It could function regardless of the changing political circumstances: it suited nineteenth-century nationalists seeking to maintain the vitality of Polish culture in the absence of the Polish state as well as postwar Communists seeking to rally Poles to a new national ideal under the traditional guise of service to the nation. Sometimes it was noble, sometimes kitschy. Sometimes it was reinforced by periods of genuine oppression (such as the Nazi occupation), sometimes it was simply rejected (as in the short period of independence in interwar Poland), and sometimes it was mocked in gestures of cultural self-reflexivity (Witold Gombrowicz's anti-Romantic provocations are just one example). In all cases, however, the Romantic paradigm remained the ever-present reference point for Polish national and cultural identity.

The greatest trap of the Romantic paradigm, which became clear to Poles themselves, was constructing a national identity by valorizing the position of the victim as, to use Sandoval's words, "epistemologically privileged."[11] The heritage of Romantic Messianism, condensed in Adam Mickiewicz's famous line "Poland is the Messiah of all nations," found its reflection in a perception of historical suffering as a source of national identity and moral superiority. Such a self-image allowed little room for growth and change. Sławomir Mrożek, a postwar playwright, mocked this self-image in the play *Moniza Clavier* (1963), a biting satire directed at East and West alike. His Eastern European hero, feeling inadequate when interacting with the glamorous Westerners, resorts to presenting himself "not as an individual, but as a representative of an insulted society. As the son of a northern nation, austere, severely tried by history, with its distinct character, with its particular wisdom dearly paid for, inaccessible to others."[12] Mrożek satirizes the oppressive nature of Polish collective identity, which colonizes individual impulses; his hero, full of "Polish complexes," lacks sufficient symbolic capital to construct an alternative identity. Yet, his best option for hiding his Eastern European barbarism is to offer exactly what the Western audience expects from him: a display of ostensible suffering attesting to a "particular wisdom" inaccessible to others, in this case to those from the other side of the Iron Curtain.[13] For Mrożek, the cultural tendency to conflate the individual and the collective is grotesque; he mocks the Romantic paradigm with its central notion of redemptive suffering. By the same token, his very choice to satirize this paradigm showcases its ubiquity.

Białoszewski is a rare voice from outside the Romantic paradigm.

He disengaged from it by constructing the project of life-writing, in which countless events of everyday life are reenacted in the cadences and tones of oral delivery.[14] Unlike the literature of moral dissent, in which the ordinary merely encodes the political, Białoszewski's everyday is not a backdrop for conveying something else; ultimately, it does not point toward something of transcendental importance.[15] When Białoszewski represents a domestic space, he also positions it as alternative to the public sphere and by doing so implies a new set of political questions. This space, however, is worlds apart from a traditional representation of domesticity as an "underground home culture," a private sphere and simultaneously a revolutionary space in which to debate Polish fate in "the compatriots' nighttime conversations," to use Mickiewicz's expression.

Polish culture has found it challenging to integrate Białoszewski's project into its symbolic vocabulary. The institutional standing of Białoszewski's writing is symptomatic in this regard. Since he has been critically acclaimed, some of his works are included as required readings in Polish gymnasium and lyceum (middle and high school), but which ones is telling.[16] *A Memoir of the Warsaw Uprising*, Białoszewski's idiosyncratic take on the literary testimony of this iconic event in Polish history, is most frequently included. The *Memoir* is a counternarrative to numerous literary accounts of the uprising, which tend to replicate the Romantic paradigm. To teach the *Memoir* entails, then, first of all projecting its singularities upon a screen of other works on the subject. Another reading in high school curricula consists of a selection of Białoszewski's early poetry, mainly his first two volumes, which fall into the avant-garde spectrum. In these poems, the ordinary is transformed into a sphere of unexpected artistic explorations; in the avant-garde idiom, Białoszewski elevates the objects of daily use, say a fork, to the status of the sacred. What is not included in the high school curricula, even though they form a major portion of Białoszewski's oeuvre, is the small narrations. I take this omission as a sign that the small narrations resist the Polish canon and its synchronic order; it also signals the challenge of putting Białoszewski 's prose in dialogue with other Polish works, simply because Białoszewski's work is unprecedented both in its scope and its consistency in attention to the everyday. The uniqueness of Białoszewski's voice in Polish literature has been a critical topos since his debut in 1956, but it has generally been refracted through the evocative metaphor of "withdrawal" coined by Janusz Sławiński in 1976. In "Białoszewski: Sukces wycofania się" ("Białoszewski: The Success of Withdrawal"), his introduction to an anthology of Białoszewski's poetry, Sławiński encapsulates the most persistent interpretation of Białoszewski's modus operandi:

> By inhabiting a kingdom of insignificance . . . Białoszewski ensures his freedom from any expectations that could interfere with his privacy; he protects

> himself from obligations that would force him to pull faces [*pozy i miny*]. Where he lives (and here I am talking about the world of his writing), there is no need to bother with requests to "participate in life"; the level of existence he claimed for himself lies beyond the immediate pressure of these sanctioned behavioral patterns—Białoszewski is not elevated by the controlling interests of others. He is free "to be a singular self" ["*być sobie jednym*"] without fighting for his singularity [*jedność*]. His autonomy is synonymous with marginality, and with consistently falling shy of the norm.[17]

Białoszewski's withdrawal from mainstream literary culture and his freedom in creating an alternative literary niche became the operative principle of his reception. This principle presupposes a synthesis of the aesthetic and the existential; it abounds in the vocabulary of agency and self-control. Białoszewski's self-distancing from public life has been time and time again expressed in terms of autonomy, authenticity, singularity, separateness, and withdrawal (*osobność, autetyczność, bycie sobie jednym*). His writing—which he himself labeled as *życiopisanie* (life-writing)—has been understood as a gestalt of life and writing that originates in his sovereign gesture of claiming his artistic and existential territory. The concept of withdrawal employed by Sławiński to indicate Białoszewski's impulse to free himself from the "sanctioned behavioral patterns" of the Polish literary scene as well as from the cultural imperative that writers serve as public intellectuals often became an all-encompassing paradigm. Withdrawal has become an integral part of the cult of the writer about whom, as his friend and critic Anna Sobolewska put it, "stories circulate in the similar manner to stories about famous tzadiks or Hasidim. What's important in these stories is not just what [the tzadiks and Hasidim] taught, but how they lived as well—the way they brew their tea or tied their shoelaces."[18] Even when surrounded by a circle of loyal friends, Białoszewski is perceived as someone who functions within his own niche. His "maximally successful existence" is conditioned by the freedom of withdrawal and withdrawal as a form of freedom.

A telling account of how Białoszewski was perceived by people who knew him emerges from a conversation between two of Białoszewski's friends. Tadeusz Sobolewski met Białoszewski in 1970 when, as a college student having read the just-published *Memoir of the Warsaw Uprising*, he knocked on the writer's door to express his admiration. He became part of the writer's circle—and one of his literary characters.[19] Olgierd Wołyński was, from 1958 to 1968, Białoszewski's next-door neighbor on Dąbrowski Square in the center of Warsaw.[20] In an interview that Wołyński gave to Sobolewski for a book of remembrances of Białoszewski (*Miron: Wspomnienia o poecie*)[21] gathered from his relatives and friends, Wołyński reacts curiously to Sobolewski's claim about the sense of security that supposedly characterized Białoszewski's immediate environment:

> Sobolewski: At Miron's one felt a sense of complete safety. . . . When Leszek [Soliński] saw us he said that we looked like a sow with piglets. It was like a family for us, a kind of home. And the important thing was that you were completely accepted.
>
> Wołyński: . . . You talk about the sense of safety you felt at Miron's. For me it was sometimes the dangers and complications of this type of life that stood out. The downstairs neighbor complained about the noise at night. The building management accused him of trashing the apartment. Some guys were banging on his door. This was not a safe place at all. One day I come home and someone had written FAGGOT on Miron's door. . . . And Leszek was painting over it. See, these are the kinds of things that I remember.
>
> Sobolewski: We knew about it. About the administration, even about the word on the door, but because we thought of him first and foremost as a writer who had already processed it all, and therefore tamed and defused it, we felt that nothing could happen to him, that he wasn't in any danger. Even the police interrogations he described to us in his own way—with a light touch. He seemed happy.[22]

We can learn much about Białoszewski's life from this interview, and I will return to it later, but it is worth signaling at this point that Sobolewski's view of the writer as a "happy" person presupposes a perception in which Białoszewski functions as a "textual/bodily being,"[23] that is, someone whose existence is read like a text, but also someone who models his life with text in mind and lives his life thinking that others will read it like a text. As a result, Białoszewski, the author of his existential narrative, is viewed as someone who "processed it all and so tamed it and defused it." But what is this "all" that gets tamed and defused? Who were the "guys" banging on the door of Białoszewski's apartment? Why was he interrogated by the police? What or who motivated the accusations from the building management? Both Sobolewski and Wołyński omit as much as they reveal. The reader of the interview senses that the two men speak primarily to those who already understand what they are talking about. Their pattern of speaking resembles, to an extent, the double gesture of Białoszewski's writing: it says everything to the knowing reader while not saying much to the "naive" reader. This double gesture is particularly striking when the theme of homosexuality is concerned, which I discuss in chapter 3. This pattern of hiding through a full exposure becomes clear only to the reader who is able to "look awry," that is, "at an angle [which shows] the thing in its clear and distinct form, in opposition to the 'straightforward' view that sees only an indistinct confusion."[24]

My main interest is neither to fill in Białoszewski's omissions and silences, nor to exhibit what is hidden in plain view. No utopian wholeness awaits us after we decode Białoszewski's self-censorship. What is worth considering, however, is the mode of reception Białoszewski asks of his reader. What kind of knowledge can we arrive at through Białoszewski's narration? How is "not-knowing" part of this knowledge, and what kind of knowledge is "not-knowing" in the first place? I take Głowiński's imaginary challenge quite literally: how can we explain the appeal of Białoszewski's writing to a "foreigner"—where "foreigner" is also meant figuratively as someone who does not have access to the works' context, whether cultural or biographical? What are the sources of the "something more" so succinctly expressed in Głowiński's phrase that in Białoszewski's work the "everyday doesn't stop being the everyday, but it simultaneously becomes something more"?

I part ways with previous approaches in that I refuse the "withdrawal" metaphor, because it a priori idealizes Białoszewski and in this way prevents us from engaging with the complexities of his "bodily" and "textual" existence. Instead, I propose to see in his writing a complex oscillation between the traumatic and the quotidian, the banal and the extreme, the sense of total disclosure and a mode of narration that denies any stable knowledge about the narrator. This oscillation is subtle and often almost imperceptible. Although my use of the word "and" (as in "the traumatic *and* the quotidian") suggests opposing qualities, I argue that what happens in Białoszewski is a fusion of the seemingly mutually exclusive that neither "and" nor "as," which connotes substitution (as in "the traumatic *as* the quotidian"), accommodates quite adequately. The three chapters of this book explore through the lenses of trauma, everyday, and queer how these paradoxes function in Białoszewski's writing, and how their cumulative effect contributes to the quality of the "something more" in Białoszewski's writing.

RECONFIGURING THE AUTOBIOGRAPHICAL PACT

Białoszewski presents us with a puzzling regulatory fiction, by which I mean a certain view of reality that naturalizes its own pattern to such an extent that these patterns cease to bear any traces of strangeness, and instead seem natural and inevitable. In the small narrations, the reader becomes acquainted with the narrator's reality, and with each consecutive volume the relationship strengthens between the narrator and the reader. Although Białoszewski's narration is full of tensions, incongruities, and ruptures between qualities that seem mutually exclusive (such as the traumatic and the everyday), they disappear from the reader's field of vision, and the reader experiences a smooth narration, building a unified story from Białoszewski's fragments. I believe that Białoszewski's consistent use of the narratorial "I" and his autobiographical "signature," and, first of all, his narrator's ongoing "performance" of the quotidian neutralize narrative ruptures, those moments when the reader could be asked to confront something singular (i.e., something "resisting calculation" and, thus, by definition subversive). They disappear not because they are encoded in, for instance, a system of hermetic cultural references, but because they create a coherent and tight "code of obviousness," in which the non-normative and the normative perfectly blend together in a non-hierarchical, horizontal manner. Through this horizontal exposure, what could strike us as subversive becomes naturalized. Białoszewski's series becomes a norm sui generis; the reader is "always displaced—the one who knows and the one who doesn't."[25]

My discussion focuses on *A Memoir of the Warsaw Uprising* (1970) and the small narrations, though I refer to Białoszewski's earlier (pre-*Memoir*) poetry and theater as well as to his later poetry and "cabaret" (written in the late 1970s and early 1980s). I focus on the small narrations because I am interested in the way Białoszewski constructs his narrator and the modes of knowing—and not-knowing—that the reader gets from such construction. I treat the *Memoir*, often considered an exception in Białoszewski's oeuvre as the only work in which Białoszewski addresses a historical event, as the very center of gravity in his writing. The *Memoir* is a dividing point between Białoszewski's early poetry and his later prose, but Białoszewski's attention to the quotidian in his life-writing is inseparable from the *Memoir*'s testimony on the traumatic everyday of the Warsaw Uprising.

Białoszewski's life-writing eludes the criteria of traditional autobiography and becomes its own genre according to the etymological and literal take on life-writing—*bios*, or "life," and *graphein*, "to write"—as writing about life, writing with life, and life as writing.[26] Yet, Białoszewski encourages his reader to approach life-writing within the autobiographical horizon. Throughout the small narrations, the mode of first-person narration, the use of the present tense, and the employment of dates and biographical realia lead the reader to assume that the narrator is Białoszewski himself. But this identification does not follow the "autobiographical pact," famously formulated by Philippe Lejeune, in which the text promises to reveal to the reader a self-evident and self-sufficient "truth" about the author.[27] With Białoszewski, we are too aware of the figurative nature of language and how utopian is such a proposition of autobiographical mimesis. In this sense, even Głowiński's claim that since *Było i było* (1965; *There Was and There Was*), "the majority of Białoszewski's writing constitutes one immense intimate crypto-diary" is too straightforward an identification of Białoszewski-the-author with "Białoszewski"-the-narrator.[28] It also builds on an assumption of priority and causality: it assumes that the writer's life leads straightforwardly into his work—while in Białoszewski's case both writing and theatricalized life are mutually interdependent and constitute what some critics called "the project of existence" ("project egzystencji"). We must always remember that the "autobiographical" self of Białoszewski's life-writing is illusory, imbued with a sense of distance and irony with respect to its own textual status and with awareness of Białoszewski's multiple levels of semiotization. The way Białoszewski repeats his writer's "signature" creates a peculiar effect, in which the repetitions do not add up to some total cumulative value, that is, they do not lead to the progressive emergence of a "full" narratorial self. Rather, every "Miron" seems to confirm the one whom we already think we know. Białoszewski's narrator consistently "creates his own image[,] adding new scenes to the spectacle played in front of the reader. These new images carry within themselves memory about their previous incarnations [and] form a kind of palimpsest."[29] This palimpsestic mechanism is particularly visible in the small narrations, in which the "seriality" of the works facilitates and forms a sustained relationship of learning between the text and the reader. Each new volume is constantly teaching the reader how to read the whole. All the small narrations share a number of features that gradually train the reader how to perceive the series: for example, Białoszewski reduces the distance between the time of the event and the time of writing, and the distance between the teller and the told, which creates an effect of immediacy, as if speech were being reenacted in writing. Further, the narrator's attention is horizontal, that is, every quotidian event seems equally important. As the narrator accumulates details in his drive for accuracy, it is as if the reader were accompanying him in his daily activities. Although every volume of the small narrations has its own thematic preoccupations and differs from its predecessor, the repetition of "Miron's" performance has a homogenizing effect. The reader presupposes that the series is unified by the subjectivity who "keeps staging his words, building an image of 'Miron Białoszewski' that is partly real, partly fictional (but is immediately incorporated into the sphere of the poet's artistic personality)."[30] Thus, Białoszewski consistently trains his readers to make a mental leap between the textual fragment and the imaginary whole and to incorporate every episode of the small narrations into the larger project of "life-writing." As a result of this mental operation, regardless of changes and variations, consecutive volumes of the small narrations constitute a regulatory fiction according to which the reader knows the narrator.

By regulatory fiction I am referring not so much to the characteristics of the text itself as I am to the intersection of textual qualities and the reading experience. Two things happen at this intersection. First of all, every textual performance contributes to the further integration of "Miron Białoszewski"—"partly fictional, partly real"—into the Gestalt of life-writing. The seriality of life-writing creates a sense of an all-embracing project through which the reader in regulated and consistent ways accumulates knowledge about the narrator's world. In the process of building a sense of intimacy with "Miron," who in a consistent yet variegated pattern repeats his performance of the Mironian quotidian, this quotidian becomes, in turn, naturalized for the reader. Białoszewski acclimatizes readers to the text and consequently leads them to overlook its inconsistencies as well as its subversive charge. In fact, Białoszewski's performance of the quotidian is fluid and unstable and creates a disjunction between what the reader receives as the author's projected self-knowledge and the very possibility of a stable interpretation. The very seriality of the small narrations on the one hand integrates the diversity of Białoszewski's writing while on the other suggests open-endedness and undermines the self-sufficiency that is characteristic of individual volumes. The text seems to promise a self-contained "truth" about its author, but keeps breaking the promise; the narrator keeps inviting the reader into his "private" world, but then frustrates every attempt to grasp anything certain about himself. The same narrator who maximalistically postulates that he will "write everything" ("spiszę wszystko")[31] in fact subtly and carefully circumscribes his reader's field of vision.

The greatest challenge in reading Białoszewski is thus to avoid two extremes. One is to avoid biographical mimetism by looking at Białoszewski's writing in a bio-chronological way and for a source of information on his life. At one end of the spectrum is, hence, the intentional fallacy, the idea of authorial intention controlling the meaning of the work. On the other end, we have a post-structuralist discussion of the tropological character of literature, in which the constant doubling of subject/object; creating/being created; "I"/"not I"; and the permeability of binaries of writing/living and written/lived (à la de Man and Derrida) dismisses the very possibility of biography. Neither of these extremes presents an adequate way to read Białoszewski's work. No work springs from one author only—if by "one author" we understand a unified creative self whose essence reveals itself to us through his writing—and Białoszewski's autobiographical project asks for multiple paradigms of selfhood and authorship. At the same time, to know about Białoszewski's biography—for instance, about his homosexuality—and, first of all, to know how this biography was unfolding in his specific cultural and political context is a condition sine qua non to understand the complexity of Białoszewski's project. The biographical aspect of Białoszewski's writing cannot be disregarded, and yet it needs a different model of biography, one that (in the spirit of Ann Jefferson's "expressive biographism")[32] would not be afraid to appreciate the dependencies of Białoszewski's writing on his life or even make his writing more intelligible by pointing out these dependencies. Most of all, such a different model would point out our presuppositions and the categories of knowledge we engage when analyzing Białoszewski's life-writing and how the modification of these categories may change our understanding of the role of the biographical in literature as such.

I will examine some of the contradictions and ruptures in Białoszewski's writing and show why and how they have been occluded in the categories of reading that dominated Białoszewski's reception in Poland. My focus is on Białoszewski's representation of the war and of himself as narrator-survivor; equally important for me is his status as a homosexual writer who in his construction of the everyday is not as invested in betraying or occluding the homophobic culture that contextualizes his writing as he is in circumventing the gender and sexual normatives and subverting them in his own alternative communities. As I examine how Białoszewski refigures, refracts, and reconstitues "Białoszewski" in his work, it becomes clear that neither a seamless connection between life and literature nor the hyper-tropologism of post-structuralism can adequately address a complex dynamics between his life and life-writing. To explore this "in-between" territory of Białoszewski's writing presents both a great challenge and a great opportunity. It asks us to reclaim the complexities of Białoszewski's freedom, too often treated as a self-explanatory fact or, at least, as a fact that exists outside of specific historical delineations; it intensifies a need for interpretive self-reflection on our categories of knowledge, which often presuppose different binaries to smooth over the rough edges of Białoszewski's writing; finally, it urges us to retrieve the full potential of Białoszewski's ethical claims—his reimaging of the cultural place of the extreme and the everyday experience, and of the communities in which these experiences take place.

THE TRAUMATIC, THE QUOTIDIAN, AND THE QUEER IN BIAŁOSZEWSKI'S LIFE-WRITING

This book explores the dynamics of seemingly mutually exclusive narrative and stylistic strategies in Białoszewski's writing. I examine these dynamics in three major thematic categories: the traumatic, the everyday, and the queer. In "The Glaring Identity of 'Now': *A Memoir of the Warsaw Uprising* as a Reenactment of the Traumatic" (chapter 1), I use the framework of trauma studies to discuss how Białoszewski reenacts traumatic testimony and how he simultaneously obfuscates the radicality of his narration. "Something More from Almost Nothing: The Paradoxes of Białoszewski's Life-Writing" (chapter 2) discusses the saturation of the post-*Memoir* small narrations with traumatic features and how these traumatic features transform the everyday, usually understood as a sphere of repetitions and inertia, into a sphere where banality and uniqueness are interdependent. Imperceptibility is at the core of "Miron at the Margins, or Can We Queer Białoszewski?" (chapter 3), in which I focus on how Białoszewski inscribes a non-normative representation of gender and sexuality onto the quotidian of his small narrations. All three chapters are bound by an attention to paradoxes and subversions and direct our attention to how the positionality of Białoszewski's "autobiographical" narrator and his narrative strategies make these paradoxes and subversions escape our attention. The valorization of the everyday, which more than any other feature distinguishes Białoszewski from other Polish writers, is a leitmotif of my argument. This valorization both persists and evolves, developing from the avant-garde approach of Bialoszewki's early poetry to the "banality" of the small narrations.

Throughout my discussion I return to *A Memoir of the Warsaw Uprising,* Białoszewski's best-known book and an apple of discord in the periodization of his oeuvre. The *Memoir,* published in 1970, is usually granted an exceptional place among Białoszewski's works. It is a dividing line between Białoszewski's first four volumes of poetry, on the one side, and, on the other, his theatrical work and his life-writing, which, as mentioned earlier, also included poetry later in his life. Głowiński calls the *Memoir* "a separate thing";[33] Barańczak also considers it an exception, which, in turn, allows him to propose a coherent chronology of Białoszewski's oeuvre in which he treats the first book following *Donosy rzeczywistości* (1973; *Reporting Reality*) as a model for the rest of Białoszewski's work.[34] Barańczak's distinctions are driven mainly by what he considers the genre markers of the *Memoir* ("a relative continuity of the narration, action based on the chronological order, and an illusion of the temporal perspective typical for memoirs") as opposed to the more fragmented small narrations. My explorations of Białoszewski's representation of traumatic memory and its aftereffects, however, suggest a different periodization: the *Memoir* is neither an exception nor a dividing point between Białoszewski's poetic and prosaic periods, but is rather the core of his writing. Treating the *Memoir* as a "separate thing" in Białoszewski's writing trajectory reaffirms the view of the historical trauma of the Warsaw Uprising as a self-contained reality and depreciates its formative power. I, on the other hand, consider this experience and its aftereffects as fundamental to Białoszewski's psychology and aesthetics. It is through this experience and its transformation in the *Memoir* that Białoszewski finds his idiosyncratic voice for his portrayal of the everyday. Rather than just thinking about the *Memoir* as a shift toward prose, I understand it as a shift toward the everyday—a shift that is inseparable, in my mind, from the *Memoir*'s testimonial qualities. Although the *Memoir*'s historical subject seemingly points to a preoccupation with the non-quotidian, the mode in which Białoszewski reenacts traumatic testimony in the *Memoir* becomes an idiosyncratic reconfiguration of the historical trauma into the traumatic everyday. As literary artifact, the *Memoir* simultaneously encapsulates the event and its memory, the dialectics of remembering and forgetting, (re)living trauma, and post-traumatic living. The *Memoir* also showcases the poetic skills Białoszewski acquired in publishing the four volumes of poetry he wrote prior to the *Memoir* (in which he also introduced the motifs and characters that resurface fully developed in the *Memoir*). This work is the fullest realization of Białoszewski's linguistic strategies and the most striking manifestation of his fusion of the traumatic and the everyday. It encapsulates the paradoxes of Białoszewski's writing and radicalizes the notion that the everyday can be "only" the everyday and yet always already "something more" than the everyday. As a traumatic reenactment, the *Memoir* amplifies Białoszewski's representation of the everyday, governed by the non-teleological, non-apocalyptic, and non-redemptive view of time on which he will insist in his later works.

In its form and diction, the *Memoir* directly reenacts the struggle between Białoszewski the trauma survivor and Białoszewski the writer and narrator. Białoszewski replays the interaction between traumatic and narrative memory, showing us a traumatic "shimmering"—an alternating opening and closing of the event in the survivor's memory. The narration simultaneously encapsulates the event and its memory, remembering and not being able to remember as the two processes of working through the past. This interplay between the narrative and traumatic aspects of memory is strikingly performed in the *Memoir*'s diction, which reenacts orality. The *Memoir*'s idiosyncratic genre of a "pamiętnik gadany"—a "talking memoir"—recreates a conversation in which the audience (the reader) is positioned as a witness to the traumatic testimony of the narrator, who claims that "for twenty years I could not write about this. Although I wanted to very much. I would talk. About the uprising. To so many people. All sorts of people. So many times." In its reenactment of orality, the *Memoir* shows how memory negotiates between the traumatic "remembering too much" and "forgetting enough" to allow narrative sequences to form from traumatic flashbacks. On the psychobiographical level, we can read the *Memoir* as a text which testifies to the impact of Białoszewski's experience and which thematizes his own struggle with the transformation of his open-ended traumatic memory into a self-contained artistic product.

To understand the *Memoir* as an organic part of Białoszewski's development rather than a separate, self-contained, chapter in his oeuvre unlocks rich interpretative possibilities for the works that follow its publication—and, in a different sense, for those that precede it, as well. The *Memoir* intensifies what is more or less visible in his other works and is a pivotal moment in Białoszewski's evolution from writing poetry marked by avant-garde aspirations to transform the everyday into something else, to his intermediary cutting-edge performance of colloquial banality in *Było i było* (*There Was and There Was*), and, finally, to the quotidian of the small narrations. The puzzling quality of the post-*Memoir* small narrations (the everyday is "only" the everyday and yet it is always already "something more"), which I discuss in chapter 2, relates to Białoszewski's traumatic experiences and the poetics with which he represented them in the *Memoir*. The repetitive, banal, and familar surface of the everyday is actually permeated by traumatic traces. "Struggling with memory," the leitmotif of the survivor in the *Memoir*, resonates in life-writing in the double identity of the narrator and/as survivor. The everyday of the small narrations repeatedly returns to the place of trauma; some of these returns are thematic (as, for instance, in the form of traumatic flashbacks, nightmares, and memories of the past), but often they manifest themselves in less direct forms: the narrator's agoraphobia, his sensitivity to sounds and voices, his hypervigilance. On a subtler level, these returns are embedded in the narrator's sense of temporality, which resembles traumatic belatedness, and in his fear that quotidian reality could, at any moment, disappear. Głowiński's claim that Białoszewski "plays out life in the everyday" could thus be rephrased: almost imperceptibly, Białoszewski plays out the traumatic in the everyday.

In chapter 3 ("Miron at the Margins, or Can We Queer Białoszewski?") my argument is also concerned with Białoszewski's mode of almost-imperceptibility, but this time related to his representation of gender and sexuality in the small narrations. We cannot overlook the role of Białoszewski's homosexuality in his aesthetic choices and the impact of the homophobic culture of Communist Poland on his life-writing and on his reception. Białoszewski's representation of gender and sexuality demonstrates more strikingly than other aspects of his writing the paradox of a seemingly "autobiographical" narratorial subjectivity that unifies the series of the small narrations while in itself being all "blurred up."[35] Białoszewski desexualizes his narration by erasing from his narrative "persona" any traces of desire and by granting this persona a non-normative community. At the center of this community is a narrator who bears the name of the author and whose behavior does not fall within the acceptable bounds of the hetero-normative and patriarchal spectrum; in fact, it is unclear which categories could be used to define the narrator who represents, to use Kaja Silverman's expression, "male subjectivity at the margins."[36] The narrator favors the world of women and represents them more vividly and with a greater engagement than he does with the world of men, yet without desiring women. He builds an alternative family around his friends, and he blends into his narrative "queer" moments, which, when noticed, destabilize normativity without suggesting a counter-narrative. I analyze this mode of "blending in" and propose a mode of reading—borrowing the metaphor of the "purloined letter" from Edgar Allan Poe's famous detective story—that allows Białoszewski to naturalize subversion. My contention is that this naturalization is related to Białoszewski's "counterfeited autobiographical pact,"[37] which promises to the reader knowledge about the narrator but delivers it only—and even then indirectly and incompletely—when the reader is able to "look awry."[38] Looking awry excludes a probing stare that demands truth; rather, its angled position allows one to see moments when the text becomes opaque and when it displaces the reader and shows the oscillation of knowing and not knowing about the author's biography.

What is really at stake for me is how our ways of reading are implicated in the ways we "see" and "do not see" Białoszewski's construction of homosexuality in his writing. I am, therefore, not interested in the moments we can "out" Białoszewski. I am appreciative of this tendency in the recent scholarship as it offers a critical counterproposition to the earlier tendency to treat Białoszewski as a de-sexualized, if not de-gendered "subject" of his writing. I believe, however, that a shortcoming of this approach is that it does not further our understanding of how Białoszewski operated within complex historical, sociological, political, biographical, and textual networks of power. To understand these networks means that we need to assess how our own critical positions are implicated in and limited by our systems of knowledge. Białoszewski had to operate in his systems of knowledge—*his* "epistemological regime," to use Foucault's expression—and so do we in ours. In the post-Communist period we can see how dramatically these systems shift. Witkowski's incorporation of Białoszewski in his queer novel *Lubiewo*, for instance, forges a new set of questions about intertextuality as an instrument of symbolic capital to be instrumentalized by emancipatory movements in Poland (in this case, the movements of homosexual minorities) in their struggle for social visibility. At the same time, it is just as crucial to recognize how Białoszewski's idiosyncratic strategies differ from contemporary works that validate minorities by the creation of a homosexual counter-narrative as it is to recognize how these strategies differ from the aesthetics of sublimation, which remained a model in Polish literature until recently and in which homosexuality was displaced, coded, and projected upon acceptable modernist topoi. I'm not interested in giving a univocal answer—to queer or not to queer—especially as the very notion of "queering" presents a serious problem when imported from a Western context to the political and social context of Polish literature. What interests me is an interrogation of the very notion of queering by confronting it with the elusiveness and obviousness of Białoszewski's writing.

"I DIDN'T SERVE IN THE CAVALRY, I DIDN'T TRAVEL THE ANTARCTIC": BIAŁOSZEWSKI'S UNEVENTFUL BIOGRAPHY

However, before we can delve further into the complexities of Białoszewski's writing, a few more words are in order about his biographical and artistic trajectory. "Born in July, on Sunday, in Warsaw, at the corner of Leszno and Wronia, in 1922" is how, with his usual attention to topography, Białoszewski described his arrival into the family of Kazimiera and Zenon, a homemaker and a postal clerk, respectively. His life was relatively uneventful—if by "events" we mean exciting personal developments. Born and raised in the independent Poland of the interwar period, Białoszewski came of age during the Nazi occupation of Warsaw (1939–45), lived through the utter destruction of the city in the Warsaw Uprising of 1944, and experienced both the poverty of the postwar period and the restrictions of the Communist system, whose fall he did not live to witness. During the occupation, Białoszewski graduated from a clandestine lyceum and began studying Polish philology at a clandestine university, but he did not complete the program. After the Warsaw Uprising, he was deported to Germany as a forced laborer but escaped and returned to Warsaw. He worked as a postal clerk before finding employment as a journalist for the daily papers *Kurier Codzienny* (*The Daily Courier*) and, later, *Wieczór Warszawy* (*The Warsaw Evening*). Forced out from this line of work in the Stalinist era, Białoszewski suffered extreme poverty in the early 1950s. He was living in desperate conditions and often literally starving. His situation improved when he began to receive revenues that allowed him to live from his publications and was granted a disability pension because of the effects of the chronic tuberculosis he suffered in his youth. The publication of *Pamiętnik z powstania warszawskiego* (*A Memoir of the Warsaw Uprising*) in 1970 brought him wider recognition, including an award from the Ministry of Culture. Later in life he did some traveling, visiting several Mediterranean countries on a boat cruise; he also came to the United States to receive the Jurzykowski Literary Award (Nagroda Jurzykowskiego) from a Polish-American audience in New York in 1982. He described these trips in two posthumously published diaries, *Obmapywanie Europy: Dziennik okrętowy* and *AAAmeryka* (1988; *Mapping Europe: A Ship's Log* and *AAAmeryka*).

Białoszewski claimed two events as life-changing; both involved a sense of place and displacement, and both were connected with the topography and materiality of the city of Warsaw; their incongruous juxtaposition is typical of the way Białoszewski avoids familiar hierarchies of events. The first formative event was the Warsaw Uprising of 1944 and the destruction of the city of his birth and youth; the second, incomparable in its scale to the tragic and collective dimension of the uprising and yet impacting Białoszewski's writing, was his move in 1974 from the Plac Dąbrowskiego (Dąbrowski Square) in downtown Warsaw, on the left bank of the Vistula River, to a new high-rise building on the river's right bank. Sometimes he would add to these two events his first heart attack, which he suffered in 1973 and recounted in *Zawał* (1977; *Heart Attack*). He would die of a third heart attack, on June 17, 1983.

Białoszewski belonged to the generation of Warsaw poets who debuted during the war and whom Polish readers tend to associate with the Home Army and military participation (and death) in the Warsaw Uprising.[39] Białoszewski, however, was neither a soldier nor a part of this literary and military milieu; he did not fit the group of poets and writers whom the well-known critic Kazimierz Wyka described as "infected with death." He matured as a writer outside an institutional context, although his writing was greatly influenced by his work as a reporter immediately after the war when he had a chance to witness various stages in the revitalization of the city—from the mass exhumation of the victims of the Warsaw Uprising, which he later would describe in the *Memoir*, to the construction of new buildings.

When the *Warsaw Evening* ceased publication, Białoszewski started writing for *Świat Młodych* (*The World of Youth*), a weekly for teenagers. In 1951 he was forced out of his job by the Security Police (Służba Bezpieczeństwa) because of his politically incorrect profile.[40] He began working for the children's magazine *Świerszczyk* (*The Cricket*) but lost this position as well because of his refusal to adhere to the growing ideological constraints of Stalinism and socialist realism. The system was as externally oppressive as it was internally seductive; it captivated many minds with ideology as well as with various perks and inducements, and with the most enticing gift of all: statewide publishing houses that could guarantee a mass readership for cooperating writers and intellectuals.[41]

In post-Communist Poland, there have been intense discussions about the writers who cooperated with the regime, especially in the Stalinist period. The issue is intimately entangled with the ongoing debate over the continuity between post-Communist Poland and the Communist period, and cooperation (or "collaboration," as many would choose to say, implying a betrayal) is a thorny issue in a view of a collective identity as organized around the binary of "we" (the people) and "they" (the regime). The interpretations of cooperation range from straightforward moral sell-outs (or "domestic shame" ["hańba domowa"]), to a double game of "Ketman" (a notion introduced by Miłosz to indicate the practice of paying lip service to the regime while in fact opposing it), to sometimes tragic—as in Tadeusz Borowski's case—entanglements with the regime. Białoszewski's specific case is not part of these discussions; in fact, it does not fall within the usual coordinates. He did not cooperate with the regime and did not follow the precepts of socialist realism; he was in fact prevented from publishing during the Stalinist years and spent them in extreme poverty. As the story goes, most of the time he was lying in bed, often starving and living on strong tea and psycherine, a stimulant and appetite surpressant. Yet, his non-cooperation was not constructed as an act of defiance the way it was, for instance, for his famous poetic and generational peer, Zbigniew Herbert, whose refusal to cooperate (regardless of the fact that, as it turned out later, he did publish in the Stalinist period) became part of his poetic image and later his political cachet. Białoszewski's refusal became part of his legend only insofar as it reinforced his cult status as a self-marginalized outsider. Białoszewski himself never made any gestures that would indicate that he was even vaguely interested in capitalizing on an oppositional or "dissident" stance, and he was never inscribed, nor did he inscribe himself, into the Polish catalogue of persecuted writers. In fact, he promoted an image of himself as a man seeking internal freedom and impervious to the restrictions of the Stalinist period.

A quarter of a century after the end of Stalinism, in the volume *AAAmeryka* (published posthumously in 1988), he presented such an image of internal freedom, when his narrator recalls a meeting with the audience in New York City:

> They asked about my impressions of America. I tell them what I can. And about the idea of traveling in general. Then about the years I spent in bed in a dark room, the meditations, weird states, visions, writings, the not leaving the house. And I say that this too was like traveling, only better.
>
> Pytają o moje wrażenia z Ameryki. Mówię jak potrafię. I w ogóle o idei podróży. A potem o swoich latach leżenia w ciemnym pokoju, namysły, dziwny stan, wizje, pisania, niewychodzenia. I mówię, że to też było jak podróże, a nawet lepsze.[42]

"It was like traveling, only better." The years of solitude and hunger become here a form of creative self-confinement unrelated to socialist realism or political oppression. No socialist realism or any kind of "oppression" is even signaled. For the audience, "Białoszewski" the narrator remains a free agent. But in his reception Białoszewski the author, too, is perceived as someone who transforms external restrictions into an internal stimulus to explore the unknown territories of his psyche. Emphasizing his dislike of any forms of collective behaviors and exultant displays of patriotism, Białoszewski cultivated an apolitical image, and his critics trusted this self-presentation. When asked why he did not participate in the anti-Communist demonstrations popular during the "carnival of Solidarity" (a time between the birth of Solidarity in August 1980 and the martial law of December 1981), he responded, "I cannot sway with everybody else" ("Nie mogę kołysać się ze wszystkimi").[43] We know little about Białoszewski's political convictions, and we can only speculate about the factors that led him to resist involvement with the life of the collective. This resistance became part of his image as an autonomous artist withdrawn from public life, although it was, most likely, a reaction to homophobia. That Białoszewski was forced to quit his job in 1951 as a journalist is recalled by Białoszewski's friend, Krystyna Garwolińska-Błaszczykowa, who attests that Białoszewski was interrogated by Security Police because of his "politically incorrect profile"; she adds that an "additional reason was supposedly his homosexual tendencies."[44] Garwolińska-Błaszczykowa's phrase, derogatory to the English ear (and nowadays to the Polish ear also, although this was clearly not Garwolińska-Błaszczykowa's intention), points to an inability to speak about Białoszewski's homosexuality directly. It sounds vague, with the "supposedly" suggesting that Białoszewski's homosexuality was hypothetical even for his friends. Her tone, and the way she adds information as if in passing, demonstrates a general tendency in the accounts of Białoszewski's life to present his biography outside of the context of his sexual orientation. The topic is either nonexistent or treated nonchalantly (I will return to the claims of protection of the writer's privacy later); the high price that Białoszewski most likely paid for his sexual orientation remains unacknowledged.

In the many accounts of what seems an appealing space of "freedom from any expectations that could interfere with his privacy," to refer to Sławiński's formulation, rarely do we get a glimpse of the writer's vulnerability, as in an account from Andrzej Osieka, who, recalling his encounter with Białoszewski in 1951, gives us a sense of the writer's despair: "Miron stopped suddenly on the staircase and, after a moment of silence, said: 'I know I have poetic talent. And I know that they will never again print a single poem of mine.'"[45] That despair, this "never"—which in 1951 must have felt to Białoszewski like a life sentence—does not constitute part of the cult of Białoszewski, perhaps because until recently his homosexuality was not considered in critical approaches to his aesthetics. And yet it needs to be remembered, because it helps us realize how ridden with anxieties Białoszewski's "separate" identity must have been for him at times. It also makes us more attuned to the residual form of this despair in Białoszewski's strategies of coding the political in his texts.

While the role Białoszewski's sexual orientation played in his being fired in 1951 (and whether it was officially recognized) remains an open question, there is little doubt that Białoszewski's aesthetics in all respects contradicted the official guidelines of the propaganda of socialist realism: he preferred a colloquial style over pompous rhetoric and the sacralization of the quotidian over the exaltation of the ideological. His work was not aimed at mass consumption, but, in the tradition of avant-garde movements, was created for, and with, a circle of friends. It is difficult to determine to what extent Białoszewski's creation of an exclusive and alternative milieu of artistically experimental friends was an artistic response to compensate for his forced exclusion from mainstream public life and to what extent it was simply his aesthetic predilection. Between 1949 and 1956 he wrote "for the drawer," with an exception of three poems, all published before 1950.[46] Many of the poems from that "silent" period appeared in Białoszewski's later volumes. His first poetry collection, *Obroty rzeczy* (*The Revolution of Things*), appeared in 1956.

Białoszewski's debut was considered part of the emergence of the Generation of 1956, a group of influential writers whose debut in a new post-Thaw environment delineated new horizons for literature free from the precepts of socialist realism.[47] Although considered part of this literary generation, Białoszewski was older and, chronologically, belonged to the war generation, but his debut was delayed (just as, for the same reasons, Herbert's was). Compared to his younger colleagues, Białoszewski's theatrical experience, which I will discuss in a moment, and years of writing "for the drawer" had honed his voice to maturity and compensated for the delay in his debut. His selection of poems for his first volume was greatly influenced by the critic Artur Sandauer, who became Białoszewski's self-appointed literary agent and manager, to use contemporary terms, and who played the role of an ambivalent father figure to Białoszewski.[48] Sandauer also insisted that Białoszewski's original title, *Słowa dodawane do rzeczy* (*Words Added to Things*), be changed to the catchier *Obroty rzeczy* (*The Revolution of Things*). While the final title emphasizes the central position that "things"[49] assume in the constellation of Białoszewski's poetics, the rejected title underlined the linguistic nature of his sacralized quotidian. Sandauer labeled this poetics "the poetry of junk" ("poezja rupieci"), a label that Białoszewski, in spite of his fondness for and fascination with discarded objects, found highly reductive, which he saw as being rooted in the modernist myth of the poet-magus and revolving around the speaker's intimate relations with inanimate objects. In *The Revolution of Things,* Białoszewski often represents objects of everyday use, which, bereft of their familiar functionality, reveal their purely aesthetic qualities. Such treatment defamiliarizes everyday reality while at the same time sacralizing and animating it. The trajectory from defamiliarization through sacralization and animation to astonishment springs from the linguistic nature of the everyday. Empirical losses become linguistic gains, as in the famous "'Oh! Oh! Should They Take Away My Stove . . .' My Inexhaustible Ode to Joy":

"'Oh! Oh! Should They Take Away
My Stove . . . ' My Inexhaustible Ode
to Joy"[50]

I have a stove
like a triumphal arch!

They are taking away my stove
like a triumphal arch!!

Give me back my stove
like a triumphal arch!!!

They took it away.

All that's left
is a grey
gaping
hole
a grey gaping hole.

And that's enough for me:
grey gaping hole
grey-gaping-hole
grey-gaping-hole
greygapinghole.

"'Ach, gdyby, gdyby nawet piec
zabrali . . . ' Moja niewyczerpana oda
do radości"[51]

Mam piec
podobny do bramy triumfalnej!

Zabierają mi piec
podobny do bramy triumfalnej!!

Oddajcie mi piec
podobny do bramy triumfalnej!!!

Zabrali.

Została po nim tylko
szara
naga
jama
szara naga jama.

I to mi wystarczy:
szara naga jama
szara naga jama
sza-ra-na-ga-ja-ma
szaranagajama

In this poem, written in Białoszewski's penurious years, the exuberant speaker substitutes the empty gray space where the stove used to be with an exotic, Japanese-sounding word game ("sza-ra-na-ga-ja-ma"). This exuberance presupposes a privatization of the high genre of the ode; note that this happens not only by the clash of high and low, but also by the ode being marked already in a title as a private speech act: "my" ode to joy is meant to disturb the intertexuality and the status of the ode in the hierarchy of genres.[52] The tone of the poem deflects the reader's attention from the unidentified "they" who invade the speaker's space and, in spite of his protests ("give me back my stove"), take away his "triumphal arch."[53] Indeed, this invasion and subsequent loss are immediately compensated by the speaker's linguistic activities, which crescendo (note the increasing number of exclamation points) in an ode to joy as "inexhaustible" as the potentially endless repetition of the word. *The Revolution of Things* is full of this powerful fusion of high and low in which exalted dialogues with floors, quilts, and drains do not express a lyrical "I," but constitute the very relationship between the subject and his own solar system. In this poetic version of the Copernican revolution, the speaker orbits around the objects. Everyday space becomes ritualized and sacralized in his paraphrases of the liturgy. For instance, the Catholic liturgy of transubstantiation ("O Lord, I am not worthy that thou should'st come to me") becomes echoed in a wordplay ("Nie jestem godny—ściano-widelcze-ojcze") through the phonic similarities between the vocative of "Father/Lord" ("Ojcze") and "fork" ("widelcze"). The speaker euphorically sacralizes the everyday; his frequent use of apostrophes emphasizes a gap between the sacred (of the object) and the profane (of the speaker). This poetic liturgy, however, has a ludic character; it is an exuberant play ("najlepsza zabawa"), which becomes a way of fighting against "getting used to things" ("do rzeczy nieprzyzwyczajenie").

This first volume of Białoszewski's poetry and, to a degree, his second collection, *Rachunek zachciankowy* (*Calculus of Whims*), are still full of recognizable intertextualities: references to literary and musical classics, mythology, hagiography, painting, and so on. This kind of intertextuality greatly decreases from the third and fourth volumes, which mark Białoszewski's shift to the type of diction that will remain unmistakably his own.[54] Already in *Calculus of Whims,* but in a more pronounced way in *Mylne wzruszenia* (1961; *Misdirected Sentiments*) and radically in *Było i było* (1965; *There Was and There Was*), Białoszewski shifts his poetry in the linguistic direction of neo-semantization, that is, preoccupation with the word formation, and experimentation with the level of articulation understood as a utilization of a variety of dictions belonging to different social groups. This poetic mode earned him a reputation as a leading poet of what came to be known as *poezja lingwistyczna* (linguistic poetry).[55] Linguistic poetry was experimental, conceiving poetry as a game aimed at laying bare the devices of language. At the same time, Białoszewski still incorporated in his poetry features from a variety of other forms and genres (e.g., epigrams, ballads, aphorisms, *fait divers,* and even philosophical theorems, as in "Wywód jestemu" ["A Treatise on I-am-ness"]).

What became his trademark, however, was the use of colloquial speech in extreme forms, especially speech that exhibits its own inability to be articulated and, like the mumblings of a drunkard, displays (or better yet exaggerates) the dynamics of speech production. Białoszewski abandons his strong lyrical "I," which was so appealing in his debut volume, and focuses on the materiality of language and the performative aspect of the spoken and colloquial.[56] He does not mimetically represent speech, but reenacts its shapelessness, its lack of linearity and precision; this hyperbolic treatment of the spoken reveals the usually unnoticed patterns of signification. By producing a deformed language Białoszewski shows what is involved in the articulation of language as such. The word in Białoszewski, as Adam Ważyk put it, "shows its inability to communicate," and the economy that usually characterizes the poetic mode of expression breaks down: the meaning either slips between the signifiers or becomes canceled by their surplus. By treating language as a structure whose separate units—even those as small as phonemes—could be arbitrarily displaced and rearranged, Białoszewski became an idiosyncratic poet-*bricoleur.*

Misdirected Sentiments also introduces a fusion of writing and autobiography under the label of "życiopisanie" ("life-writing"). The lyrical speaker from *Revolution of Things*—the "priest of the everyday" ("kapłan codzienności, as critics would have it)—now becomes "Białoszewskawy" (literally, "Białoszewskish" or "Białoszewskian"), a hero of his own linguistic inabilities ("słów niepotraf" and "niepewny cozrobień"). Minimalistic in his desires, inert, with a deficiency of will ("abulic"), Białoszewski's speaker moves away from the "active and volitional model" of the Cracow avant-garde.[57] Białoszewski's speaker functions simultaneously, and paradoxically, as an Everyman and a contemplative singular being who negotiates between the desire "to be oneself" ("wywód jestem'u") and to be indistinguishable from the crowd ("nie wychylać się").

While the notion of the everyday shifts from sacralization to (dis)articulation, the speaker's relationship to the traumatic changes as well. In, for instance, the poignant "Ballada o zejściu do sklepu" ("A Ballad of Going Down to the Store") from the *Revolution of Things,* the reader is able to reconstruct the situation: an agoraphobic speaker, forced to confront his fears of facing the outside world, models his successful trip to the store on the katabasis (the epic hero's trip into the underworld) and resurrection. The "Ballad" of the title plays, of course, on the ballad genre (another hint of Adam Mickiewicz, the Polish Romantic poet, whose *Ballads and Romances* figure prominently in the volume), but the genre's traditional folk wisdom is replaced by astonishment at one's ability to survive the confrontation with the hustle and bustle of the crowd.[58] While the "Ballad" allows the reader to clearly see the speaker's agoraphobia, a war-related poem, "Rodowód góry odosobnienia" in *Misdirected Sentiments,* actually contradicts the title's promise to explain the genesis of the mountain, which happens to be a caramel-colored blanket belonging to a character named Stefa, who returns in the *Memoir* and whose prototype was a friend of Białoszewski's. In another poem, "Cyckam Karmel" ("I'm Sucking on Caramel"), the speaker is literally reduced to a newborn attached to a breast substitute (the very same blanket with a "sweet" name). What was, in the "Ballad," highly poeticized now becomes situational, but paradoxically its referent is less clear. Białoszewski gravitates toward diary-like entries and notes-on-the-go ("zapiski") that privilege situationism and build a sense of eventfulness out of insignificant, often banal, happenings. What is gradually built in these poems, which become poetico-prosaic hybrids, is "the aesthetics of accepting everything" ("estetyka przyjmowania wszystkiego") with "Białoszewski" and his friends as main characters and Warsaw as the place of action; all of this in language shunning "literarity" and reenacting the colloquial.

These features, also characteristic of the fourth and last poetic work of this period of Białoszewski's career, *Było i było* (1965; *There Was and There Was*), were not kindly received. Critics were "outraged" by *There Was and There Was* because of the absence of traditionally accepted determinants of poetry: formal constraints, a strong sense of a poetic "I," and a distinctly poetic language. Instead, perhaps as a legacy of his journalistic manner of observation, Białoszewski employs social heteroglossia—a stratification of language into a multiplicity of voices belonging to various social groups. Sometimes, he straightforwardly provokes with his take on radical situationism, as in this tongue-in-cheek poem, which one could easily imagine performed as a cabaret piece.

"Lu. He.'s Story"

long, long ago on Spokojna
the toilet got clogged
they called in an expert, he took a look
and declared:
—too much paper!
too little water!
too much paper!
too little water!

—so what should we do?
—less paper! more water!
less paper! more water!

"Opowieść Lu. He."

dawno, dawno, na Spokojnej
zapchało się w ubikacji,
zawołali rzeczoznawcę, zbadał,
orzekł:
—za dużo papieru!
za mało wody!
za dużo papieru!
za mało wody!

—a co robić?
—mniej papieru! więcej wody!
mniej papieru! więcej wody![59]

Białoszewski sets the poem in mythical times with the words "long, long ago," a phrase that also brings to mind oral genres like fairy tales and ballads. But the contrast between style and subject matter parodies the ballad genre and, through its combination of epic, dramatic, and lyrical elements, mocks the idea of genre purity.[60] "Lu. He." is Ludwik Hering, Białoszewski's close friend, theater collaborator, and a frequent character in Białoszewski's later prose. In Hering, Białoszewski found a mentor and a critic whose judgment he valued tremendously. Hering is credited with persistently directing Białoszewski to focus on the banal and the everyday.[61] The title of the poem, "Lu. He.'s Story," suggests that what matters most is not the baseness of Lu. He.'s topic, but his approach to recounting it. By mocking the epic and the ballad, Białoszewski makes "Lu. He.'s story" an inside joke, which encapsulates and exaggerates Lu. He.'s philosophy of banality, in which he looks for the poetic viability even in clogged toilets.

Julian Przyboś, a leading critic and poet of the Polish interwar avant-garde who in the decade following Białoszewski's debut had been enthusiastic about Białoszewski's idiosyncratic voice, deemed *There Was and There Was* unworthy of even being called literature. Przyboś could not forgive Białoszewski for so radically testing the limits of the coherence and referentiality of language. The volume lacked for him an avant-garde clarity; its seemingly disorganized, colloquial language and its hybrid forms, neither poetic nor prosaic, did not allow for internal coherence, which Przyboś considered the central principle of poetry.[62] Other critics, in less sophisticated terms, labeled this collection "mumbling without making any sense."[63] Czesław Miłosz, who recognized the value of Białoszewski's first two volumes (and who, years later, would value Białoszewski's life-writing as such), described this kind of poetry as "slurping, croaking, a kind of protopolish magma."[64] *There Was and There Was* not only sealed Białoszewski's reputation as a failed poet for those who had already perceived his earlier poetry as the product of a misguided imagination and mocked it for its "salad of chopped syntax" ("sałatka połamanej składni"), but also alienated many of his former supporters. *There Was and There Was,* with its gravitation toward the radically prosaic (in the sense of its subjects and form), marked the end of Białoszewski's period of poetic experimentation. From 1965 until he returned to poetry in 1978 with the publication of *Odczepić się* (*Get Lost*), prose forms dominated Białoszewski's writing.

Before I discuss this shift toward prose, it is important to signal Białoszewski's theatrical explorations (known mainly as the Theater on Tarczyńska and the Separate Theater), which overlap with the first stage of Białoszewski's career, that is, with his first four volumes of poetry. Białoszewski started his theater work in the early 1950s when he was unable to publish and his contacts with the outside world were limited to the circle of his closest friends, with whom he started experimenting with various types of performance.[65] In 1955, the Theater on Tarczyńska Street—a small theater that fused modernist "group art" with spontaneous childlike play and performance that took advantage of the various talents of its members—was born in Lech Emfazy Stefański's apartment.[66] The theatrical experiments of those years left a permanent imprint on the visual imagery of Białoszewski's subsequent poetry and on his theatricalization of everyday events, speech, and interactions.[67]

The collaborative nature of the Theater on Tarczyńska created conflicts about authorship, leading Białoszewski to leave the group and establish his own theater, the Teatr Osobny (the Separate Theater), in his own small apartment in Dąbrowski Square in 1958.[68] The nook containing his bed served as the stage of the Separate Theater, and the entire enterprise was supported by audience donations. The theater's success was inversely proportional to the tiny space allotted to the performers and, small as it was, it became a *curiosum* that attracted not only theatergoers in Warsaw but also foreigners interested in this alternative scene in the midst of the Communist 1950s. According to both Wołyński and Białoszewski, these foreign guests included Jean-Paul Sartre and Simone de Beauvoir.[69]

The Separate Theater consisted of three artists—Białoszewski, Ludwik Hering, and Hering's niece, Ludmiła Murawska—each of whom had interchanging roles as director, actor, producer, and stage designer. Murawska was a student of painting at the time and was not only responsible for acting all of the female roles but also for both stage and costume design. Understanding of this period of Białoszewski's career is complicated because of the close collaboration of the three friends, which blurs the notion of individual authorship. Although for a long time most critics have identified the Separate Theater as Białoszewski's—as they have done with the Theater on Tarczyńska—at this point there are no doubts that Ludwik Hering exerted an enormous influence on the development of the theater and that his contribution to the textual material was more than solely inspirational. The controversy over the authorship of the plays (with the splendid "oratorio" of *Osmędeusze* at the forefront of this controversy) or, rather, Białoszewski's initial silence on the topic of coauthorship, led to a split between the two friends that lasted until 1970 when Białoszewski "redeemed" himself in Hering's eyes with the publication of his best-known work, *A Memoir of the Warsaw Uprising.*[70] In 1971, the plays from the Separate Theater were first published, and a few years later Białoszewski publicly announced that he and Hering had coauthored most of the works that we have come to know under the umbrella term of the Separate Theater.

Between the last volume of poetry, *There Was and There Was,* and the first volume of the small narrations in which Białoszewski becomes exclusively a writer of the everyday without avant-garde stylization, there lies *A Memoir of the Warsaw Uprising,* a work that at first glance seems to focus on the radically non-everyday. In the *Memoir,* Białoszewski describes the sixty-three days of the uprising using linguistic devices he had previously employed in his poetic experiments—the misapplication of idioms; the change and exchange of suffixes and prefixes; the replacement of syntactic units with isolated phonemes; the fragmentation of sentences; onomatopoeic expressions; and ellipses. All these devices are deployed in the *Memoir* to create a multi-angled, syntactically incoherent, fast-paced, first-person narrative that reenacts the event.

The Warsaw Uprising of 1944, which I will discuss in greater detail in chapter 1, persistently returns in Białoszewski's works and in interviews as *the* formative and central experience of the writer's life. It has been a critical cliché that Białoszewski's aesthetics were affected by his wartime experience, particularly by the uprising, yet the relationship between the aesthetics of life-writing and the war is frequently presented in self-explanatory terms (which I discuss in more detail in chapter 2). Few critical works, however, treat this relationship beyond the thematic.[71] Maria Janion's seminal essay "Wojna i Forma" (1976; "War and the Form"), best known for its claims about the civilian dimension of the *Memoir*, is a rare example of reading the traumatic as formative for the aesthetic. Janion interprets the experience of the Warsaw Uprising as the genesis of Białoszewski's phenomenological style and his "notion of reality" ("koncepcja rzeczywistości"). She suggests that Białoszewski's fascination with coincidence in the small narrations is directly related to the coincidental nature of survival in the uprising.

Janion's remarks about the coincidental nature of human experience resonate with my own reading of the eventfulness of the small narrations; Białoszewski's construction of the everyday is based on the representation of insignificant, quotidian events, but these insignificant events can at any moment erupt into a traumatic flashback. Moreover, as such ruptures collapse the distinction between past and present, the traumatic return becomes transformed into an epiphanic moment (for instance, "In the blink of an eye, the uprising. The courtyard after a bombing. Ruins, planks, sun. Those streets, Hożas, Wilczas").[72] I extend the notion of "przeżycie" (literally "living-through") from the context of the Warsaw Uprising and its representation in the *Memoir* to the entire project of life-writing.[73] The "living-through" affects the construction of temporality of the everyday in the small narrations, in which the banal and the epiphanic, as I discuss in chapter 2, intersect. The stylistic strategies that Białoszewski used to reenact the traumatic testimony in the *Memoir* carries over to his "życiopisanie," which is permeated by traumatic residue. In both chapter 1 and chapter 2 I refer to the vocabulary of trauma studies, which has not yet been employed to interpret Białoszewski and which I find productive not only to approach Białoszewski's writing, but also to place it in the larger context of Poland's traumatic wartime past and its culture of memory.

TRAUMA STUDIES—THEIR VALUE AND LIMITATIONS: *A MEMOIR OF THE WARSAW UPRISING* AND BEYOND

I have found trauma studies valuable to study Białoszewski's *Memoir* and post-*Memoir* works for several reasons. First of all, although trauma studies emerged in studies of individual experience, as it evolved it was applied to the field of cultural assessments. When Freud gave a famous example of the train-wreck survivor in *Mourning and Melancholia* (1917), he read the traumatic as an individual experience. Yet the term gradually became cross-disciplinary, and trauma studies became identified, as Michael Rothberg claims, with a host of issues at "the intersection of the psychic and the social."[74] Polish society, which invests its collective and national identity and, by extension, its future in its loyalty to a traumatic view of the past, could greatly benefit from using some aspects of trauma studies as tools of self-reflection.

Another aspect that makes trauma studies broadly applicable to social contexts is that its approach to traumatic experience does not limit itself to firsthand experience. In fact, as Jeffrey Alexander argues, it is a "naturalistic fallacy" to think that every tragic or disastrous experience needs to be perceived by a collective as traumatic. The perception of something as traumatic is rather the result of a "spiral of signification" that links the tragic experience to a collective identity. Trauma can be both experienced as well as transferred (culturally and transgenerationally, in public and familial settings), and the circulation of traumatic experiences in a given collective has serious repercussions on its collective view of the past and, in turn, the future.[75]

I signal this collective dimension of the traumatic because Białoszewski's *Memoir* should also be viewed from such a collective perspective, that is, from the perspective that contextualizes this text in the "spiral of signification." Indeed, it rarely happens that such an intensely idiosyncratic literary work gains as much popularity as the *Memoir*. Clearly, Białoszewski's narrative resonated with Polish readers; yet, almost seventy years after the uprising and over forty years after the publication of the *Memoir*, Polish culture still has not developed a language that would allow it to attend to the complexities of the "social production" of the uprising's memory. Białoszewski's work is required reading in Polish schools, yet, paradoxically, its civilian dimension is both well known and, on the cultural and institutional level, marginalized.[76] As I will suggest in my brief discussion of the Museum of the Warsaw Uprising, the prevailing cultural norms still privilege the Romantic model and minimize the civilian experience.

However, the first problem that we need to confront when we think about the usefulness of the concept of trauma in literary studies is the risk of essentialization. Once we know the symptoms of traumatization, it is tempting to succumb to detective impulses and begin searching for an author's traumatized psyche in his textual strategies. One could certainly think of the *Memoir* as a literary work that engages—*avant la lettre*—the precepts of trauma theory and, by extension, confirms the writer's traumatized psyche. But ultimately our analysis would only "posit retroactively its own cause,"[77] our own search for traumatic symptoms inscribed in the text. Rather than proving that Białoszewski was traumatized (and thus defined by his syndrome, as if traumatization were a category of identity), it is perhaps more productive to assume that he most likely was, but that this psychological speculation by itself does not make the *Memoir* generate different questions than it did before.

Trauma studies often seems to bring back with a vengeance the idea of individual subjectivity, making it into an object of fascination, and, at times, fetishization, as if the traumatic experience offered access to an authenticity long ago discredited in postmodern debates on the mediated nature of experience.[78] Literary texts that focus on the traumatic and involve autobiographical narration seem to assume a different ontology and are valued primarily for their documentary, historical, referential, and testimonial value. It is useful to remember the scandal of Binjamin Wilkomirski's memoirs, in which he falsely presented himself as a child Holocaust survivor; the disclosure that the author was not himself a trauma survivor discredited the book.[79] But to my mind, the demand placed on literature of trauma to provide a verifiable referential framework should instead bring to the foreground the problem of the "literariness" of literature—traumatic representations demand an investigation of form and rhetoric as much as of their referential or testimonial authenticity. Holocaust studies has often grappled with this tension between a desire to "access" experience and a frustration with the figurative nature of signification, which surfaces even in the most "direct" forms of communicating the experience, such as the oral testimonies of survivors in the presence of attentive witnesses.[80] How to interpret testimonies and how to effectively incorporate factually unreliable human memory still remains one of the main challenges for historiography. And the status of memory offers challenges for literary studies as well, but from a different perspective. In assessing the referential framework, we do not have the historian's burden of reconstructing "what really happened"; but we, too, need to consider what is at stake when we question the documentary value of a particular text and context.

Can trauma studies make us better readers of literary texts? How can we benefit from them without getting trapped by the dreaded "application"? If we were to interpret the text first, put it away, and revisit it later (in a Gadamerian spirit), what kind of reading, ultimately, would give us a sense that upon revisiting the text our initial interpretation generates new sets of questions? We perhaps cannot answer this question a priori, but we can, to an extent, evaluate a posteriori whether our original point of entry was productive. Białoszewski read via trauma studies and trauma studies read via Białoszewski prove to me a stimulating juxtaposition that keeps on generating new questions and makes each take on the text propaedeutical for questions yet to come.

I would like to refer to three constellations of questions triggered by trauma studies and persuasively delineated by Michael Rothberg in his book

Traumatic Realism. Rothberg writes from the perspective of Holocaust studies, but his reflections transcend his immediate field and may be quite useful for Białoszewski scholarship. The first constellation is "realist," in which we ask the question of reference, documentary value, what kind of history we can reconstruct from the text, and how "truthful" it would be for a historian or a sociologist. The second set of questions is "modernist," in which we reflect upon the limits of representation, and how to represent the traumatic in the first place. Finally, the third set of "demands" Rothberg labels as "postmodernist" and situates in the sphere of the public circulation of discourses; we ask questions about social mediation of traumatic experiences, and how memory is transmitted within a collective. For Rothberg, in any text representing a historical event, the "'realist' component seeks strategies for referring to and documenting the world; its 'modernist' side questions its ability to document history properly; and its 'postmodern' moment responds to the economic and political conditions of its emergence and social circulation."[81] Only when understood together can these constellations allow us to grasp the historical, social, and aesthetic particularity of the text.

In the reception of Białoszewski we encounter a paradox that Rothberg's questions help illuminate. Białoszewski has been greeted with ever-repeated claims of his "singularity," coupled with a strange erasure of history; both the author and his writing seem to occupy a place outside of history. The cult status deeply ingrained in the critical approaches to Białoszewski's writing, the myth of the writer's sovereign gesture of "withdrawal," and the assertion of his authenticity (which I discuss in chapter 2) all bar historicizing explorations. According to Rothberg's topology, Białoszewski scholarship awaits a "postmodern" reading that would allow us to understand his position in the creation and circulation of collective memory and his negotiations with the system of knowledge and power in Communist Poland.

Polish literary scholars have placed the *Memoir* so far apart from other texts on the uprising that they not only disconnect it from Białoszewski's other works but also pre-empty it by emphasizing its unique status in the social circulation. The *Memoir* is directly involved with the memory culture of Communist Poland, and it carefully negotiates between the issues connected to "double censorship" of the uprising, which I discuss in chapter 1. After its initial "scandal," the *Memoir* became not only critically acknowledged and popular among readers, but also officially recognized.[82] Yet it proposes its own alternative, intimate, and domestic view of history, which undermines official Communist sources without engaging in a counter-narrative. Białoszewski proposes a version of history that through the narrator's endless, breathless "talking" gives voice to—and constructs a representation of—collective traumatization. This is how regular people talk about the uprising, the narrator seems to say as he negotiates between a double narration in which the experience of surviving and the memory of survival intertwine. Clearly, there are no sacralized victims here; survival per se matters, but it is devoid of Romanticism, and "Polishness" becomes a modality of language, namely the language of desperate prayers. The view of the uprising from the perspective of the civilian population of Warsaw trapped in the basements during incessant bombardments challenges the reader to consider a different perspective on the event, a view that would not allow them to fall back on familiar modes of representation aimed at generating patriotic affect. In his commitment to the civilian traumatic everyday, Białoszewski needs to maneuver between the Scylla and Charybdis of traumatic representation: demonizing the experience as pure radicality or banalizing it as an extension of normality.[83] Białoszewski's solution is a fusion of the ordinary and the extreme. The rupture in the quotidian that we associate with radical experience and the open-ended continuity of the quotidian that constitutes everyday life are both embedded in the diction of the *Memoir*. The *Memoir* as a reenactment of oral testimony challenges genre categorizations, but it also challenges our conceptualization of historical traumas that tend to present the traumatic as a self-contained event and find it difficult to accommodate the open-endedness of the everyday experience. It is probably the civilian traumatic everyday that suffers most from the "collapse of witnessing" both in historiographic and artistic accounts. The question that I would like to ask, however, pertains to Białoszewski's strategies of the reenactment and how they—and the experience that shaped them—resonate in Białoszewski's later representations of the everyday.

THE POST-TRAUMATIC EVERYDAY IN THE SMALL NARRATIONS

Białoszewski's representation of the everyday in the small narrations suggests how the traumatic makes itself felt in the familiar plenitude of quotidian reality. His fusion of the familiar and the foreign undermines the common view of trauma and the everyday as mutually exclusive if only because one is perceived as intense and event-specific and the other as an open-ended sphere of unspecificity. In fact, these two dimensions pose similar challenges to representation: trauma because of its radicality and singularity, and the quotidian because of its transparent banality and repetitiveness. As the narrator of Białoszewski's small narrations is conditioned by his wartime experience, his everyday retains a residue of the traumatic. This residue has varying visibilities and is manifest in different themes; in small narrations sometimes the narrator recollects dreams about war or senses impending doom in the memories of his childhood; sometimes traumatic flashbacks erupt from the narrator's quotidian activities; or traumatic associations occur when the prosaic merges with the radical and the narrator's apartment is compared to a bomb shelter.[84] Finally, the narrator at times openly expresses his self-awareness that the psychological imprint of wartime and the uprising defies the vicissitudes of time and logic: "the Uprising always lies in wait for me" ("Powstanie zawsze na mnie czyha").

These thematized moments alert us to subtler and less immediately apparent ways in which the traumatic persists in Białoszewski's writing, and the ways in which the traumatic influences his representation of the quotidian reality. For instance, Białoszewski's treatment of quotidian temporality is similar to the structure of traumatic temporality, which is characterized, among other qualities, by a belatedness and which plays an important role in his presentation of human experiences of temporality and mortality. Białoszewski frequently uses the phrase "a to już," an equivalent of "that's it" or "here it is," but the English translation highlights the literal meaning of the phrase: "and it already was" or "and this already," This recurring phrase directs our attention to the experience of falling into the cracks of time, infinitesimal moments, which—as, for instance, an imperceptible moment of death—irrevocably change the status quo. The flow of time in the small narrations does not reveal its progress; regardless of whether the narrator is preoccupied with the elusive "nothing happenings" or reflections on himself, his reality (including his own mental processes), no matter how seemingly banal, reveals an unfailing potential to surprise him with belatedness. Here is the last vignette from the small narration *Donosy rzeczywistości* (1973; *Reporting Reality*), entitled "denunciation of himself" ("donos na siebie"), in which the narrator feels discouraged by his aged appearance, but also denounces himself by revealing his surprise:[85]

> —The nurse told me you were coming. "Some older gentleman is looking for you, doctor." I asked her what you looked like because I knew you were coming. She said "kind of bald." So then I was sure it was you.
> Jasio smiles, though he was born the same year as me.
> —Goodness me—I say—and I spent so long bracing myself for the moment when someone would describe me that way. I kept thinking no, not yet, in a few years, but here it is [*a to już*].
> —What can you do.
>
> —Siostra zdążyła mi już o tobie powiedzieć. "Jakiś starszy pan szuka pana doktora." Zacząłem ją wypytywać, bo wiedziałem, że masz przyjść. Powiedziała "z taką łysiną". To już nabrałem pewności, że to ty.
> Jasio uśmiecha się, a jest z tego samego roku co ja.

—Ładne rzeczy—mówię—tak się szykowałem na to, że kiedyś ktoś mnie tak nazwie. Ale myślałem, że to jeszcze, za ileś lat, a to już.
—Co robić.[86]

I analyze the phrase "a to już" in relation to the dialectics of two temporal modalities of *kairos* and *chronos* in the "small narrations," which I link to the notion of epiphany.

As in my reading of the *Memoir*, I do not seek clinical symptoms in Białoszewski's psychobiography in his post-*Memoir* works; rather, I am interested in the literary patterns that emerge from his narrative in relation to the traumatic and its residue. I am also interested in how the traumatic seeps into his representation of the quotidian; in other words, how it remains unthematized and yet somehow emerges from the non-traumatic settings of the text. Białoszewski's texts provide fascinating *points de capiton* (anchoring points), to use Lacan's term, in which the traumatic ties down the constant slippage of the signified under the signifier in the quilt of the quotidian. Many theorists of trauma, including Cathy Caruth, Shoshana Felman, and Dori Laub, focus on trauma as the locus of otherness, a rupture in the quotidian. They are concerned with trauma's eccentric status in the mosaic of human experiences, and therefore concentrate on the lacuna—what is missed and what, paradoxically, constitutes traumatic memory and determines its damaging impact. Yet Białoszewski's work challenges such conceptualizations of the traumatic as belonging to a radically different order from the quotidian: the traumatic as extreme and unique, the quotidian as monotonous and inert; or the traumatic as glaringly visible and the quotidian as characterized by the "essential trait of being unperceived."[87] Rather than positioning the two as mutually exclusive binaries, Białoszewski challenges both their opposition and their exclusivity.

Whether he is representing the reality of the Warsaw Uprising or the postwar period, Białoszewski's representations of the traumatic and the quotidian coexist and condition each other: the non-traumatic everyday can be perceived largely because it is interwoven with the traumatic, while the traumatic loses its otherness when it is just an everyday experience. This mutual conditioning in which the traumatic maintains its traumatizing force without being sacralized and fetishized, while the everyday—neither exalted as the locus of authenticity nor critiqued as inert—is valorized as the realm of "something more."

Białoszewski's non-teleological representation of the everyday points to the limitations of contemporary phenomenological, existential, and Marxist theories of the quotidian, which all presuppose a certain deficiency of the everyday and indicate the need to recover meaning from the everyday.

These theories evaluate the everyday through such binary oppositions as, for instance, the authentic versus the inauthentic, the active versus the inert, and the free versus the oppressive. These very binaries imply an assessment that the everyday, in and of itself, is an insufficient realm of life, whose lack of meaning should be remedied by political or philosophical transformations. And by the same token, as these transformations render the everyday meaningful, they reduce the open-ended plurality of the elusive phenomena that constitute the everyday in the first place. Within the discourse of existentialism, for example, the everyday is a repetitive, "instrumental" realm that prevents access to the authenticity of the subject (of the Heideggerian *Dasein,* for instance). In the broadly understood Marxist (or post-Marxist) discourses, the everyday is either a sphere of total control emanating from the power/knowledge structure (as in Foucault) or, on the other end of the spectrum, a sphere whose shapelessness renders it as an inherently oppositional sphere of "praxis." This "oppositional" character, which prevents the everyday from being colonized by institutional powers, is exalted by such theorists as Michel de Certeau, Saul Morson, and Michael Bernstein. Other approaches try to negotiate between the claims of total control and total opposition as, for instance, Henri Lefebvre and the situationists, who perceive the everyday as a realm commodified and manipulated by the structures of capitalism but at the same time recognize its inherent potential to become a realm of authenticity. To realize this potential, however, the everyday needs to be revolutionized, that is, freed from the all-pervasive system of control. The realm of everyday living, in these approaches, by itself is "weak," but with input from a politically conscious agent exercising his or her freedom, it can be transformed into a "strong" political sphere.

The trajectory of critical responses in Polish scholarship shows from the outset that critics were attentive to Białoszewski's treatment of the everyday. Already at his debut, a first wave of critics paid attention to Białoszewski's transformation of perception into "vision illuminating things,"[88] his elevation of everyday "junk" to the status of poetic objects, and his poetic subjectivity absorbing the everyday through the alternating modes of passivity and activity.[89] However, they were observing Białoszewski's poetry *in statu nascendi,* while the group of critics that came after them had the advantage of being able to evaluate the trajectory of the first period of Białoszewski's poetic career, up until the publication of the *Memoir.* This group (including Michał Głowiński, Janusz Sławiński, and Stanisław Barańczak, to name just a few of the most recognizable figures) initiated in the early and mid-1970s criticism influenced by structuralism and speech act theory, which to this day continues to influence Białoszewski's reception. Barańczak's typology of Białoszewski's "languages," in which he identifies three categories in his language—children's language, spoken language, and colloquial language (which Barańczak conceived as a "low" language)—became an important and lasting tool of analysis.[90] Głowiński throughout the years has maintained an interest in Białoszewski's genres and their relationship to orality; he worked since the inception of the small narrations on identifying the patterns of imitation of oral communication and the use of the most basic forms of storytelling in Białoszewski's idiosyncratic "genres of the everyday."[91] This influential group of critics has also pointed to Białoszewski's preference—closely related to the everyday—for low rather than high culture, the unofficial rather than the official, and the empirical rather than the literary. However, the unavoidable price for their typological, structuralist thinking was their treatment of Białoszewski as a disembodied voice, the language without the human.[92]

As if in response to the structuralist predilections of their predecessors, another group of critics elevated Białoszewski's representation of the everyday, moving from the study of language and genre to consider epistemology and metaphysics. Anna Sobolewska linked Białoszewski's project with the ideas of Meister Eckhart and diagnosed his epistemology as a "purity of vision"—a type of phenomenological reduction—that reveals the *Istigkeit* of things.[93] In Białoszewski's broken words and anacoluthic sentences, Sobolewska saw an attempt to create a subjectivity freed from the restraints of a rationality that "search[es] for the meaning of the object even beyond the human 'psychosphere'" and yet is fully immersed in the quotidian.[94] In a similar vein, Marian Stala argued that Białoszewski is, indeed, a metaphysical poet whose "minimalism" can instantaneously "progress from a micro-observation, micro-experience to a fundamental metaphysical vision or intuition."[95] The metaphysical dimension of Białoszewski's project reveals itself, however, according to Stala, only if we resign the conviction that what Białoszewski describes is obvious and accept a type of, if you will, epiphanic defamiliarization. Such interpretations of Białoszewski were a world apart from the approaches of the "linguistic" school.[96] Not only was Białoszewski's voice recovered, but it was granted a philosophical gravitas; these critics even pointed to the "mysticism of the quotidian life"[97] with its vision of reality resembling, as Anna Sobolewska indicated, the medieval principle of "*omnia ubique*" ("all is in all" or, literally, "everything is everywhere").[98]

However, this conception of Białoszewski as a guardian of existential authenticity and a retriever of the mystical potential has its limitations as well. As Grażyna Borkowska pointed out, this exaltation of Białoszewski's philosophy "comes at the price of closing one's eyes to anxieties, tensions, and ruptures of Białoszewski's writing."[99] Joanna Orska concurs about the necessity to bring Białoszewski down from the philosophical heights in which some critics have placed him. She argues that such an approach presupposes that language is an obstacle in the search for the philosophical or mystical charge of the quotidian, whereas in fact Białoszewski's aesthetic forte lay in "a broadly understood liminality" and, thus, his writing may be better served by methodologies that do not work with the binaries and hierarchies.[100]

LIFE-WRITING THROUGH A QUEER LENS

Yet what is missing from Białoszewski scholarship is criticism that closely explores "anxieties, tensions, and ruptures" in Białoszewski's life-writing in relation to the social, material, and historical circumstances of the writer's life. There has been a tendency to treat these circumstances in a somewhat self-explanatory way and not to engage them in textual analysis, which, to some extent, can be understood as a way to avoid a naive biographical mimetism. We can see a shift in this attitude in emerging voices that intend to recover Białoszewski's life for his scholarship; these voices belong to scholars in queer studies interested in Białoszewski's status as a homosexual in Communist Poland.[101] What is at stake in this new field is understanding how Białoszewski inscribed his experience onto his life-writing; but, equally important is our understanding that the homophobic pressure also took a toll on critical approaches. After all, it is my understanding that the silence on the matter from Białoszewski's friends and critics was not only a matter of academic taboo or decorum, but it was also, as I will discuss in a moment, a polyvalent, protective gesture. When the issue of homosexuality could have been broached, however, the "epistemic regime," to use Foucault's expression, persisted and the protective silence became oppressive. New methodologies entered the field, yet the mechanism of circumventing the "inconvenient" by deeming it irrelevant continues.

A force that reinforced such silence was the notion—accepted by default—of Białoszewski's self-willed authorial withdrawal introduced in the early 1970s by Janusz Sławiński. This potent formulation replicated, in various configurations and levels of intensity, Białoszewski's own peculiar and tautological positions: his critics/readers needed him to have constructed an aesthetic space in which he supposedly cultivated his artistic singularity and authenticity, precisely because they wanted to claim him as an existential inhabitant of this space. "Where else if not here [i.e., in his language]," Sławiński asked in the last sentence of his popular essay, "could he [Białoszewski] cultivate 'being his own self,' not depending on anybody and, therefore, authentic . . . ?"[102] Sławiński suggests, thus, a self-limiting characteristic of Białoszewski's practice, but does not tell us why Białoszewski's autonomy must be identified with marginality and from which socially "sanctioned behaviors" that he mentions earlier in his essay this marginality presents a refuge. Białoszewski's "withdrawal" remains vague, yet pure and free. Obviously, the moment we historicize Sławiński's essay, we understand that politically, Sławiński could not be anything but vague in his treatment of the social and cultural forces that shaped Białoszewski's negotiations between socially sanctioned behaviors and his individual choices, including homosexuality. If some of Białoszewski's critics once avoided mentioning his homosexuality because of the anticipated homophobia of Białoszewski's readers and other critics, not to mention the regime, now this avoidance has become its own form of repression, a refusal to discuss Białoszewski's sexuality even though it was clear that it was relevant to his aesthetics and to his lifestyle. Both notions—withdrawal and uniqueness—perform a double task of simultaneously elevating the writer and excusing one's own omission of this writer's status as a member of a sexual minority.

The paradigm of withdrawal is problematic for many reasons, the most basic being that it implies an impenetrability of the space of resistance to outside pressures and, on an even more fundamental level, it constitutes the space of resistance in the first place. This model (and such is, indeed, Sławiński's model) identifies artistic independence with freedom, with "separateness/singularity" ("osobność"), and with authenticity, both in the aesthetic and existential senses. Authenticity, in turn, presupposes a static subject able to free himself from the constraints of hegemonic normativities and to function autonomously. Only such a subject has the power to create and maintain an alternative space—both aesthetically and existentially—protected from cultural norms. This alternative space becomes a self-willed counter-narrative in which the subject celebrates his own sameness. Clearly, such a counter-narrative presupposes a simplistic model of causality in which external oppression leads to internal freedom. We can postulate such a model only if we conceive of identity as self-contained and impenetrable to systems of power and knowledge (in the Foucauldian sense) and, thus, as autonomous.

In my view, this autonomous view of identity, and the individualist notion of an essence lying at the core of an autonomous identity, has contributed to the formation of an unhelpful cult around Białoszewski. Even the most insightful works on Białoszewski's writing and biography favor the notion of authenticity and existential success. Białoszewski's declarations that he happened to be "his singular self" ("być sobie jednym/taki traf mi się"), or that he was translating factuality into expressibility ("faktyczność na wyrażalność"), have often been received in a utopian way (utopian in the aesthetic, sociological, and psychological senses) as the expressions of aesthetic and existential satisfaction. Yet no writer is able to absolutely control his own signification, and no withdrawal, however deliberate and intentional, is ever complete. The spaces from which and into which one withdraws interpenetrate. Not even a "kingdom of insignificance" guarantees the authenticity of the subject.

Białoszewski's freedom to be "separate" ("osobny") in the uniform grayness of the Polish People's Republic and to be able to transform this grayness into "maximally successful existence" was at the core of his appeal. The fact that his audience, including his closest circle of friends, eagerly accepted and reinforced the image of Białoszewski as a symbiosis of life and art even though they were perfectly aware that Białoszewski was repressed for his homosexuality reveals more about the audience's desire than about Białoszewski's choices. Białoszewski's homosexuality was not discussed in terms of the writer's negotiation of his image with the public and the authorities, but it was viewed as another factor that reinforced the utopian vision of an artist creating a free inner space.

To be fair, Białoszewski himself did try, actively and persistently, to maintain his image as a writer with a sovereign gesture, immune to external circumstances. He circulated this image regardless of whether he was addressing his friends or readers and critics. For instance, Białoszewski never draws an explicit connection between, on the one hand, the Stalinist years that he spent in relative seclusion after being forced out of his publishing career and, on the other, his decision not to adhere to the official aesthetic ideology of socialist realism. On the contrary, any sign that could be read as potential resistance is preempted by being incorporated into a story of Białoszewski's creativity, a story designed to reinforce his position of minimalist with the creative freedom of a maximalist. In a well-known, playful eulogy to his bed in the cycle "Leżenia" ("Lying Downs," in *Mylne wzruszenia* [*Misdirected Sentiments*], 1961), published just five years after the Thaw, he presents his speaker as blissfully contemplating the world from his bed. A quarter of a century later, when Białoszewski writes about his reading in New York City, he repeats the pattern of "Lying Downs" and presents, as I discussed, the years of solitude and hunger as a form of creative self-confinement.

Thus, accounts of Białoszewski's biography rarely acknowledge his hardships and the price he paid for his, in contemporary terms, uncloseted sexual orientation. Białoszewski's homosexuality represents the aspect of his biography that transpires to life-writing in a fascinating mode of what I call "hiding through exposure" or a "code of obviousness." I discuss this code in chapter 3, but what interests me is not what signs of homosexual desire we can detect in Białoszewski's life-writing, but what modes of reading emerge from the interaction between our knowledge about Białoszewski's homosexuality and Białoszewski's self-revelations and self-deference in the text. Thus, when I refer to "queering" in the title of the chapter, I am referring both to Białoszewski's strategies of writing as well as to our strategies of reading. And when it comes to our reading, what tools from "Western" queer studies should we use, and how should we use them, in reading a writer whose work emerged from a cultural and political environment quite different from the one in which these tools were developed?

Białoszewski's sense of social exclusion is usually treated perfunctorily. Anna Sobolewska, while reminiscing about the writer, recalls his self-referential joke at the wedding of a mutual friend: "I'm outside of the social brackets" ("Jestem poza nawiasem społecznym"), and then his immediate self-correction, "Let me correct myself: I'm outside of the social hinges. But no, I am just in/on the social hinges" ("Chciałem się poprawić: poza zawiasem. Ale nie, ja jestem właśnie w zawiasie społecznym").[103] In a typical gesture reminding us of his poetic word-games, Białoszewski recasted what sounded like a quasi-confessional (and perhaps melodramatic and self-pitying?) statement into a metaphor of his "in-betweenness" that played with the sounds of "nawias" ("bracket") and "zawias" ("hinge"). But he does not entertain such confessional modes in his writing and, even from the sources closest to him, we rarely learn about the homophobic pressure that Białoszewski experienced, such as the slur painted on his door, as recalled by Wołyński in his conversation with Sobolewski. Wołyński, nota bene, in this very conversation provides information about Białoszewski's life that is, in most accounts, either only hinted at or presumed to be well-known facts. He acknowledges, for instance, that Leszek Soliński (who later inherited the rights to Białoszewski's works, and who appears in the life-writing as "Le.") was Białoszewski's former partner and that "it was probably because of Leszek that Miron found his place in life" (a statement that a "naive" reader could take in general existential terms).[104] And in talking about the dramatically poor living conditions of Białoszewski's younger years, a fact emphasized by critics and biographers, Wołyński also acknowledges a different hardship, namely the need for a family that in a traditional form he could never have: "Miron badly needed something resembling a family—this was Ludwik's [Hering] observation, by the way—and he would get attached to these guys like they were family."[105]

Wołyński also presents us with a unique assessment of Białoszewski's withdrawal from public life, which is far from the romanticized notion of "separateness" or a dissident-like resistance to ideological restrictions:

> Of course, there were other distinguished individuals who did not take on any public roles, but in Miron's case this bothered me somehow. I was bothered by his fear of the police. And suddenly I saw his writing as a kind of refuge. That it was not just done for its own sake, but was a means to go through life painlessly—writing poems like these, which in the period of Socialist Realism seemed to go against the grain, but later became a comfortable refuge. It wasn't fair to think of it this way—I see that now.[106]

Wołyński's thinking presupposes the binary of public/private and the notion of different roles played in each sphere. He perceives Białoszewski's disengagement as a mode of escape from the complications associated with public roles and political choices although such an escape is clearly a political choice per se. The "fear of the police" reminds us that the image of homosexuality propagated in Communist Poland was pathologizing and criminogenic, and ranged from "everyday" forms of persecution such as having neighbors whisper behind Białoszewski's back, being bothered by the administration of his building, and having the already mentioned invectives scrawled on his door, as well as the constantly looming threat of institutional violence and interrogations by the police.

Incidentally, Wołyński (just like Sobolewski, for whom Białoszewski presented himself first of all "as a writer who had already processed it all, and therefore tamed and defused it") treats literature as a coping technique; both read Białoszewski's life-writing as a compensatory strategy. For Wołyński there is too much "humanity" in Białoszewski's escapist attitude, while for Sobolewski, Białoszewski is always already "Białoszewski," a "dehumanized" product of his own autobiographical project and, thus, untouchable ("we felt that nothing could happen to him, that he wasn't in any danger"). Both interpretations presuppose that literature functions as a safety net allowing a successful removal from "life" and creating a hiding place from public pressure and responsibilities. Neither asks about the price exacted on Białoszewski for acting "happy" and for writing poems in order to "go through life painlessly" or about the impenetrability of the public and private spheres in the writer's (and any writer's) life. The result is a biographical disconnect between the fascination with Białoszewski's creative niche—his withdrawal from public life and his refusal to play the role of public intellectual—and the limitations that homosexuality must have imposed on his ability to acquire an identity in the public sphere. In chapter 3, I pay close attention to the representation of private and public spheres; I see it as part and parcel of Białoszewski's subversive narration of gender and sexuality in the small narrations.

It is important to stress that I am reluctant to interpret Białoszewski's writing as a counter-narrative. In my understanding, the notion of counter-narrative presupposes an agent with an autonomous subjectivity composed of self-contained units of existential value—a subjectivity that I discredited earlier in my discussion of "withdrawal." Moreover, counter-narrative presupposes an emancipatory context, which was not part of Białoszewski's historical and social milieu. Hence, I disagree with German Ritz's influential statements on Białoszewski's writing as "the" counter-narrative (one based on "privacy without confession") to the mainstream of Polish literature.[107] Although the notions of confession and privacy are necessary, I see Białoszewski as proposing a more complex mode than the counter-narrative, a mode which is neither emancipatory nor sublimatory.

Instead, Białoszewski's mode is subversive, and I analyze it by employing the tools proposed by gender and queer theories—notably Judith Butler's notion of performativity and David Halperin's notion of "queer" as positionality. These notions allow us to reconceptualize our approach to Białoszewski and his "withdrawal" and to explore his writing without resorting to the vicious conceptual circle of authenticity, agency, and static subjectivity. My goal is to trace Białoszewski's textual strategies in order to better understand how the aesthetic subjectivities are performed in his writing. At the same time, I want to show how Białoszewski's treatment of gender and sexuality in the small narrations exhibits a resistance to the tools of contemporary critical theory pertaining to sexual minorities and to the notions that are its hallmarks (e.g., camp, counter-narrative, emancipation). Białoszewski's own strategies can thus help us reflect upon the categories that organize our reading.

In a much-needed and quite recent development, a number of Polish critics have undertaken the task of interpreting the legacy of "autobiographical" life-writing in the context of Białoszewski's homosexuality. Piotr Sobolczyk traced the trajectory of Białoszewski's early poetic language from modernist sublimation to more straightforward moments of disclosure in his later writing.[108] Białoszewski's private diaries, published in February 2012, have already spurred some discussion in this territory as well.[109] Out of necessity, these first interpretations, while opening up a new field, still have undertones of detective work, which will most likely disappear as the approach accrues greater interpretive capital.

This recent interest in Białoszewski's ways of "coding" homosexuality should be read in the context of a growing "queer literature" in Poland. It was certainly intensified by the heated discussion around Michał Witkowski's *Lubiewo* (2005; *Lovetown*), a queer novel in which Witkowski employed a large segment from Białoszewski's *Szumy, zlepy, ciągi* (1976; *Hums, Lumps, Threads*).[110] In chapter 3, I discuss *Lubiewo*'s intertextuality at length, in order to reflect upon the limitations of reading Białoszewski's texts through the lenses of emancipation, which do not do justice to the material, historical, and semiotic circumstances of Białoszewski's milieu. The surrounding homophobic culture is embedded in Białoszewski's self-censoring aesthetic choices, and without exploring both the culture and the choices it offered, we will be unable to understand this writer who declared an inseparable bond between the lived and the represented.

The issue of interpreting Białoszewski's textual strategies vis-à-vis homosexuality opens up greater challenges of finding an autobiographical model capable of addressing the complexities and idiosyncrasies of Białoszewski's writing. Białoszewski created an all-encompassing model of writing that makes the notion of self-censorship appear mechanical and inadequate, as self-censorship connotes a loss of something that could be voiced but instead is omitted. But a knowing reader immersed in the small narrations does not see gaps and repressions; on the contrary, Białoszewski's represented world lacks nothing. It stands on its own, fully sufficient and obvious, but ultimately hermetic. The effect of the tight code of obviousness lies partly in the seriality of the small narrations and in the way Białoszewski trains his reader to naturalize the subversive character of what he represents. This regulatory mechanism includes, for instance, his non-patriarchal, non-hetero-normative (but also not homo-normative) representation of the family throughout the series. Equally interesting is Białoszewski's consistent focus on women, yet the attentiveness of the narrator's gaze lacks any trace of sexual desire. The effect is a fascinating representation of gender without sexuality. The more straightforward and often hilarious homosexual "moments," as I discuss in my analysis of the passage used by Witkowski in *Lubiewo,* are fully visible to "knowing" readers and easily overlooked by the "naive" ones. Białoszewski generates this effect by using many techniques, including the horizontality of his attention (i.e., the "disclosing" passages get buried in the details with which Białoszewski saturates his narration) and the non-psychological portrayal of his characters.

At the core of the challenges that Białoszewski's maximalist project of life-writing presents to his critics is the problem of autobiography, which surfaces more strikingly—and more politically—in the sphere pertaining to Białoszewski's homosexuality. I focus primarily on the parts of the small narrations which engage an autobiographical narrator (even if at times the "I" expands into the intimate "we" of the narrrator's most immediate circle) and which have the character of, as Michał Głowiński put it, a "crypto-diary" (although I discuss the problems with the use of this term in chapter 3). It is difficult not to see Białoszewski, as I mentioned earlier, as "always already" a "textual-bodily being," where "always already" denotes a mode of reading that is marked by the hermeneutic impossibility of return to Białoszewski from "Białoszewski," the writer's creation.

My interest lies in Białoszewski's insistence on his "signature," that is, on the creation of the narratorial subjectivity that encourages the reader to treat life-writing as Białoszewski's autobiography. In this regard, I find a sylleptic understanding of narratorial subjectivity, which has already generated engaging critical works in Białoszewski scholarship, particularly applicable.[111] Sylleptic subjectivity is marked by the use of the author's real name that needs to be simultaneously understood as fictional and real (i.e., identified with author), textual and empirical. This kind of construction of subjectivity presupposes that the "I" of the narrative "imitates and creates, i.e., that its function is simultaneously mimetic and semiotic." Syllepsis suggests a zeugmatic relationship between writing and biography, that is, both sides of the equation—I/author/life and "I"/"Białoszewski"/life-writing—are mutually dependent and reinforcing. Such a dynamic is particularly suitable for the writer who, from what we see in his oeuvre (and by all biographical accounts as well), favored performative and theatricalized approaches to creativity. The sylleptic view of Białoszewski's narratorial "I" allows us to avoid the mimetic approach to autobiography (from the self to creation; from the subject to the object, etc.), the trap of the post-structuralist death of the author (Barthes), and a view of authorship as a function of discourses (Foucault). Białoszewski and "Białoszewski" do not seem satisfactorily accommodated by the notion of the "scriptor";[112] Białoszewski's "I"s and the political, sociological, and cultural circumstances of his life do not seem to be satisfactorily addressed in reading his creative space as purely intertextual. The sylleptic perspective dismisses the "I" which is not the "I" of the Cartesian "cogito" (that is, "I" of intact, "internal" subjectivity that precedes the "external" and is constituted by a clear divide between the me and the not-me) and proposes an "I" simultaneously engaged in the empirical and in the process of constituting itself in the process of writing. The inherent doubleness of such "self-creating subjectivity" (or "podmiotowość autokreatywna," as Polish critics also call it) resonates well with Białoszewski's project of life-writing and presupposes a more dynamic understanding of its documentary value (including the veracity of the *Memoir*). The sylleptic understanding of Białoszewski's narrative positionality that respects both his textual as well as biographical performance can also produce interesting results in gender and queer theory. Białoszewski's homosexuality simply cannot be displaced anymore under a general category of artistic "individuality" or silenced by the notion of "privacy," or identified, as it used to be, in a convenient gesture of essentialization, with, to use one critic's expression, "separateness, which in Białoszewski's case probably had a psychosomatic background."[113]

Perhaps the greatest challenges for a future scholarship on Białoszewski are to return it to the mud of history, to historicize and to politicize. Białoszewski, when taken at his own word, makes us forget the "details" and challenges of his moment in history; nevertheless, we need to saturate our scholarship with these details, in the spirit of Białoszewski's own words that "every little detail is important, otherwise the writing isn't saturated and without this saturation there is only literature, the absence of the human." I propose to look more closely at the dynamic interrelations between contradictory impulses in Białoszewski's writing, to see him as a writer who ultimately affirmed life, but whose affirmation—and the power of it—sprang from traumatization (of a historical, political, and cultural nature). I see Białoszewski oscillating between the traumatic and the quotidian and negotiating between the queer and the hegemonic, assimilation and "self-othering." The appeal and elusiveness, the "puzzling quality" of this writing, springs precisely from Białoszewski's ability to smoothly and consistently integrate such contradictions and destabilize his own authorial position between fiction and autobiography. As this destabilization turns into his own regulatory fiction, Białoszewski succeeds, like no other Polish writer, in naturalizing what could otherwise be perceived as radical and, at times, subversive.

"Nobody has yet attempted to delineate the degree of radicality and courage of Białoszewski's enterprise in the sphere of literature and—simultaneously—in the sphere of life," said Stanisław Rosiek. This book aims to contribute to a much larger communal project of recovering this radicality without romanticizing and heroicizing Białoszewski's existential and literary project. Although I believe that, as Anna Sobolewska affectionately assessed it, Miron Białoszewski, in spite of everything, practiced and represented a "quiet freedom," I also think we must remember how difficult, how fraught with anxieties and self-limitations, this freedom was. This does not make it any less valuable; on the contrary, it makes it even more deserving of our grateful recognition.[114]

Chapter 1

“The Glaring Identity of ‘Now’”: *A Memoir of the Warsaw Uprising* as a Reenactment of the Traumatic

Znów zaczął się dygot. Osuwanie się z szumem. Coraz większym. Swen ściskał mnie ręką za kolano. Ja wciskałem w siebie oczy i wtuliłem w kołnierz głowę: “Więc to już? To już? tak, trudno, tylko czy ściśnie od głowy? spłaszczy? i żeby tylko prędko.” Dwa sklepienia razem runęły z pierwszego piętra na parter, więc teraz my. Swen wciskał glowę gdzieś pod moje kolano. Matka Swena stała bez zmiany. Było cichutko. Była kompletna cisza. Tylko coś szumiało, osypywało się, jeszcze osypało się, osypało . . .

Again the vibrations began. A noisy moving about. More and more. Swen squeezed my knee. I winced and hid my head in my collar. “Is this it already? Already? Yes, it’s hard, only will it strike from the head? To the feet? Will it knock you flat? If only it could be quick.” Two ceilings collapsed from the first floor to the ground floor, so now it was our turn. Swen pressed his head against my knee. Swen’s mother stood there without changing her position. It was very quiet. There was absolute silence. Only something rumbled, was crumbling, still crumbling, crumbling . . .
—Miron Białoszewski, *Pamiętnik z powstania warszawskiego* (1970)

—Zdrowaś, Mario, łaskiś pełna, Pan z Tobą . . .
—Święta Mario, Matko Boża, módl się za
nami grzesznymi teraz i w godzinę śmierci
naszej, amen.
Pamiętam jaskrawą tożsamość "teraz" i "w
godzinę śmierci" – ile razy ją odczuwałem przy
odmawianiach, a wciąż się odmawiało, słyszało,
tu, obok, tu drugi raz, na spacerze, u tych obok,
i obok dalej, i jak przejść dalej, i jak iść, jak coś
tylko głośniej waliło, to to jak fala:
—Zdrowaś, Mario, łaskiś pełna . . .
—Teraz i w godzinę śmierci naszej, amen.

—Hail, Mary, full of grace. The Lord be with
Thee . . .
—Hail, Mary, Mother of God, pray for
us sinners now and in the hour of our
death, amen.
I remember the glaring identity of "now" and
"in the hour of our death." How many times
did I feel it during the prayers, but people
prayed constantly. You could hear them. Here
beside you or, during a walk, among those near
by, or somewhat distant, as you walked ahead,
and as you just wandered about, whenever
something exploded a little more loudly than
usual. Then it was like a wave:
—Hail, Mary, full of grace . . .
—Now and in the hour of our death, amen.
—Miron Białoszewski, *Pamiętnik z powstania warszawskiego* (1970)

BETWEEN MOURNING AND FETISHIZATION: THE WARSAW UPRISING IN POLISH CULTURAL MEMORY

The posters announced, "They were dying in the sun" ("Umierali w słońcu"), but the images were of contemporary young Varsovians. They were dressed like twenty-first-century urban youths, and they faced the camera in the frontal, still posture typical of the tradition of photographic portraiture. These black-and-white images were punctuated by the white-and-red armbands of the Polish Home Army. The posters—accompanied as they were by a statement whose grammatical subject ("they") was left vague, yet in its vagueness invited a sense of communal understanding of what it pertains to—were displayed throughout Warsaw to mark the sixtieth anniversary of the outbreak of the Warsaw Uprising of 1944. The afternoon of August 1, 2004, was bright and hot, just like the afternoon sixty years earlier when the Home Army rose up against the Nazis who had occupied Warsaw for almost five years. The months of August and September 1944, through the uprising's capitulation on October 2, 1944, are still remembered as particularly sunny.

The ceremonies of 2004 might be the last major anniversary of the uprising in which surviving insurrectionists participated. The occasion, one of the most elaborate and carefully choreographed state events in recent Polish history, was designed to display the inchoate contours of the country's post-Communist cultural memory. Led by the mayor of Warsaw, Lech Kaczyński (who later became the country's president and died tragically in a plane crash in 2010),[1] and attended by the country's leading political and cultural figures, the events took place just three months after Poland joined the European Union (EU). The former German chancellor Gerhard Schröder attended, as did U.S. Secretary of State Colin Powell and British Deputy Prime Minister John Prescott. Despite the ongoing debate concerning the role of the Soviet Union during the uprising and the invitation from the Polish government to attend the ceremonies, Russian officials were conspicuously absent. The celebrations were designed to simultaneously emphasize Poland's new standing within the international community as well as to reinforce a traditional view of Polish identity and, hence, also to reassure those Poles who feared that joining the EU would weaken their national identity.

The authorities of Warsaw, together with the governmental agencies that organized the ceremonies, sought to create an anniversary that conveyed historical continuity, emphasized the legendary patriotism of its participants, and represented the foundational dimension of the uprising for the city's identity. Words and images of the uprising—posters with lyrics of iconic songs and poems of the uprising along with photographs of their young authors, most of whom died fighting—became part of the capital's landscape. *Kotwica,* an anchor combining letters the "W" and "P" signifying Poland Fighting (Polska Walcząca)—a symbol of the Polish wartime underground that was well known to every Pole—became the all-pervasive logo of the ceremonies. On the anniversary of the uprising, 5:00 p.m., the very hour at which the uprising broke out, the Polish translation of *Rising '44: The Battle for Warsaw,* by the popular British historian Norman Davies, hit the bookstores.[2] The day before the anniversary, Mayor Kaczyński inaugurated an institution that was his idée fixe for years: the new Museum of the Warsaw Uprising (Muzeum powstania warszawskiego), probably the most interactive museum in Poland.

With their splendor and range, these commemorative celebrations seemed more to express the Polish need for an international audience to recognize the staggering impact of the event than to serve as a reminder of what happened for the benefit of Polish society. Clearly, there was no danger that the uprising would be forgotten at home. Sixty years after its outbreak, the uprising was still considered by 45 percent of Poles as one of the most important events in Polish history, and some 30 percent of the population regards it as an event that directly affected their lives in one way or another.[3] To a large extent, this persistence of the uprising's position in the communal memory may be a reaction to its convoluted post-memory, that is, to the fact that for decades during the Communist regime, its losses were neither properly mourned nor were the multiplicity of its political and symbolic dimensions openly acknowledged and publicly discussed. In other words, the communal memory of the uprising, due to the role Soviet Russia played in the event, was only partially institutionalized. The reductive debate on the uprising reflected the complexities and miseries of postwar Poland's situation as a Soviet satellite country. The communal memory of the uprising was to a large extent transmitted "under the table" with all the consequences that unofficial modes of transmission entail. Before I discuss these consequences, a brief review of some basic facts about the uprising, which contributed to the later symbolic status of the event, is in order.[4]

THE HISTORICAL CONTEXT OF THE UPRISING

The Warsaw Uprising erupted on August 1, 1944, on the orders of Poland's London-based government-in-exile in response to the Soviet Union's establishment of a pro-Moscow government in Poland's liberated eastern provinces. The military aim of the uprising was for the underground Home Army, loyal to the London government, to end the German occupation of Warsaw. This military aim to liberate the city by Polish hands before the Soviet army entered it overlapped with the uprising's political aim: to force the Soviet leader, Joseph Stalin, to recognize that Poles regarded the London government as their legitimate leader, thus preventing Poland from being forced into the Soviet orbit. The Home Army's forces were remarkably well organized considering that Warsaw had been under German occupation for five years, but the determination of the 55,000 young insurrectionists, lightly armed, often with homemade munitions, was no match for the aerial bombardments, heavy artillery, and the well-equipped elite SS units deployed by the Germans.[5]

The uprising, which was planned to last for a maximum of seven days, continued for sixty-three days. Historians still argue about the political and military reasons for the failure of the Western Allies to provide substantial help to the insurrectionists who fought—first in the hope that this help would come and later in desperation that it never materialized. Stalin repeatedly thwarted the Allies' attempts to help the uprising by not allowing British and American planes to land and refuel on territories liberated by the Red Army, which reduced the number of aid deliveries. Meanwhile, the Red Army that approached the city famously waited on the left bank of the Vistula River for the uprising to meet its end, prohibiting the Polish troops that were part of the Red Army to cross the river to aid their compatriots and shooting those who tried.[6] However, it is still a matter of dispute whether the spiral of death and utter destruction that followed the first victorious days of the uprising could have been avoided through the Allies' diplomatic means. We know, though, that as the events of the uprising unfolded, the scale of the calamities only increased, and as the uprising stretched into weeks, the testimonies of its participants show how the initial sense of elation and hope was gradually transformed into a growing sense of inevitable doom, and how waiting for help that never came intensified the desperation and alienation of the insurrectionists and the Warsaw population.

By the uprising's end on October 2, 1944, some 225,000 Polish soldiers and civilians lay dead amidst the ruins of Warsaw. After Polish capitulation, the Germans deported the remaining population to labor camps and burned and dynamited the remains of the city. The order to completely level the city came from Hitler himself, whose desire to take revenge on the city in a pure display of power was greater than the more pressing needs of deploying his troops to fight the war. His orders were executed systematically and thoroughly. Buildings—especially archives and libraries—that had survived the bombardments were repeatedly set ablaze until they were utterly destroyed. In December 1944, the Führer announced to the Reichstag, "Warsaw is only a geographical point on the map of Europe."

Almost immediately after its conclusion, the uprising acquired legendary status in the communal memory. It became an immensely loaded point of reference on the map of Polish collective memory and a repository of values associated with national identity. Its status was only reinforced by the fact that throughout the Communist period, the memory of the uprising was either actively repressed or, at best, politically censored and manipulated. Fluctuations in the modes of representing and officially commemorating the uprising reflected the country's political situation and ranged from the direct violence of incarceration and execution of the Home Army soldiers in the Stalinist period to, in happier periods of "stabilization," a political manipulation of preserving the anti-Nazi aspect of the uprising while censoring common knowledge that Soviet Russia capitalized on letting the Nazis do "the dirty work" in Warsaw and eradicate the Polish leadership. The basic fact remained that, except for a short period of Solidarity's "carnival" (August 1980–December 1981) and until the fall of the Berlin Wall and the change of the system, the historical, political, and moral complexities of the uprising could be addressed only selectively.[7] It is quite telling that the first monument of the Warsaw Uprising was erected in Warsaw only in 1989; as if to gesture to a historical justice, the Supreme Court building is visible in the background.

This selective presence of the event in the public arena and its selective integration into society's commemorative practices and institutional memory was reinforced by the tendency of Communist propaganda to circumvent inconvenient aspects of the uprising by conflating it under the larger category of the "heroism and courage of the Polish soldier." While it was acceptable to address the uprising's immediate goal of liberating the capital from German occupation, the uprising's origins and political dimensions were either silenced or presented as the irresponsible decision of the London government. What remained intact even in these official narratives was the military valor and patriotic devotion of the Polish nation in its "fight with the Nazi invader" ("walka z hitlerowskim najeźdźcą"), in the propagandistic idiom. This vocabulary of unspecificity facilitated a conflation of the uprising with other, politically appropriate, displays of heroism.[8] Both modes of selectivity and conflation had a profound impact on the configuration of the uprising's communal memory and its symbolic reverberations.

First of all, this partial presence of the uprising only strengthened the predominant view of the event as a moral triumph despite the irony, which most historians now agree upon, that the uprising ultimately contributed to the political outcomes its initiators had sought to avoid: as a result of its failure, it was easier for the Red Army to enter the city and to establish the U.S.S.R.-affiliated local government, which discredited the London-based government-in-exile, while the death of the young intelligentsia participating in the uprising deprived Poland of its human potential for political opposition in the postwar Communist years.[9] Yet, in spite of—although, as I would ultimately like to claim, because of—the sheer volume of the loss, being "one of the greatest political and military failures [Poland] suffered throughout its long and often tragic history,"[10] the collective and cultural memory of the uprising is permeated by compensatory mechanisms, in which moral gains substitute for human, material, and political losses.

Beginning as early as 1945 (and thus in the short period between the end of the war and the beginning of Stalinism in Poland in 1947), the uprising was cast in ethical categories as an event that demonstrated the Conradian ethics of faithfulness. The best-known proponent of this view was a recognized interwar writer, Maria Dąbrowska, whose 1945–46 debate with a young Marxist essayist, Jan Kott, encoded in Conradian terms the most urgent moral issues of the Polish "uprising tradition" ("tradycja powstańcza") and the uprising itself. Conradian faithfulness means that, writes Dąbrowska, "without sanctions, without obligations, without hope, without price, and without fear of punishment we are to be moral out of the very sense of responsiblity for our own fate and the fate of another human being."[11] Such an interpretation of the uprising shifted the weight from the event's political and military failures to the unquantifiable realm of ethics. In this realm of ethically privileged categories, honor meant unflinching faithfulness to one's community and to one's task regardless of the final outcome of one's action. The model of acting outside of a pragmatic economy of gain and loss resonated with the cultural memory of the earlier failed uprisings against Russian rule in the nineteenth century (in fact, the very word "powstanie"—"uprising"—immediately invokes this tradition).[12] In fact, in *A Memoir of the Warsaw Uprising,* Miron Białoszewski remarks that during the Warsaw Uprising, Varsovians expected it to be known as the August Uprising, thus already pointing to the communal sense that the Warsaw Uprising, like the January Uprising of 1863 and the November Uprising of 1830 before it, is another repetition of the sacrificial pattern of Poland's tragic history.[13]

Indeed, the notion of repetition is not surprising in a nation that—since 1795, that is, the final partition of a sovereign Poland until the end of Communism in 1989—could boast few political successes but numerous historical tragedies including the two aforementioned uprisings followed by decades of Russian retributions, the battles that raged across Poland during the First World War, two decades of crisis-filled independence in between the two world wars followed by the immense traumas of the Holocaust and the German occupation (in which Poland lost approximately six million citizens, half of whom were Polish Jews), and, finally, the territorial surgeries of the Yalta agreement and more than forty years of Communist rule. National identity forged in the process of these historical traumas thus manifested in what Dominick LaCapra calls a "tendency in modern culture and thought . . . to convert trauma into the occasion for sublimity, to transvaluate it into a test of the self of the group and an entry into the extraordinary."[14] This elevation of the traumatic to the level of the sublime, the traumatic sublime, became a compensatory cultural mode that served a vital function in Poland, and the historical context of the losses in the Warsaw Uprising made Poles particularly susceptible to such compensation. As if performing the words of the great Romantic Juliusz Słowacki—"let them watch us when we are dying" ("niech nas widzą jak konamy")—the trauma and losses of the uprising were elevated to the level of the sublime as "an uncanny source of elation or ecstasy" (to which I will return later when discussing the uprising's literary representations).[15]

The compensatory transformation of the traumatic into the sublime (which also functioned as a defense mechanism alleviating confrontation with unimaginable human and material losses of the uprising) manifested itself in the predominance of a rhetoric that disregarded pragmatic calculations. Engaged in the symbolic exchange of empirical loss (human, material, etc.) for symbolic (moral, religious) gain, this rhetoric transformed the political and military failure of the uprising into a moral triumph by enshrining its young participants' patriotism, heroism, and sacrifice. In light of the official sanitization of the uprising, the elevation of the uprising became associated with, if not political dissent, at least moral opposition against Russia. In a complex turn, the decades of suppression reinforced what Tomasz Łubieński aptly describes as "a double censorship" of the uprising, one from the Communist state, which censored its political dimension, and the other from a large section of the citizenry, whose unspoken agreement was to preserve the unofficial heroic memory of the event by refusing to discuss the uprising's raison d'être even in the underground "public" sphere.[16] Such censorship from the inside manifested faithfulness to the dead and became loyalty to the event itself. In this logic, to critique the event by questioning its significance or justification threatens the economy of the sacrifice: for there to be a symbolic gain, the meaningfulness of the loss cannot be questioned.

Such a compensatory manner of remembering was still tangible in the celebratory strategies sixty years after the event of which the posters with the inscription "They were dying in the sun" serve as a telling example. Clearly, the weather was not at stake in the message of this inscription, although it was suggestive of the summer's heat recalled by the survivors. More to the point is its evocation of one of the most persistent myths of the uprising—the myth of the "beautiful death," a Polish version of the Latin patriotic exhortation, *dulce et decorum est pro patria mori*—which became the motto associated with the uprising's generation, that is, the only generation born in an independent Poland and brought up in the zealous atmosphere of freshly regained independence. The imagery of the sun gracing the death scene, with its connotation of divine light, transforms dying into a moment of transcendence. Such aesthetically elated visualizations of dying (note the use of the past continuous in "they were dying"—*umierali*) compensate for—and distract from—the horrific ways of dying inscribed by the actual nature of the event: in the sewers, which served as evacuation paths; in provisional field hospitals, which lacked basic anesthetics and whose many patients met a horrifying death;[17] under the collapsed buildings or in the flames of accidentally self-set "Molotov cocktails."[18] Only for a few lucky ones did death come in the fervor of battle. Sunshine, we may suspect, was hardly the last image on earth for some 200,000 civilian casualties who spent the uprising in basements, terrified by the incessant bombardments—many of them had to await their deaths while buried alive under the collapsed buildings. Yet, sixty years after the uprising, the poster still succeeds in creating a sense of continuity between the tradition of unconditional patriotism attributed to the young members of the Home Army and the youth of contemporary Poland.

The mechanisms in use here are the de-historicization of the past and a conflation of contemporary youth with their wartime peers and their "sweet and honorable death for the homeland." The armbands with Poland's national colors on the living and the evocative inscription of the dead suggest an idealization of the traumatic past, with the intent to trigger an immediate emotional response. Rather than blending pathos with historical reflection, the pathos is generated to summon identification. Such de-historicization is characteristic of the collective memory since, as Maurice Holbswach tells us, collective memory tends to be ahistorical and forgetful of both the passage of time and the complexities of historical events.[19]

A similar de-historicization of the collective memory is encouraged by the Museum of the Warsaw Uprising, which caters both to Polish and foreign visitors and is, in a sense, designed to "export" the memory of the uprising to an international audience. Technologically savvy, the museum presents a consistent, streamlined, and engaging narrative; however, in spite of its technological sophistication and its self-proclaimed educational mission, the museum fails to present the historical complexities of the uprising and insists on the reinforcement of the emotional, not to say at times titillating, presentation of the event. It merely alludes to controversy over the purpose and results of the uprising, but its main effect is to induce in the viewers a sense of awe for the insurrectionists' sacrificial spirit. By brushing over the controversies surrounding the uprising by invoking the emotional impact of death and destruction and, first and foremost, with a romanticization and aestheticization of the insurrectionists' sacrifice, the museum fully reinforces a vision of Polish history as a series of repeated sacrificial gestures whose sheer traumatic dimension silences any rational debate. The uprising is to be admired in awe and not debated in reason; the museum situates patriotism outside rational debate. The impressive museum store offers a range of patriotic memorabilia including some coloring books for children, in which they can color brave scout boys and girls, the Gavroches of Warsaw; and the models of Liberty planes—the same planes that for the insurrectionists were too long-awaited and too scarce signs of hope—thus engaging the youngest generation of contemporary Poles in the re-creation of the uprising's iconic images. Clearly, this heroic and primarily military narrative comes at the price of minimizing the losses of Warsaw's civilian population, which paid the highest price for the uprising.[20]

THE PINNACLES AND NADIRS OF REPRESENTATION

Most literary treatments of the Warsaw Uprising tend to have a compensatory function and perpetuate what Maria Janion calls "the mythical imperative,"[21] stressing the youth and dedication of the insurrectionists, the beauty of their heedlessness, and the meaningfulness of their deaths. In "Wojna i forma" (1976; "War and Form")—a study that has become fundamental to a critical understanding of Białoszewski's *Memoir*—Janion analyzes the tradition of uprising representations in the light of war representation. Her main point is to demonstrate the pinnacles and nadirs into which war has been cast in order to show the uniqueness of Białoszewski's deeply civilian perspective. In Polish literary tradition, a predominant mode has been to represent the uprising according to the Romantic paradigm, in which suffering has a redeeming value and the traumatic is aestheticized and theatricalized. Such redemptive narratives have had various forms and permutations. At the most extreme, they manifest a martyrological "desperate Romanticism" ("romantyzm straceńczy") in which death becomes an occasion to deliver an exquisite, unforgettable gesture and a spectacle that shames an indifferent world—"let them watch us when we are dying" ("niech nas widzą jak konamy"). In a more popular form, they can exhibit what Janion evocatively names the "uhlan western" ("western ułański"), in which war becomes an occasion for a community of "strong men" to test their courage, stamina, and heroism. In the "uhlan western," *jouissance* of death substitutes for erotic *jouissance*.[22]

In its most sympathetic manifestation, Romantic rhetoric ensured the psychological survival of those whose losses were greatest. In his 1951 autobiographical novel, *Ziele na kraterze* (*The Grass at the Edge of the Crater*), written abroad and first published in London, Melchior Wańkowicz (1892–1974) incorporates the story of the uprising into a loving tale about his two daughters who belonged to the same generation as Białoszewski. Wańkowicz's older daughter, Krystyna, was killed in the uprising at the age of twenty-four while serving as a Home Army nurse. A juxtaposition of the pastoral landscape with the implicit destruction in the book's title reflects the clash of Wańkowicz's memories of the girls' happy childhood and adolescence in interwar Poland with heart-wrenching passages describing his wife's futile search for Krystyna's body among the thousands of bodies exhumed after the end of the war. Wańkowicz's approach is symptomatic of a cultural tendency to fuse personal mourning with a redemptive vision of Polish history. The parent's immense grief is alleviated, and he finds purpose in his child's death by treating the uprising as a historical manifestation of the ethos of sacrifice for one's homeland. A Conradian faithfulness to oneself becomes an essential ingredient of this ethos and of the upbringing of the uprising's generation. Wańkowicz characterizes this generation as breathtakingly brilliant in its readiness to confirm the noble principle of the Thermopylae, in which the community's raison d'être validates individual death.[23] This tautological thinking—patriotism validates death and death validates patriotism—prevents any exploration of the event that would not have predictable answers already inscribed in the questions. The author's grief bars the reader's right to explore the non-redemptive.

The novel's most memorable passages merge descriptions of eight couples (friends of Wańkowicz's daughter) as they dance a mazurka a few days before the uprising with descriptions of their fate in the uprising. The beauty, youth, and carelessness emanating from the dance scene are projected onto the next section. Preceded by the motto of *non omnis moriar* ("I shall not wholly die"), the section provides the reader with a specifics of the death of each dancer while at the same time treating their deaths as the ultimate bonding experience. In highly aestheticized descriptions, the beauty of the insurrectionists' sacrificial deed radiates through the horrors of violent death and later through the horrors of exhumation. Wańkowicz's grief does not contribute to an innovative treatment of the uprising. On the contrary, *Ziele na kraterze* is a good example of how a psychological need to make sense of the loss reinforces a cultural tendency for redemptive readings of the traumatic. In some sense, loss and redemptive readings are mutually conditioning and powerful enough to override a confrontation with the past that would resist symbolic compensation; this power is particularly striking in writers who, like Wańkowicz, proved their prowess in documentary genres.[24]

In the predominant representations of the uprising, we can see a tendency to place the event in a redemptive framework, that is, to create a narrative that compensates for loss with the symbolic gain of a reaffirmed Polish identity.[25] Such a framework resembles what Eric Santner labeled as "narrative fetishism" characterized by "the construction and deployment of a narrative consciously or unconsciously designed to expunge the traces of the trauma or loss that called the narrative into being in the first place."[26] Thus, instead of binding the already excessive pathos, portrayals of the uprising tend to generate even more pathos, which in turn serves as a defense mechanism against confrontation with the impact of loss. Pathos grows from a kernel of fetishization of death that is strikingly visible in the "myth of the beautiful death." On the most basic level, this myth had to do with the demographics of the uprising troops—mostly consisting of people under twenty-four years of age; on a more complex level, the myth treats the uprising as a holocaust. I use this term not to suggest a parallel with the historical event of the Holocaust, but in its etymological Greek sense of *holokauston* that signifies "a thing wholly burnt," a sacrifice to the gods that is completely burned to ashes; this sacrifice presupposes a moral sovereignty and an agency which a conscious choice of death confirms.[27]

In the sacrificial economy, something is willingly lost to enable something else to be gained. In the Polish tradition, the Warsaw insurrectionists are iconic self-willed sacrificial figures. What constitutes them is their sovereign gesture of the "total" (*holos*) "burning out" (*kaustos*) of life at the altar of fatherland. Their actions and their agency situate them at the same time in the order of the living (the "here and now" of fighting the uprising) and in the order "beyond" (being always already implicated in the transcendence of sacrifice). This liminal position is precisely what facilitates a paradoxical mechanism of simultaneous sacralization and identification. In the iconic representations of the uprising's participants, beauty and death merge, placing the reader and the viewer in a transgressive position of a voyeur terrified, yet erotically appealed to by life on the verge of disappearance.[28] The traumatic loss is compulsively staged and repeated—in other words, "acted out." "Acting out" presupposes a symptomatic relationship with the past; its mechanism is transferential and identificatory. In "acting out," the contours delineating past and present lose their definition and the observer is intimately implicated in the observed. A good example of implicating the observer in the observed are the photographs included in the collection of the Museum of the Warsaw Uprising and displayed and disseminated in various forms (from billboards on the museum grounds to postcards in its store) under the title "The Color of Freedom. Warsaw 1944" ("Kolor wolności. Warszawa 1944"). Digitally altered colors of the original black-and-white photographs juxtapose shades of sepia with a touch of color that emphasizes small elements of the image—a child's pink hair ribbon, a white-and-red band on a soldier's arm, the blueness of a girl's eyes. Explaining the idea of coloring the pictures, the museum declares, "Traditional black and white images made the past an isolated and self-contained territory, separated from the present with impermeable border . . . Color erases distance, which separates us from the past. Human faces, the streets of that Warsaw, scenes caught by a reporter, are immersed in the same presentness [*teraźniejszość*] as the one that we are experiencing right here and right now. It's August, it's September 1944. We are in Warsaw, which will disappear but only in a few weeks, in a few days." This emotional rhetoric guides the viewer to look at the photographs from an apocalyptic perspective. The "presentness" that the viewer is summoned to share with the subjects of the photographs is conditioned by the viewer's knowledge of imminent destruction of the reality that the photograph represents.

By summoning the viewer, these photographs encourage "acting out" and emotional identification with the past. "Working through," on the other hand, is a mode of critical distancing; it implies an ongoing dialogue between the traumatic past and the present. This dialogue disrupts the otherness and self-contained nature of the traumatic and gradually shifts it into the realm of the narrative, which frees the victim from the cycle of uncontrollable returns. A goal of "working through" is to have an awareness that no matter how connected we are to the past, our present identity cannot and should not be conflated with the identity of the victim (regardless of whether we were the victim or whether we experienced a so-called secondary traumatization by witnessing the trauma of others). To gain a critical perspective on the experience, to put it in the broader context of the victim's life and the life of the collective allows a gradual "overcoming" of the traumatic. The notion of overcoming should be qualified, however; no overcoming is absolute and no traumatic story gets fully integrated into the narrative. Yet the gradual and open-ended process of working through allows enough control over the memory—at the very least over the unexpected "acting out" of memory and its returns in the form of traumatic flashbacks—to allow a victim to lead a so-called normal life.

It is important to remember, however, that these psychoanalytic distinctions of "acting out" and "working through," which are fundamental for memory and trauma studies, are analytical and differential in nature, that is, they are to be treated as conceptual tools to differentiate between processes of memory and not as ontological categories.[29] No category of memory exists in a pure form, and neither on the individual nor on the collective level can they ever be separated. Every process of relating to the past and "working through" it involves a dynamics of distancing and identification; after all, the open-ended nature of memory allows no mastery over the past. "Acting out" thus can be viewed as part of the process of "working through," which becomes detrimental only when not critically bound and not accompanied by other processes. On its own acting out may become a process of never-ending transference—a repetitive identification with the past and the victim that becomes the main vehicle for a confirmation of one's identity, both on the individual or collective level.[30] The distancing that "working through" entails bars the mechanism of transference, yet such distancing does not have to exclude empathy. Ideally, a relationship with the past should balance empathy and criticism (the attitude LaCapra terms as "empathic unsettlement"): empathy for the victims and mourning for the losses merged with a sense of the historical context for the traumatic. Only by binding the impulse to respond to the traumatic with pure affect and with transference can we create a politically and culturally viable collective identity.

The case of the uprising shows, unfortunately, that even in post-1989 Poland, not to mention the Communist period, transference is actually encouraged and institutionally reinforced. Transference is a seductive proposition: it offers emotional stimulation and demands nothing more than the repetition of the same. It often makes for a secondary traumatization, that is, the traumatization that occurs from the identification with an experience that one did not share. Transference may even have an irresistible and transgressive erotic charge: the gazes of the soldiers, nurses, and messenger girls staring directly into the camera, and the words of the uprising's poets always resonating in the impending silence have a transfixing and bewitching power. It is not surprising that in postwar Poland "acting out" took precedence over working through the memory of the uprising. A tendency toward narrative fetishism was a logical consequence of double censorship, but the mechanism of double censorship was perhaps slightly different than what Tomasz Łubieński proposes in his approach. For Łubieński, double censorship works like a steam engine: a repression of memory on the official, public level powers its unofficial elevation. However, narrative fetishism may be viewed not only as a compensating response to the restriction on representation, but the very repetition of the mechanism governing such restriction. As I have mentioned, one of the most successful tactics of Communist propaganda while dealing with inconvenient historical events was to promote a conflation of historical memory.[31] Thus, inconvenient events would be "folded over" into the category of convenient events. The category of the "heroism of the Polish soldier," for instance, allowed one to mention in the same sentence the Battle of Monte Cassino and the participation of General Anders's army (the memory of which was censored), or the Battle of Berlin and the participation of Polish troops incorporated into the Red Army (the memory of which was politically advantageous), as long as both events proved to serve a teleological pull for the existing political status quo. Avoiding specifics facilitated a homogenization of history that was less conspicuous than the simpler, blunter mechanism of prohibition and compensation.[32]

Thus, the redemptive patterns that could be found in such novels as Wańkowicz's existed regardless of whether the uprising was approached (that is, when it could be talked about, after the Stalinist period) from the officially encouraged Marxist evaluation ("heroic soldiers" with "cynical leaders") or from the unofficial perspective of the Polish government-in-exile that validated the uprising's reason d'être. Whether it was to be a historically regressive attempt to stall the Hegelian march of history toward a new social formation and a politically irresponsible event generated by the London government or, on the contrary, a historically necessary and morally unavoidable attempt to defend one's national sovereignty, structurally the patterns remained the same: in both cases it demanded idenitification with a given political take on the event and, regardless of the ideology, it sacralized patriotic dedication.[33]

There are rare works that avoid heroicizing, sacralizing, and romanticizing the uprising, to mention only a novel by Aleksander Ścibor-Rylski, *Pierścionek z końskiego włosia* (*The Horse Hair Ring*), which was written in the early 1970s but was banned due to its representation of postwar Communist Poland and published posthumously in 1991. Ścibor-Rylski demystifies the "beautiful death" and projects the uprising onto the larger screen of pointless and senseless history. His characters are insurrectionists stranded at the end of the uprising at the outskirts of the city, frustrated and unsure whom and why they should keep fighting; they feel locked in the trap of history, which pulls them through a chain of events to the inevitable submission to the Soviets. Prohibiting his reader from enjoying any sense of elation inscribed in the cultural memory of the uprising, Ścibor-Rylski imbues his narration with a Kafkaesque flair. His uprising is a grotesque nightmare that evades rationalization and idealization alike—it makes no sense and yet it must be continued. Nothing in Ścibor-Rylski's narration suggests that war facilitates the discovery of human authenticity.[34] While removing the uprising from the sublime and portraying it as pointless chaos, Ścibor-Rylski counters the predominant redemptive patterns but still focuses on military experience, which removes the narrated experience from the practices of everyday life. Białoszewski's *Memoir of the Warsaw Uprising* does something else. Not only does it ignore redemptive patterns and counter-patterns, but with the attention paid to the civilian experience of the traumatic and to the everyday dimension of the traumatic, Białoszewski creates a work that stands on its own; his treatment of the event is incomparable to any other representation of the uprising.

REDEEMING THE CIVILIAN EXPERIENCE

What makes the *Memoir* stand apart from other canonic texts on the uprising is its deeply civilian character. Białoszewski does not represent military experience and makes no political claims about its value. The political aspect of the *Memoir* is not thematized, but rather subtly embedded in the voice of its civilian narrator and in his choices to circumvent what was at the core of the event's mainstream representations. One can find in Białoszewski's narration no affinities with the patterns of romanticization and aestheticization of the uprising, or, to use Janion's binary, with the "systems and anti-systems" of the "uprising tradition" ("tradycja powstańcza"). The *Memoir*'s innovative colloquial diction, its focus on civilian experience and preoccupation with the everyday create a vision that retrieves the uprising from the pinnacles and nadirs into which Polish national tradition has cast it.

The civilian experience could not share in the same economy of sacrifice as culturally valorized military experience, so there has been a tendency to approach the former as a foil and, in most representations of the uprising, place it in the background.[35] In the redemptive and compensatory modes of representation, the civilian aspect of the uprising simply could not be integrated into the main narrative as it contaminated the pure categories of the "heroic death" and "heroic deed" and, by extension, the aesthetics of the sublime.[36] The civilian experience lacked the self-contained quality related to the "deed" that allows for the process of symbolic compensation; it was too scattered and elusive to fit the familiar patterns of representation. It was overlooked precisely because as an experience it was open-ended, shaped by coincidence, chance, and unpredictability and, thus, resisted teleology.[37]

In his *Pamiętnik z powstania warszawskiego* (1970; *A Memoir of the Warsaw Uprising*), Białoszewski chronicles the Warsaw Uprising of 1944 as it was experienced by a civilian witness and articulates an entirely new set of representational possibilities. In the *Memoir*, the uprising does not so much rupture the familiar framework as transform it into an uncanny, traumatic everyday. In this everyday, what used to be culturally marked as hidden (for instance, the scatological) becomes visible. The traumatic quotidian also brings to the foreground activities usually perceived as routine and monotonous, such as procuring food and water, and imbues them with the radical. The predictable nature of non-traumatic time becomes loaded with a multiplicity of possible outcomes in the traumatic everyday; getting water from a street pump can lead to a range of outcomes, from the desired result of obtaining water to being wounded and killed, and anything in between, such as running from enemy planes and forming "herds" with other runners, or being unable to return to the place of departure because it was bombarded in the meantime. In the everyday of the uprising that the *Memoir* represents, there are no great deeds, but routine activities acquire the status of life-changing events.

The narrator's "ideology" of war is rather simple: war "happens" and descends on people like a force of nature. Left without a choice, people live through it as their everyday. This "happening" stands outside of historical determinants: purpose, ideals, and political speculations become irrelevant amidst the everyday survival of war, while traumatic experiences are not experienced as traumatic but rather as organic parts of that everyday. Regardless of how extreme the situation becomes, the tools for survival derive from ordinary life. Civilian living is unheroic and its main purpose is self-perpetuation; if heroism happens, it happens almost by accident and presents no theatrical potential. The traumatic dimension of the civilian experience emerges only when one steps outside of the experience; it emerges not from the process of living itself, but from the mechanisms of memory, which is what Białoszewski explores in his *Memoir*.

Because of the celebratory position the uprising had assumed in postwar Polish memory, the publication of his *Memoir* brought Białoszewski's name to the attention of the general public in a way that his avant-garde poetry could not. It also forced critics to reevaluate his writing and cease regarding it as dominated by linguistic self-indulgence, which many saw as a pointless—albeit harmless—language game. Marking both the end of Białoszewski's poetic experimentation and the beginning of his preoccupation with the everyday that would last until his death, the *Memoir* extended Białoszewski's audience beyond the hermetic circle of avant-garde poetry lovers.[38] The *Memoir* proved that the "salad of chopped syntax" of Białoszewski's earlier work may actually lead to the "juicy beefsteak of reality."[39]

Yet, it was the particularity of Białoszewski's brand of reality that stirred controversy. After the book's publication, Wojciech Żukrowski wrote a review entitled "Mironek w powstaniu" ("Little Miron in the Uprising").[40] The vitriolic character of this review is symptomatic of Białoszewski touching a nerve in the mythical order of the uprising. Żukrowski finds it provoking and offensive that the narrator, Miron (or rather "Mironek"), does not consider his civilian living inferior to military living, which destabilizes the hierarchy that privileges the military ethos. The aggression in the review toward "the embryo floating in the solution of others' fight, instinctually crouching and searching for his mother" ("embrion pływający w roztworze cudzej walki, kulący się odruchowo i szukający mamy") attests to how threatening to the reading public Żukrowski found the contamination of the patriotic sublime with the civilian will to survive.

In the condescending use of the diminutive of Białoszewski's first name, Żukrowski disparages Białoszewski's account of the uprising as infantile and compares its author to an "overgrown baby" ("wyrośnięty niemowlak") and the value of the *Memoir* to kids drawing on the wall ("bazgranie po ścianie"). This infantile quality shows itself in the narrator's "amputated memory and amputated capacity for associations." Białoszewski's account, Żukrowski claims, reduces its protagonists to "their digestive functions" and presents Warsaw's population as "little humans who are neither the most interesting nor worthy of remembering." Żukrowski reacts against Białoszewski's projection of his "politically bleached" ("odbarwiony politicznie") narrator onto the civilian population in toto. That "the author represents himself as more stupid than he really is," rages Żukrowski, "is his own business. But that he does the same to the Warsaw population, which, even though it participated only passively in the Uprising, was emotionally fully engaged supporting it, fluctuating from despair to hope, this, to put it delicately, is far from truth."[41] Interestingly, the claim about the quality of Białoszewski's voice, which is established as autobiographical ("the author represents himself") and intentionally "stupid" and which supposedly leads to a representation which is "far from truth" is contradicted by the end of Żukrowski's review. After railing against the *Memoir* for its historically false and psychologically improbable representation of the Varsovians' experience ("I know what's going on in the human brain," he asserts on the basis of his own war veteran's experience), Żukrowski grants the *Memoir* permission to exist.

This permission strangely undermines his earlier claim of its falsehood. Żukrowski admits that after all civilians, with amputated memories and, like the narrator himself, "dragged by the current of events" ("wleczony prądem zdarzeń") "constitute the majority, so let us let them live on the pages of this novel, searching for food, squashing fleas, squeezing a girl, and sighing with relief under the burial pile of ruined Warsaw, 'good, not us yet.' This, too, offers some truth about the Warsaw Uprising, although we would not like to pass this as its heritage."[42] The disdain for those sighing with relief "not us yet" positions Żukrowski as the guardian of the great divide between the uprising's exceptional and the uprising's ordinary. "The grand vision of the uprising tragedy" ("wielka wizja powstańczej tragedii") requires that the efforts of its military participants be mirrored by the civilian population's emotional engagement and support for the uprising. Although the majority may have actually behaved the way Białoszewski describes, the dominant "truth" (as opposed to "some truth" ["jakaś prawda"]) about the uprising's "heritage" belongs to those who shape history. At the same time, Żukrowski's contradictory reaction (outrage at Białoszewski's representation and questioning its truthfulness followed by a condescending recognition that Białoszewski's vision actually may have some historical value and reflect the majority's behavior) shows that Żukrowski is not able to control his reaction to the *Memoir.* His review functions like a litmus test indicating that the *Memoir*'s subversion reached well beyond its stylistic properties and well beyond a simple counter-narrative to the Romantic myth. In some sense, Żukrowski's assessment of Białoszewski's treatment of memory and cognitive abilities as "amputated" is right. In order, however, to appreciate what this amputation entails and signifies, Żukrowski would need to—and this is what he is clearly unable to do—legitimize the will to survive and approach the *Memoir* beyond the closed system of mythical representations. He cannot fathom a representation of the uprising without the redemptive strategies of aestheticization and moral valorization that would bring the extraordinary to the fore. The scandal of the *Memoir* lies precisely in its immunity to narrative fetishism.

The lack of fetishization manifests itself in the most unique quality of the *Memoir,* which is also the most difficult to conceptualize: the organic fusion of the traumatic and the everyday. Białoszewski approaches the traumatic experience from the "inside" of its everyday, as an open-ended process that has not (yet) been molded by reflection, cultural norms, and values. In his treatment, the traumatic does not rupture the preexisting framework of the quotidian, rendering it irrelevant; rather, it "charges" the quotidian, forming a new everyday that is—simultaneously and paradoxically—radically different and radically the same as the one of the non-traumatic times. Białoszewski's feat as a writer is to immerse his reader in traumatic memory by, on the one hand, representing traumatic experience from within while, on the other, showing that the traumatic becomes traumatic only in retrospect when the experience itself is over.

To represent this paradoxical position of experiencing "now" and witnessing "later," Białoszewski shuns discursive, abstract language and constructs a double narrator. Charged with emotivity, the language of the *Memoir* propels the reader into the uprising's ordinary and sensory, its "here and now." Yet, this "here and now" is characterized by a paradoxical temporality and agency: the *Memoir* reenacts the traumatic everyday, which does not (yet) traumatize as it is being experienced by its young narrator, while at the same time, it shows a traumatized older narrator who recounts the story of his survival from a place of safety decades after the war is over. This insider's tale of the everyday experience of a traumatic time and the traumatic residue in the post-traumatic everyday puts the *Memoir* simultaneously in two seemingly mutually exclusive dimensions: it belongs to both the literature of trauma and of the everyday.

TRAUMATIC MEMORY AND BIAŁOSZEWSKI'S ALTERNATIVE HISTORY

Already the notions of "trauma" and the associated notion of "traumatic memory" present great challenges. In strictly medical terms, "'trauma' refers not to the *injury* inflicted but to the *blow* that inflicted it, not to the *state of mind* that ensues but to the *event* that provoked it. The term 'post-traumatic stress disorder' . . . is an accommodation to that medical convention."[43] However, most culturally driven theories question such distinctions. Although most theorists would agree that "trauma" signifies an experience in the life of the individual "in which a person feels utterly helpless in the face of a force that is perceived to be life-threatening,"[44] most would also agree that "trauma" also pertains to the aftereffect of such experiences, a long-term response to "an unexpected or overwhelming event or events that are not fully grasped as they occur."[45] The dominant tendency in trauma and memory studies is to use the notion of "trauma" as an umbrella term that conflates post-traumatic stress disorder—the psychological injury that in the medical convention is a consequence of trauma—with the trauma-inducing event.

Such a conflation led Cathy Caruth to talk about trauma in ahistorical terms as a *structure of experience* which is characterized by specific temporality. Trauma is characterized by its belatedness, which is related to the dissociative nature of the traumatic experience. In a protective mechanism, a psyche dissociates itself from an event.[46] However, "unexperienced" experience "return[s] later in repeated flashbacks, nightmares, and other repetitive phenomena."[47] The experience is thus not fully registered while it is happening, but becomes accessible only in the belated forms of mental and somatic returns.[48] These returns include hypersensitivity, constant alertness to potential dangers, and persistent flashbacks that, to various extents, disrupt the victim's attempts to lead a normal life and may make him or her feel powerless.[49] Trauma's temporality is, therefore, already unsettled and displaced yet paradoxically central to its experience: although the traumatic event belongs to the victim's past, the traumatic memory of the event ruptures the present. L. L. Langer observes that "[trauma] stops the chronological clock and fixes the moment permanently in memory and imagination, immune to the vicissitudes of time."[50] In Langer's view, trauma exists outside temporal categories, and traumatic experiences acquire an otherness that cannot be comprehended and recounted, an otherness that has no closure but invades the present and "spills over" every sphere of life. Trauma, says Caruth, "does not simply serve as a record of the past but precisely registers the force of an experience that is not yet fully owned."[51]

The emphasis on the universal nature of belatedness inscribed in the "structure of experience" allows this ahistorical notion a wide applicability. But this very applicability is also problematic as it erases the idiosyncrasies of the traumatic event (or trauma-inducing event) and the idiosyncrasies of the response to it. It homogenizes individual responses and a plurality of historical events. A great challenge facing trauma studies, therefore, is adopting a theoretical vocabulary that would allow us to historicize trauma, if only to accommodate the basic axiom that natural disasters and human-caused events may traumatize in different ways. Perhaps allowing for the multiplicity and heterogeneity of traumatic memory does not need to annul the basic idea behind the *structure of experience,* but it would make it more dynamic and extend its analytical parameters. These extended parameters would take into consideration variables such as the duration of the traumatic experience, or the degree of agency left to the victim: the sixty-three days of the Warsaw Uprising do not compare, for example, to a rape both in terms of duration and the agency (or lack thereof) of the victim, just as these two differ from the experience of long-term abuse or life in a concentration camp. Each of these experiences traumatizes in its own unique way, regardless of the structural similarity in the psychological and somatic symptoms of their aftermaths.[52]

The specificity of these aftermaths escapes Langer's and Caruth's evocative—and absolutist—statements. They emphasize the victim's lack of control over what returns in somatic symptoms and mental images that disrupt the present with the full force of the painful past. In their view, somatic, pre-representational, and non-reflective, "traumatic memory" stands in stark opposition to its narrative and habitual counterparts.[53] It resists being integrated into the trajectory of the survivor's life and being governed by such basic categories of human experience as causality. From such a perspective, the contours between the "fully traumatic" ("fixed in memory," "immune to the vicissitudes of time") and fully narrative (integrated, fluid, relative, and contextual) are clear. This, in turn, presupposes that traumatic memory can become fully sublated into narrative memory and the traumatic experience completely worked through.[54]

The value of literary works that focus on trauma and traumatic memory, such as Białoszewski's *Memoir*, lies also in their ability to demand from us subtler ways of understanding the "hard categories" of theory and their dynamics.[55] Traumatic memory and the process of transforming it into narrative memory govern the complex narrative strategies of the *Memoir;* its narrator is at once "in good health and spirits"[56] and repeatedly returning to the place of trauma. In a narrative that reenacts the struggle with being possessed by the past (according to the definition that "to be traumatized is precisely to be possessed by an image or event),"[57] Białoszewski does not grant his reader a sense of final sublation of the traumatic into the narrative. Rather, in his simultaneous encapsulation of the event and its memory, remembering too much and not remembering enough, the *Memoir* becomes a literary artifact that works through an alternative vision of Polish history. This vision—self-deprecating, domestic, quietly subversive to the official idiom, and deeply traumatic—relies on the refusal to privilege the extreme dimensions of the event over its everydayness. Białoszewski's idiosyncratic intersection of the traumatic and the everyday makes the uprising and the ensuing memory of it radically *specific* and, therefore, unharnessable for the myth and redemptive teleology. The *Memoir* constitutes a performative act of "working through" that presents a challenge to the vocabulary of experience and representation for the literary critic and the trauma scholar alike; but it also proposes a mode of reading Polish history whose ethics and politics stand apart from the clichéd morality and the valorization of national identity. No other writer in Polish literature had conceived of writing about the uprising—or about war in general—in this way.

TRAUMATIC TIME AND THE HISTORICAL TESTIMONY

A Memoir of the Warsaw Uprising was published in 1970, but on the opening page the narrator specifies the exact time of his narration—twenty-three years after the uprising: "it's October, nighttime, 1967." The dynamics between three temporal planes—the "now" of the traumatic event, the repetitive "now" of traumatic memory, and the dialectics of "now and then" of the narrative memory—make Białoszewski's *Memoir* particularly resistant to genre classifications. The title—*A Memoir of the Warsaw Uprising*—suggests a broad narrative horizon typical of the genre of memoir that combines an autobiographical perspective with a historiographical slant, that is, a memoir that traditionally recollects a personal experience of a historical event. The twenty-three-year gap between the event and its narration signaled at the very beginning of the work suggests a possibility for such a recollection, yet the urgent immediacy of the present tense, employed by Białoszewski, subverts one of the most important characteristics of the memoir as genre—marking the temporal distance between the time of the event's narration and the time of the event's occurrence. This marking is challenged by the oscillation of narration between the "now" of quasi-documentary recounting (i.e., the "now" of the narrator's self-awareness of recalling the experience from the past) and the "now" of the experience, whose "oral" account throws the reader in medias res. Hence, for some critics, the *Memoir* is characterized by the "narrow narrative horizon," which resembles a diary;[58] others perceive it as a mixed form—a fusion of diary, memoir, stream of consciousness, and "spoken monologue" ("monolog wypowiedziany").[59] While the *Memoir* partakes in features of both diary and memoir, it also escapes clear genre classifications. What may actually be useful is reading the title outside of genre markers, but within Białoszewski's own tradition of inventing genres, which sometimes take the form of gerunds, to mention a well-known early poem, "Leżenia" ("Lying Downs"), in which the title marked not only the theme, but functioned as a genre comparable to "odes" or "ballads" and indicated reflections on the state of lying down.[60] Białoszewski trained his reader to defamiliarize familiar notions by reading them literally, so if we were to employ this strategy we could say that literally the "memoir" means the state, or rather the process, of remembering.[61] Such a performative understanding of the title better reflects the processual character of Białoszewski's work that represents a complex dynamics of traumatic and narrative memory, as well as a fusion of psychobiography, historical trauma, and representation.

The symbiotic relationship between Białoszewski's aesthetic strategies and the structure of memory manifests itself in the author's oft-quoted explanation of the genesis of the *Memoir*:

> For twenty years I couldn't write about it. Although I wanted to—badly. I would talk. About the uprising. To lots of people. All sorts of people. Over and over. And the whole time I was thinking: I have to describe the uprising, really *describe* it. I didn't realize that those twenty years of talking (I have been talking about it for twenty years, because it is the most important experience of my life—a closed experience), precisely that talking was the only possible method for describing the uprising.[62]

> Przez dwadzieścia lat nie mogłem o tym pisać. Chociaż tak chciałem. I gadałem. O powstaniu. Tylu ludziom. Różnym. Po ileś razy. I ciągle myślałem,

> że mam to powstanie opisać, ale jakoś przecież *opisać*. A nie wiedziałem, przecież, że właśnie te gadania przez dwadzieścia lat—bo to jest największe przeżycie mojego życia, takie zamknięte—że właśnie te gadania, ten to sposób nadaje się jako jedyny do opisania powstania.[63]

Usually this statement serves to explain Białoszewski's stylistic decision to render the reality of the uprising in an imitation of the spoken language, but it also reveals the symbiotic relationship between the structure of traumatic memory and Białoszewski's aesthetic choices. The passage brings out the opposition between "talking" and "writing" ("gadanie" vs. "pisanie"), to which Białoszewski often returns when reflecting on his creative process. The reenactment of speech becomes, simultaneously and paradoxically, the tool and the goal of representation: "talking" reflected in the medium of writing becomes "the only possible method for describing" the experience. Speech is constructed as a medium whose emotive force has the ability to grant the audience direct access to experience, but also the only medium through which the narrator can experience his own process of remembering.[64]

However, in the quote above Białoszewski also identifies for the reader the specific site from which the *Memoir* was born—the narrator's "possession" by the memory of his life's "greatest experience" and its demand to be rendered by the narrator. The twenty years of compulsive "gadanie"—"talking" or even in a more precise English equivalent "chatter"—acquires the air of an ethical imperative—"And the whole time I was thinking: I have to describe the uprising, really *describe* it." This emphatic imperative—"I have to"—is the sign of the narrator's inability ("I cannot, therefore I must," we could add) to close the experience by rendering it, as it were, once and for all ("I couldn't write about it."). The desire to give the experience a written representation becomes the desire to contain it, yet despite the twenty years of repetitive recounting and reenactments ("over and over . . . to lots of people. All sorts of people") the experience remained open.

Such repetitive reenactments suggest the characteristic susceptibility of oral transmission to modification by external influences, while Białoszewski's author-narrator defines the site of this memory as a self-contained experience ("takie zamknięte," literally "a closed experience"). Thus, we have the paradox that the experience is on the one hand obsessively recounted (and, thus, opened to the audience), while on the other considered closed and self-contained. What does this paradox tell us about the structure of memory and the nature of Białoszewski's traumatic representation? First, the narrator situates the experience of the uprising simultaneously in the past and in the present; the uprising's consuming memory reverberates through all spheres of the narrator's life and oppresses him with the need to contain it in the representation. If we were to think about this passage from a clinical perspective, we could say that it shows the repetitive nature of traumatic returns and, presumably, their fragmentary character, since the narrator stresses that in spite of talking "so many times" to various people, his desire to *describe* the uprising was never fulfilled. Here the traumatic returns do not so much help to complete the memory of the experience, as some theorists would have it,[65] but in themselves—in their very structure, we might say—become the representation of this memory, which further sustains the performative reading of the title.

MEMORY AS FORM AND THE FORM OF MEMORY: NARRATIVE TRANSFORMATIONS OF THE TRAUMATIC

The brilliance of Białoszewski's writing lies in his ability to represent the survivor's ongoing struggle to transform his traumatic memory into narrative form. This struggle is embedded directly in the form and diction of the *Memoir,* which, rather than showing us the traumatic as if it were not yet a narrative, gives the reader a sense of traumatic "shimmering"—an alternating opening and closing of the event. The "shimmering" between narrative and traumatic memory is strikingly performed in the reenactment of orality in "gadanie." The *Memoir*'s idiosyncratic genre of a "talking memoir"/ "chattered memoir" ("pamiętnik gadany")[66] re-creates a monologue in which the reader is positioned as a listener who witnesses a traumatic testimony. For the testimony—meant here as a survivor's attempt to confront and externalize the traumatic—to happen the presence of witness is crucial. The diction of "gadanie" inscribes the impact of experience into the heart of Białoszewski's linguistic practices and creates an effect of eyewitness "reportage." Although Białoszewski codes emotions in a complex way, it is safe to say that he emotionally engages his reader via the *Memoir*'s "narrow narrative horizon" that erases the temporal distance between the occurrence of represented events and the time of writing. This engagement is complex as well; the reader is thrown into the narrative in medias res, yet is repeatedly reminded of the belatedness of the work through the recurring theme of the work's genesis in the twenty-three years of struggle with the memory *as* form.

Białoszewski enacts the problem with memory as form, and with the form of memory, on several levels. He has his narrator speak about it in self-reflexive passages; he "traumatizes" language via his employment of enunciative strategies (about which later); and he configures two narrators—one who is a survivor, who has already experienced the uprising and comments on his struggle with the transformation of the traumatic into the narrative, and another who is "naive," and in the midst of the present tense experiences the traumatic.[67] The presence of the two narrators is already signaled on the opening page of the *Memoir*:

> In recollecting that other self in small facts I shall be frank, perhaps too detailed, but on the other hand I shall write only the truth. I am forty-five years old now—it's twenty-three years later; I am lying on my couch uninjured, alive, free, in good health and spirits; it is October, nighttime, 1967.
>
> Będę szczery, przypominający sobie siebie tamtego w fakcikach, może za dokładny, ale za to tylko prawda będzie. Teraz mam czterdzieści pięć lat, po tych dwudziestu trzech latach, leżę na tapczanie cały, żywy, wolny, w dobrym stanie i humorze, jest październik, noc, 67 rok.[68]

The naive narrator's narrative horizon is narrow. He is thrown into an incomprehensible event without knowing whether he will survive it and what will happen after the conclusion of the uprising. As this naive narrator experiences the uprising, his senses are bombarded with stimuli—he sees, feels, hears, and smells—and he runs around ("lata," literally "flies around").[69] The experienced narrator—or "meta-narrator"—reflects upon what happened; it is he who has survived the uprising and its aftermath, and it is he who brings back a version of himself from twenty-three years earlier.

While through the eyes of the naive narrator and by means of his "gadanie," the reader experiences the *Memoir*'s emotive force and witnesses to the everyday of the uprising, the experienced narrator keeps scuffling with memory, and this everyday is transformed into the *traumatic everyday.* In other words, living through the event, the naive narrator is not (yet) traumatized, whereas the experienced narrator, "lying on [his] couch uninjured," having (already) lived through the event, is (still) traumatized.[70] The naive narrator lives through the experience according to the mechanisms of the traumatic experience, that is, without fully experiencing it; the experienced narrator remembers the experience and, thus, traumatically relives it. Because the experienced narrator remembers and reexperiences by situating himself in the position of the naive narrator, whatever "was common *then*"—the extreme as the ordinary—retains its force of incomprehensibility. At the same time, the experienced narrator reveals his consciousness of the mechanisms of traumatic memory, marks the gap between "then" and "now," and anticipates his reader's reactions in statements like, "Don't be surprised. This was common then." Such statements also emphasize the doubleness of the narrator; in the midst of the naive narrator's account, we get glimpses of the experienced narrator's awareness. Although it is the naive narrator who reenacts the traumatic, he is "always already" part of the experienced narrator's worked-through memory.

This reenactment presupposes a narrative integration of the traumatic memory, which is defined by its belatedness. Belatedness also structures the interaction between the two narrators. For instance, while the naive narrator expresses his desire to write a poem about the uprising as he witnesses it, the experienced narrator stresses that "for twenty years [he] could not write about this." Such statements, expressing the imperative and the inability to write, make the narrator's testimony always already belated. When Białoszewski commented on the genesis of the *Memoir* in an interview, he repeated his narrator's gesture and stressed his inability to write it earlier. But, while the narrator leaves us with a sense of impasse—"I wanted to but I couldn't"—Białoszewski is able to define what kept him from writing, and what he says bears a striking resemblance to the nature of traumatic memory: "Before it had seemed too difficult. I remembered too much. I had too much of it in myself. As the years went by it became clearer. More writable." ("Przedtem wydawało mi się to za trudne. Za dużo pamiętałem. Za dużo miałem tego w sobie. Po iluś latach zrobiło się to przejrzystsze. Możliwe do napisania.")[71]

Remembering "too much" and thus not being able to recount is a well-known phenomenon in trauma studies. It is particularly well attested in the case of Holocaust literature, in which belatedness seems to be built into the genre.[72] Such belatedness also characterizes the very memory of the traumatic experience, which can remain latent for a prolonged period of time and return mainly in its unmediated and uncontrollable somatic form. Only when the event has been partially forgotten, that is, when its sensory surplus is contained and there is no longer "too much of it in myself," can the experience be integrated by narrative memory and, consequently, represented.

These paradoxical features of traumatic memory make the "memory" portion of the term "a kind of oxymoron; the traumatic event is not initially remembered or represented but is held at bay by dissociation and reenacted without remembering. It is the narrative integration that produces the memory of the traumatic event. It is when they become full-blown narratives that these memories tell stories."[73] What returns, then, in involuntary traumatic recollection is not a repressed or forgotten experience in toto but "an event that is itself constituted, in part, by its lack of integration into consciousness . . . Not having been fully integrated as it occurred, the event cannot become, as Pierre Janet says, a 'narrative memory' that is integrated into a completed story of the past."[74] One of Białoszewski's goals in his representation of the uprising is precisely that: to throw the reader into the seemingly unmediated, somatic, and sensory past and to show how the traumatic event is *not* integrated as it occurs. At the same time, he aims to show, through the interaction between his two narrators, the process of narrative integration, however incomplete. This incomplete and open-ended memorial process is *the* story of the *Memoir*.

TRAUMATIC SEQUENCING AND THE SCUFFLE OF MEMORY

When Białoszewski was asked how he managed to remember the uprising after so many years, he identified the process of narrative integration with the process of memory production:

> The memory stayed. This was possible because it had already been shaken down. I finally stopped thinking about the uprising as an unbroken sequence [*nieprzerwany ciąg*], which, in the first years, had seemed impossible to circumscribe. I had not yet developed a form—that's another thing, this obvious form for that, but the memory [literally, "it"] grew clearer through all the little remembrances and through conversations with people, and also through my own telling of the uprising.

> To zostało, jak, to było możliwe właśnie dlatego, że trochę się już utrząsnęło, już przestałem myśleć o powstaniu jako o nieprzerwanym ciągu, który wydawał mi się przez pierwsze lata nie do ogarnięcia. Wtedy jeszcze nie miałem wyrobionej formy, to jest druga sprawa, do tego, tej oczywistej, tylko to się utrwalało poprzez przypominki sobie i poprzez rozmowy z ludźmi, poprzez opowiadania—moje—o powstaniu.[75]

This fascinating reflection on the process of remembering and the process of conceptualizing the act of remembering presupposes a recasting of the event's narration in different forms and to different audiences. This recasting ranges from unexpectedly recalling details or episodes with (presumably) close friends and relatives (note that the diminutive of the neologism, "little remembrance" ["przypominka"] suggests both an intimate setting and a sudden recollection that is shared with others); conversations with unspecified "other people," which presumably allow a comparative perspective; and finally a crystallization of one's own story (*moje opowiadania*). The unspecified setting of these narrations and the unspecified identity of their participants add a political slant to Białoszewski's "unofficial" approach, as I will discuss later. What is important now in the context of reading the *Memoir* as a reenactment of traumatic testimony is that all these modes enable the gradual individuation of memory: the memory of the uprising *and* the story of the uprising emerge in the process of social circulation. The fusion of memory with the story is reflected in an unclear syntax: "I had not yet developed a form—that's another thing, this obvious form for that, but the memory [literally "it"] grew clearer through all the little remembrances." From the context, the reader assumes that "it" ("to") pertains to memory, although it may also pertain to the "not yet developed form." Both assumptions make sense, as the memory and the story are represented in the *Memoir* as simultaneously produced. Białoszewski uses the phrase "to się utrwalało," where "utrwalać" is a transitive verb which in non-reflexive form means "to preserve something" (as in preservation of memory) or, in a similar context, fixing a photographic image in the darkroom. This photographic dimension suggests that the process of memory and story production means simultaneously "emerging" and "fixing" to prevent it from fading. The fixative in this case is the modes of oral transmission, but the reflexive form of "utrwalało *się*" suggests that the whole process is somewhat involuntary and that it takes place outside the author's sphere of intentionality.

In trauma studies, the transmission of memory to others is considered a vital ingredient of "working through" the traumatic past. The presence of an audience—provided the audience is willing to function as a witness, that is, to recognize and acknowledge the story—forces the victim to face and articulate the traumatic—to name it, literally, and to locate it in place and time. This naming corresponds to the loss of the traumatic precision of the traumatic memory as it initiates the process of introducing changes and alterations, in other words making the story flexible for the sake of collective, and not traumatic, ownership. Ideally, individual healing enriches communal memory.

Białoszewski's statement on the "sequence" may actually point to the mechanism of the loss of precision. He says that the memory of the uprising "stayed with him" because it became contained, "compressed" ("trochę się już utrząsnęło," but note that "utrząsnęło," literally "shaken down," implies a violent motion), and because he stopped thinking about the uprising as an "unbroken sequence" ("nieprzerwany ciąg"), which, "in the first years, had seemed impossible to circumscribe." "The unbroken sequence" became sequenced into smaller "units" of memory, whose details were gradually modified as they were shared and discussed with others. The traumatic memory begins to show cracks only when it stops being a parallel psychic reality dissociated from other realms and becomes integrated in one's life story. Its "compressing" or "shaking down" allows remembering *enough* (in "little remembrances" and "conversations") in order to remember in a flexible, integrated narrative mode as opposed to remembering *too much* in an unembraceable, and non-represeentional, traumatic way.[76]

Sequencing is a persistent trait of Białoszewski's work as such.[77] In the *Memoir,* it is marked by dates whose correctness (or rather they are to be as correct as possible) is emphasized by the narrator as both a matter of memory and a matter of form:

> I'm having problems again with the sequence of events between August 12 and August 18. I know that for my readers it's not important exactly what happened when. But they shouldn't be surprised. It is important for me; that precision of dates and places (as I think I have already indicated) is my way of holding on to the pile of construction.[78]

> Mam kłopot znów z kolejnością pewnych faktów, które działy się między 12 a 18 sierpnia. Wiem, że dla moich czytelników nie jest ważne, co kiedy dokładnie. Ale niech się nie dziwią. Dla mnie to jest ważne—ta dokładność dat i miejsc (jak już chyba zaznaczyłem), to jest moje trzymanie się kupy konstrukcyjnej.[79]

The narrator shares here how he negotiated between his memory and his articulation of memory. He presents the establishment of narrative sequences as relying on the contradictory notions of a "disorderly accumulation of things" ("kupa," literally "pile" or "heap") and order ("konstrukcyjna").[80] This contradiction is significant, as the sequence of events, its progression along the linearity of dates, marks for the narrator the sequence of memory forced into the markers of time. What we learn in this passage is not what actually happened, or might have happened, between August 12 and August 18, but about the narrator's "problems . . . with the sequence of events between August 12 and August 18."

But what is this "pile of construction"? Can the precision of dates be identified with a "pile of construction"? Surely, dates serve as reference points and facilitate the organization of the material of memory into a streamlined narrative. But "that precision of dates and places" serves as a *means* of "holding on to the pile of construction." If that is so, then the orderly (the dates) helps to hold on to the disorderly ("pile") order ("[of] construction"). Note, however, that in the Polish phrase "kupa konstruktcyjna" (literally "constructive pile"), "konstrukcyjna" ("of construction") is an adjective modifying "kupa," which implies that the function (or, perhaps, essence) of the pile is its construction. One way to approach this puzzling sentence is to go back to the idea of the survivors retelling their stories many times before they can produce their memory, that is, a picture of the past that makes some sense and has a sequential order. The retelling and the introduction of the sequential order enables the loss of (somatic) precision of the traumatic memory and the development of a narrative precision of chronology. Paradoxically, this type of narrative precision is an agent of flexibility and modification that helps to unfix the frozenness of traumatic memory. With this unfixing (i.e., with the loss of the somatic precision of traumatic memory), "there is another, more profound, disappearance: the loss, precisely, of the event's essential incomprehensibility, the force of its *affront to understanding*."[81] This, in turn, facilitates the externalization of events, offering parameters that the survivors can share with their witnesses. The narrator of the *Memoir* stresses to his reader an awareness of his own process (as if anticipating the reader's frustration with surplus information) and again, as before, he thematizes his memory as the form of the book.

Thus, the chronology of dates that facilitates the narrator's externalization and transmission of memory also becomes a mode of the narrator's own stability—the narrator does not seem to have control over the pile of construction; rather he "hangs onto" or "holds onto" it as the only mode of continuing the narration. In this somewhat desperate expression, the reader gets a sense that what is being narrated is not some kind of already externalized "full" memory. On the contrary, the process of narration signifies an attempt to externalize memory; it is only in this process of being narrated that the gaps of memory can resurface.

As a result, in his insistence on dates, the narrator reconstructs not only what he remembers but also the very mechanism of simultaneously remembering *and* not remembering. The "constructive pile" thematizes the dialectics between representation and "scuffling with memory." The guiding principle of Białoszewski's narration is to reconstruct events as they emerge in the narrator's memory, which is why the narrator reminds us that what he is recording is "uncorrected"; his memory oscillates between the precision of chronology—crucial for him to externalize the experience—and the gaps, which emerge as suddenly as his remembrances:

> After the surrender of Żoliborz on September 30 the weather was clear, and it was hot. (Don't be surprised that I remember all of a sudden. That's how it is. And I make no revisions, so as to convey that scuffle of memory and that distinctness of neighborhoods.)[82]

> Po kapitulacji Żoliborza—30 września—była pogoda, upał. (Nie dziwcie się, że pamiętam nagle. To tak jest. A poprawek nie robię, żeby wyszło to szamotanie pamięci i ta oddzielność dzielnic.)[83]

While the precision of dates in the *Memoir* enables recollection, it leads not to the full reconstruction of the memory of the event but, on the contrary, to the reconstruction of the scuffle of memory,[84] which is another way of expressing the idea of the "pile of construction." Levine, in introducing her translation of the *Memoir*, emphasizes that the most pervasive category of words in the *Memoir* are those that express hesitancy—"I don't know" ("nie wiem"), "perhaps," "probably" ("chyba"), and "I don't remember" ("nie pamiętam"). By using these words of hesitancy and "not making any corrections," Białoszewski emphasizes the process of producing and *not* completing the memory. Moreover, words like "I don't know" and "perhaps" suggest that what *really* happened may never be accessible, so memory tries to re-create the experience that, by itself, is incomplete. Thus, the *Memoir*, if we return to a performative reading of the title, also implies *creating* the (incomplete) experience of the event itself.

The potent construction of the two narrators, or a double narrator—to stay true to the dynamic nature of memory—reinforces this oscillation between the re-creation of memory in the *Memoir* and conveying the inaccessibility of memory *and* experience. Białoszewski re-creates the impact of the events via the "naive" narrator whose "oral testimony" presents events as if they were transparent and accessible, while also conveying the impossibility or, at least, the hesitancy of such transparency via the "experienced" narrator. This sense of impossibility comes not only from the narrator's awareness that no language is transparent, but also from the experience itself, which, while it is being experienced, is not transparent even to the one who experiences it. In other words, a traumatic experience presents problems both with the type of memory it leaves behind (i.e., its resistance to becoming narrative memory) and with the nature of the experience itself, which is characterized by loss or gaps. Thus, the "pile of construction" points to the memory of events being unabsorbed while they were happening. The experience is constituted by a sense of dissociation, disjuncture, and discontinuity; the subject lives the experience—the processual aspect of the Polish "przeżycie" ("survival") comes to mind—and yet does not believe that it is real. The narrator declares: "Mąciło się w głowie" ("Our brains were reeling"):[85]

> The heat, that sun, the blue sky mangled with fires, smoke, explosions, falling plaster—all this added a touch of the exotic to what was happening (hard as even that was to believe). Namely, a further multiplying in one's brain.[86]

> Upały, to słońce i niebieskie niebo zmaglowane z pożarami, dymem, hukiem, zasypaniem, to jeszcze dodawało temu, w co i tak trudno było wierzyć, chociaż było, czegoś egzotycznego. Czyli dodatkowego trojenia się w głowie.[87]

The passage depicts a sensory overload (note that all the senses are simultaneously engaged) that breaks familiar mental processes; the event's combination of sensory experience (summer heat overlapping with the heat of fires, the blue of the sky, and the noise of bombardments) further defamiliarizes the already defamiliarized landscape of war and produces an additional effect of displacement and confusion, thus generating a "further multiplying in one's brain." The dominance and intensity of sensory perception creates a sense of incredulity and self-alienation ("hard as even that was to believe"). The sensory surplus of reality—the "too-muchness" of its somatic absorption—contributes to the hallucinatory effect and results in a dissolution, or at least a distortion, of the categories that organize everyday experience.

The *Memoir* represents many of these categories, including the crucial category of time, which, following the pattern of somatic reception, is tangibly experienced. The experienced narrator claims that, during the uprising, the passing of time was experienced as simultaneously slow and fast. In the experience and in the memories of its participants, the uprising escapes the everyday markings of the passage of time and assumes a timeless quality. Time, too, is something to be scuffled with:

> For in the memory those two days seem like a good several days. Almost like a week. And not only in the memory. Then, too. Back then, before the worst on Rybaki Street, we began counting time differently, more quickly. It seemed to pass more slowly. But that was how it appeared. As a thickening [*Zagęściło się*].[88]

> Bo w pamięci to wygląda na kilka dobrych dni, te dwa dni. Prawie na tydzień. I nie tylko w pamięci. Bo i wtedy. Czas wtedy, w tym przednajgorszym okresie Rybaków, zaczął się liczyć jeszcze inaczej, szybciej. Schodził niby wolniej. A to i tak na pozór. Zagęściło się.[89]

Contradictory adverbs convey the perception of time as imbued with contradictory characteristics—time is counted faster ("szybciej") but passes more slowly ("Schodził niby wolniej"). Even this paradoxical statement does not adequately express the narrator's experience of time and requires the qualification "that was how it appeared." Finally, as if to point to the source of this inability to maintain time as an organizer of experience, the narrator transforms it into a substance, "as a thickening" (literally, "things thickened").

This "thickening of things" relates to the experience both of time and of events. A "thickening" implies an intensity of experience that alters and confuses the experience of time, which cannot anymore be organized by familiar external measures of "counting time." Throughout his oeuvre, but particularly in his post-*Memoir* small narrations, Białoszewski represents the experience of time (similar to the mechanisms of traumatic memory) in terms of the narrator's surprise at events that take place in infinitesimal moments and whose significance hits the narrator only a posteriori—even when he partakes in them. In this treatment, change as a process, not result, remains unnoticed because it takes place in the untraceable divisions of time. Such a concept of time resembles what is described in the *Memoir* as the traumatic experience of time. The intensity of this experience lengthens each moment into infinity, breaking it up and segmenting it with the relentless logic of Zeno's paradox into always divisible—and always unbearable—units of "now-ness":

> That a little scrap of time seemed long is no cause for wonder. Every day people would say,
> —it's already day twelve of the uprising . . .
> —it's already day thirteen of the uprising . . .
> And it was as though whole years of this were already behind us—and what lay ahead? As though there had never been, nor ever would be, anything else—only the uprising. Which was impossible to endure much longer. Every day was the last we could endure. Then every night. Then every two hours. Then every fifteen minutes. Yes. People kept track of time incessantly.[90]

> A to, że mały kawałek czasu wydawał się wielki, to nic dziwnego. Każdego dnia się mówiło:
> —Już dwunasty dzień powstania . . .
> —Już trzynasty dzień powstania . . .
> I wydawało się, że już całe lata tego za nami, i co przed nami?, że nic innego nie było i nie będzie, tylko powstanie. Którego już nie można było dłużej wytrzymać. Każdego dnia nie można było dłużej. Potem każdej nocy. Potem każdych dwóch godzin. Potem każdych piętnastu minut. Tak. Liczyło sie czas bez przerwy.[91]

The uprising resists being integrated into the temporal progression of life, which roots itself in the past and stretches into the future. It obliterates both the memory of a pre-uprising reality ("as if we already had entire years of this behind us") and appropriates visions of a future ("and what lay ahead of us? As though there had never been, nor ever would be, anything else—only the uprising "). Such a totalization of the past and future into a sense of perpetual "present-ness" removes any sense of an outside frame of reference delimiting the temporal boundaries of experience: the participants of the uprising no longer recognize a beginning, middle, and end, and have lost their sense of a sequence of events. The community of the *Memoir* lives a-temporally through an event that engulfs the past and washes away the very possibility of a future. This scuffling with time (lack of temporal references, condensation of time, etc.) overlaps with the need to "[keep] track of time incessantly." This need to quantify time's flow in increasingly smaller units manifests the growing difficulty of psychological survival.

The absence of a referential frame and the inability to envision something outside the uprising confuses ("scrambles together") the community's mental processes and affects the mechanism of reflective thinking and memory:

> Imagining what might take place or what would surely take place a moment later occupied at least half one's thoughts. The rest went to satisfying various immediate needs—food, shelter, clothing. . . . Memories forced the rest back. Not really "memories" in the strict sense of the word. Because some are from the day before yesterday. Others from an hour ago. Some are from Wola, and others fresh from Mostowa Street. All of it scrambled together. In circles. Together with possibilities, with what might have been. Against the backdrop of what was happening. And obviously, there must have been a gap for talking too. And a rather long one at that. Considering that our talking dealt precisely with those subjects. By and large.[92]

> Wyobrażanie sobie, co może być albo co na pewno będzie za chwilę, zajmowało chyba połowę myślenia. Reszta szła na załatwianie bieżących spraw różnych, a to jedzeniowych, a to położeniowych się, nakryciowych. . . . Resztę dopychały wspomnienia. Trudno mówić "wspomnienia" w ścisłym sensie. Bo i te z przedednia. I sprzed godziny. I te z Woli, i ze świeżej Mostowej. To wszystko się międliło. W kółko. Razem z tymi właśnie możliwościami, co może być. Na tle tego, co się działo. No i oczywiście musiała być i luka na gadanie. I to jeszcze jaka duża. Z tym, że gadanie było właśnie na te tematy. Głównie.[93]

Long- and short-term memory are conflated by the collapse of temporal planes between past and future and the awareness that each moment is pregnant with the possibility of being the last. The future is reduced to imagining possible scenarios of "what might take place or what would surely take place a moment later," just as the past is reduced to the "memories" of events that have taken place just an hour ago.[94] At the same time, with "all of it scrambled together," the narrator hesitates to label these mechanisms "'memories' in the strict sense of the word." This hesitancy reflects the experienced metanarrator's recognition that this foreshortening of time and its condensation describes phenomena beyond the habitual concepts of human behavior, and in this anticipation of the reader's potential reluctance to accept his choice of terms, he mediates his other self's experience.

There are several occasions in the *Memoir* in which the narrator describes his body as dissociated from his mind and as if it belonged to someone else: "the hands are working, the legs are moving" ("ręce pracują, nogi w czymś").[95] The most striking example of the dissociation of the sensory from the conscious occurs in a passage describing the bombardment of the city. This passage also involves counting time in a literal sense, when the shell-shocked narrator and his friends sitting in a basement count the seconds between the dropping of bombs (which they can recognize by a specific sound) and their explosion. After one close explosion, the disoriented narrator asks, "*Us*? *No,* next door, *it seems;* no, because we are still here. There was no other proof." The disjuncture between sensory input and conscious output is so radical that the mind only hesitantly accepts the existence of the body as proof of the existence of the subject. Showing the delay between seeing one's living body and recognition that one is still alive in the one-word question "Us?" also exemplifies Białoszewski's strategy of encoding emotions in his language without sentimentalizing his characters' feelings.

This lack of sentimentalization contributes to the overall effect of the uprising's radical otherness. The narrator experiences himself outside of the familiar framework of emotional reference. His feelings are contradictory and spread between an experience of sensory overload (and oversensitivity) and mental numbness (and detachment). The experienced narrator comments on the lack of psychological depth:

> Actually it all feels like one long hallucination. A terribly banal tale. But this alone suits me. It fits what I felt then. Because you didn't have to be a poet to have things multiplying in your head. And if I write very little about my impressions. And all of it in ordinary language. Like nothing had happened. Or like I hardly ever look inside myself, so it seems like I'm all surface. It's only because it can't be done any other way. Because that is exactly how it felt. And generally speaking, that is the only way that is not contrived, but completely natural. For getting all of this across.[96]

> To wszystko zresztą zupełnie jakby jednym złudzeniem. Strasznie oklepane powiedzenie. Ale tylko to mi pasuje. Do tego, co wtedy się odczuwało. Bo nie trzeba było być aż poetą, żeby troiło się w głowie. A jeżeli mało piszę o wrażeniach. I zwyczajnym językiem wszystko. Tak jakby nigdy nic. Albo nie wchodzę w siebie prawie, czyli jestem jakby od wierzchu. To tylko dlatego, że inaczej się nie da. Że zresztą tak to się siebie czuło. I w ogóle to jest jedyny sposób, zresztą nie sztucznie wykombinowany, ale jedyny właśnie naturalny. Przekazania tego wszystkiego.[97]

Writing "like I'm all surface" (or "on the surface of things") and "in ordinary language . . . like nothing had happened" is how Białoszewski's narrator declares the "completely natural" way of conveying "how it felt." The experience of the uprising, the narrator claims, was an experience of living "inside out" and, therefore, calls for a language of surfaces, not depth. Through his narrator, Białoszewski positions himself as a writer who does not construct a new aesthetic realm, but solely responds to the demands of the reality he represents. It is the nature of reality and the nature of experience itself that guide him, he tells us, and it is faithfulness to them that leads him to exclude high diction, psychological depth, and reflections ("writing little about impressions and "not looking into himself"). Białoszewski's ongoing struggle against literature as a high mode of "literariness" (or "contrived" language) finds validation in his re-signification of his highly idiosyncratic choices as mimetic. At the same time, the call for ordinary language coexists with an insistence that the experience of the uprising was surreal and poetic ("You didn't have to be a poet to have things multiplying in your head"), yet "a terribly banal tale" as well. It is this fusion of "ordinary language" in a "terribly banal tale" of highly traumatic (and highly poetic) experience that becomes Białoszewski's "completely natural" and unique performance of memory.

THE HYPER-ORALITY OF TRAUMATIC TESTIMONY

The most striking stylistic feature of this performance of memory is Białoszewski's choice of diction, which re-creates the effects of orality. Through this re-creation, the *Memoir* becomes a reenactment of traumatic testimony. Throughout his career, Białoszewski stressed his belief in the power of orality, which was directly related to his experimentations with the situational contexts and to his theatrical experience, in which text fully realizes itself only when it is in direct contact with the audience.[98] His penchant for theatrical readings and singing his own works both during formal and informal meetings with his audience became legendary, and the existing recordings of his work clearly demonstrate that Białoszewski acted out his writing even without the presence of an audience. In the 1970s, reading and recording became an integral part of his process of writing and revising. In keeping with this spirit, the *Memoir* was meant to read as a rendition of speech. In an interview given in 1978, Białoszewski stresses the oral core of the work's composition:

> My point was so that it [the *Memoir*] will not be worse than talking. This is a common sin. A grievous one. Someone is great at recounting his experience. But, often when he writes it down, it turns out that he deadened the entire thing. Talking was better. The point is not to make it better. To give and not to stint people and oneself. The *Memoir* was first written in longhand and then I taped it so that someone else could type it. So, the entire *Memoir* went through the ear.[99]

Rendering the uprising with features characteristic of "talking" ("gadanie") was part of the *Memoir*'s scandal. In the preface to the first edition, Janusz

Wilhelmi, in a peculiar mixture of disdain and promotion, described the *Memoir*'s language as "artificially mangled . . . artificially crippled . . . [and] artificially overblown in its complex colloquial [syntax]." He also warned readers that they would encounter a work that is "distinctly annoying."[100] Thankfully, critics who were not officially appointed to critique the book quickly realized the revelatory qualities of Białoszewski's diction, and a clash between the subject and the low diction of "chatter" ("gadanie") was acknowledged as truly innovative.

Białoszewski's diction in the *Memoir* was often described as a written imitation of the spoken language or, as Barańczak put it, a "semantically saturated" imitation of orality. Some critics also compared the *Memoir* to *l'ecriture automatique.*[101] Although there is some truth in both statements, they do not point to a hyperbolic quality of language in the *Memoir.* Białoszewski does not only re-create the qualities of spoken language, but he exaggerates them and by doing so, he brings the essence of the oral and the colloquial to the fore. The language of the *Memoir* is seemingly chaotic and imprecise, but upon a closer examination one realizes that it oscillates with great precision between different registers and that what seems at times like a breathless narration of great speed and semantic approximation in fact carefully balances each and every word.[102] The condensation of the qualities of spoken language exposes the very mechanism of the generation and articulation of language. This emphasis on how language is produced directs the reader's attention to the very working of language vis-à-vis memory and, ultimately, re-creates the force of traumatic recall As if condensing twenty-three years of "gadanie" that the narrator declares as the story of the uprising, the text positions the reader as the witness-listener whose experience parallels the fluctuating tension and release of the narrator.[103] The effect of the *Memoir* is both of orality and aurality, and their combination contributes to the *Memoir*'s ethical impact as a reenactment of traumatic testimony.

Białoszewski defines for us the danger of writing: it is a mode that often "deadens" narrated experience. He qualifies the lack of emotional impact as a "grievous sin" and conveys the empathetic and participatory character of oral communication. Only in such communication is sound "poured into" the listener, which allows him or her to interiorize the impact of the narrated events.[104] The form of the *Memoir*'s reenactment of orality fulfills two functions: on the one hand, it reenacts the process of the individual recovery of memory via sharing it with others and, on the other, it aims at the emotional effect of creating a witness for the traumatic testimony.

The *Memoir*'s reader "listens" to a virtual performer whose main concern is to sway and overwhelm the reader. This performance takes place on three levels: first, it reenacts the experience of the uprising (via the naive narrator); second, it reenacts the traumatic memory of this experience (via the experienced narrator); and third, it reenacts the transformation of the traumatic memory into a narrative memory through the text's emotional impact upon the reader, which is encoded in Białoszewski's linguistic choices, particularly those that pertain to the reenactment of orality. The process of reading parallels the act of listening to a survivor's testimony, which entails the rhythm of exteriorization and interiorization, proximity and distance. These oscillations also reflect the emotional relationship with the double nature of the *Memoir,* a text that asks the reader for oral/aural openness to it, but can convey this request only through its highly literary mode. The reader, therefore, is cast as a key player not only in the narrator's "recovery" of memory, but also as a witness to Białoszewski's ongoing articulation of the doubleness of his language.

The re-creation of the effect of a spoken recollection relies on the "tightness" of the narration. Białoszewski remarks:

> The question of form. I was mainly interested in conveying things, and the form got pushed to the side. But in spite of myself, when I was writing, and later revising and taping, I would try to make it tight. When a situation or occurrence [literally: "situation and little situation"] came out sounding too descriptive and the sentences dragged on. For example—on entering the basement on Miodowa Street, there's a wounded man lying there and a woman in a slip dressing his wounds. Initially, it was written situationally, almost sequentially. But then I thought to myself—I've got to give it as I had it. And the first thing was that I stood at the top of a dark staircase, burnt out in the bottom. And then what I saw: unclearly at first. Something was moving. Someone wounded. Someone taking care of him. And later—what that was. I wanted to write it as I had felt it. With wound-up senses. The nose on top of the head, the ear in the belly. We were bundles of perception. At the sight of a tank on Miodowa Street, I was in pain.
>
> Temat formy. Mnie chodziło bardzo o przekazanie, a forma szła do kąta. Ale mimo woli jak pisałem, a potem poprawiałem, przedyktowałem, to starałem się, żeby to było spięte. Kiedy jakaś sytuacja, sytuacyjka, wychodziła za bardzo opisowo i długo wlokły się zdania. Dam przykład—wejście do piwnicy na Miodową, jak leży ranny i kobieta w halce go opatruje. Z początku to było opisane sytuacyjnie, jakby po kolei. Ale potem myślę—trzeba dać, jak ja to miałem. A najpierw stanąłem z góry w ciemnych schodach na dole wypalonych. I to—co widziałem: Najpierw niejasno. Coś się tam rusza. Że ranny. Że opatrują go. A potem—co to jest. Chodziło o to, żeby było, jak to wtedy odczułem. Na jakichś zakręconych zmysłach. Nos na czubku głowy, a ucho w brzuchu. Było się takim kłębkiem odbioru. Od czołgu na Miodowej dostałem boleści.[105]

Białoszewski identifies such tightness with "giv[ing] it as [he] had it," meaning with abandoning the rationale of narrative sequences ("jakby po kolei") in order to convey the experience of sensory disorientation. His choice is to re-create a perceptive confusion that makes it difficult to identify the situation, or a sensory overload, as when the sight of a tank causes pain, obliterating the somatic boundary between the inside of the subject and the outside of the situation. In this sense, the *Memoir* reenacts the physical experience of the traumatic event as much as the struggle to articulate it through traumatic recall. Both these phenomena resist stable understanding, yet Białoszewski aims to convey them through an "oral" diction that allows language itself to become the carrier of the emotivity that is shunned on the discursive level. Białoszewski's diction hides no secrets, yet it deprives the story of the pacifying quality of narrative comprehensibility. Oral diction is the medium and the message of the traumatic reenactment. In short, the experience of the uprising is felt rather than told.

THE EMOTIVE INTONATION

The most striking elements of Białoszewski's re-creation of orality are his fragmentation of sentences and his use of ellipses. These devices dominate Białoszewski's performative utterances and foreground a primary feature of the oral: intonation. In the *Memoir*, the intonation achieved with this strategy becomes a type of semantic organizer that carries the message not in syntactic-logical units but "over" these units, by charging them with the intensity of the present and by forcing the reader to relive the experience of the uprising in the present tense as the narrative unfolds. As a result, the uprising is witnessed rather than comprehended, empathized with rather than understood. Białoszewski's brief, choppy sentences lack subordination and are often no more than fragments or noun phrases. In this respect, they resemble the spoken diction Julia Kristeva analyzes in Louis Ferdinand Céline's description of shell shock in *Voyage au bout de la nuit* (1932; *Journey to the End of the Night*).[106] Kristeva calls Céline's linguistic strategy "enunciative," a strategy characterized by musical qualities and employing (as in the *Memoir*) intonation as the dominant carrier of emotivities that would otherwise remain unexpressed. Rather than explicate the narrator's mental state, Białoszewski's sentences perform the narrator's sense of disorientation, breathlessness, and fear, as in this passage describing the fleeing of civilians:

> Again people. Buckets. And nothing. And planes. Bombs. There was no sense in thinking about taking shelter. Where? When? Already there were explo-

sions. Bursts. And again. Again they're flying over. Diving. Whining. Bombs. The only thing to do was to run even faster. With the bucket.[107]

Znów ludzie. Kubły. I nic. I samoloty. Bomby. Nie ma co myśleć o schowaniu się. Bo kiedy i gdzie. I tak już huki. Wybuchy. I następne. I znów nadlatują. Zniżanie. Wycie. Bomby. Jedyne, co można było zrobić, to jeszcze szybciej lecieć. Z kubłem.[108]

With the water cut off in the buildings, civilians would line up with buckets around street pumps, which became strategic targets for German planes. In accordance with his promise to describe "how it felt," Białoszewski describes the chaotic flight of these civilians from the bombers by staying "on the surface of things" and piling up noun phrases that position buckets, bombs, and fear on a single horizontal plane of importance. Such noun phrases contain the raw, immediate information, but it is the intonation that conveys the narrator's internal states.

The narrator does not indicate a specific musical register of this intonation and, thus, of his emotions. Through the silences, Białoszewski as a narrator positions his reader as listener who must fill in the emotional gaps in the narrative. The lack of exclamatory marks in this passage allows us, for instance, to read it as much less eruptive than Białoszewski's onomatopoeic expressions (which are, per se, enunciative, as they perform rather than describe sound) in other fragments of the *Memoir.*[109] Yet the choppiness coupled with a powerful emotional silence succeeds in conveying a paralyzing sense of helplessness, as a few short noun phrases reflect how the senses simultaneously register the falling of bombs and the absence of shelter. As if responding to a listener's unspoken question "So what did you do?" the narrator explains, "The only thing to do was to run even faster. With the bucket."

The fragmented sentences make the experience feel close to the reader, and they resist being totalized in an act of comprehension. More than fragmentation, however, ellipses typify Białoszewski's strategy of enunciation. Ellipses, broadly understood as any deliberate pause or omission of words required to complete a grammatical construction, are essential for colloquial language; they participate in its economy (when we speak we usually omit words whose meaning is clear from the context) and in its ambiguity. In the *Memoir,* however, ellipses function not as linguistic shortcuts or creators of conceptual ambivalence, but as gaps that charge language with an overflowing emotive force. Their strategic function is to move the reader closer to the represented events while at the same time allowing the narrator to refrain from any overt commentary. Ellipses shift the emphasis of the text from a logical progression of thought, which requires fully developed syntactic units, to an eruptive emotivity befitting the violent reality that Białoszewski represents.

The emotive function of ellipses emerges with particular clarity in Białoszewski's treatment of temporality, especially in one of the most dramatic parts of the *Memoir*, a description of the incessant bombardment of the Old City. During the bombardment, the narrator and his circle count the seconds—"aloud in a family chorus"[110]—during each gap of time between the moments they hear the specific sound made by a bomb being released from a plane and the moment of its detonation. If Białoszewski's goal had been to tell the reader about behavioral patterns during bombardment, there would have been no need for the extensive use of repetitions and ellipses in this passage; his employment of ellipses in the counting of time, however, charges the language with intensity, which, on the one hand, reflects the perception of the lengthening of time during the traumatic experience, and, on the other, brings the reader into the immediate vicinity of the "family chorus" and makes the reader count along. In the following passage, Białoszewski separates a series of repetitions with ellipses to underscore the tension of waiting. With every elliptic omission in the counting, the reader experiences the tension and the emotions of those awaiting the bomb's explosion:

> But soon the airplanes would fly over once more, screeching; the bombs being released, the whining, the silence, and:
> "One, two, three, four, five, six, seven, eight, nine, ten, eleven, twelve . . ." And then—Bam!!!—all of a sudden, as it often happened.
> They mostly exploded at eight or nine. Yes. But the planes would fly over again and: "One, two, three, four, five, six, seven . . ."
> Bam!!
> Us? No . . . Now the whining again.
> "one, two, three, four, five, six, seven, eight, nine . . ."
> Bam!!
> No. Next door, it seems; no, because we're still here. There was no other proof. And again they're flying, whining . . .
> "one, two, three, four, five, six, seven, eight, nine, ten . . ."
> Bam!!
> And again:
> "one, two, three, four, five, six, seven, eight, nine, ten, ele-ven . . . tweeelve . . . thir-teen . . ."
> "Oh . . ."
> Then all of a sudden there might be a pause. Half an hour. An hour. And:
> "one, two, three, four, five, six, seven, eight, nine, ten . . ."
> ssss
> and right away:
> "one, two, three, four, five, six, seven, eight nine, ten, eleven, twelve . . . thirteen . . . oof . . ."
> and already new ones were diving down

"one, two, three, four . . . Oh gosh." pause—and again
"they're back"
"oh Jesus"
and
"one, two, three, four, five, six, seven, eight, nine, ten, eleven, twelve . . . thirteen . . . oof."[111]

Ale niedługo zlatywały samoloty, świdrowały, to odłączanie się bomb, wycie, cisza—i:
-Raz, dwa, trzy, cztery, pięć, sześć, siedem, osiem, dziewięć, dziesięć, jedenaście . . .—i tu nieraz potrafiło nagle—jak grzmotnąć!
Przeważnie wybuchało przy ośmiu, dziewięciu. No tak. Ale samoloty znów zlatywały i:
-Raz, dwa, trzy, cztery, pięć, sześć, siedem . . .
Trzask!
W nas? Nie . . . Ale już wycie.
Raz, dwa, trzy, cztery, pięć, sześć, siedem, osiem, dziewięć . . .
Trzask!
Nie, obok, chyba—no bo jesteśmy. Innego dowodu nie było. I już lecą, wyją . . .
-Raz, dwa, trzy, cztery, pięć, sześć, siedem, osiem, dziewięć, dziesięć . . .
Trzask!
Ale już następne:
-Raz, dwa, trzy, cztery, pięć, sześć, siedem, osiem, dziewięć, dzie-sięć, jedenaście . . . dwa-naś-cieee . . . trzyna . . . ście . . .
-O . . .
Potem mogła być nagle przewa. Pół godziny. Godzinę. I . . .
-Raz, dwa, trzy, cztery, pięć, sześć, siedem, osiem, dziewięć, dziesięć . . .
sss—i zaraz
-raz, dwa, trzy, cztery, pięć, sześć, siedem, osiem, dziewięć, dziesięć, jedenaście, dwanaście . . . trzy-naa-ście . . . o . . .
i już zlatywały nowe
-raz, dwa, trzy, cztery, . . . o rany! . . .—i znów za trochę
-o już są
-o Jezu
i
-raz, dwa, trzy, cztery, pięć, sześć, siedem, osiem, dziewięć, dziesięć, jedenaście, dwa-na-ście . . . trzy-naa-ście . . . o![112]

The longer the wait, the more it is marked by suspenseful ellipses between the numbers and by a lengthening of the numbers, either by the insertion of dashes to segment the word itself or by the repetition of vowels ("dwa-naś-cieee . . . trzy-na-ście . . ."). After the addition of the vowels ("dwa-naś-cieee . . ."), their absence (in "trzy-na-ście") strikes the reader as suddenly as the bomb's explosion. The exclamations ("they're back," "oh Jesus") function as the breaking point—the tension has grown so strong that fear bursts out of the language.

The elliptic representation of the articulation of numbers blends a description of reality with a performance of the internal states of its participants precisely by articulating the passage of time. The emotional intensity of waiting to see whether one has survived the bomb's blast is expressed by a time punctuated with pauses between the counting of time's passage. Even visually, these fragmented sentences disappear into the blank spaces around them, allowing ellipses to take over signification. This creates a cumulative effect of time as a series of lengthened, highly charged moments (and highly charged dots). The visual representation of the spoken words ("dwa-na-ście . . . trzy-naa-ście . . . o!") shifts the passage's emphasis from the logic of signification to the affect of intonation.

Ellipses also convey the narrator's disbelief in his sensory perception; in this function, they are often combined with exclamatory phrases, question marks, and onomatopoeias that set the language, the narrator's senses, and his surrounding reality into motion:

> God, how those walls moved . . . One time, I'm watching them—and it looks like they're moving a meter back and forth . . . and back . . . and forth . . . are we flying apart?! . . . nooo . . . they were seesawing . . . a little less, still less, and they've stopped . . . just where they were before. I rubbed my eyes in amazement.[113]

> A jak te mury chodziły . . . raz patrzę—a one chodzą chyba na metr w tę i w tę . . . i w tę . . . i w tę . . . rozlatujemy się?! . . . niee—pohuśtały się . . . trochę mniej, coraz mniej, i ustawiły . . . tak jak stały. Przecierałem oczy ze zdumienia.[114]

In this passage, brief statements replace syntactic subordination. The very brevity and fragmentation of these statements convey the resistance of the narrator's experience to any speculative process. For the narrator, everything becomes a fact, even his own amazement; but, at the same time, these facts do not add up to a generalizable knowledge. The reader, like the narrator, is only to rub her eyes "in amazement"; Białoszewski's strategy is to make the reader believe the narrator's experience and yet resist making any larger claims about the uprising.

In this stylistic strategy, where everything is narrated as if it were happening before the reader's eyes, the staccato rhythm of elliptic sentences carries the very energy of the narration and allows the reader to link the heterogeneous sensory experiences of the narrator into an unbroken flow of experience—that is, elliptic blanks provide "energetic" fillers. These fillers give the narration a sense of continuity despite the fragmentary nature of the traumatic experience. As in the fragmented sentences used to convey the experience of fleeing (with the bucket) from the German bombing of a street pump, ellipses also produce a suspenseful intonation that invites the reader to fill in the blank of the narrator's mental and emotional states. In one of the rare internal "monologues," the narrator describes his thoughts about parting from his relatives during the uprising:

> "'Oh God,' I thought to myself, 'they're back there on Miodowa—and the sign of the cross when we're saying goodbye . . .'"[115]

> "Oj . . .—myślałem sobie—zostały tam na Miodowej—i te krzyżyki przy pożegnaniu . . ."[116]

The passage tells us nothing that we do not already know (that the narrator's family is left on Miodowa Street and that the farewell scene involved the sign of the cross), yet the very repetition of the information as a thought process punctuated by ellipses allows a reconstructive reading of the narrator's internal state. The register of his varying mental states (wistfulness, despair, fear, or resignation) is left to the imagination of the reader, directly engaging him or her as an emotional participant in the action of the *Memoir*.

Because of their nature, Białoszewski's linguistic devices—fragmentation, repetitions, onomatopoeias, ellipses—belong to the "naive" narrator whose function is to totally immerse the reader in the uncanny everyday of the uprising and to speak from the position of eyewitness. Białoszewski's openness to language and his seemingly frantic way of exploring its possibilities can be metaphorically compared to his narrator's roaming through the streets of Warsaw and exploring its hidden secrets revealed in the process of destruction. The reader, along for the journey, is asked to take it all (i.e., the language and/as the event) with its violent power, without conceptual control, without distancing himself, and without understanding.

HISTORY AVOIDED AND HISTORY SUBVERTED

Orality is represented in the *Memoir* and in Białoszewski's statements as a mode of communication that enables "re-presenting" the event to the audience. Białoszewski puts his reader in the position of listener and employs various strategies to avoid a "common sin" of "deadening the whole thing." However, bringing the experience closer to the reader does not necessarily mean that the *Memoir* showed that "behind the salad of chopped syntax one finds a juicy beefsteak of reality,"[117] if by "reality" we mean, simply, the topic whose referent—as opposed to Białoszewski's pre-*Memoir* work—was clear to his readers. This is perhaps why it is tempting to look teleologically at Białoszewski's artistic trajectory and see in the *Memoir* a representation of a collectively shared historical event, for which Białoszewski gathered tools in the period of his earlier linguistic experiments. This sense of the indisputable "reality" of the referent is what endeared the *Memoir* to an audience that was unreceptive to a similar style in Białoszewski's earlier work.

However, Białoszewski does not so much treat his reader with a "juicy beefsteak" of reality as with a concoction of memory whose stylistic and narrative ingredients are potent enough to blur the reader's vision. While the *Memoir* brilliantly actualizes the logic of traumatic testimony, at the same time, in this very actualization, it remains hermetic, and hence protected from a demand to engage in historical and political interrogations. Białoszewski generates his own discursive regime ("regime" in the Foucauldian sense) in which his stylistic reenactment of orality—the flow of vivid, hyperbolically colloquial, highly enunciative, obsessive, and, at times, almost claustrophobic sentences—increases the emotivity of the work in the same way a green paper under an emerald increases the perceived authenticity of the stone.[118] This sense of veracity shifts the reader's attention away from the fact that the *Memoir* does not contextualize itself, that is, it does not offer to put itself in a framework that would allow for a comparison to any other source of "truth" about the uprising other than itself. In a dazzling spectacle of authorial control, Białoszewski engages the reader in the theater of traumatic memory, which becomes an absolute, autonomous truth in itself.

The *Memoir*'s claims to the truth of history are embedded in its very form. The narrator describes "talking/chattering" ("gadanie") as the genesis of the text, and this talking is presented as a collectively circulated testimony, itself already embodying the "genre" of oral memoir. We learn little about the context in which the construction of memories of the uprising takes place: the narrator tells us only that he talked to "lots of people" during the twenty-three years in which he struggled to articulate his memories. Sometimes he tells us that he checked his memories against that of his friends and relatives ("When I recently asked [Halina] about it she didn't remember it at all").[119] Infrequently, he refers to external sources, but when he does so, what he seeks is a confirmation of something that becomes self-evident (for instance, in the Weapon Museum he confirms that "cows," a nickname for the missile used to bombard Warsaw, was well-chosen because the missiles reminded him of milk cans). The collective of the narrator's interlocutors is not bound by any national characteristics but by its experience of the uprising. This way, the uprising made the collective; it is not something that happened to a specific collective. What emerges is a view of history that is collective and private at the same time. Its private dimension pertains, on the most basic level, to the fact that the memories of friends and relatives emerge in the domestic setting; however, the history is private also because it does not justify itself in relation to outside sources.

The narrator together with "lots of people" contributes to a single story and history, but their account of the uprising seems to be suspended outside any recognizable frame of reference; that is, it resists being compared with or verified against other accounts. Białoszewski creates a narrator whose language of "how it was" gives the reader a testimony that operates in self-referential terms. The memory of "small facts, perhaps too detailed" ("w fakcikach, może za dokładny")[120] becomes a way to validate the promise of providing "only the truth" ("tylko prawda będzie"). In the *Memoir* Białoszewski exhibits a strategy similar to the one we can see in his later small narrations (which I discuss in chapter 3 through the metaphor of the "purloined letter"): while claiming to offer the reader full visibility and exposure—being "all surface" and "writing everything"—Białoszewski creates a code of obviousness, which conditions the reader's field of vision. The highly controlled stylistic devices masterfully reenact the traumatic on the level of style; simultaneously, they allow the narrator to assume the position of a transparent medium for the testimony that contains truth and nothing but the truth. "Wszystko na wierzchu" promises everything and makes us overlook what is missing. This applies not only to the avoidance of a political commentary, but also of the topics that could potentially take the narrator from the microhistories of everyday situations to a more panoramic vision of suffering or, surprisingly (considering the nature of the event), to the close-up of a dead body. For instance, Białoszewski only hints at such horrifying episodes of the uprising as the Wola massacre ("what happened in Wola happened again" ["powtórzyły się wolskie sprawy"]),[121] and although he describes a reality where death abounds, his narrator's vision comes out of focus in the description of the body (for instance, "people are digging something white and something else in white is lying there" ["wydobywają coś białego i coś jeszcze białego leży"]).[122] An extreme instance of a defamiliarized body is the exhumation scene where the decomposed body brings to mind an image of a breaded piece of meat "with a single bone sticking out."[123]

The narrator defines his voice as the voice of the layman and reasserts his right to attest to the past on behalf of those who simply "were there." By appointing himself as a spokesman for the Everyman, the narrator naturalizes his account by disclaiming any agency over his language, which is not "contrived" ("sztucznie wykombinowany"), but the only "natural language" to convey the experience and its memory. Białoszewski makes the act of putting the memory in motion the drive and the logic of the *Memoir*, and he makes us trust the narrator's "gadanie" as a "naive"—hence, straightforward and authentic—glimpse of history. Much like the mechanism that I discuss in chapter 3 wherein any sense of incongruency could be answered by what Sobolczyk calls the "dictate of reality" ("dyktat rzeczywistości"), this time, too, the "truth of the event" protects the storyteller's "blurred up" subjectivity[124] and bars our questions about his experience of the event, while also redirecting our attention from the subversive charge of Białoszewski's narration and its political and historiographical implications. In the culture of "double censorship," Białoszewski circumvents both the official historiography and the counter-narrative, and he eludes known qualifiers and categories in his approach to the representation of the uprising. If the "author-function" is to "characterize the existence, circulation, and operation of certain discourses within a society," then the picture that emerges from Białoszewski's account is at once blurred and vivid.[125]

Yet, in spite of this unspecificity, Białoszewski signals to his reader that he wants his double gesture—merging blurriness and vividness—to be recognized. He subtly leads the reader to the realization that his reenacting of an individual testimony enmeshed with collective voices and his "naive" affirmations of "only the truth" are to be read as an ethical and political gesture. When at one point the narrator says that the continuation of the uprising seemed pointless because there were no weapons left, he immediately restrains himself, suggesting a self-awareness that he went too far with his assessment:

> There is no need for me to play a sage. Others have long since made history of this, have drawn their conclusions and publicized them. So it's well known. I'm speaking for myself—a layman. And for others. Also laymen. Inasmuch as we can speak because we were there. Laymen and nonlaymen. All condemned together to a single history.[126]

> Niepotrzebnię mędrkuję. Dawno inni już zrobili i historię, i wnioski z tego, i ogłosili. I rzecz jest znana. Tak mówię od siebie—laika. I od innych. Też laików. O tyle nam wolno mówić, że tam byliśmy. Laicy z nielaikami. Wszyscy razem skazani na jedną historię.[127]

The word choices—"laymen and nonlaymen"—base the right to the memory of the uprising on some criteria of historical professionalization that remains undisclosed to the reader. The "they" who "made history" of the uprising are not specified; note, however, that the word "ogłosili" (here "announced" or "publicized") brings to mind a biblical "głosili," or "spreading" (as in "głosić dobrą nowinę," "spreading the gospel") and thus combines a kind of institutional announcement with a proselytizing flair. Białoszewski's vocabulary thus subtly suggests an ironic view of official historiography, although it immediately protects this view by the self-deprecating statement that "I am speaking for myself" ("tak tylko mówię"). This "speaking for myself" is juxtaposed with "making history"; thus the narrator claims that he speaks from a non-historical position, a position that does not purport to offer conclusions and is therefore non-threatening in relation to the historical conclusions drawn from official sources. At the same time, the self-consciousness of this feigned ignorance is emphasized by the narrator's claiming his right to speak "inasmuch as we can speak" by the very virtue of experience and survival.

There is a contrast of tones in the way Białoszewski talks about "speaking for myself" and "for others" ("tak mówię od siebie—laika. I od innych"). "I speak for myself" has a nonchalant quality of "Don't mind me, I'm just talking. I'm just mumbling my own non-professional opinion," while the phrase "and for others" brings an air of ethical responsibility and collective gravitas. This unattested community stands outside official history, yet it has access to its own unquestionable truth provided by the fundamental fact of "being there." Against "well-known conclusions," the narrator of the *Memoir* sets an alternative of "being there," which he presents as the only undisputable "history" of the uprising. "Inasmuch as we can speak" points to the suppression of the voices of those who do not make history but are "condemned" to it, while "being there" does not discriminate.

Thus, the narrator simultaneously suggests that the *Memoir* is subversive in relation to the official historiography and softens his claim by extending its testimony to "all condemned together to a single history." Note that in typical Białoszewskian fashion we do not learn the content of the dominant historical "conclusions" that the *Memoir* is positioned against. All we learn is that they are "well known," which allows the readers to understand the dominant discourse in whichever terms they choose. This is a possible wink to readers and to their awareness of the uprising's double political status, but this is also a gesture that is consistent with the narrator's expression of annoyance with the abstract, the general, and the speculative, that is, a framework—if not to say, any framework—that is not his own. By delineating the narrow horizon of his explorations, Białoszewski stays in control of what questions can and cannot be asked.[128] By the same token, he leaves himself free to claim his own private history and witness "being there" that disregard official historiography and mythical imperative alike.

Chapter 2

Something More from Almost Nothing: The Paradoxes of Białoszewski's Life-Writing

> My heartburn is at its peak and I'm thinking to myself:
> "ten o'clock . . . night . . . quiet, I'll go throw up, put a record on, and write . . . everything . . . all of this . . . all . . .
>
> Zgaga sięgła szczytu, a ja se myślę tak:
> —dziesiąta . . . noc . . . spokój, pójdę się wyrzygać, puszczę płytę i będę pisał . . . wszystko, to wszystko . . . wszystko . . .
> —Miron Białoszewski, *Szumy, zlepy, ciągi* (1976)

> I know very well that I belong to those in the coats, those from the ditches. Like them I am a dug up, half-buried corpse, basically, and I must at all costs pretend to be alive, and more or less fit to use a shovel. I am neither scared nor desperate. Resigned to my fate. The resignation—everything—is long past.
>
> Wiedziałem dobrze, że należę do tych w paltach, tych z rowu. Sam jestem taki wykopany, niedogrzebany, po prostu trup i muszę za wszelką cenę udawać żywego, jako tako zdolnego do kopania łopatą. Nie jestem ani przestraszony ani zrozpaczony. Pogodzony ze swoim losem. Jest dawno po rezygnacji, po wszystkim.
> —Miron Białoszewski, *Szumy, zlepy, ciągi* (1976)

Chapter 2

THE "EVERYTHING" OF THE SMALL NARRATIONS: MAXIMALISTIC MINIMALISM

What is this compulsively repeated "all" that we see in this passage from the second volume of the small narrations? Clearly, it does not mean a thematic all-inclusivity—an impossibility in any case—but rather a specific kind of relationship between the narrator and his project of life-writing. The low register of a need for bodily purgation juxtaposed with a diary-like specification of date and time and the maximalist ambition of "all" signals to the reader that *Szumy, zlepy, ciągi* (1976; *Hums, Lumps, Threads*) follows the mode of narration of the everyday inaugurated by *Donosy rzeczywistości* (1973; *Reporting Reality*). In this mode, the narrator, bearing the name of the author, takes the reader through his quotidian activities, paying attention to countless insignificant events, encounters, and reflections.[1]

From 1970 until his death in 1983, Białoszewski wrote a series of works for which, for lack of a better word, critics tend to employ the umbrella term "małe narracje" ("small narrations"), introduced in 1973 by Michał Głowiński. Although difficult to define generically, thematically these works seem to hide no secrets; they revolve around such quotidian subjects as passersby the narrator observes from his window, daily events in the lives of the narrator and his friends, a hospital stay after a heart attack, bus trips, and flashes of memories from his childhood and wartime youth. Focused on daily life, Białoszewski describes in his works the ordinary, the mundane, and the prosaic—the everyday life of undramatic times. The post-*Memoir* works also include prose and poetic travel diaries from the writer's trips to Egypt and the United States as well as from his boat trip along the coast of Europe. Those who look for exoticism in these travel accounts will be disappointed—for the narrator, traveling to Garwolin (a small town in the suburbs of Warsaw) is as stimulating as his journey to New York. Then, there are "transy i transiki" ("trances and little trances"), meditative reveries that arise from observing such everyday objects as the poplar tree in front of his window. This tree becomes a leitmotif—the narrator maintains a close relationship with it, and its seasonal transformations lend themselves to what may be the most visionary passages in all of Białoszewski's work. The small narrations inaugurate Białoszewski's preoccupation with the everyday, which differs from his earlier poetry, in which, in the spirit of avant-garde poetics, the everyday (as in the poem about the stove) was (literally) transformed into an exotic construct.

Through the names of the genres that Białoszewski invents for his writing, he emphasizes that each of them signifies a particular situation or mental state or, à la Bakhtin, individual types of speech. And so, we find in the small narrations both "spacerownik" (a "walking diary") for descriptions of situations the narrator observes during his daily walks, and "ojcownik" (a "father diary/fatherbook") that focuses on the narrator's father. Even more innovative are genres such as "cytaty" ("quotations"), "przecieki" ("leaks"), "frywole" ("frivolities"), "transiki" ("minitrances"), and "wyrwy z zamyśleń" ("plucked from musings"), which all have their own idiosyncratic diction. The "minitrances," for instance, indicate contemplative speech, while "quotations" are reserved for bits and pieces of conversation overheard on the street. Sometimes, the narrator functions like a microphone picking up fragments of conversations and street life; often the small narrations bring to mind the automatic recording of ordinary activities, but the narrator also shares with his reader his dreams and reflections. Through this proliferation of genres, Białoszewski embraces the multitude of everyday interactions and points to the limitations of established literary classifications. His genres seem not to be invented but instead autochthonic, that is, arising from the soil of specific situations. They contribute to the overall effect of life-writing that does not seem so much to translate life as to grow out of life organically.

Which works should be included in the small narrations has been a subject of critical contention. Barańczak thinks that from *Donosy rzeczywistości* (1973; *Reporting Reality*) we can see that the norm for Białoszewski becomes fragmentary, diary-like entries, and temporal leaps (while, for Barańczak, the *Memoir* was characterized by a continuous narration and a chronological order). From *Donosy rzeczywistości,* Białoszewski moves freely between prose, drama, and poetry, and this is why for Baranczak a "small narration" "may take a graphic form of a poem, short story, anecdote, or even a small drama piece."[2] Thus, the term also encompasses Białoszewski's later poems (e.g., *Odczepić się* [1978; *Got Lost*], dramatic pieces such as "Kabaret Kici Koci" ["The Cabaret of Kicia Kocia"] in the volume *Oho,* and large prose pieces with more extensive plots. In other words, Barańczak qualifies everything that Białoszewski publishes after the *Memoir* as belonging to the category of small narrations and treats any differences between these works as essentially graphic, rather than genealogical. What matters in Barańczak's eyes is that with the first volume of the small narrations published in 1973 Białoszewski becomes "the Białoszewski as we knew him later, the Białoszewski who is not only a linguist and an experimentator, but simultaneously a great and revelatory realist."[3]

Głowiński claims a different divide in Białoszewski's ouevre. He notes that already from his pre-*Memoir* poetry (fully from *There Was and There Was,* 1965), Białoszewski initiates the transformation of his writing into what Głowiński labels an "intimate crypto-diary."[4] This crypto-diary is characterized by the employment of dates, fragmentation, and biographical realia. The diary-like effect is emphasized by the erasure of anything that would help the reader to identify the context of what is narrated or give some kind of introduction into the situation. Finally, crucial for this writing is a drastic reduction of the distance between the teller and the told, which manifests itself primarily in the eternal present of the story. With the distance between the time of an event and the time of writing disappearing, the small narrations, like the *Memoir,* reenact a process of speaking directly to the reader-listener. This principle of narrating events as if they were happening simultaneously with the act of narration is, according to Głowiński, an unshakable rule in the small narrations, even in the volumes of small narrations, such as *Heart Attack* or *Konstancin* (bound by the topic of the narrator's heart attack and his convalescence in the sanatorium), that have a more cohesive and extensive narration than shorter vignettes of other volumes.[5] The principle of "here" and "now" that defined the *Memoir* is continued in the small narrations as well. However, while through these oral characteristics Białoszewski erases traces of writing, at the same time he emphasizes them by the attention he pays to dates and to the diary-like fragmentariness of expressions. Thus, Białoszewski brings attention to both oral and written mediums of communication and underscores the very process of reenacting speech.

One of the features that I find particularly important in relation to the reenactment of speech is, in Głowiński's words, "the constant tension between the continuous narration, which provides the global sense of the work, and the narration broken down into fragments governed in some cases by the given dates and in others by left-out dates. In this kind of narration what matters is not to narrate from the position of someone who is able to control events and their participants, but someone who speaks in such a way as if there were no gap or cracks between the act of speech and the event."[6] This quality is sometimes thematized as in the playful beginning of *Hums, Lumps, Threads,* when the narrator hurries to add final notes to his manuscript in front of the publishing house and asks rhetorically, "what author writes this way?" These qualities of narration greatly affect the reading experience and are particularly important in light of the seriality of the small narrations. This seriality, as I signaled in the introduction, facilitates a sustained relationship between the text and the reader, and with the progression of each volume the reader is invited to accumulate his knowledge about the narrator, whose name and characteristics indicate that Białoszewski makes a biographical pact with the reader. The illusiveness of this pact and the controlled nature of Białoszewski's self-exposure are topics that I discuss in chapter 3, where I address the self-revelation and self-concealment of his homosexuality. What is important for me in the context of the everyday is that this narrator creates for the reader an illusion of a unified vision of the everyday, which otherwise is as fragmentary as the form itself. The narrator promises a horizontal attention to "everything" (as in "I will write down everything") and a continuous attention, but the flow of his narration is not only interrupted by the diary-like fragmentariness; it is full of ruptures and gaps from within, and I see these ruptures as emerging from the traumatic. The quotidian quilt that Białoszewski weaves throughout the small narrations owes its appeal to traumatic stitches.[7]

The uniqueness of the representation of the everyday in the small narrations depends on a fusion of seemingly mutually exclusive qualities of the traumatic and the quotidian. As in the *Memoir,* in which the radical and the banal constitute the same reality, the post-*Memoir* works, albeit in a less striking way, show one through the other. The small narrations continue what the *Memoir* so dramatically inaugurated: a shift toward the particular—names, places, objects, situations, and perceptions; each of them can, potentially, erupt into something traumatic or show its traumatic underpinnings. The "revelatory realism" of Białoszewski emerges from these paradoxes; it is also related to the testimonial qualities of the narration that Białoszewski developed in the *Memoir.*

Białoszewski gives visibility to the realm of quotidian experience often characterized by inertia, monotony, and repetitions. The striking, revelatory character of Białoszewski's everyday—its cumulative effect of "something more"—lies in his interweaving the quotidian and the traumatic; it is directly related to the formative experience of the uprising, which resonates in many forms and permutations in all of Białoszewski's work. "Life-writing," seen through the prism of the continuum of the writer's psychobiography, shows no division between the Białoszewski of the *Memoir* and the Białoszewski of the small narrations. The *Memoir's* reality was one of radical potentiality. Every moment in time, with its "glaring identity of 'now,'" carried within itself an unpredictable eventfulness that imbued the flow of quotidian time and routine activities with traumatic visibility. That sense of eventfulness remained at the core of Białoszewski's post-*Memoir's* representation of the everyday.[8]

That the experience of the uprising was formative for Białoszewski's life and writing (and life as writing) has been noted by his critics. Yet, this experience is treated as a self-contained event rather than as a force that continuously shaped his writing. *A Memoir of the Warsaw Uprising*, approached as a separate work in the writer's oeuvre, creates a gap between its historical subject and Białoszewski's later focus on the quotidian.[9] From such a perspective, the *Memoir* utilizes the linguistic experimentations present in Białoszewski's earlier writing[10] with later works merely echoing the *Memoir* rather than being shaped by it. The notion of traumatic memory and its impact on representation allows us to bring the *Memoir* and life-writing together and, in fact, to see the *Memoir* as an integral part of life-writing. Indeed, the shift in Białoszewski's writing from pre-*Memoir* poetry to episodic prose afterward could be read on the psychobiographic level: from the pattern of the "unbroken sequence" of the traumatic Białoszewski moves to multiple sequences—"hums, lumps, threads"—of narrative memory. It may be that in this way the small narrations continue the therapeutic process of working through the past that the *Memoir* epitomizes.

That wartime experiences had a lasting effect on Białoszewski became a cliché in critical works. It is usually stated in a self-explanatory way, and it does not take into consideration that formative experiences are open-ended; that is, they do not shape someone once and for all but are dynamic and reverberate throughout the person's life. In other words, they are formative because they keep on having a formative impact. Several of the author's critics have acknowledged the deep imprint of the war on Białoszewski; however, this acknowledgment usually does not take into consideration how long-lasting and dynamic are the implications of an experience that is deemed formative. With the exception of Maria Janion's study that takes the sensory imprint of the uprising as the origins of Białoszewski's phenomenological poetic, most critics approach the idea of the formative as a set of topoi in Białoszewski's imagery.[11] For instance, throughout his writing Białoszewski returned several times to the motif of sewers, as he himself had escaped during the uprising to a safer part of the city through Warsaw's sewers. This motif occurs a few times in unexpected moments, for instance, during the narrator's trip to Egypt when his friend refuses to enter the pyramids; the incident is recalled both in poetry and prose (see *Rozkurz*). In fact, Białoszewski's post-*Memoir* writings contain many "doubles," that is, the same themes are worked in both prose and poetry (to mention only both prosaic and poetic accounts of Białoszewski's travels). Similarly, the themes and characters that appear in the pre-*Memoir* poetry, but in somewhat obfuscated form (for instance, the speaker's Jewish friend Stefa and her blanket "Karmel"), become clarified in the *Memoir* and continue to appear in the small narrations. The doubles work like a palimpsest and a map simultaneously; there are textual variations, but the reader also learns how to decode them.

The war topoi also vary throughout Białoszewski's writing, although not all of them are obvious. Jarosław Fazan has emphasized the recurrent motifs of "identification of the human being with the home" and the uprising's apocalyptic character through the "vision of a primal 'pre-uprising' happiness, which ends with the destruction of the city of Warsaw and exile from the familial community."[12] The traces of Białoszewski's wartime experience have been indicated in the narrator's drive "to stay in the herd" (i.e., to form interdependencies in the group) as well as in his agoraphobic tendencies, which are manifested in the leitmotif of hiding (often expressed through the desire to escape from the outside world and to "return to the womb"—the narrator's bed).[13] The ambivalent relationship with home as a place of safety and as a place that can disappear in the blink of an eye has also been considered as a legacy of the wartime experiences.[14]

I would like to suggest a greater complexity in the intersection of the artistic, psychological, and ethical spheres in Białoszewski's work. This complexity is related to my understanding of what it means for an experience to be formative. In an insightful study of Białoszewski's poetic subjectivity, Jacek Fazan suggests:

> For Białoszewski, literature was an attempt to rebuild a world destroyed by the war; this imperative to write reflects his constant drive to build a form of life that could substitute for the one destroyed in the Warsaw Uprising. The annihilation of the city—the space of Białoszewski's physical and spiritual life—triggered the poet in him.[15]

Echoing Janion's definition of Białoszewski's origins as a writer, Fazan points to the deep imprint of loss on Białoszewski's poetics where the drive to represent is conceived as an ethical imperative to substitute for the loss of the "physical and spiritual life" of the city with its symbolic life in the representation. It is unclear whether we are to relate this ethical imperative to the author's intentionality or to a post-traumatic compulsion as Fazan does not elaborate on the traumatic origins of Białoszewski's poetic impulses. We should pause, however, at the notion of the traumatic as a "trigger point" for Białoszewski's drive to substitute one form of life for another. The idea of "trigger point" presupposes a certain linearity of cause and effect, in which trauma is recognized as the point of origin for something that follows. What gets overlooked in this approach is trauma's residual (and repetitive) effect that may not be visible on the thematic level. Also, the belatedness of the traumatic memory that I discussed in chapter 1 complicates a linear chronology.

I would like to propose a more dynamic approach to the notion of the traumatic as formative; the traumatic did not form Białoszewski's poetic once and for all, but kept on forming it throughout his career. As the structure of traumatic memory folds together its origin and its aftereffects, it is unavoidable for Białoszewski's writing to be contextualized by the traumatic regardless of whether he represents the reality of the Warsaw Uprising or the banality of the everyday. The small narrations exhibit complex dynamics by which the traumatic makes itself felt in the familiar plenitude of quotidian reality. The traumatic and the everyday are usually perceived as mutually exclusive spheres—trauma's intensity and uniqueness versus the everyday's unspecificity and repetition—yet they pose similar interpretive challenges. I focus in this chapter on the traumatic related to wartime experience, but in chapter 3 I will discuss the possibilities of engaging the notion of the traumatic in reading the small narrations in the light of Białoszewski's homosexuality. This experience was, after all, part and parcel of Białoszewski's quotidian as an individual living in a homophobic environment. In both cases, I understand the traumatic (and, simultaneously, according to the paradoxes of traumatic temporality, post-traumatic) as the context for Białoszewski's writing on the everyday. I would like to keep in mind, however, Jonathan Culler's caution that context is not "fundamentally different from what it contextualizes."[16] In other words, the traumatic and the everyday are not the "inside" and the "outside," but are instead interpenetrating spheres. The traumatic and the everyday inseparably "frame the sign" under which Białoszewski writes. This permeability of context and the contextualized means that the everyday and the non-everyday condition each other's visibility.

However, in what sense is the traumatic implicated in the representation of the everyday in the small narrations? Does this mutual implication mean that they are part of each other (and if so, how does this impact their inherent differences?), or does the traumatic retain its interruptive quality and resist integration? How do they coexist? To start answering these questions—and indeed to begin posing them in the first place—requires that we look at the small narrations through the lens of the *Memoir.* The perspective it provides is valuable not because the *Memoir* directly preceded the small narrations, but because the post-*Memoir* works display a similar logic of interpenetrability of the radical and the ordinary as we observe in the *Memoir;* the strategies that Białoszewski developed to represent the traumatic in the *Memoir* shape his representation of the quotidian as well. In the small narrations trauma becomes a modality of the everyday.

The representation of the post-traumatic everyday in life-writing involves qualities similar to the representation of the traumatic everyday of the Warsaw Uprising. The experience in the *Memoir* is neither a reversal of the quotidian nor an annihilation of all familiar frames of reference. The sixty-three days are lived as a fusion of the extreme and the familiar, or an uncanny familiar. Just as in the *Memoir* Białoszewski attests to the traumatic everyday—not a rupture, but a lived everyday experience—in the post-*Memoir* works he attests to the everyday not filled with any special events, but permeated with traumatic residue.

This residue conditions the narrator's mode of narrating and has varying visibilities; sometimes Białoszewski incorporates the theme of war into the dreams his narrator recollects; the presence of the war manifests itself in the sense of impending doom that taints memories of childhood; traumatic flashbacks erupt from the narrator's quotidian activities; or traumatic associations occur when the prosaic merges with the radical and the narrator's apartment is compared to a bomb shelter.[17] The "communal life against the background of the possibility of death" (to recall the "definition" of the uprising by the *Memoir*'s narrator) shapes the narrator of the small narrations in his relationship to his community (about which more in chapter 3) and the city. This includes his constant awareness of the Warsaw that is no more, the one that disappeared in the uprising and yet which permeates the materiality of the existing city. This materiality can, at any moment, trigger in the narrator a traumatic flashback; he is hypersensitive to sound, and in his attention to the nearly inaudible one can hear an echo of the bombardment; in general, the narrator's hypervigilance transplants the qualities of the *Memoir*'s narrator to a quotidian setting. These qualities also contribute to a testimonial character of life-writing where there is a sense of exposure and proximity to "everything" regardless of whether it is something eventful or banal, animate or inanimate. Finally, sometimes traumatic residue is manifested in the narrator's statements such as "the Uprising always lies in wait for me" ("Powstanie zawsze na mnie czyha"), in which he expresses his self-awareness that the psychological imprint of the war and the uprising defies the vicissitudes of time and logic.

All these qualities alert us to the aspects of the traumatic that are more difficult to grasp and yet fundamental for Białoszewski's treatment of the quotidian, particularly quotidian temporality. This temporality has a similar structure to that of traumatic temporality characterized by belatedness. It manifests itself in a sense of a missed encounter with experience; thus, the leitmotif of "a to już" (or "to już"). The phrase appears both in the small narrations and in Białoszewski's earlier poetry. In the poem from *Misdirected Sentiments* (*Mylne wzruszenia,* 1961), for instance, "a to już" serves as the title of the poem and conveys a sense of the belatedness of death; we encounter a similar pattern in the description of the death of another friend of the narrator, Baśka (which I discuss later in this chapter), in the small narrations as well:

"this is it" ["and it already was"]

I'm looking at Janek with
the oxygen tube
he's falling asleep
what'll happen?
not yet not yet
I'm thinking
when will it happen
I arrive
I'm looking   with an
oxygen tube
he's falling asleep
when will it happen
not yet not yet
I'm leaving for a moment
I'll come back soon
I'm asking over the phone
—how is Janek?
and it already was

"a to już"

patrzę na Janka z rurą
tlenową
zasypia
co to będzie?
jeszcze jeszcze
myślę
kiedy to będzie
przyjeżdżam
patrzę   z rurą
tlenową
zasypia
kiedy to będzie
jeszcze jeszcze
odjeżdżam na chwilę
wrócę jeszcze
pytam przez telefon
—co z Jankiem?
a to już

In the *Memoir* the phrase appears many times. It is particularly striking when it expresses the narrator's fear and disbelief that he is about to die. For instance, when waiting for the ceiling to collapse with other civilians in a crowded basement during the bombardment, he keeps repeating, "Is this it already? Already?" ("więc już? to już?"). But the phrase also occurs in a context pertaining to the experience of the sacred. Describing the "communion out of hunger" (i.e., a ritual of holy communion performed in extreme situations when no wafer can be provided) given by a priest to the entire community in the basement, the narrator relates the experience as characterized by its imperceptibility and a sense of belatedness: "Short prayer. Silence. Everyone bowed his head. And it was over" ("Krótka modlitwa. Cisza. Wszyscy pochylili głowy. I już").[18]

Although "a to już" can be colloquially translated as "it's over/it was over" or "this is it," its literal meaning is closer to "and it was" or, to convey its sense of completed action, more precisely, "it already was." This indicates that the event has always already happened without the narrator's—and the reader's—participation. In the life-writing, the completion of the action rarely appears before our eyes, which poses the question of what actually drives our reading and understanding of events, if we cannot anticipate a reliable conclusion.[19] Such challenging questions often escape our attention because Białoszewski accustoms his readers to his fragmentary style and narrative leaps; he trains them to stitch his narrative pieces into a coherent mental fabric. He also makes it easy to read, or rather misread, his residually traumatic quotidian as space "safe as an imaginary mother's womb."[20]

"THE UPRISING ALWAYS LIES IN WAIT FOR ME": TRAUMATIC FLASHBACKS

The publication of the *Memoir* marks a change in the presence of the uprising in Białoszewski's work. No longer veiled in avant-garde language as in Białoszewski's pre-*Memoir* poetry, the experience is thenceforth treated thematically and constructed as central to the narrator's life. Nowhere is this centrality more straightforwardly expressed than in the passage from the volume *Rozkurz*:

> Whenever things don't go well for me and I—consciously—play at putting on a good face, the subconscious starts ruling my dreams mercilessly. It synthesizes everything in torture, blackmail, and ultimately in the uprising. The uprising always lies in wait for me.

Jak tylko gorzej mi się powodzi i ze sobą świadomym toczę grę o dobrą minę, to podświadomość zaczyna się rządzić w moich snach w sposób bezwzględny. Syntetyzuje mi to wszystko w tortury, szantaże i ostatecznie w powstanie. Powstanie zawsze na mnie czyha.[21]

The narrator's self-diagnosis of the direct relationship between conscious activities and subconscious reactions emphasizes the ambiguous nature of his memories: they are at once constant and interruptive. Thus, the narrator feels not only that traumatic memories of the uprising are "lying in wait" in his subconscious, ready to attack, but also that they are "always" lying in wait. This acknowledgment of constantly being prey to the traumatic works of his own subconscious and the narrator's accounts of traumatic dreams exemplify a powerful self-knowledge.

The experience of the uprising and, in general, of the German occupation often returns in the narrator's nightmares. He dreams, for instance, about being bombarded during a Third World War[22] or about being dead and pretending to be alive:

About a year and a half ago I'm dreaming, as if it were perfectly real, that it is autumn; I see cold, wet, ruddy earth, lots of sticky mud, ditches. Some awful clothes. Gray day. I'm sneaking out of the ditch. I can see that somewhere they're hiring laborers, for digging. I'm anxious to get the job. I pass some suspicious-looking coats lying around, not coats, but tattered rags, and perhaps rags with people . . . I stealthily approach the man who's giving out jobs, writing something down. I am worried that he might recognize me, that he might know. Because even before I reach him, I know very well that I belong with those in the coats, those from the ditches. I'm the same way; dug up, half-buried, a corpse, basically, and I must at all costs pretend to be alive, and more or less fit to use a shovel. I am not scared or desperate. Resigned to my fate. Resignation—everything—is long past.

Z półtora roku temu śni mi się jako zupełna rzeczywistość, że jesień, zimno, mokra rudoczarna ziemia, dużo gliny, lepi się, rowy. Jakieś ciuchy, straszne. Szary dzień. Ja wychodzę chyłkiem z rowu. Widzę, że tam gdzieś angażują do robót, do kopania. Zależy mi na tym, żeby się do tych robót dostać. Omijam leżące podejrzane palta, nie palta, ostatnie łachy, a może to łachy z ludźmi . . . i podchodzę chyłkiem do faceta, który angażuje, coś spisuje. Chodzi mi o to, żeby mnie nie rozpoznał, żeby się nie kapnął. Bo nim doszedłem do niego, już wiedziałem dobrze, że należę do tych w paltach, tych z rowu. Sam jestem taki wykopany, niedogrzebany, po prostu trup i muszę za wszelką cenę udawać żywego, jako tako zdolnego do kopania łopatą. Nie jestem ani przestraszony ani zrozpaczony. Pogodzony ze swoim losem. Jest dawno po rezygnacji, po wszystkim.[23]

Although in the small narrations Białoszewski includes many accounts of his narrator's dreams, this account is particularly telling. The mere fact that the dream is remembered "a year and a half ago" directs the reader's attention to the fact that this specific dream defies the main characteristic of dreaming, that is, the tendency to forget upon waking what one dreamed. The terrifying vividness of the dream is fused with the imprecision of the dream vision. This vision is processually presented to readers so that they partake in the narrator's focalizing gaze: first the narrator sees some "coats lying around," then adjusts his vision to the "tattered rags," and adjusts it again to "perhaps rags with people." This type of hesitation and "zooming in" resembles the phantasmatic character of Białoszewski's phenomenology in general, which relies on the constant expression of doubt and mistrust in the narrator's sensory experience. The final sentiment of the dream—resignation and the sense that "everything—is long past" ("po wszystkim" means literally "after everything")—resembles the emotional state that often characterizes the narrator in the *Memoir.* Also, in the final "po wszystkim," we can detect a hint of "and it already was" ("a to już"): something shifts within the dream in an indiscernible and yet fundamental way—as fundamental as the gap between the desire to "pretend to be alive at all costs" and a sense of "resignation to one's fate."

The flow of the everyday in the small narrations is interrupted by traumatic flashbacks. These flashbacks are often triggered by a phenomenological association. For instance, the narrator sees a courtyard under construction and it brings him back to the uprising ("In the blink of an eye, the uprising. The courtyard after a bombing. Ruins, planks, sun. Those streets, Hożas, Wilczas").[24] As in the case of "and it already was" and its connection with the changes in infinitesimal segments of time, here Białoszewski indicates an "almost" indiscernible notion of time. *Augenblick*—the blinking of an eye ("mgnienie oka")—becomes an important modality of Białoszewski's construction of temporality. The passage of time between one blink of an eye and the next is experientially almost imperceptible, just as the "snoring on Próżna," which I will discuss later, is almost inaudible. Here, however, this almost imperceptible unit—"for a blink of an eye"—is charged with the "return" of the uprising. What is left unspecified is the nature of this return, and indeed what it is that is returning. What first comes to mind is a phenomenological association, a visual affinity between a courtyard under construction and a courtyard ruined after bombardment. It is interesting, however, that the very expression—"In the blink of an eye" ("przez jedno mgnienie")—suggests an interception, that is, something is brought into the field of mental vision, during an interruption of visual perception. Does the narrator simply associate two distinct realities during this interception, or does he experience a "return" of the past in a traumatic flashback? We cannot quite say; the sentence lacks a verb, and the "return" is not linked to one specific image but becomes a totalized vision of the ruined city emphasized by the plural form of each proper street name "those streets, Hożas, Wilczas" ("te ulice, Hoże, Wilcze"). Such pluralization of proper names locks peculiar; it defamiliarizes the street names and multiplies the loss. The succession of nouns, "ruins, planks, sun" ("rozłupki, dechy, słońce"), a stylistic device familiar to readers of the *Memoir,* immediately evokes a feeling of sensory overload. In typical fashion, Białoszewski leaves the reader with the suggestive power of a short sentence fragment.

The Warsaw of the small narrations is a double of the Warsaw of the *Memoir.* The narrator's flashbacks exteriorize this doubleness and transform the quotidian encounters with the materiality of the city into traumatic encounters with the materiality that evokes and embodies the traumatic past. Their uncontrollable character "scares" the narrator:

> The tram crosses Jerusalem Boulevard; the sun is yellow, half-warm. Out of habit I look at the Boulevard wall, this time in the direction of Ochota. At a glance. Yellow. Familiar. And sinister. It scared me, even. Is it that full of bad associations? There were so many views of hunger, cold, fear.
> –But how many!
> A whole wall of suffering. The tram had already crossed the intersection.
>
> Tramwaj przecina Aleje Jerozolimskie, słońce żółte, półciepłe. Z przyzwyczajenia spoglądam na ścianę Alej, tym razem na tę w stronę Ochoty. W jednym rzucie. Żółta. Znana. I niedobra. Aż mnie przeraziła. To aż tyle z nią niedobrych skojarzeń? Tyle było widoków z głodem, zimnem, strachem.
> –Ale ile!
> Jedna ściana cierpienia. Już tramwaj przeciął skrzyżowanie.[25]

This passage contains the narrator's experience of the city in one short moment, and although the translation of "w jednym rzucie" as "at a glance" accurately reflects the ephemeral dimension, literally "w jednym rzucie" contains an additional spatial dimension. "W jednym rzucie" means literally "in one throw" and signifies a momentary gaze, but the connotative value of the expression extends the gaze into the object, making the gaze into something bodily as well. At the same time, the wall responds to this projection/extension by scaring the narrator ("aż mnie przeraziła") with its "projecting back" the traumatic recollection of the war ("hunger, cold, fear"). Thus, the encounter with the wall resembles a pattern typical of somatic memory, which is characterized by a blurring of the Cartesian distinctions between mind and body, subject and object, inside and outside. The encounter also represents the traumatic as visible, as an experience that is "stored" in an object whose materiality at any given moment can transform itself into a traumatic impact.[26] Interestingly, the passage about the wall is preceded (all in the same episode, "10th of July," "10 lipca") by the description of the narrator's illness, so that his trip downtown and the encounter with the "wall of suffering" is linked to his own suffering body. This linking, or even projecting, of pain from the organic to the inanimate continues when the narrator returns home and is "circling [his] bed as if it were a land mine" ("chodzę koło swojego łóżka jak koło niewypału").[27]

A traumatic visibility that can be catalyzed at any moment by the narrator's gaze brings to mind the temporality of traumatic flashbacks. Traumatic flashbacks by definition rupture the victim's perception of the flow of time. They are immobilizing in that they force the victim to experience the past not in the form of memories that are subject to the conscious, largely controllable effort of reflection, but rather in the form of a somatic assault. This surge of mental images has a physical counterpart; for instance, the victim can feel a heaviness of limbs that makes moving difficult. A flashback incapacitates because its arrival is usually unpredictable and its impact unrestrainable. In this sense, flashbacks rupture the everyday as they insert their unassimilable otherness into the everyday experience. The temporal unpredictability of flashbacks problematizes the linear view of traumatic experience. Although the traumatic event may be the *arche* that shapes the victim's later experience, this event does not stay anchored in a particular moment in the past but "spills over" and shapes the perception of reality. This means that the traumatic allows for neither closure nor a linear, causal narrative. It remains open and is always ready to be activated, while resisting being integrated into the narrative of the victim's life. In the otherness of its somatic assaults, it remains, paradoxically, self-contained.[28]

Clearly, in the representation of the post-traumatic everyday in Białoszewski's writing, flashbacks are not simply clinical symptoms but metaphoric representations of these symptoms—such as "the wall of suffering"—which at the same time point to the possibility of a different reading of post-traumatic reality. This post-traumatic reading is not so much about inserting an extraordinary moment into the banal flow of quotidian temporality; rather it is about being open to discerning the traumatic *aletheia*—a Greek term for "truth" which literally means "unconcealedness" or disclosure (I will return to this later)—when it occasionally reveals itself in the familiar. Białoszewski's quotidian Warsaw envelops the traumatic Warsaw: "suffering" is always embedded in the wall but only occasionally becomes visible and brought to the surface. This revelation of the traumatic in the object is triggered by what Białoszewski represents as an aletheic vision of his narrator, whose ocular—as well as aural—openness is coupled with his self-willed resignation from a desire to control his field of vision and sound. This resignation allows the narrator to experience the traumatic, as in the case of flashbacks, not as an insertion of otherness into the everyday, but as a moment in which the everyday in all its quotidian materiality shows itself as merging with the traumatic.

The representation of flashbacks in the life-writing shows us that Białoszewski's narrator is always already a traumatized narrator and that this traumatization defines his experience. In the *Memoir*, Białoszewski oscillates between a "naive" narrator—the narrator in medias res who is not yet traumatized because he concentrates on survival—and the traumatized narrator—the survivor who reflects on his own traumatization. In the post-*Memoir* works, there is no such oscillation; yet, the experience of the war and the uprising is embedded in the narrator's experience of the everyday in a way that escapes his control and has a potential to retraumatize him. In the *Memoir*, Białoszewski-the-author and Białoszewski-the-narrator negotiate the demands of representation of traumatic memory and of narrative memory. The *Memoir* in some sense thematizes the process of "working through" the trauma of the uprising: it shows the narrator's memories circulating and acquiring narrative flexibility ("I would talk to lots of people". . .); it also externalizes conflicting psychic forces and dynamics of memory by dividing the narration between the naive and experienced narrators. In the small narrations it is less apparent how the traumatic dwells in the world that Miron-the-narrator inhabits. Nevertheless, surviving and the survival—again as in the Polish "przeżycie," which enfolds both the experiential labor and its end result—inflects every aspect of the life-writing.

The representation of childhood memories exemplifies the all-pervasive presence of traumatic experience—it affects not only the narrator's sense of the present and future, but also his sense of the past preceding the traumatizing event. The childhood memories exemplify this mechanism:

> And suddenly the scent of wreaths hits me, envelops us, lifts us over all of Leszno . . . I'm walking next to my Grandmother Frania, completely amazed, enchanted, I can't understand it . . .
>
> I nagle uderza we mnie zapach wianków, owija nas, unosi nad całe Leszno . . . idę koło Babci Frani w zupełnym zachwyceniu, zauroczeniu, nie mogę tego pojąć . . .[29]

The counterpoint to his description of a summer church procession and the sensory bliss that it entails is an abrupt and ominous phrase a few sentences later: "only two-and-a-half months are left" ("tylko dwa i pół miesiąca nam zostało").[30] Białoszewski uses the present tense to describe the procession, enabling a stark juxtaposition between the recollections of childhood *jouissance* and the narrator's awareness of a traumatic past, which infiltrates his idyll with an anticipation of a traumatic future. Through this mechanism of grammatical present, but experiential future perfect (that is, speaking about the future as if it already happened), every recollection from the narrator's life belongs already to the memory of trauma. In this sense, trauma—by its appropriation of the time before the traumatic event and its conditioning of the time after it occurs—colonizes the entire territory of memory. The glimpses of sensations from the narrator's childhood emphasize not so much the contrast between what happened (the procession) and what was going to happen (the war), but what has always already happened, and what happened is always already traumatic. In this context, the pervasive use of the present tense so characteristic of Białoszewski's work does not distinguish between memory and the present, but points to the traumatic memory's defiance of linear temporality. The past, the future, and the present are all ingrained in the everyday, and so is trauma through all its temporal modalities. The traumatic is represented as never completely "worked through" and always in the process of intruding into the narrator's life. Such intrusion also means that, as in the case of the traumatic past projecting itself back onto the non-traumatic past perfect, the temporality of the traumatic event resembles the temporality of "a to już." That which still belonged to the unknown realm of the future for the "naive" young narrator always already shapes the memory of the past for the "experienced" one. The narrator's relationship to his own memory in the small narrations preserves the simultaneous doubleness of the naive and the experienced perspectives that governed the narration in the *Memoir.*

The narrator casts his memories according to the apocalyptic perspective of what happened next; that is, the past's past perfect always includes the future perfect. No memory can exist without being framed by the traumatic future, which has already happened at the moment of writing, but could not have yet existed at the narrated moment. No Arcadian memory stays intact, but we could also say that the memories become Arcadian because they are always already tainted by the impending catastrophe and its culminating event, the uprising. The apocalyptic undertones of the childhood recollections indicate the retroactive impact of the traumatic; they also show that Białoszewski continuously oscillates between the narrator's self-contained traumatic memory (as in traumatic flashbacks) and narrative memory already organized in a chronological and causal chain. Childhood memories are not traumatic; they do not interrupt the flow of perception the way the "wall of suffering" does, but they cannot stand on their own without the traumatic residue that shapes their contours. Białoszewski represents the traumatic as indelible traces that affect one's sense of time and give a teleological pull to one's memories as if the childhood must be Arcadian in order for the adulthood to be traumatic.

SCREAMS, SQUEALS, AND THE CIRCLING OF TRAUMA IN *KONSTANCIN*

The coexistent traumatic and everyday in the small narrations do not always present themselves in relation to the uprising. A long episode from a posthumously published volume, *Konstancin* (1991), shows the traumatic repetitively floating up to the surface of the ordinary. The title of the volume comes from Konstancin, a small town near Warsaw where Białoszewski convalesced after his first heart attack in 1974. In one scene, the narrator overhears a conversation on a local bus as he gazes into the nighttime scenery outside:

> The headlights don't take in a big slice of the road. And there's always something changing monotonously in them.
> In Chylice, the grocery kiosk is already closed, but the shop assistant is still tidying up between the shelves and wires. A man gets on the bus. A young one in a hat, with a goatee. He takes a seat, the one-seater up front left by that woman. The driver hits the gas and asks
> —So what about the kid?
> —Dead on impact.
> —A girl?
> —A girl.
> —How old?
> —Second grader.
> —They took her?
> —Yep.
> —The ambulance is still there.
> —That's for the mother.
> —Ran in front of a car too?
> —Yep. A Syrenka [a type of automobile] passed her first; the other one thought he could make it too.
> The speeding headlights catch on a bus stop with a figure. He is standing. A boy? Maybe, but—no, a grownup. But from afar? He got on. It's hard to say. We move on.
>
> Reflektor zagarnia nie taki duży kawał drogi. I wciąż coś w nim monotonnie odmiennego.
> W Chylicach kiosk spożywczy już zamknięty, ale ekspedientka coś jeszcze poprawia, między półkami, drutami. Wsiada mężczyzna. Młody, w kape-

> luszu, z bródką. Zajmuje miejsce, to osobne, na przedzie po tamtej. Kierowca rusza, pyta
> —I co z tym dzieckiem?
> —Od razu nie żyło.
> —To dziewczynka.
> —Dziewczynka.
> —Ile lat?
> —Chodziła do drugiej klasy.
> —Zabrali.
> —Bo pogotowie stoi.
> —To do matki.
> —Tak jak ona, wyleciała zza samochodu?
> —Zza samochodu, jeszcze wyminęła ją Syrenka, on myślał też, że zdąży.
> Lecący reflektor zahacza o przystanek z postacią. Stoi. Chłopaczek? Może, chociaż—no tak, dorosły. Ale z daleka? Wsiadł. Trudno rozpoznać. Ruszamy.[31]

Rather than occurring in a place where one would expect it—his sanatorium—the news of death instead catches the convalescing narrator by surprise while he is on a local bus. The overheard conversation complements the oneiric atmosphere on the bus whose self-contained environment interacts with the outside world, taking in passengers and letting them out in a familiar, yet strange, osmosis. The local news passes as quickly as the flash of the figure illuminated by the bus's headlights; the background of the overheard story, and the whole world outside the bus, literally moves to the foreground of the narrator's attention. But, just when the reader thinks that the theme of the death of an unknown child has dissolved into the description of the nighttime scenery and is forgotten in the midst of mundane activities, it returns and triggers significant responses in the narrator.

Several scenes are presented, ranging from watching a war film on television to recalling rides on a narrow-gauge railway to the difficulties of throwing out old pajamas,[32] before the child's death again intrudes on the narrator during an afternoon walk. This time, however, his response shows an emotional engagement:

> A woman with a basket stops another woman in a knitted cap coming toward her,
> —You live close by. When is the funeral?
> —They haven't arranged it yet!
> —Why haven't they arranged it?
> —Nobody to take care of it.
> —They've lost it in that house [literally: they have no head for it].
> —Lost it [literally: they have no head].
> I myself wonder how people typically manage not to lose it [literally: have a

head] after a tragedy. Tearing one's garments. Ashes on one's head, sackcloth on the body, groaning—that seems more natural. Baśka once told me how in Pionki, her sister's little boy was hit by a car. Baśka's sister raced to him, she thought he was dead because he didn't move, she clutched his hands
—Tomek's dead! Tomek's dead!
—But if you could only know how she screamed this.
When I was little, one of our windows faced Leszno, in the direction of Kercelak. Once a tram ran over a little boy. A moment later my mother closed the window
—Even in here you can hear the mother screaming!
Once my mother came back from the movies
—But how she screamed when that child of hers . . .

Kobieta z koszykiem zaczepia nadchodzącą z naprzeciwka z torebką, we włóczkowej czapce.
—Pani tam bliżej mieszka, kiedy pogrzeb?
—Jeszcze nic nie załatwione!
—Dlaczego nic nie załatwili?
—Nie ma kto.
—Tam nie ma głowy.
—Nie ma głowy.
I tak się dziwię, że ludzie na ogół mają głowę po nieszczęściu. Rozdzieranie szat. Popiół na głowę, wór na siebie i jęki—to jakieś naturalniejsze. Baśka . . . owa opowiadała, że raz w Pionkach synka jej siostry potrącił samochód. Siostra Baśki wyskoczyła, myślała, że Tomek nie żyje, bo się nie ruszał, złapała go za ręce
—Tomek nie żyje! Tomek nie żyje!
—Ale żebyś ty wiedział, jak ona to wołała.
Kiedy byłem mały, jedno nasze okno wychodziło na Leszno, to idące do Kercelaka. Raz tramwaj przejechał chłopczyka. Za chwilę Mama zamykała okno
—Słychać aż tu, jak matka krzyczy!
Raz Mama wróciła z kina
—Ale jak ona krzyczała, kiedy jej to dziecko . . .[33]

The reflections on mourning emphasize the incomprehensibility of events and the impossibility of rational behavior—of "keeping one's head"—in the face of the loss. The Polish idiom "nie mieć do czegoś głowy" ("to have no head for something"), like the English "to lose one's head," connotes a decapitated body, unable to think, but able to feel pain. To the narrator, the "more natural" response to tragedy is "tearing one's garments. Ashes on one's head, sackcloth on the body, groaning." Although these are all ritualistic gestures, they also signify responses below the level of verbal articulation; all of them involve somatic reactions. For the narrator, extreme pain and shock—

in a word, trauma—can be manifested bodily but not communicated verbally. Trauma resists incorporation into the chain of verbal signifiers, which allows us to "make arrangements" within the symbolic order.

The narrator shifts, significantly, from reflecting on the ability (or rather, inability) to articulate pain to a reflection on screams and the inability to convey the precise qualities of screams. On one hand, this reflection allows him to avoid the danger of generalization by applying his remarks to the more personal story of Baśka's sister. Yet, switching his attention to particularities only adds another dimension to his earlier reflections on responses to traumatic events. The references to Baśka's sister and her son pertain less to the death of a child known indirectly by the narrator than to the quality of the narrator's response to the death. Just as the family's grief for the death of the little girl is conveyed by their inability to attend to the funeral, the reaction of Tomek's mother—the quality of her scream—is conveyed by Baśka's inability to describe it ("if you could only know how she screamed this"). One story mirrors the other, and in both cases, between the lines of what is said, what cannot be said gains primacy.

These reflections lead the narrator back to his own childhood and to his mother's protective gesture—closing the window—used to shield her child from the horror of the scream. Again, although the scream penetrates the window, not a single adjective modifies it. We can only infer the quality of the scream from its effect on the narrator's mother, with the impossibility of describing this quality highlighted by the use of ellipses. Thus, the motif of the dead child progresses from the scene on the bus and the conversation between the two women, to the story of Baśka's sister, and finally to the narrator's own childhood memories. Every stage of the story involves aurality, either in the form of overheard conversations or in the themes of the recollections. After these brief memories, the narrator abandons the topic and continues with a description of his walk.

However, Białoszewski adds a coda to the sequence about the scream with a scene that reenacts the impasse of articulation and betrays the narrator's reaction to what was before left unexpressed. Removing himself from the space of his memories (triggered by the conversation of the women in Konstancin), the narrator seems to be forced back to the realm of the scream. While walking he hears:

> Scream. Scream or squeal. A car roars, flies past. A pig's scream.
> I look there. From the corner come two guys with this pig. Pushing her backwards. Hobbling her. She's screaming horribly.
> No wonder.
> All you can do in a situation like this is scream horribly.
> I walk on. A moment of quiet. And the burst of a new squeal. Any minute now I'll start shrieking at the top of my lungs.

> Krzyk. Krzyk czy kwik. Samochód szumi, przeleciał. Krzyk świni.
> Patrzę tam. Zza rogu wychylają się z tą świnią dwóch. Pchają ją w tył. Pętają.
> Ona strasznie krzyczy.
> Nic dziwnego.
> W tej sytuacji jedyne, co można, to strasznie krzyczeć.
> Idę. Chwila ciszy. A i wybuch nowego kwiku. Jeszcze trochę, a zacznę wrzeszczeć, wniebogłosy.[34]

The scene with the pig about to be slaughtered is unique in Białoszewski's oeuvre as it shows the narrator on the verge of a hysterical outburst. This unusual response—"Any minute now and I'll start shrieking at the top of my lungs" ("Jeszcze troche, a zacznę wrzeszczeć, wniebogłosy")—underscores the narrator's inability to separate himself from the pig's scream. The sudden encounter—the fact that the pig's scream ruptures the narrator's quotidian is important—triggers in the narrator a desire for a response that would mirror that of the pig. The vocabulary of rationality does not curb the intensity of the description. The immediacy, tangibility, and proximity of the pig's scream brings the traumatic to the surface; the narrator is trapped in a parallel of his own horror responding to the pig's horror.

While other stories of screams are experienced secondhand and thus involve distance (conveyed vividly when the narrator's mother closes the window), the scream of the pig is experienced in all its immediacy. This immediacy functions as the culmination of what was previously experienced only as a report of trauma suffered by others. Here, the trauma of others becomes the narrator's own trauma, as he has no choice but to face the pig's scream; the unendurable quality of this scream reflects the narrator's relation to the death of others. The choice of diction anthropomorphizes the animal's reaction; the narrator even clarifies that the "squealing" is, indeed, "the scream" of a pig. Yet, although this vocabulary ensures the translation of the animal's situation into human categories (such as a death sentence passed upon the innocent), the narrator not only anthropomorphizes the pig, but also intensifies his inability to translate this scream. This scream not only resists symbolization, it is also literally inhuman. The horror of the mother's scream a few scenes earlier is compressed into the horrific helplessness of a pig about to be slaughtered. The setting of the scene, which the narrator cannot avoid—the pig, its butchers, and the pig's scream—emphasizes the incomprehensible quality of a scream to which the narrator is the sole witness.

Białoszewski does not dilute his narrator's reaction with any commentary. He cuts the scream off by an abrupt tonal shift in the next sentence, "Podjechałem przystanek" ("I got on the bus for one stop"). What happens in between is left unannounced, and the lack of transition marks not only the depth of the narrator's reaction, but also imbues the scene with a striking effect of flight into the everyday from the traumatic dimension. Nevertheless, now the scenes of the scream, with the pig's scream at their apogee, contextualize the narrator's daily routines.

The story of the death of the child finds its closure a few pages later when after having discussed numerous unrelated topics, the narrator is drawn to return to it and initiates a conversation with an attendant at his sanatorium. The story of the funeral (or rather its absence) is brought up again with the phrase of "losing one's head":

> —they've lost it [literally: "they have no head over there"]. I don't blame the mother.
> —This is already the second child. Last year her son drowned.
> —The same mother?
> —The same.
> Everything got jumbled up with the Greek fates ignoring humanity, ignoring everything.
>
> —"nie ma tam głowy." Nie dziwię się tej matce,
> —To już drugie dziecko. W zeszłym roku utopił się tej matce syn.
> —Tej samej matce?
> —Tej samej.
> Wszystko skwaliło się w greckie nieliczenie się losu z człowiekiem, z niczym.[35]

In this final reflection, Białoszewski briefly allows his narrator a literary-slanted reflection about the Greek fates. The neologism "skwalić się" ("jumbled up"), however, suggests a chaotic pile, preventing the possibility of a moral order. Typically for Białoszewski, the literature is presented as growing from within the situation. Greek tragedy does not convey the incomprehensibility of human suffering; it is life itself that embodies and reenacts Greek tragedy. The *Memoir* is a blueprint for such an approach to literature. In the *Memoir,* the narrator directed the attention of the reader to the literary nature of the experience, most straightforwardly expressed in the theme of the everyday becoming defamiliarized and becoming poetic ("you didn't have to be a poet to have things multiplying in your head . . ."). Interestingly, both the traumatic as "tragic" (as in the story of the child) and the traumatic as poetic (as in the astonishment with the sensory overload during the uprising) involve expressions pertaining to the head, which suggests that the traumatic for Białoszewski is associated with the irrational, which goes hand in hand with his notion of Greek tragedy as an expression of the incomprehensibility of human fate.

The story of the child's death is paradigmatic of Białoszewski's organization of narrative. First, we do not learn the story all at once, but in bits and pieces as the narrator learns of it (first from an overheard conversation on the bus, later from the two women, and finally from the sanatorium's cleaning lady). This dispersal of the details of the story, which could alternatively constitute a single narrative unit, follows the structure of an intimate diary whose events emerge in a chronological sequence rather than in thematic units.[36] Also, by overlapping the time of narration with the time of the event, Białoszewski expresses the fragmentary nature of the story, which is never synthesized into a self-contained narrative entity. Thus, while we gradually learn about the death of the child, the problems with her funeral, and her mother's previous tragedy, we also learn about the narrator's visit to the pharmacy, the exotic flowers he bought for his room, the phone calls he made, the films he watched on television, and other matters unrelated to the child's death. Within the structure of Białoszewski's narrative, all these events coexist on a single plane. Death exists among everyday activities—it is inscribed into the mundane—and news of death is no different from any other news. Death neither ruptures the narrative nor generates moments of existential authenticity; it is granted no special status, and yet the narrator ciricles around it, approaches it again and again through the quotidian that contextualizes it.

One could think about the relationship between the quotidian and death in Białoszewski's writing in terms of Jacques Derrida's discussion of the permeability of frames (*parergon*) around a work of art (*ergon*). Derrida defines *parergon* as "neither work (*ergon*) nor outside the work [*hors d'oeuvre*], neither inside nor outside, neither above nor below, it disconcerts any opposition but does not remain indeterminate and it *gives rise* to the work."[37] Here the quotidian functions like the Derridian frames: it is neither inside death nor outside it; the quotidian and death do not belong to different orders, and neither one is more important than the other. And just as frames outline the painting and give it visibility *as* an artistic work, the silhouette of the quotidian gives visibility to the space of death *as* aporetic space. Death is like a blank canvas contained by the frames of the quotidian, but its blankness becomes visible only in relation to what surrounds it. The interpenetrability and the mutual conditioning of the two dimensions is what imbues Białoszewski's life-writing with its revelatory quality. Such representation of death goes hand in hand with what I call side-gazing[38]—persistently frustrating a potentially centralized gaze. Side-gazing distracts the reader from Białoszewski's preoccupation with human temporality and mortality and disables the reader from approaching death as radical exteriority. Death is not to be privileged, although its presence is ubiquitous and interwoven in the very texture of the small narrations. Decentralized and side-gazed, it remains on the inside of quotidian uneventfulness.[39]

The progression of the story, from the anonymous child's death overheard in conversation to the recollections of screams, also brings to mind another relationship, namely that of trauma and voice. The chain of memories and associations that orbit around the inability to articulate and even imagine a scream (recall "if you could only know how how she screamed") supplant the story of the child's death. The narrator's persistent returns to different screams bespeak of the unsettling and irreducible nature of the voice. Indeed, voice is difficult to imagine and to symbolize; it resists being incorporated into the symbolic order and its dialectics of substitution.[40] Thus, Białoszewski's approach to describing the child's death manifests both a removal from and a return to the traumatic: the death of the child is smoothly incorporated into the narrator's daily routine, and it triggers no disturbing associations or thoughts. The voice becomes, however, the carrier of the traumatic residue; it betrays the narrator's disturbance and in itself marks the limits of symbolic substitution.

Hence, more than the events themselves, their inability to be articulated is what dominates the narrative of *Konstancin.* Continuing in the tradition of the *Memoir,* the mundane is the messenger of the traumatic, and the traumatic floats to the surface of the everyday as unexpectedly as the scream of a pig during the narrator's walk. While in the *Memoir* the traumatic was experienced with sensory immediacy, now its proximity is woven into the fabric of "making arrangements" (the way the funeral arrangements are made) with the symbolic in the everyday. Framing the traumatic with the everyday and vice versa does not lead to the negation of one or the other, but rather brings to the fore the limits of representing both of them. In Białoszewski's writing, trauma becomes the radical experience of the everyday and its temporality.

"ALMOST NOTHING": THE KAIROTIC EVERYDAY

In an episode from *Hums, Lumps, Threads* entitled "Going Out," Białoszewski's narrator is filled with wonder during an evening walk through the city:

> I go home along Próżna Street. On one side, there are still three houses connected by a strange system of gates and courtyards. On the other side the houses are bigger. Two of them are old. The Secession building in particular concerns me. Five floors. With a tiny courtyard, and balconies hung skyward from the corners. When it gets a bit warmer, this is where they snore. And how. Even the walls bounce around. Afterwards I stand at the bottom of the courtyard, spellbound, and look up. I listen. I checked today. The windows were unopened. From inside I could hear nothing but breathing. Lu. told me recently, because I had reminded him of something from his walks along the street. And that they didn't have a punch line. He:
> yes—he says to me—I love it best when almost nothing is happening . . .

Wracam Próżną. Po jednej stronie ma jeszcze trzy domy połączone przedziwnym systemem bram i podwórek. Po drugiej domy większe. Dwa stare. Szczególnie jeden secesyjny mnie obchodzi. Pięciopiętrowiec. Z malutkim podwóreczkiem, z balkonami pouczepianymi po kątach, w górę. Jak tylko trochę cieplej, to chrapią tu. Ale jak. Aż mury grają. Staję wtedy na dnie podwóreczka zaczarowany i patrzę w górę. Słucham. Dziś sprawdzałem. Nie pootwierane okna. Słychać było tylko oddech ze środków. Lu. ostatnio powiedział, bo coś mu przypomniałem z jego przejść ulicą. I że to było bez puenty. On:
tak—mówi mi—najlepiej kocham, jak prawie nic się nie dzieje. . .[41]

Nothing in particular happens during the walk, but the incident constitutes a particularly meaningful place in the narrator's ritualistic revisitation of the city. "The snoring courtyard" elucidates Białoszewski's approach to the representation of the everyday. This episode, like so many in the "small narrations," borders on the trivial in the near absence of eventfulness. However, this non-eventfulness—the snoring of Próżna's inhabitants—is exactly what enchants the narrator. The significance of the emphatic closing line of the episode, which privileges the "almost nothing," is applicable beyond this particular episode; it characterizes Białoszewski's unique creation of an everyday that overflows with its own surplus—the everyday that does not cease being the everyday but at the same time becomes "something more."

This "something more" challenges the commonsense understanding of what is meant by the everyday and may well be the secret of Białoszewski's popularity as a writer. In this commonsense understanding, the everyday by definition excludes significant events amid the endless repetition of mundane tasks and activities. When events do happen, they are bracketed as "holidays," which are often nostalgically contrasted with the everyday's inertia. This inertia—the everyday's open-ended, transparent flow—resists narration; its repeatability is never considered worthy of a story since it is never seen for the first time.

Białoszewski's everyday, however, is not inert but is an all-encompassing sphere meaningful in itself, and beyond which there is nothing. In this sphere the binary oppositions of the traumatic as extreme and unique and the quotidian as monotonous and inert are nonexistent. The quotidian à la Białoszewski does not share Blanchot's "essential trait of being unperceived" because the traumatic residue gives its banality a visibility (the way the most basic daily activities in the *Memoir* gain a "glaring" visibility in the context of the "hour of our death") while the otherness of the traumatic is familiarized in the quotidian. This mutual conditioning extends into the ethical charge of Białoszewski's representation, in which the traumatic maintains its traumatizing force without being sacralized and fetishized, while the everyday—

neither exalted as the locus of authenticity nor critiqued as inert—is valorized as the realm of "something more."

One of the most important of Białoszewski's strategies is his idiosyncratic treatment of temporality, which can be better understood by distinguishing between the juxtaposition of two types of temporality, *chronos* and *kairos,* with Blanchot's view of the everyday's imperceptibility. *Chronos,* as Frank Kermode understands it, is a passing or waiting time, whereas *kairos* is "the season," a point in time "filled with significance, charged with a meaning derived from its relation to the end."[42] *Chronos* is what we usually associate with the experience of the everyday—it is just a succession, an empty period during which nothing happens—while *kairos* represents a point of concentrated time, a point of trans-temporal significance in which (usually a posteriori) the pattern of meaningfulness becomes immanent. "The divine plot," as Kermode says, "is the pattern of kairoi in relation to the End."[43]

Kermode sees the seeds of this distinction between types of time in the theology of the New Testament: in "the coming of God's time (*kairos*), the fulfilling of the time (*kairos*—Mark 1:15), the signs of the times (*kairos*—Matt. 16:2, 3) as against passing time, *chronos.*"[44] By introducing the distinction between *chronos* (time) and *kairos* (the fulfillment of time), Christian theology established anchoring points in history by which the past (that of the Hebrew Bible, for instance) was validated and the future always already imbued with teleological meaning.

In opposition to Kermode's binary view of time, Blanchot perceives the everyday as a *chronos* that leaves no room for a "holiday" (which would cancel and suppress the ordinary). For Blanchot, the everyday's essential trait is its imperceptibility; time, for Blanchot, is a pure *chronos* whose nature is quantitative and successive; it neither awaits nor permits splendid moments.[45] With such temporality, the everyday can only be intrinsically deficient, stagnant, and tedious, always in need of being filled, never sufficient unto itself. As it defies the possibility of eventfulness, the everyday defies signification; the everyday is not what is inserted between the non-everyday, but what is, in a sense, canceled and unapproachable by language and representation. Thus, Blanchot claims, "the everyday designates for us the region of speech where the determinations true or false, yes or no, do not apply—it being always before what affirms it and yet incessantly reconstituting itself beyond all that negates it."[46]

The Blanchotian view of "escaping" the everyday and the theological distinction between *kairos* and *chronos* opens up new perspectives on Białoszewski's construction of the everyday. This everyday possesses kairotic qualities, but these qualities do not belong to a distinct realm of significance that transcends temporality. Rather, the *kairos* of Białoszewski's everyday emerges from the very amorphous substance of *chronos.* Not belonging to an order outside *chronos,* Białoszewski's *kairos* seems to involve the radical experience of temporality through everyday events (or, perhaps one should say, non-events). In other words, even though Białoszewski does not distinguish between two distinct orders of time, not all moments of time are experienced in the same way.

Białoszewski's everyday involves a *chronos* whose flow becomes visible in its own kairotic moments. Thus, the kairotic moment can be identified with the moment when *chronos* discloses itself in the repeatability of everyday events. The pattern of this disclosure resembles the Heideggerian understanding of *aletheia,* "truth," which refers to the "unconcealment" of not being mediated by concepts or propositions (in its Greek etymology, *aletheia* is formed by joining the word *letho,* meaning "to conceal," with *a-*, a prefix which negates this concealment). Similarly, in Białoszewski's writing, *kairos* and *chronos* do not belong to mutually exclusive orders of time; *kairos* does not exist outside *chronos* but rather constitutes its disclosure, its "non-hiding." We might say, then, that Białoszewski's *kairos* is the *aletheia* of the *chronos.* Moreover, just as for Heidegger such a disclosure happens not in everyday praxis, but in art, so is the everyday constituted in Białoszewski's writing as a work of art. In the episode from Próżna Street, for instance, all of reality participates in an act of artistic creation. In response to the snoring of the Próżna inhabitants, the walls of the house are "bouncing around" (literally: "so that the walls are playing," in the idiomatic Polish expression "aż mury grają"). With the walls orchestrating the snoring of people, the whole of reality performs for the enchanted narrator.

The narrator poses as his task to receive as clearly as possible the "hums" of an unregulated reality that we relegate to the background—the noises of the city, the fragments of words, unexpected sounds. Even though, or perhaps because, these noises reflect the frequency of surfaces rather than of depth, in Białoszewski's work they constitute the frequency of life. This "low frequency" enchants the narrator and brings him closer to reality (as on Próżna) while he must flee the "high frequency" of the pig's screams.[47]

Aural receptiveness minimizes the degree of intervention into the world and tends to be favored over other forms of receptivity by the narrator in Białoszewski's post-*Memoir* works. Although the narrator's overtly colloquial accounts of daily conversations with his friends provide rich material for exploring Białoszewski's sense of the sociology and theatricality of language,[48] such episodes as Próżna Street and Konstancin highlight a different aspect of Białoszewski's auratic leitmotifs: namely, that neither listening to the "snoring courtyard" nor recalling the accounts of others' screams, nor hearing a pig's scream, connotes understanding. All of these sounds represent different levels of inarticulatability, and they all trigger different emotional responses. The snores of Próżna enchant the narrator, the scream of a pig horrifies him, and the reported screams of others reveal to him the symbolic untranslatabilty of pain. These screams are neither requests for mutual understanding nor for communication: they function, rather, as pure expressions of themselves that cannot be translated into any other forms, thus signifying the limits of symbolic substitution.

In this sense, the narrator's enchantment on Prózna Street is as important as his hysterical outburst after hearing the pig. The nearly subliminal level of the sounds on Prózna (the narrator's metaphor that the snoring "plays" the building's walls only emphasizes the subtlety of this sound) mirrors the stridency of the sound emitted by the terror-stricken pig. Similarly, the pig's screams are a negative double of Prózna's snores. On a larger scale, this type of doubling is significant in Białoszewski's work. A similar form of negative doubling can be seen in the contrast between the aural assault on the narrator of the *Memoir* and the near caress of the narrator's ears on Prózna Street. The walls, too, in these works double each other, with the walls of Warsaw under bombardment swaying and tottering, and the walls of Prózna resounding playfully with snores.

The inhuman (literally and metaphorically) materiality of the pig's scream in the narrator's ears can be read as the always present traumatic/real invading the narrator's everyday life, as if the hobbled pig were sneaking up "from around the corner." Prózna, for its part, a place to which the narrator regularly returns, represents an "almost nothing" in terms of sonics. This "almost nothing" is an "event" to witness and watch over. What is most enchanting on Prózna is that listening yields nothing that can be understood. To listen to the "almost nothing" of snoring is the narrator's way of receiving and responding to reality in which the very passage of time becomes kairotic.

To expand our exploration of Białoszewski's treatment of kairotic moments as chronotic it might be useful to look further at his representation of death—traditionally understood as a radical kairotic moment or, as Lefebvre calls it, "the distinctly non-everyday."[49] The recurrence of the phrase "a to już" in the description of death points to a larger issue in Białoszewski's treatment of temporality, namely, his insistent return to changes that go unnoticed because they happen in—or rather between—infinitesimal units of time. This fascination with the micro-temporal reduces the traditionally privileged status of death to an always already belated recognition of its occurrence. Thus, in one small narration, Lusia describes with the words "to już" her a posteriori recognition that her sister Baśka, the narrator's close friend, has died:

> Lusia rushed up and stood in my doorway.
> —It's over [*to już*], Miron.
> Basia died at four, a little after four. Lusia with Mira, her other sister, rushed

immediately to the hospital because they'd been sleeping in their coats by the telephone. Baśka was sitting up, her head swaying. Lusia started to cry. Baśka said to her.

—Dummy.

She pointed to the tiny radio borrowed from her tiny neighbor

—Remember the radio . . .

Then she lost consciousness. Lusia ran to fetch a priest.

—Don't tell mother he didn't make it.

Mira held Baśka's hand.

—At one point I couldn't tell if it was her pulse or just mine. And imagine—me, who's so frightened of the dead.

Lusia wpadła, stanęła w moich drzwiach.

—To już Miron.

. . . Basia umarła o czwartej, po czwartej. Obie z Mirą, drugą siostrą, przyleciały do szpitala natychmiast, bo spały przy telefonie w paltach. Baśka siedziała, chwiała jej się głowa. Lusia zaczęła płakać. Baśka do niej

—Głuptas.

Pokazała na radyjko, pożyczone od małej sąsiadki

—Pamiętajcie radio . . .

Potem straciła przytomność. Lusia poleciała po księdza.

—Mamie nie mówcie, że nie zdążył

Mira trzymała Baśkę za rękę.

—W pewnej chwili nie wiedziałam, czy to jej tętno jeszcze czy tylko moje. Pomyśl i to ja, co się boję umarłych.[50]

Baśka's death is granted no visibility. Rather than constituting a kairotic rupture in the chronotic everyday, it is always already embedded in the fabric of *chronos*. Although Lusia and Mira witness Baśka's death, it actually goes unnoticed, its precise moment unrecorded—". . . at four, after four." Even Baśka's body does not signal a moment of clear passing from life, but almost in a symbolic act of transmitting life, her fading pulse merges with her sister's. Baśka never becomes the Other, and her place never becomes "the place where I am not."[51] On the contrary, when her pulse merges with Mira's, Baśka's place becomes the place "where I am," not because death renders itself as a means for experiencing existential authenticity but because the invisibility of the border between life and death is rendered as familiar. Mira's astonishment at the experience ("And imagine—me . . .") only deepens the familiarity and ordinariness of death. The very manner in which Baśka's death is related brings it from the sphere of potential ontological inquiry to the sphere of an animated conversation between friends.

The narration of the death firmly embeds Baśka's last moments in the realm of the profane through her focus on mundane responsibilities (her concern for the borrowed radio) and Lusia's concern lest her mother discover that the priest had not arrived in time to administer the last rites. Baśka's death is also domesticated because the narration is focalized by her sisters, avoiding psychologizing and pointing toward the otherness of death. In a sense, the possibility of relating Baśka's death is determined on positioning it in the everyday's open-ended flow, as if positioning it outside of the everyday, as in kairotic rupture, would render it abstract and thus deprive Baśka of it.

In Białoszewski's world, the (potentially) eventful moments of rupture are short-circuited—the event of death always already incorporated into the open-ended flow of the quotidian and recognized from the quotidian only a posteriori. Thus, nothing "authentic" is learned in moments of crisis, and indeed the very word "crisis" proves inadequate. The lack of an epiphany does not, however, signify that human life is inauthentic; rather, in Białoszewski's all-embracing quotidian, the category of authenticity proves useless as it presupposes a distinction between the inauthentic (traditionally associated with the quotidian and non-eventful) and the authentic (the non-quotidian and event-full). Białoszewski's treatment of death shows that even the most extreme events do not anchor his everyday, as if the very idea of anchoring negated the open-ended flow of the everyday. The elusiveness of this flow is manifested by a repetitive belatedness, by an endless repetition of "to już," to which even something as radical as death cannot grant the visibility of "now." On the contrary, if we adopt Blanchot's view that the nature of the everyday is its invisibility, in Białoszewski's works death's imperceptibility represents the quintessential everyday. In the absence of any panoramic vision, death becomes a vanishing point where change is infinitesimal, hardly palpable, and always already disappearing between one heartbeat and the next. And yet, between these beats, the status quo is irrevocably changed and that which is invisible is not made visible but is made part of the everyday. Death's presence is as subtle as life's, but it is a presence that is present in life not as the boundary *of* life.

While Białoszewski glosses over significant changes such as death with a lack of eventfulness and a non-climactic tone, ordinary, even banal, events generate an excess of eventfulness. Thus, in *Hums, Lumps, Threads* the sudden experience of a spring day elicits epiphanic exaltation. Sandwiched between the narrator's memory of his youthful days as a journalist in "the rural story" ("Dispatch from the Countryside") and an episode about a Swedish hotel in Warsaw in "Looks like it's not just Swedes' faults" ("Podobno to nie tylko Szwedzi winni"), the episode "When will we say so again?" ("Kiedy znów tak powiemy?") is written in the form of a diary entry. Its title does not signal the subject matter and it carries no connection with the episodes preceding and following it.

Sunday March 31, 1974

"When will we say so again?"

After that non-winter the world opened up gently, unhurriedly. Birds began to sing. The sun struck. So that we knew. We watched.

And suddenly, today—the weather brought warmth to the shade, people came out . . . bit by bit; Sunday. I'm standing at the window: the trees burst forth here, and here, and my saved maple has budded, and my poplar has furry buds today. I lean out the window . . . and three willows are hanging there, green, all in leaves.

So it's already happened. Just like that. And it's only March 31. Like in a dream. I can't believe it.

—What a moment! what a moment!

All is still before us—the dream is fulfilled.

niedziela 31 marca 1974

"Kiedy znów tak powiemy?"

Po tej nie-zimie łagodnie, długo świat się rozchylał. Ptaszki dośpiewywały. Słońce uderzyło. Tak, że wiedzieliśmy. Patrzyliśmy.

Ale dziś nagle—pogoda z ciepłem w cieniu, ludzie wyszli . . . pomału; niedziela. Staję w oknie: drzewa ruszyły i tu, i tu, i mój klon odratowany wypuścił, i topola ma dziś bazie, wychylam się . . . a trzy wierzby wiszą zieloniutkie, całe w liściach.

Więc już. Już! Stało się. Jest. A to dopiero 31 marzec. Jak we śnie. Nie wierzę.

—Co za chwila! co za chwila. Wszystko jeszcze przed nami, a sen spełniony.[52]

The episode is suffused with the elation, ecstasy, intensity, and mystery that typify literary epiphanies. The ordinary world "opens up" ("rozchyla się") to reveal—if only for a moment—its hidden potential in the miraculous force of spring. In an episode that could easily slip into a literary cliché, Białoszewski condensed the complexities of his representation of temporal experience: belatedness, epiphany, kairotic time, and the totality of future. What is striking, however, is that the narrator's amazement at this bursting vitality manifests itself in language similar to that used to describe Baśka's death, as if both events fall into the same category of temporality. While Baśka's death is marked as "to już," spring's epiphany is, "Więc już. Już! Stało się. Jest"—literally, "So it already was. Already! It happened. It is." The coming of spring, like that of death, has occurred between heartbeats. In his belated recognition of the change, the narrator can only repeat in amazement, "What a moment! What a moment."

As in the teleological view of *kairos,* the special position of the moment in the flow of time is viewed in this exclamation a posteriori, after the moment has passed. Białoszewski's *kairoi,* however, do not contribute to the future's meaningfulness, and thus differ from the apocalyptic *kairoi* of Christian theology. The concluding sentence of the episode—"all is still before us, the dream is fulfilled"—presents the fulfillment of time in which the future still lies ahead unchanged and not organized and prefigured by the kairotic "moment." The use of the same language to express the infinitesimal units of time in the scene of Baśka's death and in the epiphanic moment of spring's arrival demonstrates that, regardless of their character, the specific moments of transformation—life into death, winter into spring—always pass unnoticed and unrecorded. However, only the spring day generates an epiphanic feeling in the narrator; the discreet scene of Baśka's death is marked neither by this intensity nor even by the active presence of the narrator, who only relates the events in a subdued tone. In a reversal of hierarchy, Baśka's scene is marked by a deficiency of eventfulness whereas a spring day on which nothing remarkable happens overflows with kairotic charge. Although the narrator recognizes the moment as cyclical and thus anticipated ("So that we knew. We watched"), he nonetheless configures it as kairotic. With his emotional exhilaration, he imbues this cyclical transformation with the significance of an unexpected event overflowing with its own surplus. By specifying the date at the beginning of this passage, Białoszewski indicates his desire to trace the pattern of the repeatability of his *kairos,* its cyclical nature which, per se, excludes an apocalyptic view of time. This cyclicality, however, only contributes to the narrator's always fresh and always repeatable amazement. The response to the title of the episode—"When will we say so again?"—could well be "Next spring."[53]

This reversal is also how Białoszewski departs from a traditional notion of epiphany, which reconfigures a cognitive event into atemporal, expansive, and heightened intensity that points beyond itself. Epiphany, according to Ryszard Nycz, is the "regulatory ideal of Białoszewski's writing, its central technique, and the main axis of its semantics."[54] Nycz approaches epiphany in the tradition of the Joycean "profane" epiphany, as he calls it ("epifania świecka"), which conveys or rather creates within the quotidian banality a sense of proximity to the existential experience of "radical temporality and chance." By linking Białoszewski to the avant-garde tradition of writing from "within" life and creativity in the middle of everyday life, Nycz is able to investigate the revelatory quality in Białoszewski's work without engaging in the binaries of author/narrator, life/text, experience/interpretation, and so on.[55] In this perspective, we are not invested in extracting the meaning out of phenomenological perception (à la Sobolewska) since the springtime epiphany is self-referential, not transcendental. It does not direct us to any external point of reference; what matters most is the narrator's performance of his own astonishment: "What a moment! What a moment!"

These affirmations—note the theophanic resonance in a playful take on the biblical "consummatum est" in "stało się" ("it happened")—create the epiphanic moment in the first place. Such epiphanies are "happenings" in the narrator's speech-acts; his "epiphanic sequences" attest to the experience of temporality, which is radical and banal at the same time.[56] They continue the mode of poetic "astonishment" with the ordinary that characterized the speaker in Białoszewski's early poetry.[57] While in his poetry an encounter with objects was configured as an "event" (often a sacralized one), now the very experience of time is performed as event. In this performance, however, Białoszewski reverses our expectations about the repeatable and the revelatory: he imbues the repeatable with the attributes of the revelatory, while the unique and extreme are imbued with the attributes of the familiar. Hence, cyclical seasonal experience such as the arrival of spring is granted the uniqueness of epiphany while the unique situations (such as Baśka's death) are framed with mundane preoccupations and the narrator's restrained tones. The language employed for each type of temporality is divided between epiphany and elation, in the case of the chronotic, and everydayness and restraint, in the case of the kairotic. Both Baśka's sister and the narrator of the spring day experience perform for the reader their surprise at this reversal (of the kairotic in the cliché and the chronotic in the unique). In both cases, the reversals notwithstanding, the change in the status quo always occurs on the scale of the infinitesimal and is only recognized post facto. The experience is always as "untimely" and "nonsynchronizable with presence and representation."

Thus, epiphanies do not so much punctuate life-writing's open-ended chronotic sequence ("one damn thing after another," to use Kermode's expression) as imbue this very chronotic sequence with kairotic value. The reversals of hierarchies convey, then, the repeatability of the ordinary as unique. Białoszewski is not invested in representing the *chronos* of inertia illuminated by the *kairos* of meaning, and thus in freezing *chronos* in an atemporal moment of meaningfulness. Rather than trying to grasp the everyday by making it into an "event"—a moment creating personal or communal history in the otherwise shapeless realm—Białoszewski strives for something seemingly banal: to show that, indeed, the everyday escapes. But it is only in the ordinary that Białoszewski's narrator can see this escape and perform it—and life-writing is this performance—as a source of meaning and elation. This is an alternative proposition to the binaries that organize the conceptualizations of the everyday and which usually deem the everyday, because of its open-ended temporality, as inessential and inert. Białoszewski's gesture is a gesture of hope vis-à-vis the realm of human experience that Blanchot deemed inexpressible. Białoszewski does not recover the everyday through kairotic moments of meaning but through the narrator's permanent state of alertness to the ever-present possibility that *chronos* will imperceptibly slip into *kairos*. This insistence on domesticating life into the all-embracing everyday points not only to an affirmation of life but also to a resistance to configure the traumatic as the radically non-everyday.

Thus, with no central events amid a proliferation of non-events, Białoszewski's life-writing actualizes the everyday as the only realm of life. It is precisely the banality of the everyday "without a punch line" that leads Białoszewski to affirm, "yes, life everywhere." This astonishment that permeates many of Białoszewski's narrations often conceals their unrealistic settings. How easily the reader passes over the narrator's claim that he could hear the breathing of the sleeping inhabitants of Próżna Street through their closed windows ("The windows were unopened. From inside I could hear nothing but breathing"). But to ask whether this is a realistic or unrealistic situation is irrelevant simply because, throughout several volumes of small narrations, Białoszewski's narrator has accustomed his reader to the extraordinary receptivity of his ear. This ear catches not only language but also random sounds and the residual noises of life—like the snoring on Próżna Street—as a frequency of life. Life, like traumatic trace, can be residual. To Blanchot's claim that "nothing happens; this is the everyday,"[58] Białoszewski emphatically responds, "I love it best when *almost* nothing is happening."

What is the critical value of this "decod[ing] of the world according to the everyday"?[59] Perhaps the word "decoding" is somewhat misleading—Białoszewski, after all, decodes nothing. His everyday is an all-encompassing, fully exposed realm that conceals neither secrets nor deeper structures. No event, as the *Memoir* most radically attests, can change the everyday into the non-everyday for Białoszewski. In a parallel to his treatment of genres, in which he obliterates the temporal gap between the time of event and the time of writing (and thus anything that would create distance between the narrator and the everyday), Białoszewski erases from his everyday anything that could create the impression of a "panoramic vision" that would deprive the everyday of its transparency and repeatability. The cumulative effect of this representation of the everyday is not knowing it as a "Great Pleonasm,"[60] but understanding the everyday in the Heideggerian sense of knowing what it means to stand in its presence rather than grasping it as an object of knowledge. Such an understanding presupposes a subject far removed from the Cartesian ego or the transcendental subject; Białoszewski's narrative subjectivity has no mastery or agency over the world. His subject is characterized by situatedness, finitude, and temporality; in short, by his "belonging" to the world.

"Whatever its other aspects," writes Blanchot, "the everyday . . . allows no hold. It escapes. It belongs to insignificance; the insignificance being what is without truth, without reality, but also perhaps the site of all possible signification. The everyday escapes."[61] The open-ended repetitions that consitute Białoszewski's small narrations do not offer us a theory of the everyday that would counter Blanchot's skepticism about its meaning. Yet, life-writing shows a process in which the everyday keeps on becoming "the site of all possible signification."

To be astonished by the everyday requires a special type of attentiveness to its alterity that resurfaces in "almost nothing"—to the non-events, the subtle presences, the barely perceptible voices that resonate with traumatic screams. "Almost nothing" is, in Białoszewski's writing, "always something changing monotonously."[62] The "almost" is a crucial qualifier, for it is not that "nothing" happens in the everyday. This "almost" is the foundation on which Białoszewski builds his everyday. Changes in the everyday happen, as in Baśka's death, in infinitesimal spaces between one heartbeat and another. In this sense, life itself is the everyday; as Lefebvre would say, "The days follow one after another and resemble one another, and yet—here lies the contradiction at the heart of everydayness—everything changes."[63] In this static dynamism, the everyday is never seen for the first time but is always already there.

Despite its not being seen for the first time, however, the quotidian life of the small narrations is far from a repetitive, stagnant realm that, as Blanchot puts it, only opens itself into history in moments of effervescence.[64] Białoszewski's everyday is constituted by lateral gazing and by decentering the very events, objects, and phenomena that literature tends to position centrally and endow with kairotic value. One aspect of this decentering tendency is a focus, marked by a lack of distinctions or hierarchies, on barely traceable signs of life like the animated blob of marmalade in the volume *The Heart Attack* or the merging of Baśka's pulse with her sister's, or the snores heard through courtyard windows.

This consistent incorporation of everything into the narrative flow makes it familiar and domesticated without depriving it of its power to astonish. Instead of noticing moments in time—the *Augenblick* of presence and meaning—Białoszewski wants us to notice the interstices between moments and their all-encompassing flow. In these interstices and in this flow dwells both enchantment with the snoring on Próżna Street and fear of falling bombs during the uprising. To live in time means refusing to allow this flow to escape our attention. For a writer who spent a good portion of his career on minimal things, this is quite a maximalist postulate. "The aspects of things that are most important to us are hidden because of their simplicity and familiarity. One is unable to notice something—because it is always before one's eyes," observed Wittgenstein, "and this means: we fail to be struck by what, once seen, is most striking and powerful."[65]

Chapter 3

Miron at the Margins, or Can We Queer Białoszewski?

—What a big ass—says Le.—Even he says he's put on weight, but that ass is too much. Short. Mid-calf boots with some kind of lining—cat, probably. Pleather. He's standing in front of a mirror. Turns to me and asks "Am I pretty? In this latex? I'm still attractive, yeah?" Another Redemptorist. A boy in latex. Lavender. Every time it's someone different, either perfumed or clueless, at best subtle . . . as a brick. But he's aware—hence the nuances, the scholasticism. Sometimes he wears a sweater, sometimes a mesh t-shirt, sometimes moonglasses and a briefcase under his arm—once he even came in robes.

—Dupska takie urosłe—mówi Le.—Sam mówi, że zgrubł, zad niepotrzebny. Mały. Buty z cholewkami na pół łydek, z jakimś kotem. Ta niby skóra. Stoi w lustrze. Obraca się i pyta mnie „ładny jestem? w tym skaju? jeszcze się mogę spodobać, prawda?" Redemptorysta drugi. Chłopiec w skaju. Lawenda. Co za razem, to inny, albo się perfumi, albo nigdy nic nie wie, najwyżej diskresją, tak, aż tak do nosa, ale ma poczucie, więc te subtelności, scholastyka. Ubierze to sweterek, to koszulkę siatkowe uwidaczniającą, to okular przeciwksiężycowy, teka pod pachą, raz nawet był w sutannie.

—Michał Witkowski, "Redemptorysta," *Lubiewo* (2005)

THE *LUBIEWO* EFFECT

This passage is entitled "Redemptorysta" ("Redemptorist"), after the character of an effeminate male theology student belonging to the order of "redemptorists," in *Lubiewo*—a 2005 novel by Michał Witkowski.[1] *Lubiewo,* in an unprecedented way, envisions the life of Polish *cioty*—a word that might be translated as "fags" or "queens"—under Communism and their contemporary counterparts, the Westernized and globalized, post-Communist "gays" ("geje"). The book has become a sociological phenomenon in itself. It has achieved huge popularity, won prestigious awards, and celebrity status for its author, who cultivated with relish his image of Polish literature's enfant terrible; it has been translated into several languages and in Poland has gone through seven reprints and five editions, each with extensive textual modifications. Discussed on Internet forums and in major cultural magazines, and reinforced by the flamboyant public presence of its author, the novel has been received as a sociologically accurate representation of two major types of homosexual minorities in Poland. With its dramatic clash between the milieu of the "queens" who lived through the Communist period on the society's margins and the young, progressive, Westernized gays whose social status is damaged by the very affiliation with *cioty* that *Lubiewo* represents, the novel was interpreted as an apt indication of ongoing post-1989 cultural changes: "*Lubiewo,*" as one critic remarked, "is about the world that is in the process of transformation from faggot-ness [*pedalstwo*] into gay-ness [*gejostwo*]."[2]

It takes a reader familiar with Białoszewski's work to realize that "Redemptorist" is in fact an extensive quotation from the episode "Blokada" ("Blockade") included in Białoszewski's *Donosy rzeczywistości* (1973; *Reporting Reality*). Although Białoszewski's life-writing is separated from Witkowski's novel by over thirty years, the incorporated quotation fits Witkowski's text in a strikingly smooth fashion. This fusion of the two texts—one from an author celebrated for his unique mode of representing the everyday and the other from one celebrated for his breakthrough representation of homosexual minorities—presents us with a complex case of intertextuality.

The insertion of Białoszewski's text into a novel, the reception of which was contextualized by the emancipatory movements of sexual minorities in post-1989 Poland, displaces Białoszewski's work and gives it a different slant. The basic result of the "*Lubiewo* effect" is that it does not allow us to turn a blind eye to the issue of sexuality in Białoszewski's works; after Witkowski's intertextual intervention, we cannot return to reading Białoszewski "naively," that is, as if this intervention had not happened and as if the subject of homosexuality were not on the table in Polish cultural criticism.[3] Witkowski's incorporation of Białoszewski invites questions about Białoszewski's narrative strategies and, simultaneously, about our own interpretative tendencies. What is Białoszewski's strategy regarding his homosexuality in the life-writing, built on the "I" and promises of an autobiographical disclosure? What are the approaches through which we can best discern the different languages of gender and sexuality that emerge in Białoszewski's writing? Do the small narrations harbor a homosexual counter-narrative, which resurfaces like a palimpsestic layer only when we superimpose on them contemporary narratives like *Lubiewo*? Finally, what kind of interpretive adjustments does Białoszewski demand of his readers if they are to recognize the subversive charge of his project but also avoid conflating it with new literary developments? I'm not interested in giving a univocal answer to the title of this chapter—can we or can we not queer Białoszewski? What interests me is exploring the qualities of Białoszewski's writing that emerge when we juxtapose in our approach a constellation of notions associated with "queering" (such as "coming out," "counter-narrative," and "emancipation") with the notions that organized our traditional reception of Białoszewski (such as "withdrawal").

While Białoszewski's small narrations hardly aim for shock value, *Lubiewo* clearly intends to provoke; its campy descriptions and brazen language employed to nostalgically validate the subculture of Polish queens under Communism are a studiously limp-wristed slap in the face[4] of the new post-1989 Polish reality or, at the very least, that facet of the new reality that insisted on a clear-cut separation from the Communist past.

Lubiewo thematizes the clash between a globalized view of emancipation and the practices of the local community, in this case predominantly the community that belongs to the bygone era of the Polish People's Republic. Through its narrator who is hyper-aware of "theory," it playfully showcases the clash of the Western theories of gender and sexuality with the Eastern reality.

Witkowski consciously plays with the notion of the counter-narrative (including the narrator's ironic remarks on Polish academia's fascination with Judith Butler) and is also hyper-conscious of *Lubiewo*'s sociological position. Yet, the novel anticipates cultural developments. Its status is paradoxical: on the one hand, *Lubiewo* gives visibility (and I put aside the documentary value of this visibility) to a homosexual subculture in the Communist Poland of the 1970s, and this very fact makes it an emancipatory text; on the other hand, however, it subverts this emancipation in its representation of this subculture. The novel's appeal lies precisely in its subversion of emancipation as it is traditionally understood, in which disenfranchised groups struggle for equal rights and public voice. *Lubiewo* affirms subcultural self-marginalization. It imagines—and nostalgically privileges—the Communist-era "queens" who, in all their mannerisms and self-fashioning, represent "queer" par excellence;

it contrasts the freedom that the flamboyant "ciotas" find in their exclusion from society with the image of men without qualities—the post-Communist "gays"—trapped in the brave new world of post-1989 assimilation and consumerism. Hence, within the logic of the novel, queer precedes gay: "ciotas," with their post-emancipatory drive to differ, precede gays, with their emancipatory aspirations to be equal.

The phrase "queer precedes gay" is paradoxical in the Western context, in which the distinction between the notions of "gay" and "queer" and the trajectory from "gay" to "queer" organized Western theories of homosexuality and the activism of homosexual (or, to use a contemporary term, LGBT—"lesbian, gay, bisexual, and transsexual") minorities. This trajectory, however, does not hold true in Poland, where the distinctions between the two notions are not made. In fact, in ample reception of *Lubiewo*, both "queer" and "gay" are used interchangeably, usually to denote the post-1989 middle-class (assimilated) homosexual male minority, while the term "ciota" is reserved for the pre-1989 "queens" whose social status is presented as willfully marginal. Such interchangeability of "queer" and "gay" indicates that the notion of "queer" was transplanted into a Polish context (and, basically, semantically sublated by the more popular term "gay") without the historical trajectory of its semiotic re-signification. Remembering this trajectory is quite telling when we approach texts that, as in the case of Białoszewski and Witkowski, mark different periods in the history of emancipation. The debate surrounding the novel showed the deficiencies of analytical categories that would allow critics to explore textual, historical, and cultural avenues in a way that would do justice to Polish cultural and political idiosyncrasies. In other words, the reception of *Lubiewo* pointed to problems with the globally distributed vocabulary of queer theory. It therefore may be useful to review basic facts about the notion of "queer."

QUEER/GAY

"Queer," which originally meant "strange" or "odd," has become in the twentieth century a homophobic slur used primarily against homosexual men. Only since the 1980s has it become re-signified as a term of defiant self-affirmation denoting resistance to any type of gender and sexual identities. Although even in English it is often mistaken for an umbrella label to designate male and female homosexuality and one can hear it sometimes used as a colloquial substitute for "gay," queer actually proposes something altogether different. The field of "queer theory" (and, interchangeably, "queer studies") and queer activism advocate a rejection of the very notion of sexual and gender identities, including the identities represented by various LGBT movements. Queer theory has been reclaiming "difference" and stressing aspects of difference that are most uncomfortable for the majority—for example, the fluidity of gender and its markers and the broad range of libidinal economies—and also radicalizing these aspects, performing them in a camp aesthetics. Whether its postulates are utopian and whether it is possible to resist normativities without surreptitiously engaging in the construction of one's own identity have been topics of many debates. What is important for my discussion is the fundamental fact that in the Western context, queer theory followed the accomplishments and developments of "gay and lesbian" activism. It had the luxury of returning to an emphasis on "difference," which their predecessors tended to abandon for the sake of ideological coherence and political efficacy.

Such an evolutionary path—from emancipation based on political demands for equal rights, to the cultural performance of one's "separateness" and difference—occurred in most Western societies. The notion of queer, then, marks a post-emancipatory stage for sexual minorities, transcends the binary of homo- and hetero-normativity, and subverts any type of sexual normativity. In this way, "queer" turns away from the category of gender and valorizes the notion of fluid sexuality; that is, it returns to the politically uncomfortable notions of the (unassimilatable) body and desire. The emancipatory agenda of the gay and lesbian movement relied on the rights and regulations of civil society and on replicating institutions accommodating hetero-normativity (e.g., in the institution of homosexual marriage). Such an agenda basically had to minimize what was uncomfortable—and unproductive—in the public debate, namely sexual difference. Queer, on the other hand, emphasizes a departure from the struggle of sexual minorities for civic recognition; it affirms difference and does not pursue political valorization and social integration. To be queer—or to queer—means to celebrate otherness by valorizing the polyphony of voices, which subversively react to various pressures toward the homogenization of minority groups arising from mainstream culture.

How does this largely Western historical trajectory compare with what happened in Poland? The Communist period in Poland was characterized by a tendency to homogenize *all* types of cultural and sociological difference. The collapse of Communism brought long-awaited opportunities for minority groups to gain public visibility and to explore issues that could not have been addressed earlier. As a result, post-Communist culture is characterized by the "coming out" of various minority groups—not just sexual minorities, but also religious and ethnic ones (to mention only the revival of Jewish and German communities). At the same time, the first years of the post-Communist era saw the sudden absorption and circulation of Western cultural and academic vocabulary, particularly of French and American provenance (e.g., postcolonial studies and feminism), with one of the most active fields being queer studies. This vocabulary, however, preceded activist movements: while Poland's sexual minorities were mobilizing to gain basic rights, the visibility of their Western counterparts was a fait accompli. Western minorities could afford generating polyphony of voices and engaging in scholarly debates on the nuances of sexual and cultural identities; in other words, they could afford internal differentiations and strive for a theoretical self-awareness. This, however, in cultures like Poland's—where even "coming out" still posed a major problem—was politically unproductive.

Poland did not have the social and cultural—and indeed academic—capital that the gay liberation movement, coupled with LGBT studies, had acquired in Western societies. I stress academic capital because the notion of "queer" refers not only to a minority group or to a variety of lifestyles that gain social visibility, but also to an intellectual engagement—in this case, predominantly in American academia—in the production of a language of "queer difference." In the American context, social engagement and the evolving academic language (roughly, from feminism to gender studies to LGBT studies and, finally, to queer studies) were interdependent and conditioned each other. This wasn't the case in Poland simply because the sudden import of theories concerning gender and sexuality followed the Communist period, when all forms of socially emancipatory activism were muffled. Queer vocabulary transplanted onto Polish soil was insufficient to articulate local experience given the principles on which this vocabulary relied, namely that it is post-emancipatory (in the sense that it follows emancipatory movements), and that it problematizes and subverts its predecessors' claims and accomplishments (mainly related to striving for middle-class civic equality through advocating homo-normativity). In Poland, there was no emancipatory capital and no predecessors to rebel against. Unable to speak the vernacular, queer theory in Poland—regardless of its intellectual appeal—could not retain the subversive character it had in its original context. In some sense, the conflation of queer and gay perfectly befits a culture in which much remains to be done in the sphere of rudimentary recognition of minority rights; such a distinction simply does not yet have its raison d'être.

The incongruity between the imported vocabulary and local realities revealed itself on the basic level of terminology: to begin with, finding an equivalent to the humiliating label of exclusion that could become successfully re-signified the way "queer" did. Although the word "queer" is usually employed in Poland in its English original, some critics like to use as its native equivalent the notion of "odmieniec" (literally "that-who-differs").[5] This equivalent, however, is already symptomatic of the problems with cultural translation, because "odmieniec" suggests any kind of difference and, first of all, does not encompass the history of its own re-signification, that is, it is not retroactively affirmative as the English "queer." Such re-signification, as I discussed earlier, is not a matter of a linguistic agreement, but a result of a gradual evolvement of activism and theory.[6]

Hence, the labels of exclusion and the categories of emancipation are historically dynamic and codependent; their international/global provenance becomes at times incongruous when applied to the specific cultural situation. A clear-cut emancipatory narrative would be politically driven and would argue in favor of social visibility and equal rights. In the world according to Witkowski, however, such emancipation is resisted, and this resistance is thematized in the character of the narrator, who deliberates about whether he should address issues of civic inequality among current gays or follow his drive to represent the underworld of Polish "queens." Although the fictional world of *Lubiewo* should not be treated as a litmus test for the activism in situ, some of the dilemmas that it represents are pertinent to the political situation of the gay movement, whose struggle for recognition still depends on stressing that which could be safely incorporated into mainstream Polish society. Witkowski chooses to emphasize in *Lubiewo* precisely what the gay movement had to minimize in order to pursue its political agenda: the body and desire. Instead of a story about "two middle-class, educated gay men [who have] established a solid, long-term relationship, and now they want to adopt a child,"[7] that is, a story about the limitations of civil rights (such as family rights to wed, inherit, adopt, etc.), *Lubiewo* narrates stories of "queens," who celebrate their non-assimilation and who insist on bringing to the fore their sexual desires and practices. Therefore, the reader cannot—even under the provision of bracketing out the choice of the sexual object—assimilate the world of *Lubiewo* as one that structurally resembles monogamous hetero-normativity (two middle-class gays in a long-term relationship). Witkowski's choice of privileging the world of queens/fags (*cioty*) over the world of gays (*geje*) denies the reader the comfort of recognizing the patterns of the majority in the practices of the minority.[8] Thus, *Lubiewo* is not so much an emancipatory "gay" counter-narrative as it is a post-emancipatory "queer" narrative.

Yet the novel aims at the reader who can hardly see himself or herself surrounded by a post-emancipatory culture. The popularity of *Lubiewo* is indicative of the Polish reading public's readiness to embrace another form of "otherness"; it is also symptomatic of the scarce alternatives in the representation of homosexuality and the lack of historical treatments of homosexual minorities during the Communist period. It is quite symptomatic that the binaries between *ciotas* and *geje* became surreptitiously naturalized in the course of the novel's reception. Both in critical reviews and in the many online discussions of the novel, Witkowski's vision of the Communist-era queens and their post-Communist successors acquired a quasi-documentary flair (hence, the very question whether representation of *ciotas* has a detrimental impact on the emancipatory advancement of sexual minorities). Undoubtedly, Witkowski's brilliant vision of "queer ciotas," which constructs them predominantly as members of a homosexual minority in a bygone Communist era, presents a fictional history of Polish emancipatory discourse. But it is this fictional history that allows Witkowski to subvert the Western pattern of "queer after gay" and write in an "as if" mode—as if there existed a body of representations of sexual minorities that needed to be subverted.

Where does the "*Lubiewo* effect" leave us in terms of our approach to Białoszewski? By the "*Lubiewo* effect," I do not mean solely the textual qualities of Witkowski's novel but the novel as a phenomenon that engages the sociocultural context of the "coming out" of homosexual minorities in Poland in the 1990s.[9] *Lubiewo* marks *the* emancipatory moment of Polish homosexual literature, and with this moment comes a new cultural vocabulary that shifts our interpretative practices. Białoszewski, however, belongs to a different historical milieu, and it is problematic to approach him as emancipation's precursor. A teleological lens through which Białoszewski initiates what finds its fulfillment in contemporary writing (a presupposition that does not work in any case if we disclaim *Lubiewo*'s emancipatory status) is self-congratulatory in relation to contemporary writing and restraining in terms of the multiple approaches that Białoszewski's writing invites. At the same time, this new vocabulary, challenging as it is in its conflation of its foreign genealogy and local transmogrification, cannot be bracketed out. Whether we want it or not, it superimposes itself over traditional approaches to Białoszewski, forming a new palimpsest layered with the vocabularies in which native and foreign contexts intermingle. We cannot afford to disregard it, but even more so, we have to tread lightly when we engage it if we want to explore the rich and complex terrain of Białoszewski's texts.

QUEER *AVANT LA LETTRE*?

What needs to happen in order to productively read Białoszewski's texts as queer *avant la lettre*? First of all, "queering" Białoszewski will yield predictable results if we assume that there are in his writing some essentialized qualities that define it as "queer" (or as "gay," for that matter). We need to make a couple of caveats in our use of the notion of "queer." First and foremost, we cannot treat "queer" as an identity label (let alone an umbrella term for homosexuality as such) but rather as a hermeneutical modality. In this sense, I find useful David Halperin's flexible understanding of queer as

> by definition *whatever* is at odds with the normal, the legitimate, the dominant. There is nothing in particular to which it necessarily refers. It is an iden-

> tity without an essence. "Queer" then, demarcates not a positivity but a positionality vis-à-vis the normative . . . [Queer] describes a horizon of possibility whose precise extent and heterogeneous scope cannot in principle be delimited in advance.[10]

Although Halperin anchors "queer" in questions of sexual marginalization, his views on positionality allow us to extend its application beyond the realm of hetero-normativity to any type of normativity. I find the possibility of such an extension particularly useful in approaching Białoszewski's work because the positionality of the narrator, for instance, destabilizes not only the normativity of gender and sexuality per se but also other normative dimensions related to them. The narrative position, rather than the narrative identity, undermines patriarchy in Białoszewski's life-writing and facilitates a construction of alternative communities; in turn, alternative communities that emerge in this non-patriarchal sphere function according to their own regulations of what constitutes private and public sphere. Such issues (and I discuss them later) have political and ethical resonance and imbue Białoszewski's writing with a distinct, yet subtle, subversive flair.

Another assumption that I make (and which goes hand in hand with the Butlerian notion of performativity) is an understanding of "queer," after Janet Jakobsen, as a verb and not a noun.[11] In other words, "queer" is not a concept of identity but a type of action contributing to the formation of identities that rupture various gender norms.[12] In light of Nikki Sullivan's explanation, such an understanding of the queer allows us to move beyond the notion of identity as the source of signification—even when it is an identity characterized by fluidity, instability, gaps, and ruptures. Combining the notions of "queering" and "positionality" with the Butlerian notions of performance and performativity enhances how we explore the fluidity of Białoszewski's textual strategies. In this chapter, I discuss Białoszewski's construction of "Miron" in the small narrations in relation to his representation of gender and sexuality. For the purpose of my discussion, it is important to take into account what I emphasized in previous chapters, that in the small narrations Białoszewski encourages the reception of his life-writing as an autobiographical enterprise, a "crypto-diary," in which the process of creation of a symbolic biography is naturalized. I refer again to the notion of sylleptic subjectivity, which I discussed in the introduction in relation to Białoszewski's creation of a symbolic biography.[13] Clearly, this symbolic biography displays a creative reciprocity between the author and the narrator. Białoszewski creates his own symbolic biography, in which he naturalizes for his reader mimetic and semiotic functions of the sylleptic subjectivity of life-writing.

My point of departure presupposes that Białoszewski encodes his sexuality and that examining how he does so is crucial for the interpretation of the dynamics of the small narrations as such. Therefore, I am not interested in celebrating the moments of disclosure, which others have already indicated, but instead in the way the narrator represents gender and sexuality and what kind of proposition about human relationships emerges from this representation.[14] I analyze how we insert our knowledge about Białoszewski's homosexuality into our reading and how we can accommodate such categories as "coming out" and "emancipation" in our interpretation. When employed in a de-historicized manner in the case of a writer who made no emancipatory claims, these categories closet rather than out the multiple meanings of Białoszewski's texts. I explore Białoszewski's intentionality as an author: was he "simply" self-censoring or was he creating a "counter-narrative" or perhaps something different altogether? I make a point to show that the complexities of Białoszewski's life-writing cannot be accommodated by the dynamics between the normative and repressed entailed by the categories of self-censorship and counter-narrative. Finally, I suggest that questions related to Białoszewski's homosexuality affect the way we see his artistic trajectory. This trajectory has already been altered by an intense anticipation surrounding the publication of Białoszewski's "secret diary," as I discuss later. A speculation on the diary's disclosure of Białoszewski's homosexuality indicates a great pull toward the vocabulary of revelation in his critical reception.[15] Yet, Białoszewski proposes in his writing multiple paradigms of gender and sexuality and multiple paradigms of selfhood. In order to fully appreciate these paradigms, we need to pluralize our approaches to his work.

COMING-OUT, COUNTER-NARRATIVE, AND WITHDRAWAL

I will begin by attempting to locate Białoszewski on the map of Polish "gay" literature according to Witkowski's intertextuality. When Witkowski inserts a passage from Białoszewski into his "queer" novel, he simultaneously maps out his own self-appointed position and remaps the position of his "predecessor." This juxtaposition creates, according to Błażej Warkocki, a trajectory of literary identification.[16] Warkocki regards the effect of Witkowski's strategy as a "coming out" of Polish modernism, as if *Lubiewo*'s intertextuality were saying, "Białoszewski and Breza would have been writing as openly as I do if only they could."[17] Witkowski's use of passages from Białoszewski invites the reader to imagine literary continuity: a flamboyant representation of Polish queens is legitimized by its identification with the work of well-established writers.

However, we should be careful about putting too much weight on the "*Lubiewo* effect," that is, rereading Białoszewski through the lens of the "coming out" literature of the past two decades and using the critical vocabulary proposed by queer studies. This kind of reading invites the reader to accept the premise that Witkowski openly displays meanings that would otherwise remain closeted by those whom he appoints as his predecessors. According to this premise, Białoszewski represents a category of writers whose meanings were closeted; those meanings "come out" only in juxtaposition with works that wear emancipation on their sleeves. Marian Bielecki expresses this logic when he claims that Witkowski "reveals the real and concrete semantic shape of that which Miron Białoszewski concealed many times in his poetically unique style, namely the rustic reality of the homosexual world in the communist times."[18] Bielecki's reading has a double effect: on the one hand, it "reveals" what Białoszewski supposedly masked through his stylistic idiosyncrasies, while delineating a territory for interpreting Białoszewski's work. Through his engagement in a binary of "masking" and "revealing," Bielecki suggests that Witkowski "outs" Białoszewski. This kind of interpretation has the effect of restricting the interpretative range that Białoszewski's work invites; it takes Białoszewski out of one "closet" only to put him into another.

As Eve Kosofsky-Sedgwick argued in her pathbreaking work on the epistemology of the closet, the metaphor of the closet and coming out—the unknown and the known—demonstrates the very structures according to which we construe and negotiate (psychologically, socially, culturally, etc.) such basic notions as identity, truth, and power. The moment we engage in the notion of "revelation" of Białoszewski's homosexual identity hidden in his texts, but revealed with the key of intertextuality, we homogenize his multifaceted work and make him "write under the sign" of homosexuality, to refer to Judith Butler's expression. Such a reading is a form of colonization; it gives the reader a peculiar power to treat texts as a treasure island that promises a reward of homosexual disclosures for the reader's exploratory labor. However, to find in Białoszewski's life-writing moments in which he "reveals" his otherwise "carefully hidden homosexual desire" (to refer to Ritz's formulation)[19] is, ultimately, to miss more interesting questions—or more to the point, to miss the way Białoszewski's work challenges the very way we formulate our questions.

To examine how we formulate our questions and according to what categories we organize our knowledge and reception of Białoszewski means opening up to Białoszewski's "multiple authorships."[20] Białoszewski's homosexual identity does not preclude his other identities; neither is homosexuality a self-explanatory concept, but rather one that needs to be historicized and culturally contextualized. In order to mediate between what we know about Białoszewski's biography with what we find conveyed to us in his texts we need to take a closer look at the material (cultural, social, political, etc.) circumstances of sexual minorities in Communist Poland (an under-researched area) to understand how Białoszewski performed and negotiated his position both as a public and a private figure At the same time, to know that there is more than one authorial identity and to remain aware of the need to culturally and historically contextualize homosexuality "does not mean that sexual identity is of no cultural and historical consequence."[21]

Lastly, as we cannot step outside the context in which we approach a text, it is helpful to remember how we project ourselves onto our reading of Białoszewski's textual and biographical self-censorship, disclosure, and subversion. Because queer studies in Poland has been a growing and rapidly changing discipline, Białoszewski's reception has been affected by the strengths and weaknesses that characterize a young field. Notions such as "emancipation," "queer," and "camp" in a culture in which these notions did not develop in sychronicity with other social developments affects their very semantics. Every reception creates its "epistemic regime," and as we create new interpretive practices with a new set of notions, it is important to remember how dynamic these notions are and how susceptible they are to semantic shifts in the process of transcultural borrowing. It is also vital to remain cognizant of the fact that new frameworks merge with the concepts and metaphors that organized our previous readings; we should also pay close attention to which earlier presuppositions become solidified, which become marginalized, and why.

The metaphor of withdrawal that I discussed in the introduction as an organizing principle of Białoszewski's reception presupposes Białoszewski's freedom to create his own artistic and existential niche. "Withdrawal" presumes that the space of writing is impenetrable to outside pressures and that Białoszewski freely cultivates his "separateness/singularity" ("osobność"), and, above all, authenticity (in both the aesthetic and existential senses). Authenticity, in turn, assumes that the subject is static, able to free himself from the constraints of hegemonic normativities and to function autonomously. Only such a subject has the power to create and maintain an alternative space—both aesthetically and existentially—vis-à-vis the cultural normative. The paradox of the counter-narrative, in which the subject celebrates his self-willed difference from the dominant narrative, is that in its very existence it presupposes a replication of itself, a repetition of sameness. Moreover, it predicates a rather straightforward mechanism of cause and effect, in which external oppression leads to internal freedom. It can be postulated only if we conceive of identity as self-contained and impenetrable to systems of power and knowledge (in the Foucauldian sense) and, thus, as autonomous.

This autonomous, self-willed separatism was usually identified in Białoszewski's reception with the notion of the "private," although that private was treated as if it were a self-explanatory idea. In Sławiński's view, "withdrawal" marked both movements of freedom—*from* the well-established, normative patterns and *for* "marginality," "autonomy," and "being a singular self"—but not the dynamics between them, as if both spheres had clearly delineated boundaries of "inside" and "outside" and could be inhabited independently, purely dependent on Białoszewski's "successful" exercise of his intentionality. This intentionality suggests on the one hand that the "kingdom of insignificance" is an aesthetic space ("where else if not in his works could Białoszewski do it?" Sławiński ends his essay), but at the same time is marked by a distinctly existential vocabulary of "authenticity" and "singularity," which blurs the borderline between Białoszewski's work and life and makes him into a textual-bodily being. Białoszewski corroborated this self-image in his private circles, to refer again to the conversation between Wołyński and Sobolewski, in which Białoszewski's experience of homophobia (e.g., a homophobic slur on his door, interrogations by the police) is aestheticized, that is, viewed from the perspective of its aesthetic transformation:

> We thought of him first and foremost as a writer who has already processed it all, and therefore tamed and defused it; we felt that nothing could happen to him, that he wasn't in any danger. Even the police interrogations he described to us in his own way, with a light touch. He seemed happy.[22]

Białoszewski is "first and foremost a writer who has already processed it all, and therefore tamed and defused it," not someone who pays the price for both sexual discrimination and his self-presentation as a "happy person." Sobolewski's remarks not only tell us about the writer's experience, but also symptomatically reveal the mechanism of Białoszewski's reception. One cannot blame Sobolewski for such views because Białoszewski himself corroborated them; the secret of Białoszewski's "separateness" ("osobność") lies in his ability to present to his readers simultaneously Miron Białoszewski the author and "Miron" the narrator, whose hardships are never seen for what they are, but for what they become, a piece of literature. Białoszewski remains consistently "Białoszewski": "simultaneously the bodily and the textual being."[23] While the notion of withdrawal situated Białoszewski's uniqueness on the map of Polish literature by indicating his departure from the national paradigm of literature, the notion of textual-bodily being, albeit a potent one, discreetly omitted the impact of Białoszewski's experience as homosexual on his aesthetic choices

While I think it is time to humanize Białoszewski and not to take him, as his self-narration has it, as impervious to society, it is also necessary to be aware with what intentions we read his nonchalant self-presentation recounted by Sobolewski. Białoszewski exhibited himself as a product of his own narration, that is, someone immune to a homophobic society and in firm control of his narrative. He was able to convincingly shift the emphasis from the events in his life, such as police interrogations, to "his own" mode of narration, "with a light touch." To understand the nuances of Białoszewski's political position, one needs to resist the opposite impulse, that is, to read his nonchalance as masking his victimhood and as an indicator of an experience whose shape and form is clear to us. The term "police interrogation" may signify a variety of experiences; it can range from physical abuse to a "polite" questioning. All of its forms are repressive, but each implies a different dynamic of power and control. We do not know what exactly Białoszewski was interrogated or questioned about, nor how his encounters with the police changed over time, nor how they were related to his files from Stalinist times, nor how (if at all) Białoszewski's experience as a homosexual writer differed from the experience of the homosexual minority in general. We would need to know much more than what we know, and we would need corroboration from various sources (e.g., police files, Białoszewski's correspondence, witnesses' reports) in order for us to have a better understanding of the entire canvas of his life.

The point is not to conflate under the rubric of homophobic discrimination the complex interactions and dynamics between writer and regime; these interactions may be more intricate than what we associate with homophobic discrimination when we examine their contingencies and complexities. Białoszewski's homosexuality and the way it enters his writing needs to be explored; but it needs to be explored with caution so that our explorations do not surreptitiously become another reinforcement of the notion of Białoszewski's "separateness," this time separateness as an escape from the homophobic mainstream.

To privilege Białoszewski's homosexuality is, however, also a natural reaction to decades of discreet omission of the topic in Białoszewski's scholarship. Piotr Sobolczyk harshly judges Białoszewski's critics "who knew, but preferred to stay silent either because it wasn't important for them or in the name of the poet's own well-being, or for the sake of the purity of scholarly discourse."[24] His assessment needs to be softened. Clearly, the issues of sexuality were considered rather insubstantial in the field of Polish literary criticism until relatively recently. The more canonical the writer, the more he was treated as a disembodied voice. The labels of "privacy" and "private author" functioned as an elegant camouflage for the taboo of homosexulity. Protecting the "poet's well-being," nonetheless, was not an abstract demand. Not only was there no public discourse of sexual minorities in the 1970s or even in the 1980s in Poland, but the tendency was to pathologize homosexuality. It is illustrative enough to mention the police's gathering of data on the homosexual population in the 1970s and the infamous "Hyacinth" campaign ("akcja Hiacynt") conducted in the second half of the 1980s. During this action homosexuals were arrested and forced to fill out—often under the threat of being publicly disclosed—a "karta homoseksualisty" ("homosexual form"), or as it became popularly known, a "pink file."[25] It is in this context of pathologization and the state's representation of homosexuality as criminal and criminogenic that we should look at the silence of Białoszewski's critics. Although a large portion of Polish society even today continues to manifest a homophobic attitude and much remains to be done for tolerance to become social reality, it is easy to forget the power of the societal paranoia spread through a propaganda about homosexuality some thirty or forty years ago.[26]

Białoszewski's complex negotiations between his textual and bodily identities require a more dynamic reading than the notions of withdrawal or revelation can afford. The very notion of counter-narrative—a counter-narrative to the national grand narrative and a homosexual counter-narrative resurfacing with an intertextual catalyst—is likely to tell us more about our own cultural positioning than Białoszewski's. Counter-narratives imply writing against the main narrative, and usually from one's position as a member of a politically engaged group or community. Frequently counter-narratives contribute to the political, social, and cultural capital of a community and are part of its emancipatory drive. In a sense, counter-narratives are triggered by the need for emancipation, and they create non-normative discourses to validate alternative identities in the early stages of emancipatory movements.[27] Whether successful or not—that is, whether or not they give sufficient visibility to a minority—counter-narratives seek to represent what has been silenced, omitted, repressed, or sublimated by the main narrative. At the same time, the notion of counter-narrative suggests a return to the notion of an autonomous and authentic identity and the belief that counter-narrative comprises self-contained units of existential value. If, indeed, *Lubiewo* unveils what Białoszewski had no choice but to veil, then both works belong to the same constellation of counter-narratives and dovetail with strategies of self-liberating. From this perspective, the incorporation of Białoszewski in *Lubiewo* suggests a split between the narrative of the majority and the counter-narrative of the minority, and thus demands an interpretation similar to Sławiński's celebration of agency and withdrawal: if Białoszewski writes a counter-narrative of an unrecognized minority, then his agency and freedom are still maintained. Such a view of closeted meanings assumes similar binary oppositions that organized a celebratory reading of Białoszewski's "withdrawal" as a mode of artistic self-emancipation. The campy aesthetics of *Lubiewo* allows the reader to enter inside the outside—that is, inside the subculture of the abject and marginalized. According to the logic of *Lubiewo*'s intertextuality, Białoszewski is also a camp writer who shows us that the outside can function from the inside; in other words, Białoszewski's queer passages "pass" inside of the socially accepted aesthetics.

Rather than locking Białoszewski into a particular meaning, the *Lu-*

biewo effect reveals a surplus of meaning in Białoszewski's text. By multiple authorships, I mean our understanding that, as Dryer reminds us, there is no one "sole and all determining authorship" and that "claims of authorship" happen in various performances and in diverse languages: that of mainstream and of counter-narrative; of disclosure and of exposure; of limitations and of freedom. Every representation is marked by the author's sexuality and gender in both culturally and historically specific modes, all of which have cultural and historical consequences [28] These consequences include how we read Białoszewski and how we project him into the future of Polish literature (and also the future history of Polish literature).

Hence, instead of a strategy of self-liberation, I see Białoszewski's withdrawal as a tendency toward "self-othering," to which homosexuality contributes but which it does not predetermine. It is a possibility that this "self-othering" was a coping strategy in order to avoid full closeting or sublimation, but if we claim homosexuality as the factor predetermining Białoszewski's work, we reduce the author to an essentialized subject and his authorship to a mimetic externalization of the internal; such a claim reinforces the legend of Białoszewski, but limits our explorations of a man and his fascinating aesthetics. Białoszewski's success lies in the expansiveness and coherence of his project, which naturalizes the subversive and creates a code of obviousness that he inscribed upon his life-writing. The uniqueness of Białoszewski's oeuvre springs, that is, from the particular way in which he "queers" the normative. The language of gender studies and queer studies can be a useful hermeneutic tool in creating an optics that helps us to see this obviousness as an aesthetic strategy, but it needs to be employed cautiously and with a sense of historical particularities. To "queer" Białoszewski means that we immediately fall into sociological and cultural categories such as emancipation and post-emancipation, which are not, at least not *sensu stricto,* relevant to the author, who did not function within a political framework of self-awareness of homosexual rights nor claimed "withdrawal" as a label of sexual identity. It is important to keep reminding ourselves of the basic fact that our critical vocabulary is culturally conditioned. To pause before applying it to an author whose social and cultural circumstances could not permit them in the first place means to acknowledge that Białoszewski was more than a textual-bodily being, but a person who had to live in a given reality. He lived courageously, to be sure, but we cannot assume that he transcended all the limitations of this reality. In other words, in looking for "Witkowski in Białoszewski" (both intertextually and metaphorically) one risks a sensationalistic reading of Białoszewski's texts.[29]

Clearly, Witkowski's text circulates in a cultural milieu dramatically different from that of Białoszewski's. The very success of *Lubiewo* and the demographics of its audience—most of its readers are under forty years of age and many of them discuss the novel on Internet forums—indicates that *Lubiewo* responds and caters to a need for the public visibility of sexual minorities coming from a generation that has little experience with Communist homophobia. Regardless of whether *Lubiewo* is (still) a discursive "coming out" gay novel or (already) a performative and subversive post-emancipatory queer novel, it showcases—also on the thematic level—the author's awareness of the audience's horizon of expectations.[30] *Lubiewo* is a sociological phenomenon: as there was no body of work that represented homosexual minorities in Communist Poland, the novel was a "coming out" of these (imagined) communities. Witkowski ironically plays out, in terms of plot and characters, various possibilities for mapping out the situation of sexual minorities in Poland. This awareness helps him create a vision of the local brand of "queens" while, at the same time, subverting our expectations about what should constitute a "coming out" novel. With this in mind, it is useful to ask what kind of paradoxes of emancipation we encounter in Białoszewski's narrative, which cannot rely on any emancipatory precedent, and what type of reading horizon these paradoxes require in order to be read.

REVISITING THE AUTOBIOGRAPHICAL PACT

Białoszewski's representation of gender and sexuality strikingly demonstrates the paradox of "autobiographical" narratorial subjectivity, which I discussed in the introduction. Białoszewski's narrator—"Miron Białoszewski"—is a unifying figure of the series, and through his character Białoszewski trains his reader to take mental leaps between the textual fragment and the imaginary whole and to incorporate every episode of the small narrations into the larger project of "life-writing" ("życiopisanie"). As a result of this mental operation, regardless of changes and variations, consecutive volumes of the small narrations constitute a regulatory fiction of knowing the narrator.

Yet we know very little about this narrator, whose subjectivity is "blurred up."[31] In the complicated dynamics of sylleptic subjectivity—a subjectivity that presupposes working with the reader's expectations about the interaction between textual and biographical references—"Miron Białoszewski" intends on "writing everything" except himself. This quality becomes visible especially when we think about the representation of the narrator's sexuality. Białoszewski desexualizes his narration by erasing from his narrative "persona" any traces of desire, heterosexual and homosexual alike; in fact, it is unclear which sexual and gender categories could adequately define this narrator, who represents, to use Kaja Silverman's expression, "male subjectivity at the margins."[32] This unspecificity is further emphasized by an unspecified community that forms around the narrator. The narrator is surrounded by friends and relatives, all of whom constitute his alternative family; some of them are heterosexual couples, but symptomatically the institutional aspects of relationships (such as "husband" and "wife") among the narrator's most immediate circle are mentioned infrequently. The narrator is encircled by female friends (and fans), and he favors the world of women—or "baby"[33] as he calls them; he represents women with more curiosity and engagement than he represents men. Yet throughout the small narrations one cannot find a moment when the narrator's gaze would be desiring toward women. Similarly, with few exceptions (like *AAAmeryka,* which, I will argue later, can be read as an attempt to come out), no situation nor the narrator's self-reflection allows the reader to learn about the narrator's sexuality. The desire toward men is conveyed in a manner that escapes the mode of sublimation or projection. Rather, it is blended into the narrative, which destabilizes normativity without proposing a counter-narrative. In what follows, I will analyze this mode of "blending in" and propose a mode of reading—with the metaphor of the "purloined letter," referring to Edgar Allan Poe's detective story—that allows Białoszewski to naturalize subversion.

Through the seriality of the small narrations Białoszewski builds on the reader's sense of presence and intimacy with "Miron," who in a consistent yet variegated pattern repeats his performance of the Mironian quotidian. Although the very fact of seriality suggests open-endedness and undermines the self-sufficiency of individual volumes, the reader experiences a sense of accumulated knowledge and gets acclimated to the text. The text of the small narrations becomes naturalized; as an imaginary whole, its inconsistencies are homogenized. Białoszewski's performance of the quotidian is fluid and unstable and aims at creating a disjunction between what the reader receives as the author's projected self-knowledge and the very possibility of a stable interpretation. The promise that the text presents an access to a self-contained "truth" about its author is frustrated: on the one hand, the narrator repeats his invitation to take the reader into his "private" world, but on the other, he frustrates every attempt to grasp something certain about himself. The same narrator who maximalistically postulates that he will "write everything" ("spiszę wszystko")[34] in fact carefully delineates the boundaries of his inaccessibility and resists the confessional.[35]

These repetitions do not "add up" to some total cumulative value, that is, they do not lead to the progressive emergence of a "full" narratorial self. Rather, every "Miron" is to confirm with his return the one we already think we know and about whom we actually know little. When changes in the formation of subjectivity occur, they happen surreptitiously and the new becomes embedded with the memory of the known. The "I" of Białoszewski's narration with every new image of itself carries within itself the "memory about [its] previous incarnations," which forms a kind of palimpsest.[36] Białoszewski forms a sustained relationship of learning between the text and the reader through the "seriality" of the small narrations. There are some features that every volume of the small narrations shares: to refresh them, Białoszewski reduces the distance between the time of the event and the time of writing, and the distance between the teller and the told, which creates an effect of immediacy and of a written reenactment of speech; his narrator's attention is horizontal, that is, every quotidian event seems equally important, and the narrator's perception is based on the accumulation of details and the drive for accuracy, which also contributes to the effect that the reader accompanies the narrator in his daily activities. Although every volume of the small narrations has its own thematic preoccupations and differs from its predecessor, the repetition of "Miron's" performance has a homogenizing effect. In spite of changes and modifications in the mode of narration, the reader presupposes that the series is unified by the subjectivity who "keeps staging his words, building a partly real, partly fictional (but immediately incorporated into the sphere of the poet's artistic personality) image of 'Miron Białoszewski.'"[37] Through this "immediate incorporation into the sphere of the poet's artistic personality," Białoszewski consistently trains his readers to make a mental leap between the textual fragment and the imaginary whole and to incorporate every episode of the small narrations into the larger project of life-writing ("życiopisanie"). As a result of this mental operation, regardless of changes and variations, consecutive volumes of the small narrations constitute a regulatory fiction of knowing the narrator.

The subversive charge of the small narrations is easily overlooked because Białoszewski makes it difficult to localize. I agree with Piotr Sobolczyk that Białoszewski "counterfeited the autobiographical pact"; he presents to the reader an autobiographical "I," yet this "I" is "blurred up" ("rozmyta podmiotowość").[38] This blurred-up subjectivity is a way for Białoszewski to conceal the control he has over the narrative: we can hardly say anything about the narrator's qualities and characteristics. He functions like a medium to transparently channel the reality around him. Whatever happens can be attributed to the nature of reality itself and not to the narrator's choices. Białoszewski's autobiographical "I" is seemingly passive, and even in the small narrations carries the characteristic of the abulic speakers from his early poetry. It is such an unclear subjectivity that unifies the small narrations.

I would like, however, to look at Białoszewski's construction of the narrator not solely as an alibi to protect this sylleptic narrator from disclosure or to safely "sneak in" moments of disclosure, but as a narrative tool that allows him to consistently destabilize the representation of gender and sexuality and, through this consistency, naturalize this destabilization. Białoszewski's strategy becomes visible when we approach the small narrations in toto rather than as individual works. The reader is unable to anchor knowledge of the narrator, whose blurred-up subjectivity becomes a norm in itself; in fact, the most appealing quality of Białoszewski's narration—his narrator's horizontal attention to "everything"—prevents the reader from grasping a hierarchy of the narrator's wishes and desires. The libidinal economies are excluded from the narrator's self-presentation in a narration that yet claims the "autobiographical signature."

BEYOND COUNTER-NARRATIVE: NATURALIZING SUBVERSION

According to an often-cited assessment by German Ritz, Polish literature deals with homosexuality "discreetly." It is permeated by homosexual tension, which is sublimated and, therefore, able to enter the canon (more so than in other literatures of Europe and America), and it remains unnoticed by the unaccustomed eye.[39] But Białoszewski's literary project follows neither the order of sublimation nor that of suppression. Both orders assume that we could find a treasure, the textual presence of homosexual love, if only we knew where to look. Białoszewski's writing preempts such a mode of reception. His life-writing is constituted through thematic, stylistic, and formal repetitions and relies on a cumulative effect more than moments of revelation and depends on a reader who has gotten accustomed to this type of narrative flow. The technique of repetitions with slight variations precludes a reading experience that leads to a culmination of understanding; rather, the reader becomes familiarized with the text's sense of open-endedness. The punch lines that often conclude individual situations (such as "I love it best when nothing is happening," which I discussed in chapter 2) do not progress toward a moment where the reader's illumination unifies the narration.

Such writing resists a vertical mode of reading in which one probes through the cracks of the text to find a slipped-off meaning; it instead invites a horizontal reading in which one approaches the text like a tapestry always fully available to one's gaze, but in which individual threads are indistinguishable. The horizontal nature of Białoszewski's writing relies on the interwoven character of all textual threads; contributing equally to the overall effect, the threads are interwoven so skillfully that their blending does not allow one to notice that they are actually differentiated. Thus, even if Białoszewski gives us a non-normative image of sexuality, it easily blends in with other normative images. Seemingly everything in life-writing is open and fully exposed, and only when we slightly change our optics can we see what we had overlooked because it blended in.

What is the source of this change of optics? It presupposes a double knowing: on the one hand, we must already know about Białoszewski's homosexuality; on the other, however we must abandon our suspicion and disengage our detective skills and, rather than looking below the surface, look through the lenses that Białoszewski constructs for us. In other words, acknowledging "knowing" as a point of departure frees us from focusing not on the silenced or encoded, and allows us to focus on that which is visible at the surface of the text. The uniqueness—also on the ethical level—of Białoszewski's text lies precisely in its full exposure.

However, to allow this proposition to manifest its alternative meanings requires that we give up the traditional reading of Białoszewski in the light of the harmonious symbiosis of text and authorial existence.[40] The task is not to unveil a homoerotic desire camouflaged in Białoszewski's writing but to read him also—although by no means exclusively—as a writer who negotiates his textual identity between the hegemony of cultural norms (of heteronormativity, patriarchy, etc.) and otherness. This negotiation, by definition, does not create a counter-narrative—it does not validate the non-normative (for example, by replacing heterosexuality with homosexuality) but rather destabilizes normativity itself, by relaxing the categories that structure it.

As I discussed earlier, the predominant trend in the reception of Białoszewski was to emphasize his "separateness" and "withdrawal" and thus to maintain a myth of Białoszewski's full agency in his "bodily-textual" existence. At the same time, it is important to remember that the whole generation of Polish critics and readers in the last twenty years of Communism was trained to read literature through "Aesopian language," in which the writer encoded political messages through metaphors, symbols, and allegories, while the reader assumed that the text was saying something other than what it appeared to say, and that one's task was to decipher the code. The idea of Aesopian language presupposed a mutual pact between the writer and the reader; the limitations that this "winking" to each other placed both on writing and reading strategies have been discussed by many critics. What is important in this case is that not only was there a shortage of modes of seeing and reading homosexual motifs in Polish literature, but also that Białoszewski's writing was "anti-Aesopian": its insistence on surfaces went against the grain of the literary normativity of his milieu.[41]

Białoszewski constructs a non-normative male narrator. This male's unclear libidinal patterns do not organize themselves around a male/female binary; his most immediate social structures are an alternative to the heteronormative, patriarchal family, and, as this male identifies with the world of women, his sense of public and private space is also reconfigured. His subversive positionality destabilizes the normative in a subtle but consistent way; as a result, the reader becomes accustomed to Białoszewski's textual strategies and, in some sense, blind to their subversive cumulative effect. This effect becomes more easily perceptible when we put aside the vocabulary of authenticity, agency, and static subjectivity and employ, instead, the concepts of "performance" and "performativity."

CIRCUMVENTING VOLUNTARISM: BIAŁOSZEWSKI'S "PERFORMANCE"

"Performance" and "performativity," originally employed in speech-act theory and later adapted by Butler and gender studies, help to circumvent the trap of treating the author's biographical identity as the source of textual identities.[42] Speech-act theory showed how we employ language to accomplish an intended action and how language itself becomes a performance that creates social facts, as in the classic example "I now pronounce you husband and wife." In Butler's approach, the emphasis shifts from the impact of individual performances to "performativity," understood as a repeatability of linguistic perfomances and behavior. This repeatability is what shapes social understanding of gender and sexuality and sustains the expectations of male and female roles and identities in any given cultural context. A variety of social performances ranging from the most quotidian behaviors and divisions of male/female roles to institutional performativity and internalized beliefs do not arise from an innate, essential male/female identity. Rather, the repeated performance constitutes what we understand as the female and the male and engenders hetero-normativity as a sort of aftereffect. Hetero-normativity then is not a universal, ahistorical, and natural phenomenon, but a phenomenon that in its very constitution depends on the illusion of universality and naturalness.

Not only does performance/performativity generate the subject but also—and this is crucial—the subject has an ongoing relationship with his/her own performance and its cultural context. The cultural context prescribes specific forms of performance or, at the very least, delineates their range. Thus, the performance of hetero-normative identities in Communist Poland had to happen within the boundaries of existing social models of Polish patriarchy, and these models were constructed in their idiosyncratic local context. What gender and sexual identities could be performed was not a matter of a free play of possibilities, but was delineated by the cultural context. It is important to remember this non-voluntaristic understanding of performance and performativity, because it affects how we understand anything that does not fit an expected performance. The idiosyncratic and the unique are not external to the normative; on the contrary, they are produced within a hegemonic code, and their resistance to the hegemonic, in the Foucauldian tradition, takes place internally in the normative, rather than externally to it. Butler thus engages the idiosyncratic and the unique in a dynamic relationship with the normative, which is important in our discussion of "queerness" and "gayness" as historical and culturally specific notions rather than universal terms that, like hetero-normativity itself, can be naturalized and dehistoricized.

The Butlerian notions of performance and performativity help us to go beyond reading Białoszewski voluntaristically, that is, as a free subject who chose his alternative artistic and existential performance. He neither chose to withdraw in order to embody a myth of the absolute artist who sacrifices everything to his totally autonomous work, nor did he set out to create a gay counter-narrative. Emphasizing Białoszewski's separateness and sovereignty will not allow us to see the full scope of his project. When we keep performance and performativity in mind, though, our knowledge about Białoszewski's homosexuality becomes secondary and we can assign primary importance to his particular strategies of representing gender and sexuality. These strategies are repeated throughout the small narrations and—like social performances—create their own aftereffect. These aftereffects are non-normative, yet, they are not counter-normative; Białoszewski does not offer us an alternative vision of gender identities and sexual identities to counter the dominant narrative, but rather destabilizes the normative as he inserts the idiosyncratic into the normative. This insertion is visible, yet it presents a greater challenge than would a search for the hidden and undisclosed, as the metaphor of the purloined letter shows.

THE IMPENETRABILITY OF OBVIOUSNESS

Edgar Allan Poe's well-known detective story "The Purloined Letter" (1844) describes the search conducted by Detective Dupin for the story's title letter, snatched from the Queen by an evil Minister who uses the letter to blackmail its addressee.[43] The story stages a competition among different optics through which the main characters try to outsmart one other by anticipating one another's expectations. First of all, the Minister outsmarts the police, who helplessly search for the letter in places typically used for concealing something, by hiding the letter in plain sight, next to other papers, so it blends in with its background. This hiding by leaving in full view outsmarts the common optics according to which the hidden must be invisible—the letter becomes hidden by its exposure. The detective finds the letter by, on the one hand, understanding how the Minister's psychology works, and on the other, by taking into consideration that while looking for the letter he needs to expect that the letter may look slightly different from its initial description. In the midst of other papers, he notices a letter whose appearance has been modified—the paper is chafed, refolded, and sealed with a new seal. This is the very letter that was stolen; the thief had modified its appearance to help it blend in with its surroundings.

The fascinating dynamics of hiding and searching that organize Poe's story can help us understand some of Białoszewski's narrative strategies as well as the type of reading dynamics Białoszewski creates for his readers. When it comes to the representation of homosexuality and sexuality in general, Białoszewski, like the Minister, hides his letter in plain view by blending it with other objects. Passages such as "Blockade" show us that the "queer" is not hidden—that is, repressed, suppressed, or sublimated—but fully exposed while blending with the non-queer. Białoszewski plays with the long-established expectations that meaning needs to be buried in allusions and vague references that require special decoding in order to be uncovered. Moreover, like the Minister, Białoszewski complicates the act of identification by modifying the "look" of the objects we are looking for.

He does this by frustrating two expectations. First, as readers, we expect the act of identification to be both temporally and spatially distinct, that is, we expect the moment of identification to be distinguishable for us in the process of reading. Second, we expect that such identification points to spaces in the text that are localizable. Białoszewski's writing relies neither on self-contained textual loci nor on a "eureka moment" that would satisfy our detective faculties. No direct, probing gaze will show us anything, because Białoszewski neither sublimates nor suppresses, and thus he frustrates his reader's desire to engage in the hunt and to experience the pleasure of the find. Białoszewski's mode of writing can be compared to glazing, a painting technique made famous by Dutch painters in which a transparent paint is imposed on layers of colored paint to give depth to the lower layers and slightly change their colors. Białoszewski's glazing covers the entire surface of his text and imperceptibly affects our optics. We cannot notice the modification of colors because—if we look straight—we cannot localize it. To notice Białoszewski's strategy of modification, we need to change our angle of vision. Not only do we need a knowing gaze, but also the gaze which Slavoj Žižek describes as "looking awry." Žižek writes:

> If we look at a thing straight on, i.e., matter-of-factly, disinterestedly, we see nothing but a formless spot; the object assumes clear and distinctive features only if we look at it "at an angle," i.e., with an "interested" view, supported, permeated, and "distorted" by *desire*.[44]

While for the straightforward gaze, Białoszewski's everyday does not invite any questions about the representation of sexuality, for the gaze that looks awry he destabilizes the normative in a way that resists questioning (and this is why we should question it in the first place) and presents us with an approach to sexuality that is surprisingly opaque, elusive, and even subversive.

Nevertheless, what Białoszewski hides through exposure is very different from the object of desire in Poe's story. While in Poe's story the search is teleological (that is, the letter must be located and identified among many other, similar objects only once), Białoszewski's textual exposure ensures an open-ended search. The process of searching is never-ending and always already frustrated, if only because Białoszewski's work is serial and repetitive. His texts are not maps replete with secret signs that, when decoded properly, will lead a perspicacious reader to the treasure of the authorial "coming out." There is no single purloined letter—a key to the rest of the text—nor are there multiple letters; the metaphor must be modified, because Białoszewski does not hide anything the way the Minister does, but instead frustrates the search and makes it pointless for the reader to play detective. The small narrations do not suggest the crisis of loss at their origin, nor do they promise a *jouissance* at the end. In some sense they invite us to read "naively," that is, to abandon the idea of playing the role of the police in Poe's story or the Aesopian reader who finds a "key" to the mystery of homosexual desire; they invite us to read "na wierzchu," or on the surfaces, to use the narrator's expression about his way of accessing the truth of the story in the *Memoir.*

The traditional search is futile because predictable hiding places imply verticality (they are located deep "beneath the surface"), whereas Białoszewski writes horizontally—that is, he suggests to the reader that the author is exposing everything on the surface of the text. Such horizontality preempts the *jouissance* of finding something because everything seems to be treated in self-explanatory terms. This being "on the surface" was a self-declared principle of Białoszewski's representation of the traumatic in the *Memoir,* and it governed the rest of his writing as well. In the *Memoir,* "being on the surface" is explained as having being triggered by the event itself and its sensory overload. In the small narrations we are not reminded of this explanation, but the principle stays the same. The blurred-up subjectivity of the narrator channels the everyday to us in ways that make its "superficial," self-explanatory quality the property of the everyday itself. As such, it is nothing to question: Białoszewski's writing becomes an impenetrable code because his narratorial position and the language his narrator employs are shown to us as "obvious" traits of experience and of reality itself.

The effectiveness of Białoszewski's deception manifests itself, among other ways, in his critics' treatment of the autobiographical aspect of his work. As I argued in my discussion of the *Memoir* in chapter 2, there is a tendency to acknowledge the impact of the Warsaw Uprising on Białoszewski's writing while at the same time reducing this impact to war-related topoi or general statements about the author's sensibility or sensitivity. As in the case of the traumatic traces, issues of gender and sexuality also permeate Białoszewski's writing in complex ways that on the one hand are hard to localize and, on the other, are redisplayed on the surface. Let us now return to Witkowski's *Lubiewo* in order to understand his use of Białoszewski. Witkowski quotes a passage from the small narrations that draws attention to the futility of the search by serving on a silver platter, so to speak, plenty of information about the narrator's domestic space and milieu. If we wanted to read it using the category of disclosure, we could borrow from the literal meaning of the title of the volume, *Donosy rzeczywistości,* as "denunciations of reality" and suggest that it shows the narrator's self-denunciation. In "Blockade," the narrator mentions an anonymous letter written to denounce him and talks about being interrogated, together with his roommate Le., by the police. We do not know what the letter contains, why the police are coming in the first place, or what the topic of the interrogation is. *Donosy rzeczywistości* opens the series of the small narrations and establish the leitmotif of the "blockade" that appears in later volumes and concerns the narrator and his roommate's decision about whom to grant access to their apartment. This leitmotif itself may be seen as an attempt to demonstrate agency that the characters might not have, particularly in this case: though the police may enter on their own terms, their visit is shown as depending on the narrator's decision to open the door or not. Since the reason for the visit is not given, the reader does not know how to interpret the inquisitive gaze of the policemen who, while surveying Le.'s room, "were transfixed by a pair of panty hose" ("u Le. w saloniku wpili się oczami w damskie pończochy").[45] The narrator adds that "Le. was supposed to mail the hose this evening to his sister," so only a knowing reader can laugh at this ironic quid pro quo, in which searching reveals exactly the opposite of what one intended to prove in the first place. The narrator tells the reader that the police are deceived by their own findings and, hence, suggests not to trust the female panty hose as a proof of Le.'s heterosexuality. The whole situation is described by a series of omissions and playful double-gazes for the knowing reader and the "not-knowing" police. The reader is left to wonder, along with the narrator, whether the police arrived because the music was being played too loudly, or whether the music itself, as the narrator remarks, was "an alibi."

The disclosure of doubleness to the knowing reader is striking—the noise is an alibi for the police to knock on the narrator's apartment, but the fact that it is, or at least may be, an alibi is thematized by the narrator in his question to himself and the reader. The real reason is not spelled out, but the narrator invites the reader to ask the question. The search and interrogation part of "Blockade" culminates with the nonchalant, over-the-top ("campy," as I will discuss in a moment) behavior of Le., who after being taken with the narrator and questioned at the police station (for the loud music? the reader may ask) repays them with an improvised recital of Romantic poetry. While a knowing reader can interpret Le.'s behavior at the police station as a conscious performance of campy resistance to a homophobic reality, the unknowing one finds the whole situation unclear, but funny and perhaps even grotesque. "Blockade" is full of sexually related disclosures (of a bisexual doctor who makes advances to his patients; a priest sexually harassing young seminarians; Le. using public saunas as a cruising ground, etc.), but Białoszewski writes it as one comic stream, in which characters and events pile up, but because the context is missing it is unclear who is who and what is really happening. Białoszewski's prose is usually characterized by rich details, the use of proper names, and a seeming drive to be phenomenologically accurate, but without providing any background for the story its singularities confuse rather than increase precision. The not-knowing reader sees a blurry picture that combines vague plots with comic tones; for such a reader, the comic tones preempt questions about the discriminatory context of the story. The main theme of "Blockade"—"the recent troubles of this household," as the narrator states it—is as indeterminate to the straight gaze as it is clear to those who look awry.

Less frequently, Białoszewski attracts the reader's attention by using language lacking in specificity. In this context, a passage from "Blockade" about the narrator's friend Włodek stands out. In language that is otherwise saturated with specificity, the failure to specify grammatical gender, and the use of the indeterminate words "person" ("osoba") and "someone" ("ktoś") makes itself stylistically visible:

> Włodek told us—regarding the recent troubles in that household—that people still find him attractive. The other day he was going home. One o'clock at night. He stopped by the Gdańsk railway station to get some cigarettes. Someone off to the side started flirting with him. Bit by bit they got to talking. But since this person's train was leaving in an hour (so how could they go back to Bielany), they made a date for tonight. Because this person is coming by train. At 22:47. And Włodek goes.

> Włodek opowiedział—w związku z problemami ostatnich czasów tego domu—że ma jeszcze powodzenie. Niedawno wracał. Pierwsza w nocy. Wstępuje na Gdański po papierosy. Ktoś stoi z boku i go kokietuje. I tak z chwili na chwilę doszło do gadki. Ale że ta osoba miała pociąg za godzinę (więc jak jechać na Bielany), to umówili się na dziś wieczór. Bo wraca pociągiem. Na 22.47. I Włodek idzie.[46]

The narrator tells us that Włodek relates his encounter at the railway station in the context of "the recent troubles in this household," yet we do not know what exactly in this story is supposed to bind the two situations. On the contrary, Włodek's report is striking for the unspecificity of the grammatically neutral "person" ("osoba") and "someone" ("ktoś"), which suggests that Białoszewski intends the knowing reader to register this unspecificity. Often, Białoszewski uses the character of Le. to comment on the situations and mark them with gender distinctions through Le.'s theatrically exaggerated—or "campy"—speech, marked by the frequent use of "baba" and "chłop."[47] Włodek's story, however, is suspended and indeterminate. Contrary to other relationships, which usually take place indoors, especially in buildings teeming with life as "kamienica," Włodek's encounter at the anonymous space of the railway station described with unclear referents seems purposefully clumsy and suggests that some information is being purposefully withheld from the reader.

Exposing indeterminacy is something different than identifying a counter-narrative. Białoszewski's texts do more than simply conceal a counter-narrative, which is not to suggest that interpretations of his texts as counter-narratives do not have a valid place in the critical reception of Białoszewski.[48] The strategy of indeterminate exposure is part and parcel of the larger vision of Białoszewski's intersubjective relationships, dynamics, and dependencies. They are ingrained in his destabilization of the binaries organizing notions of gender and sexuality. This destabilization becomes visible only when we take a closer look at Białoszewski's fascinating textual mode—or, perhaps, code—that paradoxically hides and reveals at the same time.

One of the most important aspects of this destabilization is Białoszewski's representation of the body, including the narrator's body, which marks him as an asexual being. The narrator often informs us about the state of his physical well-being and links it to his mental state (as in the opening of the *Memoir*, where it is noted that to be in good physical form means to be in a good mood: "w dobrym stanie i humorze"): we know when he sleeps well and when he sleeps badly; he tells us about colds and flu and, in one hilarious episode, "Shingles, tooth" ("Półpasiec, ząb"), the stages of his illness. Most of the time, however, the narrator's relationship to his own body (as well as to the bodies of others) is guided by the principle of distancing; the narrator does not express closeness with his body, but describes it from the position of the viewer. The mechanisms of dissociation and abstraction from one's bodily experience can perhaps be traced to the mode of representation of traumatic experience. Bodily experience in the *Memoir* is represented as a sensory dissociation, which positions the person as an external viewer of his own actions. Thus, the *Memoir* is full of metonymic passages that describe the narrator looking at himself, for instance: "Ręce pracują. Trochę jak u ślepych. Nogi w czymś. Plecy mają wprawę" ("The hands work. Somewhat like blind people's. The feet dig into something. The shoulders get exercise")[49] or "bo to ci—my, od barykady" ("they were ourselves, the men from the barricade").[50] But the passivity of traumatic experience universalizes, rather than individualizes, the body. Such a universal body, which continues in the small narrations, may experience the need for dentures and the struggle to adjust to them, but it does not experience the shapelessness of desire. The dissociation that characterizes traumatic experience persists to a degree in the post-*Memoir* works, except that the traumatic becomes theatrical and the dissociative becomes phantasmatic and phantasmagoric.[51]

The principle of alienation from the body allows the narrator to avoid addressing his sexuality. Białoszewski destabilizes the basic category organizing normativity as such, which is desire. Members of a hetero-normative society structure their community around desire that should be felt and expressed only for partners of the opposite sex. In the common understanding, desire is directly linked to biology and biology to the social understanding of gender. Historically, both desire and gender identities have been naturalized, and this naturalization fundamentally contributed to the privileged position of hetero-normativity. The notion of heterosexual desire being a socially constructed, "naturalized" aftereffect of the performance of heterosexual subjectivity is a recent development.

Białoszewski's narrator neither performs heterosexual subjectivity nor, for that matter, specifies whether he desires women or men. If, indeed, the choice of a sexual object has become, as Eve Kosofsky Sedgwick notes, "*the* dimension denoted by the now ubiquitous category of 'sexual orientation'" (emphasis Sedgwick),[52] we are given no indication of the narrator's orientation. Similarly, the narrator does not become an object of desire for any of the characters. Within the reigning frameworks of hetero-normativity, where sexual orientation became part and parcel of how society constructs gender, it becomes difficult, then, to even identify the narrator's gender. Białoszewski blurs the binary of male/female sexual orientation and of masculine/feminine social performance. Although "Miron" makes himself known as a male character, no specific social performance qualifies him as male or female. His "withdrawn subjectivity" does not present the body as a tool for governing space, which is a characteristic of patriarchal masculinity. At the same time, neither does it follow the traditionally feminine display of the body for aesthetic consumption, which characterizes a passage from "Blockade" included in *Lubiewo,* with which I open this chapter. A preoccupation with the body's attractiveness is the very reason for the narrator bringing up Włodek's railway station story. "Miron," the narrator, however, only describes others while he himself manifests no interest when it comes to his own sex appeal. We know he is male, but the only indisputable manifestation of this fact is his grammatical subject.

Białoszewski's narrator operates in the world outside male/female binaries but also outside homo-normativity (which clearly could not yet be articulated). The maleness of his narrator is simply non-normative. To return to Butler's claim that every performance of identity is defined and limited by cultural context, it is worth noting that—sublimation aside—Białoszewski had very few Polish models to draw on in representing male homosexual identity. The gender-and-sexuality-blurred narratorial position quite possibly reflects Białoszewski's explorations of alternative aesthetic routes for sexuality outside of hetero-normativity in the limited cultural context of the 1970s in Poland. He constructs a world in which several binaries (including male/female and private/public) are destabilized. This world gravitates toward women, but the narrator does not mark himself sexually nor are the women around him marked as sexual objects. In fact, he positions women outside of the binary logic of gender and sexuality and, hence, outside of the patriarchal hierarchy.

THE DESEXUALIZED FEMININE AND GENDER DESTABILIZATION

Kaja Silverman, in her book *Male Subjectivity at the Margins,* writes about the place of femininity in accounts of male homosexuality and analyzes the trope of "a woman's soul enclosed in a man's body" in her rethinking of the category of "the feminine" and "the masculine":

> The notion of inversion is probably as old as the hierarchical binarizing of "man" and "woman," and . . . human culture has to date shown itself to be stubbornly resistant to conceptualizing sexual positionality—and, more recently, object-choice—apart from the binary logic of gender. Since the category of masculinity has traditionally been a very restrictive one, those defying its conditions generally find themselves relegated to the more accommodating category of femininity.[53]

Indeed, Białoszewski's writing is full of women, a fact that has been noticed by several critics, some of whom essentialize Białoszewski's aesthetic choices. For instance, Jacek Kopciński, in *Gramatyka i mistyka* (*Grammar and Mysticism*), his monograph on Białoszewski's theater, labels women in his works as the "midwives of reality" who "protect the most important values for Białoszewski." Kopciński also rationalizes the writer's preoccupation with the characters of mothers:

> The protective mother—the aunt too, as a matter of fact—is, next to the poet himself, the main protagonist of Białoszewski's entire oeuvre. This can certainly be attributed to the poet's psychology—that of a homosexual, who all his life searched for spiritual and practical support from women.
>
> Opiekuńcza matka—choć w rzeczywistości także ciotka—jest obok samego poety najważniejszym bohaterem całej twórczości Białoszewskiego. Fakt ten ma z pewnością uzasadnienie w psychologii poety—homoseksualisty przez całe życie poszukającego duchowego i materialnego wsparcia u kobiet.[54]

Kopciński, in his otherwise fascinating treatment of Białoszewski's work, essentializes the relationship between homosexual man and maternal women, which supposedly determines Białoszewski's choices of characters and modes of representation. Are we to think that Białoszewski prefers to represent women simply because women, not men, are "natural" (another essentialization) caretakers and homosexual men are, also "by nature," unable to be independent and thus seek maternal support? Or are we, perhaps, to speculate, from the perspective of the "hidden desire," that the focus on women functions as a smokescreen and protects the writer from focusing on men and from an accidental "disclosure"? Although Kopciński indicates that the need "for spiritual and practical support from women" is tied to Białoszewski's psychology, we could redirect this psychological justification of Białoszewski's literary choices toward a sociological and cultural one. Isn't it possible that Białoszewski spent so much time describing women characters because they were the only alternative family that he could afford to represent? Without a cultural model for a non-normative masculinity, a "more accommodating category of femininity" (in Silverman's phrase) could facilitate the creation of a non-normative space whose identity does not rely on the male/female binary. Within this category of femininity, Białoszewski creates a larger vision of human interaction and familial life.

Women, whom the narrator usually affectionately calls "baby," play a special role as figures of safety in Białoszewski's representation of the quotidian. The narrator is constantly surrounded by "the entire roster of women" ("caly zestaw pań"),[55] who in various ways—from providing him with homemade meals to buying him clothing—protect his physical and psychological well-being. A woman functions like "a screen that creates for the poet a space that is tamed and organized, both existentially and socially—in other words, she fulfills for him the basic functions of personal assistant, mother, and wife," notices Wojciech Browarny.[56] Analyzing fragments from the secret diary, Browarny also comments on the double status of women in Białoszewski's narration in contrast to his representation of men.[57] While men's physicality is hardly described, women are represented as "embodied," that is, the narrator pays attention to how they look (he is particularly fascinated by physical deformities and the reflection of social class in their appearance).[58] At the same time, argues Browarny, their subjectivity ("podmiotowość") does not threaten the narrator with a narratorial domination and does not engage him in the binary of subject/object—"the old women's stories are non-authoritarian and personal. They are willing to share with another person not only their memories, but also the pronoun 'I.'" The bodies of men, on the other hand, are rarely marked with uniqueness or specificity, which complements their "cultural attachment to their subjectivity."[59]

I agree with Browarny's argument that in order for the narrator to "create along with women a common space of experience, which the 'I' of the diary can consider his own," the women can be neither desired nor idealized.[60] They can be gendered, but not sexualized, as their maternal qualities are separated from sexuality and reproduction. We find the blueprint for such gendered but desexualized representation of women again in the *Memoir*, in which women as mothers are elevated to the level of archetypal symbols, as is emphasized by the consistent use of the capital letter for the word "Mother." In the *Memoir*, civilian survival is identified with a shelter of domesticity, however brief and unstable, which women create. The leitmotif of rebuilding provisional brick kitchens and taking care of feeding the families even during the incessant bombardments positions women at the center of survival in traumatic reality. Interestingly, women in the roles of wives and lovers, that is, in roles involving their relationships with the patriarchal world, are practically nonexistent in the *Memoir*. In the *Memoir*, the women's kingdom is underground, that is, in the basements where the civilian community hides to survive, far from the world of masculine, military values.[61] With mothers at the center, survival takes the form of a regressive evolution, a return to an earlier form of social life, which brings to mind the metaphor of a "return to the womb."[62]

This cave-like matriarchy is worlds apart from the male, romantic, and heroic reality that takes place aboveground. Literally the lowest spatial dimension of the uprising's life, basements are spaces for the order of mothers—down-to-earth, protective, and bodily—limited to the most basic function of motherhood, the physical protection of the child. Women's need for emotional/spiritual nourishment also takes a form symmetrical to providing basic physical nourishment, for example,"Swen's mother used to grind out that pasta. Like all the women. Without a break. Or rosary beads. The one or the other, in tiny pieces. A similar technique."[63] The *Memoir* does not describe the psychological idiosyncrasies of particular mother-child relationships; the purely relational nature of protection is expressed in the exchangeability of the label "mother."[64] Through his representation of traumatic reality, Białoszewski reinforces what is perceived as women's traditional roles as caretakers and homemakers. The matriarchy of the uprising becomes a blueprint for a maternal role of women in all Białoszewski's works. Every volume of the small narrations repeats the role of women as organizers of the domestic sphere and protectors of the narrator's world. This protection now assumes simple forms. Beginning with the narrator's mother, who houses the narrator when he loses his keys, and extending to a group of female friends who, regardless of their age and relation (e.g., the mother-daughter tandem of Jadwiga and Ania), alleviate the trouble of the narrator's everyday life, women are still guardians of the narrator's basic physical well-being. "Miron" submits to their rule.

Nevertheless, although this conception of the women's role is traditional, their representation is part and parcel of Białoszewski's construction of an alternative type of kinship. In this kinship, "universal" mothers (who, significantly, almost always appear without their male partners) protect their familial communities, which do not rely on heterosexual and procreative sexuality. In fact, few female characters in the small narrations are young (e.g., Ania, Agnieszka, Malina), and most women are post-menopausal, that is, outside the reproductive cycle and, thus, from the patriarchal standpoint, less desirable. Białoszewski claims that "old women [*baby*] are perhaps the most interesting beings in the world."[65]

ALTERNATIVE FAMILY, AND THE DOMESTIC AS PUBLIC

As I mentioned before, Białoszewski's narrator occupies the domestic space, which is traditionally assigned to women. In his apartment the narrator finds the fulfillment of his basic need for safety. The descriptions of their space form in the small narrations a survey of his aesthetic predilections and his past preoccupations: bouquets of wildflowers and dried grasses, stage props from the times of the Separate Theater, and folk figurines from trips with Le. to the rural Polish south. The narrator organizes this space with the loving care of a homemaker, but while he finds escape at home from the hardship of the "outside," at the same time he brings the outside inside. The domestic is not a space of withdrawal from the public; on the contrary, in the small narrations the domestic becomes a reconfigured public space. The apartments become a stage (in the times of the Separate Theater, quite literally) on which the characters of the small narrations play out their lives and their everyday. "Play out" is a proper description because the narrator's community theatricalizes its internal dynamics, whether in playful conversations or at the weekly "Tuesdays" ("wtorki") during which the narrator performs his new works for his audience.

Arranging the communal life in this domestic space, the narrator shifts the character of the domestic from private into public. In this reconfigured public space, the character of Le., whose abode is the kitchen—the feminine space par excellence—plays an intriguing role. Le.'s behavior is self-consciously theatrical, performative, over-the-top, and "campy." It is in Le.'s domestic sphere that the reader catches a glimpse of the (potentially) desiring body:

> Le. brings Teresa a cup of tea. On the way to the bathroom Teresa notices someone reflected in the mirror (because the mirror in Le.'s room reflects the hall).
> —Oh!
> —What, you never saw a guy [*chłop*] before?
> —A guy [*chłop*]? No, I have. Some leg.
>
> Le. przynosi Teresie herbatę. Teresa w drodze do łazienki widzi w lustrze nieznajomego (bo lustro tak stoi u Le. ukosem, że odbija przedpokój).
> —O!
> —Co, nie widziałaś chłopa?
> —Chłopa? Widziałam. Kawałek nogi.[66]

Significantly, this body is not only anonymous and fragmented but also seen reflected in a mirror, and thus the observer is removed from a direct gaze. The language remains indeterminate, so we do not learn anything about the "stranger" except that this time Le., in response to the "Oh" of surprise from Teresa, preempts her further reaction with a provocative rhetorical question. This resistance to saying anything more about "a piece of leg" is unusual from Le., who frequently functions as the person who mediates between the narrator and the body. It is Le. who provides the narrator with the information he craves and abhors at the same time—for instance, when he touches the body of Sister Franciszka to check whether the autopsy was performed while the narrator observes him from a distance and "has to leave."[67] This time, the information about the situation is filtered through a female character, although Le.'s rhetorical question aims at a provocative naturalization of the situation.[68]

Białoszewski does not write a counter-narrative, so he does not propose an alternative form of desire (i.e., homosexual instead of heterosexual), but this only strengthens the subversiveness of his textual strategies. His erasure of desire as such denaturalizes heterosexuality and undermines it as a traditional, dominant articulation of interrelationships and a privileged framework for the formation of communities. Such erasure deprives heterosexuality of the power to function as a transparent force in social life. Stories of heterosexual relationships form important episodes of the small narrations (to mention only such episodes from *Rozkurz* as "Leszno 99" and from *Szumy, zlepy, ciągi* as "Poznańska"), but their representation is pre-emptied of sexual charge and related without judgment or evaluations.[69]

Emotions are rarely mentioned and are unaccompanied by psychological speculation. Because the narrator's attention does not discriminate in depicting various signs of communal life, sexuality appears not as a private affair, but as a part of communal life, exposed to everyone's gaze. It does not differ from other signs of life, and the fact that it does not differ empties it of both intimacy and sensuality alike and makes it disappear in the multiplicity of other anecdotes and reports. While narrating diverse stories from the lives of tenants on Poznańska Street, the narrator blends in an episode of ménage à trois:

> Behind Żenia, behind the small corridor with a john and a cold, triangular, high-ceilinged bathroom, lived the re-emigrants from France. A small policeman and his hotheaded, skinny wife. A grandfather and grandmother, parents. And little Sylvia. There was also another policeman—an ex-lover? . . . Sylvia was four, but she would lie on the floor in Żenia's room, put her legs up and say—this is what mama and papa do at night, and maybe the third guy too in turns.
>
> Za Żenią, za korytarzem z wychodeczkiem i zimną, trójkątną, wysoką łazienką mieszkali reemigranci z Francji. Mały milicjancik z krewką chudą żoną. Dziadek z babką, rodzice. I malutka Sylwia. Krecił się tam jeszcze drugi milicjancik, były kochanek? . . . Sylwia miała cztery lata, ale u Żeni na podłodze kładła się, nogi do góry i że—tak robią w nocy tata i mama, i chyba ten trzeci na zmianę.[70]

The image of a four-year-old imitating sexual positions is grotesque, and the description of a sexual position through the eyes of a child character with an accuracy that matches the narrator's usual attention to detail is disquieting. It is unclear if the narrator hides behind little Sylvia or not; we can only keep guessing whether the phrase "maybe the third guy too in turns" belongs to little Sylvia's story or to the narrator's interjection.

The narrator, with his suspended sexuality, enables Białoszewski to construct alternative structures than those linked to sexuality and hierarchy (such as biological family). Positioned in the center of a circle that includes his friends and blood relatives, the narrator privileges no one. Friendships in Białoszewski's representation have the same status as blood ties and present a full-fledged alternative to biological clans. Although "Miron" narrates the stories of his own family (to mention only "Leszno 99" from *Rozkurz* or the diptych "Poznańska" from *Szumy, zlepy, ciągi*), his immediate relations are with his group of friends. The constant formation and dissolution of this group reminds one of the temporary "herds" described in the *Memoir*—small, spontaneous, temporary communities formed in the face of danger to facilitate physical and psychological survival. In a sense, the *Memoir*'s logic of a civilian family—a flexible, fragile, non-hierarchical community whose function is to ensure the best chance for survival—still governs the narrator's construction of the post-*Memoir* family. The domestic sphere is associated with escape from external reality; it is a space to which the narrator returns to regenerate, although its safety is perceived as permanently vulnerable to destruction.[71] At the same time, the narrator invites a carefully controlled "outside" life into this domestic space. In the domestic setting, he stages his own domesticated form of public sphere, in which he and his friends and relatives act out their private affairs.

Although friends scattered on the map of the city become the destination points for the narrator's urban travels, most of the time he interacts with them in the domestic sphere, within his four walls (thus the dilemma from "Blockade" of whether to answer the knock at the door). In this space devoid of political news and public affairs, the narrator converses with his friends about more or less insignificant things that become meaningful in the very process of communication and through the bond of intimacy. The comings and goings of the narrator's friends, their repetitive disappearances and reappearances, in which there seems to be no particular pattern, create a rhythm in many episodes of the narrations.

This process of communication makes no gender distinctions. Females and males alike share this domestic space with the narrator. In the course of the small narrations, domestic space is reconfigured to function as traditional public space. This reconfiguration of the spatial binaries that traditionally assign the female element to the domestic and the male element to the public reinforces gender interchangeability in the sense that gender distinctions are not governed by an economy of desire.[72] The gender of the narrator's friends functions exactly like his own—as an interchangeable, fluid, a linguistic convention, which allows no essentialization. The narrator specifies the names of his friends, but most of his friends do not have specific qualities or speech patterns that would allow us to differentiate them; one character is replaceable by another, female or male.[73]

Therefore, one way to "infiltrate" Białoszewski's world is to enter and inhabit it with an awareness of its self-reliant character. This self-reliance comes from the persistence with which Białoszewski adheres to the regulatory fiction in the series of small narrations. The seriality of the narrations naturalizes—that is, makes transparent and indisputable—the rules according to which Białoszewski constructs his representation. Several consistent aspects of the narrations contribute to the effect of the norm sui generis, such as the indeterminacy of the narrator's sexuality, heterosexuality that is desexualized (i.e., lacking the "desiring gaze"), a destabilization of the male/female binary, a privileging of the world of women, a construction of alternative family, and a reconfiguration of public and private space. In other words, even if Białoszewski presents us with the non-normative, it does not seem to be subversive (in the Butlerian understanding of the "subversive" as something that resists calculation), because the series of performative repetitions naturalizes it and renders it imperceptible. The provocation of Białoszewski's writing lies in the fact that passages describing "boys in latex" (as in "Blockade") or Le.'s comic homosexual advances do not alert our attention.[74] The most obvious reason for this is that a different historical and cultural context (including the emancipation of minorities and intertextuality of *Lubiewo*) equips us with different reading tools; new developments in the studies of gender and sexuality also give us a new optics to discern distinctions among the threads of Białoszewski's tapestry that previously appeared to blend together. However, much in the same way that throughout the small narrations one does not find a single erotic description of the body (i.e., a description that would indicate a desiring gaze), whether homo- or heterosexual, we overlook that for the narrator women exist only in their protective, quasi-maternal roles. Similarly, we do not wonder about the alternative community formed around the narrator; nor do we register that this community is not based on gender division and sexuality, as in the traditional biological family. As readers, we project on Białoszewski's patterns our expectations that he represent human subjects according to the humanist discourse of autonomy. We presuppose that Białoszewski's characters, including "Miron," represent volitional subjects, that is, subjects whose essences precede their actions. In fact, the reverse happens. We can hardly say anything definitive about their psychology, and their subjectivity functions as an aftereffect of their linguistic performance rather than the source of it. This performance in turn is charged with non-normative possibilities in the sphere of gender and sexuality. The small narrations represent characters living outside of libidinal economies and make the non-normative become the norm sui generis. In other words, we do not notice the subversive potential of Białoszewski's representation, because the horizontality of his attention blends the subversive with the normative, subtly but persistently destabilizing it and congealing into the idiosyncratic "Mironian" everyday.

FRUSTRATED "COMING OUT": *AAAMERYKA*

Regarding this imperceptible subversiveness, *AAAmeryka*, the posthumously published "diary" from Białoszewski's journey to the United States, marks a discernible shift. *AAAmeryka* was inspired by Białoszewski's trip to New York City, in the fall of 1982, to receive the Alfred Jurzykowski literary award. The descriptions of the narrator's activities in New York—his repeated visits to and fascination with porn shows and porn shops—are striking: they break the earlier pattern in which Białoszewski's narrators were desexualized. Instead of indifference and passivity, the reader for the first time can see the narrator actively expressing his interest in and enjoyment of sexuality. For example, after describing heterosexual porn shows, the narrator nonchalantly specifies:

> There are also cinemas for men only. Labeled "*male*." You enter, you sit—just like in other theaters. Here too the reel in the projector tears sometimes and one waits, patiently. From time to time someone gets up and goes behind the curtain. This turns out to be the relief parlor. There's moaning here, too, and the whining of interplanetary rockets coming into the home stretch. I also went to a "*male*" cinema with an all-male revue. After every performance people applaud. And so I spent a delightful evening.
>
> Są i kina i dla samych panów. Z napisami na wierzchu "male." Tam też się wchodzi, siada. Też taśma się nieraz zrywa, ale się cierpliwie czeka. Co pewien czas ktoś wstaje i idzie za kulisy. Okazuje się, że to salon ulgi. Też jęki i dojeżdżania rakiet międzyplanetarnych wyjących.
> Trafiłem również do kina male z rewią męską. Po każdym występie klaszcze się.
> I tak świetnie zeszedł mi wieczór.[75]

The narrator ensures that his attention is equally directed to both heterosexual and homosexual porn movies and shows. The exactness of descriptions that characterizes the narrator's mode of representation in general also helps him here to contextualize his transitions between hetero- and homosexual domains. They, too, become part of the narrator's thoroughness. Białoszewski allows the "naive" reader to read the narrator as a curious tourist from Eastern Europe who marvels at the free market that is unknown to him—befitting the impersonal form of "wchodzi się, siada się" (literally, "one goes in, one takes a seat"). The knowing reader, on the other hand, reads the narrator's delight personally, but also in the context of a consumer who is finally able to enjoy the pleasures forbidden to him in his country of origin. At this point of the small narrations, the "naive reader" does not give a second thought to stop and contemplate the narrator who "was in this porn cinema and that porn cinema, with a curtain for relief . . . And then streets, some walking, this porn, and that porn . . . On the second day, on the third, a similar story. I'm walking in Manhattan, from cinema to records, from records to porn, from porn to window displays, from window displays to other window displays."[76] On the one hand, the repetitive enumeration of pornographic venues suggests that Białoszewski wants his audience to envision their ubiquity in the Manhattan landscape. On the other hand, these repetitions replicate the topography of the narrator's movement and remind the reader of the same cognitive strategies that he employs while "flying" in Warsaw, Garwolin, or Konstancin in the earlier installments of the small narrations. In other words, a representation of the tourist experience in Manhattan, which could have been a pretext for the exploration of the unfamiliar and for opening up a space devoted to the expression of desire, has a self-limiting quality.

The nature of this self-limitation becomes more apparent when we compare this particular passage with a similar passage from the secret diary,[77] a 2,000-page text of the journal that Białoszewski kept from the mid-1970s until his death. The entire diary came out in February 2012 (when this book was already completed), but small fragments of the diary had been published earlier as teasers. One of these fragments presents Białoszewski's experience of Manhattan, a perfect double for a passage from *AAAmeryka.* In the fragment from the unpublished diary, what used to be the narrator's equal attention to the heterosexual and homosexual porn shows becomes monopolized by porn; Białoszewski adds a memory of a homosexual encounter and writes with humor about the juxtaposition of his sexual explorations with his stay in a boarding house run by nuns. But the nonchalant description of how the tourist attends these shows in *AAAmeryka* ("you get in, you sit") becomes in the diary paradoxically both personal and self-distancing. The narrator of the diary refers to pornography with a sacralizing, modernist-style label "the cinema of my rites" ("kino mojego obrządku"). The personal "my" cannot compensate for the modernist idiom of "rites." It is as if Białoszewski could not find a way, in his "secret" diary—which one would expect to be more direct—to talk about his homosexuality without resorting to the irony of a sublimating phrase.

However, we really do not need the diary's self-disclosures to see *AAAmeryka* as a repository of clues indicating that Białoszewski intends to "come out" to the knowing reader. This impulse is thematized in a short exchange with a Polish immigrant, the narrator's old acquaintance, who asks him:

—How did it happen that you came out of the closet? Perhaps my Polish is not so good because I don't use much Polish anymore, but I hope you understand me.
—Yes, yes, perfectly.—And I explain to him that first I got thrown out of my bed into the hospital, and then into the sanatorium. And then I moved. That made it easier to travel to Budapest. And after the pleasures in Budapest, it was easier to travel somewhere else. So this is how I learned to travel even though it's still a big deal, just like with these dollars. I can't take myself so seriously with all of this.

—Jak to się stało, że pan wyszedł z szafy? Ja może niedobrze mówię po polsku, bo nie używam tu polskiego, ale chyba pan mnie rozumie.
—Tak, tak, doskonale—i tłumaczę mu, jak mogę, że najpierw wyrwało mnie z łóżka do szpitala, potem do sanatorium. Potem się przeprowadziłem. Dzięki temu już było łatwiej jechać do Budapesztu. A po przyjemnościach w Budapeszcie łatwiej było jechać gdzie indziej. I tak się nauczyłem jeździć, chociaż nadal to jest heca, tak jak i te dolary. Nie mogę siebie z tym wszystkim brać na serio.[78]

Białoszewski creates a verbal quid pro quo in which the narrator construes the question as addressing his travels abroad from behind the Iron Curtain.[79] Of course, anybody who knows the expression "to come out of the closet" will read the tourist's pleasures of Budapest quite specifically and yet still in the context of a tourism which in the 1970s and early 1980s was not a possibility for many in Poland. The beginning of the exchange, "chyba mnie pan rozumie" (literally, "you probably understand me"), presupposes the understanding of the idiom "to come out of the closet" and the speaker eagerly responds in the affirmative. Białoszewski wrote *AAAmeryka* between his visit in October 1982 and death in June 1983. At that time (and even in 1989 when *AAAmeryka* was published), most of his readers would not have understood the idiom and likely would have taken the narrator's explanation at face value as an answer to the question phrased in idiomatically incorrect Polish. We now understand the idiom, and with this understanding we are put in the position of someone witnessing, after many years of friendship, the coming out of a friend who we knew all along was gay. Eve Kosofsky-Sedgwick describes the importance of the performance of coming out, where what is at stake is not knowing per se, but a speech act itself. This speech act is contextualized by the earlier speech act, which was silence.[80] Białoszewski's speech-act performs the coming out, yet as it performs it, the language barrier—both speakers use the same language, but different idioms—frustrates it at the same time, showing that there may be no understanding even if words are openly spoken and the two speakers assume they are talking about the same thing.

That it is quite easy to overlook such passages without marking them as unusual is an effect of the serial nature of Białoszewski's narration. By the time *AAAmeryka* was published, Białoszewski had a steady readership accustomed to his mode of narration and expectant of more of the same. This "same" involves a narrator who observes others but guards himself. The disclosing quality of this American diary is thus neutralized by the context of Białoszewski's earlier works and by the fact that a potential sexual disclosure is transferred to a foreign context. Similar to the previous works in which the narrator's blurred-up subjectivity made everything a quality of external circumstances rather than his subjectivity, here moments of disclosure merge with the foreign context in which they take place and are diffused in the general excitement of tourist explorations. In a sense, Białoszewski traps himself in his own pattern, and even if passages from *AAAmeryka* were intended to have a "coming out" quality, their effect is frustrated.

Białoszewski's persistent yet subtle subversion of normativity and his claim of "writing everything" deceives the reader with the narrator's seeming horizontality of attention, which does not prioritize, but merely accumulates. Such a writing strategy elicits a specific reception, in which the reader absorbs the effect of horizontal coverage in toto, but is desensitized to moments that are out of ordinary. The reader does not privilege any particular moment in the small narrations, because the reading experience mirrors the narrator's position; in a sense, the reader becomes passive (thus, critics' understandable motivation to act like detectives) and assumes the optics of the narrator who observes but does not desire. Such a construction of narrative voice allows Białoszewski's work to be, on the one hand, easily received as a representation of the quotidian, while, on the other, encoded with Białoszewski's self-othering. The provocative value of life-writing lies in deceiving the reader with a seemingly simple quotidian mimesis.

Perhaps the challenge of this kind of writing is that while it appears to be exposed, it puzzles us with a question that we cannot formulate. In this sense, Białoszewski's purloined letter is indistinguishable from the rest of his writing because, to extend the metaphor, the letter does not reveal its silhouette among other papers. Rather, its "secret" content smoothly covers other documents like a transparent glaze indistinguishable from other layers, imperceptible until we abandon the search and look awry. Looking awry implies a willingness to look past the binary of hiding and searching where searching is identified with the desire to disclose, and hiding with the desire to prevent disclosure and an awareness of its danger. It presupposes that one enters the textual territory with a knowing gaze and yet a gaze that is not probing or detective, but rather caring and playful. Such a gaze—similar to the aletheic gaze of Białoszewski's narrator who listens to the snores on Próżna Street, which I discussed in chapter 2—enjoys the landscape rather than aims at making definite statements about the status quo.[81] So perhaps what really matters is not so much the letter—whether single or multiple, centralized or scattered—but the very mode of reading that looks past strict categories and binaries.

When reading Białoszewski we tend to accept as natural those strategies that, in the case of a less subtle writer, we would consider subversive. To look awry and see the lack of desire, the formation of alternative kinships, and the presence of campy passages does not mean, however, we need to locate the "purloined letter" of Białoszewski's homosexuality in what he repressed or encoded. We "know" (and, thus, we "saturate our gaze with desire," as Žižek would put it) but not in order to make Białoszewski's text a repository of truths whose shape and form are familiar to us before we even start looking. Even less productive is to judge this repository constructed by our own expectations according to the criteria of what Białoszewski "could have done" (such as a claim that "*Lubiewo* is a book Gombrowicz and Białoszewski did not have courage to write").[82] Rather than establishing causality for our search, looking awry allows us to notice "regions of opacity"[83] in the seeming transparency of Białoszewski's writing. The point is then not to determine how Białoszewski "as a source of an authentic gay meaning performs his identity, but what kind of identity this performance creates for us."[84]

Epilogue

"Ridiculous Places" and Queering Memory: Life-Writing, History, and How We Do Not Know

> After the war, no matter how many times I walked through that familiar park, particularly near the walled public bathroom which was badly scarred by bullets, grenades, shell fragments, I would imagine that this ridiculous place was important then, that history had touched it in those days, that for more than one person this bathroom was the last refuge or the last view of his life.
>
> Ile razy potem, już po wojnie, przechodziłem przez ten znajomy park, szczególnie koło murowanego wychodka, bardzo poharatanego kulami, granatami, odłamkami pocisków, wyobrażałem sobie, ze to głupie miejsce było wtedy ważne, że potoczyła się tędy historia, że dla niejednego ten wychodkowy budyneczek był ostatnią ucieczką albo ostatnim widokiem w życiu.
>
> —Miron Białoszewski, *Pamiętnik z powstania warszawskiego* (1970)

IT IS PARTICULARLY APT now to ask questions about how our knowledge of Białoszewski's homosexuality can most productively enter into our interpretation of his work. Białoszewski's long-awaited secret diary (*tajny dziennik*), the publication of which was delayed under the terms of his will, just became publically available as of February 2012.[1] The diary will, most likely, generate new questions for the reception of Białoszewski's work. Perhaps it will take us closer to the life of an uncloseted homosexual writer negotiating his public career and personal life in a homophobic Communist culture. Perhaps it will elucidate the dynamics between Białoszewski's early awareness of his sexual orientation and his cultivation of "separateness" ("osobność"). Will "separateness" prove to be a gesture of self-fashioning and self-othering, an aesthetic and lifestyle strategy in response to the restricting rules of the mainstream code of masculinity, or will Białoszewski surprise us with dynamics we have not yet envisioned? What will be his private account of "withdrawal"? It should be elucidating to see how Białoszewski shaped his public image, in which concern for his audience went hand in hand with a seeming disregard for achieving the public recognition and prestige traditionally granted to writers in Poland. One wonders, for instance, about the circumstances of Białoszewski's greater cultural visibility in the 1970s: how did the authorities reconcile the recognition of Białoszewski as the author of the *Memoir* with the persecution of the writer in the 1950s? Conversely, what challenges did Białoszewski face as a recognized author during the 1970s stabilization, awarded state distinction for the *Memoir* and yet with a record of his encounters with the secret police during the Stalinist period?

I hope that the diary will help us to learn about the social, political, and material circumstances of Białoszewski's life and to historically contextualize his work regardless of whether we explore his homosexuality, political views, or travels. In some cases, the lack of such contextualization in Białoszewski's scholarship is not to be laid at the feet of the literary critics; for instance, as I indicated in chapter 3, the research on sexual minorities in Poland has been undertaken only recently, and it is hard to adequately contextualize Białoszewski's life in the history of homosexual subcultures in Poland.[2] In other cases, however, our canonical views of Białoszewski as an "outsider" and as the "guardian of the everyday" often bars us from exploring his complexities beyond that, which confirms our initial position. Nevertheless, such research is critical to a deeper understanding of Białoszewski's phenomenon and its implications, both in the Polish context as well as in the framework of globalized academic vocabulary. Just as we need to be attuned to carefully nuanced shades of self-control in Białoszewski's writing—it contains many types of silence and exposures—we should also be attuned to the legacy of various pressures (and not only homophobic) on our critical approaches. We created our own epistemic regime, to borrow Foucault's expression, and either elevated some aspects of Białoszewski's work or disregarded others; sometimes for the sake of academic taboo, sometimes as a protective gesture toward Białoszewski, and most often because we reserve for him a place of uniqueness, a niche of withdrawal that gave his critics permission to disregard the larger implications of Białoszewski's aesthetic and existential project.

One epistemological hazard that became obvious in connection with the publication of the "secret diary" is reading Białoszewski within the pattern of "revelation."[3] Such reading is teleologically driven and seeks to illuminate the obscure and to clarify the ambiguous. It surfaced in the already existing scholarship on the secret diary before the diary was even published or, to be more precise, when it was published in small fragments to whet readers' appetites.[4] A rhetoric of revelation permeates these interpretations, setting up expectations that the diary will elucidate and organize our current knowledge about Białoszewski. An unspoken distinction between "the hidden" and "the revealed" divides the previously published work and the diary, imbuing the latter with a capacity for authenticity otherwise unavailable. But this rhetoric of authoritative source risks closeting Białoszewski just as much as various taboos closeted him in the past. The sheer fact of treating the diary as a hermeneutical advent to fully "out" Białoszewski presupposes a solid demarcation line between what has been said and what has been left—supposedly purposefully—unsaid. I think of "outing" here both in its narrow idiomatic sense pertaining to the public disclosure of one's sexual orientation and in a broader sense, as an expression suggesting the leaving of a constrained space and the entering of an unbounded space of social visibility. Yet, eagerness to "out" is doomed to become a form of self-fulfilling prophecy already embedded in the very category of "revelation."

The desire to bring Białoszewski to full visibility through his "secret diary" tells us that, perhaps, we crave the comforting stability of organizing our thinking around the known and the unknown that eventually unfolds into a reliable knowledge. At the same time, the status of the diary as a secret finally to be revealed puts Białoszewski on display and us, his readers, in a peculiar voyeuristic position. This position is not so much a result of how much Białoszewski discloses to us; after all, through his decision to allow the publication of the diary, Białoszewski stages his posthumous confession and retains jurisdiction over his textual dominion. Rather, it is our expectations of knowing that generate such a reading position, a position that predetermines boundaries to our understanding of the scope of Białoszewski's work.

The diary will, surely, create its own interpretive pitfalls; it arrives after a long period of anticipation, and it may become increasingly difficult not to see it as "the" key to Białoszewski. Although I doubt that "confessional" will accurately describe Białoszewski's personal history, the status of the text as "secret" (and hence, "authentic") may superimpose its voice over the polyphony of voices that Białoszewski's audience has heard from him before. The temptations of teleological interpretations are always great, and the desire for revelation often slips surreptiously into our reading only to muffle our receptiveness to anything that does not speak in the voice we expect to hear. As one can never step twice into the same reading experience—in this case, the experience of "Białoszewski-from-before-the-diary"—I find it fortuitous to be able to complete my explorations of this fascinating writer (or, at least, this stage of my explorations) before I encounter another of his textual selves. The diary will "reveal" a great deal, but we should see the "I" of the diary neither as the "real" Białoszewski, nor as identical to the "I" of the life-writing, but as yet another authorial identity, one of the multiple authorships that make Białoszewski's writing so fascinating. To avoid circumscribed reading, we must keep in mind the basic tenet of asymmetry between biography and text. In other words, it is important to treat the private diary as another voice adding a different timbre to the variety of Białoszewski's voices.

While the excitement around the diary is understandable, there is plenty to explore in Białoszewski's writing that lies hidden in plain view. The far-reaching implications of his unique construct of the everyday that encompasses the traumatic and the queer still wait to be articulated. There are "dense networks of meaning"[5] embedded in Białoszewski's polyphonic works, and his accounts of insignificant events encompass alternative views for such laden notions as history, grand narratives, and national identity. To delineate and critically reflect on these alternative propositions requires that we look closer at the ethics which conditions the life-writing and which imbues it with its idiosyncratic flair.

The elusive, yet distinct, ethical aura of Białoszewski's writing resembles the non-axiological philosophy of proximity and exposure proposed by Emmanuel Levinas. Białoszewski's ethics rarely assumes the form of statements, propositions, and imperatives, which adds to the challenge of reclaiming his writing for a systematic reflection on larger historical, social, and political frameworks. The Aristotelian rational, subject-centered, prescriptive paradigms based on binary oppositions seem ineffective when confronted with Białoszewski's model of intersubjectivity, in which there is little room for the ego's domination. Białoszewski's writing privileges openness to the other over intellectual mastery. His preoccupation with low frequencies of life—like the almost inaudible sounds that surround us and yet usually pass unregistered—manifests an impulse to attest to what is most difficult to symbolize. For Białoszewski (just as for Levinas), this impulse to witness to that which escapes our attention springs from the traumatic uprooting of wartime and the Holocaust. Although Białoszewski never expresses it in discursive terms, his ethics seems much closer to a Judaic-biblical model based on the abandonment of preexisting notions and on the vulnerability of encounter with the other than to the Greek model of philosophical knowledge based on concepts such as consciousness, will, and intentionality. The blueprint for such Levinasian ethics in Białoszewski's writing can be found in the radical everyday of the uprising in *A Memoir of the Warsaw Uprising*. The position of the witness-narrator representing, as I call it in chapter 3, "male subjectivity at the margins," shapes the ethical dimension of Białoszewski's testimony. Only through Białoszewski's disregard for the masculine ethos of heroism that constituted the myth of the Home Army can his civilian male narrator reenact the history of "communal life against the background of the possibility of death" (to quote the "definition" of the uprising from the *Memoir*) as domestic and quotidian. The aggression toward the *Memoir*'s unapologetic indifference to masculine valor and the patriotic imperative in Żukrowski's review is symptomatic of how threatening—not to say castrating—Białoszewski's vision must have been—and still is—to the traditional configuration of Polish identity. We should give more thought to the fact that the most original, and, to my mind, most ethically powerful, literary representation of this iconic event in Polish history comes from a homosexual writer who disregards the (masculine) values at the heart of the event's symbolic status.

This is not to say that disregarding these values has anything to do with sexual orientation. To suggest that being homosexual automatically redirected one from the military world of men to the domestic world of women—that is, to the world of women as understood in the *Memoir*'s cave matriarchy—would be a vast oversimplification of the *Memoir*'s complexities and an essentialization of homosexual identity as such. The point, however, is to recognize that in order to valorize survival and civilian experience, Białoszewski must bracket out traditional masculinity and create a narrator who has no interest in the heroic ethos. The category of "masculinity" operates here outside gender distinctions, as deeply rooted in Polish culture value system that constituted the ethos of the uprising, which I discuss in chapter 1, and which subsumes female insurrectionists as well.[6] "Miron," however, descends to the basements with women who cook, pray, and bicker over their children's chamber pots, and who relentlessly—if only for a moment—rebuild in the vicinity of death the illusion of everyday familial life. Through this narratorial position, a core value of Polish national identity—the sacrificial patriotic "Deed"—disappears in the ethics of witnessing to the countless quotidian deeds that ensure basic survival. Białoszewski's account circumvents the "Deed" and the "sacrifice" and pertains solely to the open-ended experience of "surviving"—where "surviving" ("prze-życie") simultaneously signifies the end result, that is, staying alive, and the process of "living through." While the traditional accounts of the uprising tend to replace proximity to the event's particularities with its symbolic dimension, Białoszewski's testimony emerges from a state of exposure to the repetitive and insignificant which resists symbolization and incorporation into a larger paradigm of national identity.

Moreover, the ethics of witnessing in the *Memoir* is more than "civilian" versus military. It is simply maximalist. It encompasses the animate and the inanimate alike. Warsaw becomes an extension of the narrator's subjectivity, its suffering a human suffering, its materiality a sentient body. Driven to witness its gradual obliteration and to create in his memory a mental equivalent of the disappearing city, Białoszewski's narrator lives in a state of permanent traumatic alertness: the surviving "we" are responsible for attesting to the non-surviving "we," regardless of the latter's ontological status. Objects (for instance, a wall, which as "a wall of suffering" I discuss in chapter 2) are neighbors who share the same fate and whose existence and death needs to be witnessed just like the existence and death of living beings. Hence, Białoszewski radicalizes what Levinas considers as "proximity" and "exposure" to the other preconditioned on the notion of the other as an incarnated, sentient being. The ethics of witnessing enacted "on the surface of the skin, at the edge of the nerves"[7] is at the core of Białoszewski's revision of the event's mainstream representations.

Białoszewski's Levinasian ethics manifests itself in proximity to the city and despair over its death (the Warsaw of the *Memoir* lies "under the ruins," and not "in ruins"). The city as a sentient being remains a permanent quality of Białoszewski's writing. Through his relationship to Warsaw, Białoszewski seems to construct a premodern type of historical memory. This memory does not rely on sites of memory (*lieux de mémoire*) à la Pierre Nora, which presuppose that unless we mark our space with collective reminders of the past the history will be forgotten; yet, in their referential function, these marks alienate us from the continuity of time and separate memory and history. Memory and history in Białoszewski are inhabited differently—in a more direct, tangible, and nondiscursive way when they are inscribed in the materiality of the city and manifest themselves in unexpected moments and everyday situations. Through the nondiscursivity of traumatic flashbacks, Białoszewski's narrator is granted continuity and immediate access to the past. This intimate and domestic history *as* memory is not localized in any memorial place, because it is embodied by the entire Warsaw understood as the narrator's space of life.

In his traumatic performance of memory, in which the extreme and the everyday do not oppose each other but seamlessly merge in the traumatic reality which evades the symbolic vocabulary, Białoszewski challenges traditional historiography and the institutionalized memory of the event. His account counters a tendency in Polish culture to overlook civilian experience (usually homogenized in the cliché of "women and children") and leave it with no witness or, at the very least, with no witness that could fully claim the legitimacy of the civilian experience to enter the Polish national meta-narrative in the way that redemptive narratives valorize the military one. Moreover, it counters another tendency, which I discussed in chapter 2 in relation to the Museum of the Warsaw Uprising, namely a tendency to grant the audience scopophilic representations of the event, which instigate secondary traumatization through the voyeuristic pleasure of watching the sacrificial offering of the uprising's military participants. Both the mode of transmitting the memory of the event and its focus on its heroic aspects that overshadow the destruction of the city and its (ten times greater!) civilian losses are problematic aspects of Polish memory culture.

I have stressed throughout this book the issues related to Białoszewski's homosexuality because these issues better than others direct our attention—to echo Kosofsky-Sedgwick's findings—to potentially larger epistemological hazards. But beyond this, they point to new ethical routes and suggest alternative ways to envision history, both Polish history and history as such. How would our interpretation of the *Memoir* shift if we allowed for the fact that onto its belated origins—the years that separate the work from the experience in which it originated—Białoszewski inscribed two different kinds of traumatization? One traumatization would be the one that I discussed in chapter 1 related to the experience of the uprising and its post-traumatic impact on Białoszewski and his writing. The other would be the traumatization that is left unarticulated and which yet from time to time resurfaces for "those who know" about the hardships of Białoszewski's life as a homosexual in a postwar homophobic society. Would an awareness of a double traumatization affect our reading of the *Memoir*? Or, perhaps, the question should be asked differently. Rather than inquiring about the psychology behind the author's choices and asking "can we queer the *Memoir*?" we should ask what emerges if we queer a traumatic representation such as the *Memoir*.

What is at stake is something other than amassing textual allusions that the narrator of the *Memoir* makes about his own homosexuality, although these subtle self-disclosures are indicative of the pattern of divulgence Białoszewski set throughout his career.[8] A more fruitful approach, however, is again to interrogate "queering" à la Halperin ("whatever is at odds with the normal"), that is, as a narrative positionality (Żukrowski recognized precisely this positionality when he chastised Białoszewski for behaving not like a man, but like an "overgrown baby"). Let us also remember Jakobsen's proposition of treating "queer" as a verb of action, not a noun of identity: Białoszewski "does" his own history of the traumatic, in which he resists the normative masculine, military, sacrificial approaches. Moreover, his version of history insists on differentiations of what became institutionalized in Polish memory as "civilian experience," a homogenized and self-explanatory part of the binary "military vs. civilian."

What can the notion of queering bring to our attention to the traumatic? Queering the traumatic and imagining the traumatic dimension of the queer open up two overlapping registers of individual as well as social and cultural experience. Queering the traumatic, as I have been signaling it, may lead us to, for instance, fresh insights into the nature of Poland's grand narratives—what they silence and what they voice as the national history. In this sense, Białoszewski's account indicates the need for the collective to redraw its memorial blueprints and to give more thought to mediation between the particularities of individual experiences and the generalities of historical understanding. In other words, working through a painful history entails not replicating the patterns already culturally imprinted but "introducing splintered or constantly recurring refractions of a traumatic past by using any number of different vantage points."[9] These splintered refractions superimposed on the institutional historiography and canonic memory become the "voice-over,"[10] to use Saul Friedlander's term, which pluralizes the experience into multiple stories, thus disrupting traumatic repetitions and helping us imagine the past through the eyes of the other. While Friedlander talks about disrupting traumatic repetitions in the context of post-traumatic syndrome, Białoszewski disrupts the mainstream narrative of Polish identity in which the myth of "beautiful death" overrides the story of everyday survival. The *Memoir* constitutes such a voice-over by reenacting the past through the eyes of the other, that is, the other who does not engage in symbolic compensation (such as moral triumph, self-congratulatory victimhood, etc.) of traumatic experience.

Disregarding grand narratives, marginalizing the masculine, and imbuing the representation with the ethics of proximity and exposure are all aspects of queering the traumatic. But how does Białoszewski traumatize the queer? I believe that a new horizon for critical explorations may open up when we attend to this question. As I discussed in chapter 2, Białoszewski's representation of the everyday is permeated with traumatic traces, which are inscribed into mundane activities. Onto what activities and exactly how they are inscribed carries great significance. For instance, the narrator of the *Memoir* tells us about his experience of passing through Skaryszewski Park after the war. No matter "how many times" he passed through the park "near the walled bathroom which was badly scarred by bullets, grenades, shell fragments, [he] would picture to [himself] how important that ridiculous place was then, that history had touched it in those days."[11] To the "naive" reader this fragment, juxtaposing the high of "history had touched it" with the low of "ridiculous place," merely illustrates that history happens everywhere. Although this is also true, the "ridiculous place" ("to głupie miejsce") is also a wink to the knowing reader who is aware that Skaryszewski Park was a popular cruising ground for homosexuals of Białoszewski's generation.[12] How can we incorporate such a specific allusion to the homosexual subculture into our understanding of traumatic representations and collective memory? How is the traumatic to condition the queer, and vice versa? What kind of historical reflection emerges from their intersection?

First of all, the subcultural specificity of the place as a trigger of traumatic memory points to alternative topographies of the city. These private, yet connected with a collective experience, traumatic, yet "ridiculous" (that is, "queer") topographies do not fall, as I signaled before, within the category of "sites of memory." Sites of memory are marked by collective reminders of history whose function is to preserve the memory of the past by institutionalizing it as history (a visitor in Warsaw feels overwhelmed by the sheer number of such historical reminders, to mention only the placards appearing on every street corner). These spatial reminders have the paradoxical effect of creating a distance between the past and its memory; they are intended to help us to remember, but as they focalize particular events in the past they also mark the lack of continuity in history and time. In the episode with Skaryszewski Park, however, something different happens: memory and history are inhabited in a direct, tangible, bodily—pun intended—way; however, only those who know about the double identity of the "ridiculous place" can share in Białoszewski's queering of history.

In the "ridiculous place" a well-known story of the past (that is, of the uprising) merges with an unknown story of the present (that is, of the cruising ground). The narrator who witnesses to the former engages here in a silent act—or surreptitious act—of simultaneously witnessing to the latter. The *Memoir* insists on historical referentiality and so the bathroom, too, becomes an object of historical knowledge and, at the same time, as Walter Benjamin stated, an "object of construction whose site is . . . time filled by the presence of the now."[13] This "now," however, is not self-identical. Rather, as the double character of the place that triggers traumatic recollection presupposes a double knowledge available only to some, the "now" in which the past reverberates becomes "a plurality of times existing together, a disjuncture of the present with itself."[14] This "disjuncture of the present with itself" on the most fundamental level can be read as different subject positions that each of us occupies while telling the story. On the other hand, the silence that frames the place's double identity silences the framework of a specific everyday—the "queer" everyday—into which the memory of the uprising returns. Such silence may also signal the traumatic splintering at the very heart of Białoszewski's life-writing in which the narratorial repetitive assertions that he "will write everything" acquire a bitter dimension. The continuum of memory that the bathroom represents merges the sexual and the historical; sexuality becomes historicized and history, sexualized.

Białoszewski's writing contains many such "life-worlds compressed in the passage"[15] through which he invites us to reflect upon alternative histories not as counter-narratives existing in their own space, but as embedded in history to which we already have access. These "life-worlds" ask us to attend to the language of historical particularity; they also ask us to look at the political in Białoszewski's writing more broadly and to read the grand narratives with micro-narratives in mind, that is, to read the marginal and the canonical—sometimes in the same source—together. Opening ourselves up to alternatives in the historical thinking permits the historical to reverberate in our everyday more subtly and in a way that promotes exposure to the past, not control over it. Such intimate coexistence of the everyday and the historical, of memory and the present is particularly important in Polish culture, in which for a long time various approaches to the past—and various collectives that inhabited it—were homogenized under the umbrella of national history.

To say that there are many textual selves in Białoszewski's writing means also that there are many modes of reading. I hope that my reading of three of them—the traumatic, the quotidian, and the queer—will invite further explorations of their symbiotic coexistence. While the traumatic and the everyday present a more organic match, the queer at face value seems to be "separate," to use this Białoszewskian term, and to belong to the dimension that we often perceive as ahistorical privacy. But, just as Białoszewski's life shows us and his reflection inscribed on the bathroom in Skaryszewski Park illustrates, this separateness is illusory, and public bathrooms too should become—literally and metaphorically—the objects of our knowledge to enter into a dialogue with other sources of our historical and cultural identity. We can learn plenty by placing Białoszewski back in his particular cultural context rather than treating him as a case study for the globalized vocabulary, whether of trauma or queer studies. Or, to put it differently, we need to remember that all theoretical frameworks fulfill their function best when through them we deepen our understanding of what it means—and what it meant—to live in a particular historical reality; consequently, their meaningfulness involves explorations of how the subject and the tools of inquiry condition each other.

The spheres of the traumatic, the quotidian, and the queer coexist and condition each other in dynamic historical ways; sexual desire is subject to history, and so is, in relation to it, identity politics. Traumatic events, especially historical traumatic events, do not all traumatize in the same way, and attending to the particularities of each of them is imperative to understanding the meanders of one's collective and individual identity. And, finally, there is nothing static about the everyday, either as a discourse or as a practice of, to quote Białoszewski, "always something monotonously changing." All three dimensions are subject to changing political circumstances; all three are "out there" while being at the same time Benjaminian "objects of construction." Finally, all three of these dimensions can be simultaneously hidden and revealed, and their dense networks of meaning are visible or invisible depending on our horizon of epistemological expectations.

Our knowledge and understanding can be closeted in different ways. After all, what closets them is not some abstract silence but "a silence that accrues particularity by fits and starts, in relation to the discourse that surrounds and differentially constitutes it."[16] We join Białoszewski's silences with our own "fits and starts" in the process of recognizing his multiple authorial selves and the multiple spheres of experience attached to them. In this process "the truth" of human experience—past and present, individual and collective—sometimes takes the shape of the walls of the bathroom reverberating with what Kosofsky-Sedgwick calls "a speech act of silence." And just as Białoszewski's account of the uprising is belated, so is our recognition as his readers that in some way he, indeed, "writes everything" and implicates spheres of life to which he seemingly makes no claims at all. If there is something we need to "out" in Białoszewski, it is this maximalist interconnectedness of things; the legacy which can impel Polish culture to redraw its blueprints so that they do not overshadow the margins.

Abbreviations

AAA	*AAAmeryka*
BB	*Było i było* (*There Was and There Was*)
DR	*Donosy rzeczywistości* (*Reporting Reality*)
K	*Konstancin* (*Konstancin*)
MWU	*A Memoir of the Warsaw Uprising*
O	*Oho*
OE	*Obmapywanie Europy* (*Mapping Europe*)
OR	*Obroty rzeczy* (*The Revolution of Things*)
PB	*Pisanie Białoszewskiego* (*Writing Białoszewski*)
PPW	*Pamiętnik z powstania warszawskiego*
R	*Rozkurz* (*Dust*)
SZC	*Szumy, zlepy, ciągi* (*Hums, Lumps, Threads*)
Z	*Zawał* (*The Heart Attack*)

Notes

INTRODUCTION

1. The title of what may be Białoszewski's most popular poem from his debut volume *Obroty rzeczy* (1956; *The Revolution of Things*).

2. Wiech (Stefan Wiechecki, 1896–1979), a popular writer of *fait divers* (*felietony i humoreski*) that preserved the dialect and lifestyle of Warsaw's pre–World War II peripheral neighborhoods.

3. Michał Głowiński, interview with Janusz Majcherek, "Niezwykłe zwykłe," *Teatr* 5 (1993): 5–7. Translation mine.

4. Stanley Cavell, *The Senses of Walden* (Chicago: University of Chicago Press, 1992), 4.

5. Ryszard Nycz reads epiphany (à la Joyce) as the principle of Białoszewski's poetics. See "'Szare eminencje zachwytu': Miejsce epifanii w poetyce Mirona Białoszewskiego," in *Pisanie Białoszewskiego* (henceforth abbreviated as *PB*), ed. Michał Głowiński and Zdzisław Łapiński (Warsaw: Wydawnictwo IBL, 1993), 179–91.

6. Michał Głowiński, "Białoszewskiego gatunki codzienne," in *PB* 144.

7. Miron Białoszewski, *The Revolution of Things: Selected Poems,* trans. Andrzej Busza and Bogdan Czaykowski (Washington: Charioteer, 1974). A small selection of Białoszewski's prose in the translation of Beth Holmgren and fragments from "The Cabaret of Kitty Katty" in the translation of Stanisław Barańczak and Clare Cavanagh were also published in *Cross Currents* 6 (1987): 195–215. A selection of reprinted and new translations of Białoszewski's poetry (trans. Busza and Czaykowski, Mark Tardi and Katarzyna Schuster, Katarzyna Jakubiak and Rick Hilles) has been published in the journal *Aufgabe* 9 (2010), guest edited by Mark Tardi and dedicated to Polish poetry and poetics. Several leading translators of Polish into English have expressed their interest in creating *A Białoszewski Reader* for American audiences.

8. I borrow the notion of "transatlantic canon" from Bożena Shallcross, who applies it to describe Polish books in English translations, which are considered

marketable for North American college and university curricula (unpublished manuscript).

9. I evoke here Czesław Miłosz's *The Witness of Poetry* (1984) and Adam Zagajewski's *Solidarity, Solitude* (1990).

10. I refer here to the well-known collection of essays *Etyka and Poetyka* (1979), by Stanisław Barańczak.

11. Chela Sandoval, *Methodology of the Oppressed* (Minneapolis: University of Minneapolis Press, 2000).

12. Sławomir Mrożek, "Moniza Clavier," in *Dwa listy* (Cracow: Wydawnictwo Literackie, 1974), 26.

13. Mrożek adds another satirical layer to the play, by having the hero impersonate a Russian because he (the hero) considers Russian identity to be more recognizable and marketable. In the logic of the play, the animosity of Poles toward Russians is overridden by the necessity to accommodate the "West."

14. I distinguish here, however, between the Romantic paradigm (à la Lyotard) and the strong influences of the Romantic imagination on Białoszewski's work. Białoszewski himself in "O tym Mickiewiczu jak go mówię" ("Of this Mickiewicz, as I speak him"), a manifesto of his relationship with the tradition, differentiated between his fascination with the power of Mickiewicz's poetry and his distancing himself from the Romantic paradigm especially as a transmission of simplified communal values. The Mickiewicz that interests Białoszewski is not the Mickiewicz of the national messianic tradition. Białoszewski is fascinated with the pre-insurrectionary Mickiewicz, with his theatricality and folkloric roots. Białoszewski both playfully and seriously reads Mickiewicz's *Dziady Part IV* (*Forefathers' Eve*) as Mickiewicz's take on opera "because there was no opera in Vilnius." The very title of Białoszewski's "O tym Mickiewiczu jak go mówię" brings Mickiewicz down from the exalted national paradigm to a level as basic and familiar as one's everyday articulation. "O tym Mickiewiczu jak go mówię," in *Debiuty poetyckie 1944–1960,* ed. Jacek Kajtoch and Jerzy Skórnicki (Warsaw: Iskry, 1972), 291–300.

15. "Aesopian language," a type of communication with the reader in which the political is encoded in allegories and allusions (supposedly in order to outsmart censors), has had a long tradition in Polish literature. In the 1970s, Aesopian language was somewhat disqualified by the poetry movement of the Generation '68, which sought to return to realism in order to represent "the unrepresented reality" of Polish life. However, commonplace themes were now charged with the political, while the everyday became configured as the sphere of dissent.

16. See the guidelines from the Polish Ministry of Education (MEN): http://wiki.wolnepodreczniki.pl/Lektury:Lista_lektur_według_spisu_MEN#Literatura_polska.

17. "Osiedlając się w królestwie 'małoznaczności' (trudno mi to jakoś inaczej nazwać), Białoszewski zapewnia sobie niezależność względem oczekiwań,

które mogłyby ingerować w jego prywatność; chroni się przed zobowiązaniami i związaną z nimi koniecznością robienia stosownych póz i min. Tam, gdzie zamieszkuje (mowa cały czas o świecie zbudowanym przez jego pisanie)—nie musi specjalnie przejmować się nagabywaniami o 'udział w życiu'; poziom bytowania, który uznał za prawdziwie swój, pozostaje poza bezpośrednią presja usankcjonowanych wzorów zachowań—nie jest honorowany kontrolującym zainteresowaniem innych. Można tu bezkarnie 'być sobie jednym' i o swoją jedność nie trzeba toczyć walki. Autonomia jest tożsama z marginalnością i permanentnym niedorastaniem do normy." Janusz Sławiński, "Białoszewski: Sukces wycofania się," introduction to *Miron Białoszewski, Wiersze* (Warsaw: Państwowy Instytut Wydawniczy, 1976), 13.

18. Anna Sobolewska, "Miron Białoszewski: Maksymalnie udana egzystencja," in *Sporne postaci polskiej literatury współczesnej*, ed. Alina Brodzka (Warsaw: Instytut Badań Literackich, 1994), 103. "Maximally successful existence" Sobolewska claims to be the phrase with which Ludwik Hering, Białoszewski's close friend and co-creator of their theater, described Białoszewski's life. Ibid., 109.

19. Anna and Tadeusz Sobolewscy are also the holders of the rights to Białoszewski's recently published "secret diary." Since the writer's death, they have been involved in preserving and popularizing his writing.

20. Wołyński recalls the times when he was befriended by Białoszewski, Ludwig Hering, and Ludmiła Murawska and how he got to know many people from Białoszewski's circle, yet—and this is important in light of the role played by Białoszewski's friends, who were also his critics—he was not directly involved in Białoszewski's artistic endeavors and their criticism. During the phase of their friendship that Wołyński recalls, Białoszewski lived with his housemate and ex-partner, Leszek Soliński.

21. Olgierd Wołyński, "Plac Dąbrowskiego: Rozmawiał Tadeusz Sobolewski," in *Miron: Wspomnienia o poecie* (*Miron: Remembering the Poet*), ed. Hanna Kirchner (Warsaw: Tenten, 1996), 189–203.

22. Ibid., 202.

> Sobolewski: U Mirona miało się poczucie kompletnego bezpieczeństwa . . . Leszek [Soliński] jak nas wszystkich zobaczył, powiedział, że to wygląda, jakby maciora z prosiętami leżała. To była dla nas jakby rodzina, jakby dom. I to ważne było, że się było całkowicie zaakceptowanym.
>
> Wołyński: Ty mówisz of bezpieczeństwie odczuwanym u Mirona. Dla mnie czasami na pierwszy plan wysuwały się zagrożenia i kłopoty tego życia. Sąsiadka z dołu protestowała, że Miron po nocy stuka. Komisja z administracji oskarżała go, że zniszczył mieszkanie. Jacyś faceci dobijali się do drzwi. Tam wcale nie było bezpiecznie. Kiedyś—wracam z miasta, a na drzwiach Mirona napis: PEDAŁ . . . I Leszek zamalowujący drzwi. Widzisz, jak takie rzeczy pamiętam?

Sobolewski: Myśmy o tym wiedzieli, o tej administracji, nawet o tym napisie, ale przez to, że stykaliśmy się z nim jako z autorem, który to wszystko już przetworzył, a więc jakby opanował, rozbroił, mieliśmy poczucie, że jemu nic się stać nie może, że nic mu nie zagraża. Nawet o przesłuchaniach opowiadał nam inaczej, lekko. Wydawał się człowiekiem szczęśliwym.

23. Stanislaw Rosiek's expression. "Pamiętnik z półgrobu," in *PB* 132.

24. Slavoj Žižek, *Looking Awry: An Introduction to Jacques Lacan Through Popular Culture* (1991; Cambridge, Mass.: MIT Press, 2000), 11.

25. This is the phrase that Michael Levine uses to describe reading Freud's metaphors whose clarity obfuscates the matter they represent. Michael Levine, *Writing Through Repression: Literature, Censorship, Psychoanalysis* (Baltimore: Johns Hopkins University Press, 1994), 8.

26. One can find an interesting discussion on life-writing in the light of biography in Ann Jefferson's *Biography and the Question of Literature in France* (Oxford: Oxford University Press, 2007), particularly in the chapter "Life-Writing in Roger Laporte and Jacques Roubaud," 371–86.

27. See Philippe Lejeune, *On Autobiography,* trans. Katherine Leary (Minneapolis: University of Minnesota Press, 1989).

28. *PB* 146.

29. Winiecka's statement about Białoszewski's poetry works equally well in relation to his prose. Elżbieta Winiecka, *Białoszewski sylleptyczny* (Poznań: "Wydawnictwo Poznańskie Studia Polonistyczne," 2006), 231.

30. "Która inscenizuje swoje słowa, buduje na poły realny, na poły zmistyfikowany (lecz natychmiast włączany w obraz artystycznej osobości poety) obraz 'Mirona Białoszewskiego.'" Ibid., 231.

31. *SZC* 10.

32. Jefferson, *Biography and the Question of Literature in France,* 2.

33. Janusz Majcherek, "Widok z mostu na M.B. (z Królikiem w tle)," interview with Janusz Głowiński, *Teatr* 5 (1993): 6.

34. Stanisław Barańczak, "Rzeczywistość Białoszewskiego," in *PB* 10.

35. I refer here to Piotr Sobolczyk's expression of "rozmyta podmiotowość," a notion that I address in chapter 3. Sobolczyk, "Hermetyczne pornografie Białoszewskiego," *Teksty drugie* 6 (2006): 175.

36. Kaja Silverman, *Male Subjectivity at the Margins* (New York: Routledge, 1992).

37. Sobolczyk, "Hermetyczne pornografie," 175.

38. Slavoj Žižek in *Looking Awry* proposes a mode of double reading to reinterpret Jacques Lacan's psychoanalytic theory. I test his metaphor of "looking awry," in which an interpretive straightforward gaze overlaps with a gaze distorted by desire, against Białoszewski's texts and his biography.

39. To mention only two iconic poets: Krzysztof Kamil Baczyński (1921–

1944) and Tadeusz Gajcy (1922–1944). Selections from Baczyński's poetry are available in English in Bill Johnston's translation. See Krzysztof Baczyński, *White Magic and Other Poems,* trans. Bill Johnston (Los Angeles: Green Integer, 2004).

40. Kirchner, *Miron: Wspomnienie o poecie,* 122.

41. The bibliography on this fascinating topic of writers' responses to Communism is immense, to mention only the influential and provocative *Hańba domowa* (*Domestic Shame*) by Jacek Trznadel (Paris: Instytut Literacki, 1986), or more recently, Anna Bikont and Joanna Szczęsna, *Lawina i kamienie: Pisarze wobec komunizmu* (Warsaw: Prószyński i S-ka, 2006). The most popular work by a Polish writer on the topic available in English is probably a probing study of intellectual seduction in *The Captive Mind* by Czesław Miłosz (New York: Knopf, 1953).

42. *AAA* 235.

43. Anna Sobolewska and Tadeusz Sobolewski, interview with Janusz Majcherek, "Nie mogę kołysać się razem ze wszystkimi," *Teatr* 5 (1993): 10–14.

44. Kirchner, *Miron: Wspomnienie o poecie,* 122.

45. Ibid., 138.

46. The only poems Białoszewski published before 1956 were "Chrystus powstania" ("Christ of the Uprising") and "Listopad popielny" ("Ash November") in 1947 in the magazines *Warszawa* and *Nowiny Literackie,* respectively, and "Fioletowy gotyk" ("Purple Gothic") in the magazine *Odrodzenie* in 1949. Seven years later, "Fioletowy gotyk" opens Białoszewski's "debut" volume, *Obroty rzeczy.* From 1952 to 1954 he published poems for children cowritten with the well-known children's author Wanda Chotomska

47. Other poets and writers in this formation included Jerzy Harasymowicz, Bohdan Drozdowski, Andrzej Bursa, Halina Poświatowska, Stanisław Grochowiak, Marek Nowakowski, and Marek Hłasko.

48. For an interesting interpretation of the relationship between the poet and the critic, see Sobolczyk's "Hermetyczne pornografie Białoszewskiego," *Teksty drugie* 6 (2006): 176.

49. The word "rzecz" in Polish can also signify an abstract notion or a set of topics, the way "res" does in Latin.

50. Białoszewski, *The Revolution of Things,* 1974.

51. *OR* 116.

52. Such privatization of genre goes hand in hand with the privatization of cultural references. Białoszewski always situates his poetic persona and narratorial subjectivity vis-à-vis history and culture that are approached in a domestic and playful mode; the most straightforward manifestation of this domestic intimacy is his use of diminutives to refer to historical figures, which puts them on the same level as the narrator's friends (e.g., King Stanisław August becomes "Król Staś").

53. The verb "zabrali" ("they took it away") could also be used to describe

an arrest in which the place of destination and the agents of the arrest are not specified.

54. In the first two volumes one can also find many affinities with the Polish avant-garde movement (particularly with the Cracow avant-garde's imagery), which decrease as Białoszewski progresses in the development of his language of the quotidian.

55. Other significant poets of this movement include Tymoteusz Karpowicz, Zbigniew Bieńkowski, and Edward Balcerzan.

56. By using these distinctions between "spoken" and "colloquial," I follow Barańczak, who distinguishes between three pairs of binaries in Białoszewski's language: spoken over written (on the level of articulation); colloquial over literary/educated/formal ("low" vs. "high" on the social level); and children's language over the language of adults (on the diachronic level of ontogenesis of human linguistic development). According to Barańczak, Białoszewski's language is governed by the logic of word formation by children, where the mistakes are logical because children do not, for instance, consider exceptions.

57. As claimed by Kwiatkowski, who coined the binary of "abulia and liturgia" to describe Białoszewski's poetic register. See "Abulia i liturgia," in *Klucze do wyobraźni: Szkice o poetach współczesnych* (Warsaw: Państwowy Instytut Wydawniczy, 1964).

58. It is worth signaling that the notion of listening to indistinguishable and inarticulate sounds so prominent in the "Ballad" ("szum toreb i ludzkie mówienie") is also thematized in several of the small narrations (as in the title of one volume, *Hums, Lumps, Threads* [*Szumy, zlepy, ciągi*]).

59. *BB* 336.

60. As pointed out by Barańczak in *Język poetycki Mirona Białoszewskiego* (*Białoszewski's Poetic Diction*) (Wrocław: Zakład Narodowy Imienia Ossolińskich, 1974), 153.

61. Ludwik Hering's mention as an influence on Białoszewski's aesthetics appears in comments by all of Białoszewski's friends, but particularly by Hanna Kirchner in "O Mironie, o Ludwiku," in *Miron: Wspomnienia o poecie*, 275–303. Ludmiła Murawska gives a fascinating account of Hering "dictating" the outline of *Wiwisekcja* (a play in which the characters were performed by Białoszewski's fingers) to Białoszewski in "Wolność w łupince orzecha" (ibid. 158).

62. Julian Przyboś, "Z powodu *Było i było* Mirona Białoszewskiego," *Poezja* 3 (1966).

63. See Jerzy Ficowski, "Trafunek zaściankowy," *Nowa Kultura* 10 (1959).

64. Czesław Miłosz, "Prywatne obowiązki wobec literatury polskiej," in *Prywatne obowiązki* (Cracow: Wydawnictwo Literackie, 1972), 130.

65. These experiments began in the Warsaw suburb of Kobyłka, where Swen Czachorowski, Lech Emfazy Stefański, Bogusław Choiński, and Stanisław

Prószyński, among others, regularly met, discussed, and tested their futurist, cubist, and surrealist sensibilities.

66. The Theater on Tarczyńska Street was as much the result of friendship as it was of artistic yearning. The creators included Lech Emfazy Stefański, Bogusław Choiński, and Stanisław Prószyński (see Stanisław Prószyński, "Wspominając Mirona," in *Miron: Wspomnienia o poecie,* ed. Kirchner, 21–59). Critics have pointed out connections between Białoszewski's poetic imagery and twentieth-century art movements such as cubism (Kazimierz Wyka, "Na odpust poezji," in *Rzecz wyobraźni* [Warsaw: Państwowy Instytut Wydawniczy, 1959]) and surrealism, as well as works of the great primitivists, especially Marc Chagall (see Jacek Kopciński, "Teatr z makaty," in *PB* 251). On cubism and impressionism in Białoszewski's ballads, see Stanisław Dan-Bruzda, "*Obroty rzeczy* Mirona Białoszewskiego," *Pamiętnik Literacki* 4 (1961): 468.

67. Białoszewski's manner of reading his work was highly theatrical. Even narrative pieces were enunciated in a manner that made them sound like a stage performance. His poetry readings often involved singing and melorecitations. Theatricalization and self-theatricalization were also integral parts of Białoszewski's creative process, especially in the 1970s, when he tested his works while performing them in private readings and taped his writing to let it "go through the ear," to use Białoszewski's expression about the process of reading and taping the *Memoir* in order to revise it before he finalized it. See Zbigniew Taranienko, *Rozmowy z pisarzami* (Warsaw: Wiedza Powszechna, 1986), 399.

68. On the problems of authorship, see Stanisław Prószyński, "Poezja, teatr, muzyka," in *Miron: Wspomnienia o poecie,* ed. Kirchner; and Jacek Kopciński, *Gramatyka i mistyka* (Warsaw: Instytut Badań Literackich, 1997). The plays from the period of the Theater on Tarczyńska Street and the Separate Theater weren't published until 1971.

69. Kirchner, *Miron: Wspomnienia o poecie,* 194.

70. The publication of the *Memoir* and Hering's experience of reading it, according to Ludmiła Murawska, triggered the reconciliation between the two friends and former collaborators; one can imagine that the *Memoir* was for Hering a realization of his artistic precepts.

71. One of the interesting essays on the features of memory as represented in the *Memoir* (although understandably without employing the vocabulary of the traumatic not yet available for cultural criticism) is Małgorzata Czermińska's "Opowiedzieć powstanie, opowiedzieć zniszczenie: O *Pamiętniku* Mirona Białoszewskiego," in *Literatura wobec wojny i okupacji,* ed. Michał Głowiński and Janusz Sławiński (Wrocław: Zakład Narodowy Imienia Ossolińskich, 1976), 269–90.

72. "Przez jedno mgnienie powstanie. Podwórko po bombardowaniu. Rozłupki, dechy, słońce. Te ulice, Hoże, Wilcze" (*SZC* 233).

73. I discuss the concept of "living-through" ("przeżycie") in greater detail in chapter 1.

74. Michael Rothberg, *Traumatic Realism: The Demands of Holocaust Representation* (Minneapolis: University of Minnesota Press, 2000), 6.

75. Neither are these transmissions reserved only for the victims. Germany's struggle with its past as perpetrators in the postwar period is a good example, as are Poland's post-1989 developments. In both cases we observe the pluralization of subject positions vis-à-vis the victimhood, for instance, in a better understanding of the plethora of Polish attitudes toward Jews during the German occupation. In Communist times, this topic was homogenized under the label of collective "victimhood."

76. By institutional level, I mean public institutions, like the Museum of the Warsaw Uprising, whose mission is to create public awareness, knowledge, and memory of the event.

77. Žižek, *Looking Awry*, 12.

78. One could see such tendencies even in most influential theorists who seem at times transfixed by the idea of suffering and often reflect their fascination in the performative style of their writing. I think here, for instance, about such passages as Giorgio Agamben's introduction to *Remnants of Auschwitz,* Cathy Caruth's treatment of the victim in the introduction to *Unclaimed Experience,* or even Claude Lanzmann's insistence on reenactments of traumatic experience in some scenes of *Shoah.*

79. Binjamin Wilkomirski, *Fragments: Memories of a Wartime Childhood* (New York: Schocken Books, 1996).

80. See, for instance, the treatment of "framework of reference" in Shoshana Felman and Dori Laub, *Testimony: Crises of Witnessing in Literature, Psychoanalysis, and History* (New York: Routledge, 1992).

81. Rothberg, *Traumatic Realism*, 9.

82. After the publication, Białoszewski received an award from the Ministry of Art and Culture.

83. Rothberg extensively discusses this stretch between the extension of the normal and the rupture of the normal; Holocaust studies were divided between supporters of the incomprehensibility and incommensurability of the "radical evil" and supporters of the "banality of evil" inscribed in the structures of normality (for instance, bureaucracy). Rothberg attributes this divide to disciplinary characteristics: writers and filmmakers tend to present the traumatic as breaking the existing frameworks of reference (e.g., Elie Wiesel, Primo Levi, Claude Lanzmann) while historians or sociologists see the radical as an extension or evolution of normality, as in bureaucratic structures (e.g., Hanna Arendt, David Goldhagen, Zygmunt Bauman). See *Traumatic Realism*, 1–17.

84. *O* 7.

85. Białoszewski often creates situations with the connotations of surveil-

lance, which constitutes part of his nonchalant political resonance that deserves a separate and extensive treatment. For instance, in the volume title *Donosy rzeczywistości*, "donos" means literally "denunciations" and adds a twist to an account of quotidian non-happenings. Barańczak discusses various possibilities of translating *Donosy rzeczywistości*. Depending on how we understand the syntax of the expression, it can mean "reality's denunciations" or "denunciations to reality," or if we prefer to maintain a journalistic connotation, "reality's reports" or "reports to reality" (*PB* 14).

86. *DR* 280.

87. Maurice Blanchot, *The Infinite Conversation*, trans. Susan Hanson (Minneapolis: University of Minnesota Press, 1993), 238.

88. Julian Przyboś, "Nowy poeta," in *Linia i gwar: Szkice* (Cracow: Wydawnictwo Literackie, 1959), 173.

89. Or, to use the expression by Jerzy Kwiatkowski, between being abulic (inert) and liturgic (i.e., sacralizing). "Abulia i liturgia" ("Abulia and Liturgy") is the title of Kwiatkowski's well-known essay on Białoszewski's poetry in *Klucze do wyobraźni*.

90. Each of these languages serves a different function. For instance, colloquial language describes street life and the narrator's desire to lose himself in the "density" ("gęściocha") of the crowd, whereas children's language often serves to describe the narrator's desire to withdraw from the crowd and hide in his bed. It is important to note, however, that although this typology has been widely used, Barańczak published it in 1974 and therefore had access to only a portion of Białoszewski's small narrations; the majority of Barańczak's material comes from Białoszewski's pre-*Memoir* poetry and the *Memoir* itself.

91. Głowiński, "Białoszewskiego gatunki codzienne," in *PB* 146.

92. I agree with Piotr Sobolczyk—although he stated this specifically within the parameters of his interests in Białoszewski's homosexuality—that what mattered to these critics was "how" things are said and not who says them (authorial position) and what actually is said (topic).

93. Anna Sobolewska, "'Lepienie widoku z domysłu': Percepcja świata w prozie Mirona Białoszewskiego," in *PB* 118.

94. *PB* 128.

95. Marian Stala, "Czy Białoszewski jest poetą metafizycznym," in *PB* 105.

96. The attention to Białoszewski's epistemology continues in more recent philosophically inclined interpretations. See, for instance, a Heideggerian reading of Białoszewski's subjectivity in Adrian Gleń's *"W tej latarni . . .": Późna twórczość Mirona Białoszewskiego w perspektywie hermeneutycznej* (Opole: Universytet Opolski, 2004).

97. I am alluding to the title of Anna Sobolewska's book, *Mistyka dnia powszedniego* (Warsaw: OPEN, 1992).

98. As pointed out by Anna Sobolewska, the concept of "omnia ubique"

reaches back to the mystical tradition of the fullness of the world in each moment of time and point of space. See Sobolewska, *Maksymalnie udana egzystencja* (Warsaw: Instytut Badań Literackich, 1997), 59.

99. Borkowska's plea not to idealize Białoszewski in her "Pędy, rytmy: Jeszcze o Białoszewskim" (*Teksty drugie* 5 [1995]: 151) is supported by Joanna Orska in her speculations on Białoszewski's "secret diary" ("Życie jako happening: O artystyczności 'tajnego dziennika'" in *Białoszewski przed dziennikiem,* by Wojciech Browarny and Adam Poprawa [Cracow: Universitas, 2010], 97–115).

100. Orska, "Życie jako happening," 99, 109.

101. I am thinking here particularly about Piotr Sobolczyk's articles. Piotr Sobolczyk, "Hermetyczne pornografie Białoszewskiego," *Teksty drugie* 6 (2006): 165–81; as well as "Homobiografia: Miron Białoszewski," *Pogranicza* 6 (2008): 15–32. Marian Bielecki's article from *Białoszewski przed dziennikiem* follows in Sobolczyk's footsteps.

102. "Gdzież bowiem, jak nie tutaj mógłby kultywować 'bycie sobie jednym' nikomu nie podległe, wiec autentyczne?" Janusz Sławiński, "Białoszewski: Sukces wycofania sie," introduction to *Miron Białoszewski, Wiersze* (Warsaw: Państwowy Instytut Wydawniczy, 1976), 17.

103. Sobolewska, *Maksymalnie udana egzystencja,* 10.

104. Olgierd Wołyński, "Plac Dąbrowskiego" in *Miron: Wspomnienia o poecie,* ed. Kirchner, 202. Equally unclear is Wołyński's remark about "Adam," another important man in Białoszewski's life. Ibid. 192.

105. "Miron ogromnie potrzebował czegoś w rodzaju rodziny—to zesztą spostrzeżenie Ludwika [Heringa] i do tych facetów przywiązywał się jak do rodziny" (*Wspomnienia o poecie,* ed. Kirchner, 192). Wołyński's remark resonates with what Anna Sobolewska recalls as once heard from Białoszewski: "for no one am I the first person" ("dla nikogo nie jestem pierwszy").

106. "Oczywiście, byli wybitni ludzie, którzy się nie angażowali, ale u Mirona jakoś mi to przeszkadzało. Przeszkadzał mi jego strach przed milicją. I naraz spojrzałem na jego twórczość jako na taki azyl. Że to nie jest samo z siebie, ale że to jest sposób na to, żeby bezboleśnie przeżyć życie, pisząc takie wiersze, które w okresie socrealizmu były jakimś tam odstępstwem, ale później zrobiły się wygodnym azylem. To był niesprawiedliwy stosunek, ja rozumiem." Olgierd Kirchner, *Wspomnienia o poecie,* 200.

107. German Ritz, *Nić w labiryncie pożądania: Gender i płeć w literaturze polskiej od romantyzmu do postmodernizmu,* trans. Bronisław Drąg, Andrzej Kopacki, and Małgorzata Łukasiewicz (Warsaw: Wiedza Powszechna, 2002), 61.

108. See Sobolczyk, "Hermetyczne pornografie Mirona Białoszewskiego," 165–81; and "Homobiografia: Miron Białoszewski." An aspect of Sobolczyk's research that I find particularly interesting is his revision of Białoszewski's image of an idiosyncratic "dandy."

109. The unpublished diary, short fragments of which have been published

in various magazines and newspapers throughout the years, has already become the subject of an edited volume, *Białoszewski przed dziennikiem*, whose contributions in terms of issues of homosexuality (as in articles by Marian Bielecki and Wojciech Browarny) I address in chapter 3.

110. Michał Witkowski, *Lubiewo* (Cracow: Wydawnictwo ha!art, 2005); in English translation, *Lovetown*, trans. William Martin (London: Portobello Books, 2010).

111. A critical study by Elżbieta Winiecka, *Białoszewski sylleptyczny* (Poznań: "Wydawnictwo Poznańskie Studia Polonistyczne," 2006), focuses on a sylleptic reading of Białoszewski's construction of narratorial subjectivity and draws from earlier work by Ryszyrd Nycz. However, Winiecka's theoretical approach (substantial and insightful as it is) again eliminates the socio-politico-cultural aspect of Białoszewski's work.

112. Barthes in his last lecture, in which he presents a typology of the narrative "I"s, disclaims his notions of "scriptor" and "the death of an author." Roland Barthes, *The Preparation of the Novel: Lecture Courses and Seminars at the Collège de France* (New York: Columbia University Press, 2011).

113. Stanisław Burkot, *Miron Białoszewski* (Warsaw: Wydawnictwo Szkolne i Pedagogiczne, 1992), 18. What is striking in such approaches is that Białoszewski is inadvertently credited with a full, utopian autonomy, in which this psychosomatically based separateness was "first of all, an individual gesture, the role played according to his own scenario."

114. Rosiek, "Pamiętnik z półgrobu," in *PB* 132.

CHAPTER 1

1. President Lech Kaczyński died on April 10, 2010, when a plane carrying the president, the first lady, and scores of military and political elites crashed near Smoleńsk, Russia.

2. Norman Davies, *Rising '44: The Battle for Warsaw* (London: Macmillan, 2003).

3. Główny Urząd Statystyczny, 2004. The political instrumentalization of the museum after President Kaczyński's death as an example of his—and by extension, his political party's—loyalty to Polish national identity and Polish historical memory is another indicator that invoking the uprising can still have great political cachet and be publicly translated as a litmus test of patriotism.

4. For a clear survey of the political treatment of the uprising in Communist Poland, see Davies, *Rising '44*; and Tomasz Łubieński, *Ani tryumf ani zgon: Szkice o powstaniu warszawskim* (Warsaw: Wydawnictwo "Nowy Świat," 2004).

5. There is an ongoing debate about the state of preparations for the uprising. To protect Warsaw and for strategic reasons, until July 1944 the city of Warsaw was excluded from Operation "Storm" (Operacja Burza), a large mili-

tary operation initiated in January 1944 by the Home Army to liberate the eastern part of the country from the Germans before the Red Army entered and claimed it for Russia. The sudden change of plans in July 1944 meant that much of the ammunition that had been first gathered in Warsaw and later smuggled out of the capital to the countryside to support the operation did not make it back to the city to help the uprising. Studies of the military and political complexities of the uprising are numerous. In English, particularly well known are Janusz Zawodny, *Nothing but Honour: The Story of the Warsaw Uprising 1944* (Stanford, Calif.: Hoover Institution, 1978); and Jan Ciechanowski, *The Warsaw Rising of 1944* (London: Cambridge University Press, 1974). Davies's *Rising '44* is an example of a recent historical work that combines the history of the event itself with the history of its memory and its evolution in various periods of the Communist regime in Poland. What is particularly appealing in Davies's treatment of the uprising is his inclusion of the uprising's culture (e.g., songs and poems), which, still popular in Poland, belong to the carriers of the event's myth.

6. The British historian Alan Bullock ironically calls this aiding of Germans by Russians "the final act in their parallel policies of destroying the existing leadership of the Polish nation" as initiated through the Ribbentrop–Molotov pact of 1939. See Bullock, *Hitler and Stalin: Parallel Lives* (London: Fontana, 1998), 935.

7. Davies's *Rising '44* includes a discussion of various stages of the treatment of the uprising in the Communist period.

8. One of the most fascinating conflations was that of the Warsaw Ghetto Uprising of 1943 with the Warsaw Uprising of 1944. The language of propaganda and the educational system in Communist Poland insisted on the obliteration of difference between the Polish and Jewish wartime experiences, merging the two into a gestalt of "Polish" experience of suffering and resistance. The Ghetto Uprising was historically decontextualized from the complexities of Polish-Jewish relations and presented as a heroic *Polish* battle with the Nazis. Such conflation can be seen as early as 1948 in a well-known film by Aleksander Ford, *Border Street* (*Ulica Graniczna*), which includes a portrayal of the Ghetto Uprising and projects Jewish resistance onto the iconography of the Warsaw Uprising. I thank Ofer Dynes for his insightful remarks on the merging of Polish and Jewish visual, as well as aural, cues in the film (private conversation).

9. On the other side of the interpretative spectrum, there is a view that the uprising was justified by its psychological impact. The scale of the uprising and the boundless dedication of its participants showed Stalin and Soviet Russia that Poles are unpredictable when it comes to defending their sovereignty. This, the proponents of this view claim, stopped Stalin from transforming Poland into, as the popular idiom has it, the "seventeenth republic," while fear of a common uprising in Poland prevented Soviet military intervention during several periods of civic unrest in postwar Poland.

10. As the uprising is called by its prominent historian and a military participant, Jan Ciechanowski ("Polityczne i militarne przyczyny powstania warszawskiego," in *Powstanie warszawskie w historiografii i literaturze 1944–1994,* ed. Zygmunt Mańkowski and Jerzy Święch [Wydawnictwo Marii Curie-Skłodowskiej, 1996], 9). Ciechanowski, who emmigrated to Great Britain, dedicated much of his academic career to studying the uprising and consistently deemed the uprising a political failure to recognize the international context of the moment, that is, the Allies' position on Poland vis-à-vis Stalin, and a military miscalculation of its direct leaders.

11. Maria Dąbrowska, *Szkice o Conradzie* (Warsaw: Czytelnik, 1974), 149.

12. Recent history shows us how important it is for Poles to have political events culturally validated via "the uprising tradition" ("tradycja powstańcza"). During the June 28, 2006, fiftieth anniversary celebrations of the "Poznań June events" ("poznańskie wypadki czerwcowe")—the bloody demonstrations against the regime in June 1956—official acknowledgment and recognition of these "events" as initiating the anti-Communist opposition involved changing the name from "the Poznań June events" to "powstanie poznańskiego czerwca" ("the Poznań June uprising"). This new name, grammatically awkward in Polish, links the local character of the event, through the name of the city, to the venerated tradition of nineteenth-century pan-Polish uprisings, through the name of the month. The function of this new name is to ennoble the Poznań events by linguistically assimilating them into a larger heroic pattern of Polish history.

13. *PPW* 65. Indeed, there is something telling in the fact that the name of this uprising (like that of the Warsaw Ghetto Uprising of 1943) includes the name of the city whose total destruction is inscribed in the memory of the event.

14. Dominick LaCapra, *Writing History, Writing Trauma* (Baltimore: Johns Hopkins University Press, 2001), 23.

15. LaCapra, *Writing History*, 23.

16. This was in spite of the fact that, as Łubieński himself notes, many critical voices came from people who had nothing to do with Communist propaganda, to mention only such an iconic figure of Polish military valor as General Anders. Łubieński, *Ani tryumf ani zgon,* 50.

17. From August 5 to August 7, during the pacification of the Wola neighborhood of Warsaw (the "rzeź Woli"—"the Wola slaughter"), 60,000 Varsovians were shot and killed in one day. Part of these systematic executions included targeting hospitals where Germans, supported by RONA troops, executed the patients, burning many of them alive.

18. The insurrectionists used bottles filled with gasoline ("Molotov cocktails") as homemade firebombs. There are many accounts of people burning to death due to tripping and falling while carrying a bottle, causing it to explode. One of the recurring adjectives of the *Memoir* is "alive/living" ("żywe") applied equally to survival as to the modes of death (e.g., "żywe ognie," "living flames").

19. Maurice Halbwachs, *The Collective Memory* (New York: Harper and Row, 1980).

20. That said, the museum is responsible for many important initiatives, to mention only the essential Archives of Oral History (Archiwum historii mówionej), which collects oral testimonies of the uprising's participants.

21. Maria Janion, "Wojna i forma" in *Płacz generała: Eseje o wojnie* (Warsaw: Wydawnictwo Sic!, 1998), 14.

22. See, for instance, the story "Lotna" by Wojciech Żukrowski, the author of the most negative review of Białoszewski's *Memoir.* The story serves for Janion as the prime example of the "uhlan western" (Janion, "Wojna" 11). It is striking how this romantic portrayal of the cavalry's attack merges death, rupture, and the sublime:

> Before my eyes flashed road maps, ambushes, and cavalry charges; above me, as though in the fluttering of the uhlan banner—something I might call inspiration. I saw how the cavalry captain pressed forward to the wicker fences, how Lotna [his horse] soared effortlessly into the air, drawing in her front legs and lifting him in a leap of crushing beauty. . . . My hand squeezing the saber's hilt grew damp. The high-pitched whistle of the bullets above my helmet only added to the beauty of this flight over the autumn field, just grazed by the hard sheen of the rising sun. My face froze in agonizing rapture. I regretted nothing. What's youth, what's love, when my nostrils were full of the smell of horse, of gunfire, of the hot blood I was to spill at any moment?

> Błyskały mi plany dróg, zasadzki i szarże, jakby z furkotem ułańskiego proporczyka krążyło nade mną coś, co nazwałbym natchnieniem. Widziałem jak rotmistrz parł na plecione płoty, jak Lotna bez wysiłku wzbija się i podkuliwszy przednie nogi—wynosi go skokiem, pełnym dławiącego piękna. . . . Ręka ściskająca szablę zwilgotniała. Wysoki gwizd kuli nad hełmem przydawał tylko piękna temu lotowi ponad jesiennym polem, ledwie powleczonym szklanym blaskiem wstającego słońca. Twarz mi stygła od bolesnego zachwytu. Nie żałowałem niczego. Cóż młodość, miłość, gdy miałem nozdrza pełne zapachu konia, wystrzałów i krwi gorącej, którą za chwilę rozleję. (Żukrowski, "Lotna" in *Z wrześniowych dni: antologia opowiadań o wojnie 1939,* ed. W. Maciąg [Poznań: Wydawnictwo Poznańskie, 1969], 14, 19–20.)

23. The uprising is sometimes referred to as the "Polish Thermopylae" in reference to what is arguably the most famous battle of the ancient world in 480 B.C.E, in which the Spartans, greatly outnumbered by Persians, fought a battle they were certain to lose in order to stall the Persian invasion. Simonides's famous inscription at the site of the battle ("Go tell the Spartans, passerby, that here obedient to their laws we lie") applied to the uprising is another manifestation of Conradian ethics.

24. Often called "a father of Polish reportage," Wańkowicz during the interwar period wrote a reportage novel, *Na tropach Smętka* (1936), in which he described the escalating tension between the German and Polish populations of East Prussia. During the war he was a chronicler of Gen. Anders's army and was especially recognized for his account of the battle of Monte Cassino (*Monte Cassino,* 1945), a book which until 1989 was published in Poland only in a shortened and censored version.

25. I stress here the representation of the uprising rather than war as such because it is important to distinguish between different wartime experiences and their modes of representation. It is significant, however, that the publication of Tadeusz Borowski's writings about Auschwitz—*Pożegnanie z Marią* and *Kamienny świat* (*Farewell to Maria* and *The World of Stone,* both published in 1948)—caused a scandal in Polish literature comparable to that of Białoszewski's *Memoir.* Borowski's works are also examples of the refusal to attribute any redeeming value to suffering; however, in contrast to Białoszewski, who shuns any historiosophic statements, Borowski diagnoses the "concentrationary universe" (to use David Rousset's expression from *Les jours de nôtre mort*) as the ultimate failure of Western civilization. However useful the comparison, Borowski's works belong to a different genre of "camp literature."

26. Eric Santner, "History Beyond the Pleasure Principle: Some Thoughts on the Representation of Trauma," in *Probing the Limits of Representation: Nazism and the Final Solution,* ed. Saul Friedlander (Cambridge, Mass.: Harvard University Press), 144. Santner discusses narrative fetishism in the context of postwar Germany's inability to confront the guilt of its Nazi past.

27. It is this sovereignty that Marek Edelman, a leader of the Warsaw Ghetto Uprising, reminisces with envy when comparing the two uprisings decades later. Edelman also comments on the myth of the "beautiful death" as an essential ingredient of Polish culture (see the interview with Edelman in Hanna Krall, *To Outwit God* [Evanston, Ill.: Northwestern University Press, 1992], 145–46).

28. The erotic charge of the myth of the uprising is captured by Darek Foks and Zbigniew Libera in their 2005 artwork *Co robi łączniczka* (2005; *What Does the Messenger Girl Do*). Consisting of sixty-three prosaic vignettes with the imaginary monologues of the eponymous messenger girl, *Co robi łączniczka* juxtaposes the musings of the messenger girl that have little to do with the military reality of the uprising with the sexy images of film stars (e.g., Sophia Loren, Anita Ekberg) superimposed onto the images of the ruined Warsaw. This subversive fantasy of the uprising, fittingly called by the Reuters agency "sex and martyrdom," is a rare example of a productive "working through" of not just the event, but the very core of its myth and its subversive "necrophilic" charge. Foks and Libera belong to the post-memorial generation, and their campy aesthetics diagnoses the transmission of the myth of the uprising in the age of mass media as a hyper-reality, which often verges on kitsch.

29. "Acting out" and "working through" are the recurring notions in numerous works by Dominick LaCapra, a historian who probes the limits of psychoanalytical vocabulary in the studies of the past and who promotes the dynamic view of memorial processes and conceptualizes "acting out" as a part of "working through."

30. Such a confirmation seemed at the core of the official celebrations of the uprising's sixtieth anniversary.

31. Among various strategies for effacing the memory of the uprising by Communist propaganda was allowing commemorations of the uprising to take place, but on the dates symbolically associated with the new regime.

32. Such a vision of ideologically driven, "unspecific" history was particularly detrimental for the educational system. Some young Poles found an alternative model of history taught at home, but this, again, replicated the structure of system and counter-system and reinforced redemptive narratives.

33. In her analysis of the "uprising myth" in Polish domestic and émigré theater, Halina Filipowicz demonstrates that the main difference between the playwrights is evident only in their stance on the political interpretation of the uprising. What remains constant in all these works is their direct or indirect insistence on the reader's and the viewer's political self-identification. Filipowicz, "Mit powstańczy w dramacie krajowym i emigracyjnym," in *Powstanie warszawskie w historiografii i literaturze, 1944–1994,* ed. Zygmunt Mańkowski and Jerzy Święch (Lublin: Wydawnictwo Uniwersytetu Marii Curie-Skłodowskiej, 1996), 167–95.

34. Unfortunately, while Maria Janion wrote her "Wojna i forma," Ścibor-Rylski's novel was not yet published. Janion discusses the expressionistic mode by referring to a classic World War I work of Henri Barbusse, *Under Fire* (*Le Feu,* 1917). The monumentalization of war as a hypnotic force devouring human identity produces, according to Janion, a mirror reflection of the romantics' beauty of war. If the romantic clichés of war overfamiliarize the subject, the expressionistic ones demonize it while carrying war's foreignness to the extreme. Unveiling the "ugliness" of war with expressionist stylistics means focusing only on those aspects of the phenomenon that can be presented as farthest removed from everyday life. Janion's claims about expressionism representing the war as a drastic rupture in the system of values and reducing the war to a gigantic slaughterhouse could have been, in some aspects, applied to Ścibor-Rylski's writing as well.

35. It is telling that a 2006 DVD published by the Museum of the Warsaw Uprising under a title suggesting the focus on civilian life ("Beyond Fighting: Everyday Life in the Warsaw Uprising"; "Poza walką: Życie codzienne w powstaniu warszawskim") does not contain a single testimony from a civilian survivor. More than six decades after the uprising, what is memorialized and institutionalized is predominantly the event's military aspect.

36. It is worth stressing that this contamination had some direct political implications. The testimonies of the insurrectionists consistently indicate that with the prolonged fighting and the bombardment of the city, the civilian population's support for the uprising was shifting to anger and resentment.

37. This is not to say that there are no literary works dedicated to the civilian experience (to mention only the treatment of the uprising in *Przygody człowieka myślącego* by Maria Dąbrowska [1970]). I look at the problem of representation from a more general perspective of cultural rhetoric, and such a rhetoric that would celebrate the desire for the preservation of life itself has not yet been developed in Polish culture. For some fundamental historical accounts of the civilian experience, see Władysław Bartoszewski, "Życie w powstańczej Warszawie," in *Ludność cywilna w powstaniu warszawskim,* ed. Czesław Madajczyk (Warsaw: Państwowy Instytut Wydawniczy, 1974); and Joanna K. M. Hanson's *The Civilian Population and the Warsaw Uprising of 1944* (Cambridge, Eng.: Cambridge University Press, 1982).

38. The *Memoir* (1970) was published at the exact midpoint of Białoszewski's career, counting from his literary debut in 1956 to his death in 1983. Although Białoszewski's first volume of poetry, *Obroty rzeczy* (1956; *The Revolution of Things*), had won the admiration of critics, his linguistic experiments in the ensuing volumes came to be considered a linguistic "storage room" ("rupieciarnia").

39. Thus remarked Stanisław Barańczak regarding the shift in the reception of Białoszewski's writing after the publication of the *Memoir* (Barańczak, *PB* 8–9).

40. Wojciech Żukrowski, "Mironek w powstaniu," *Nowe ksiażki* 19 (1970): 1191–94.

41. "Autor pokazuje siebie głupszym niż jest, to jego sprawa, natomiast, że robi to z ludnością, która nawet biernie uczestnicząc w powstaniu, w pełni emocjonalnie je przeżywała, angażowała się, ulegała falowaniu od rozpaczy po nadzieję, to powiedziałbym ostrożnie dalekie jest od prawdy."

42. "Ponieważ tacy stanowią większość, pozwólmyż im pożyć, na kartach tej powieści, pomyszkować za jedzeniem, poiskać wszy, przycisnąć dziewczynę i z ulgą westchnąć nad kopcen zgruzgotanej Warszawy—'dobrze, że to jeszcze nie my.' Bo to jest również jakaś prawda powstańczej Warszawy choć nie to chcielibyśmy przekazać jako dziedzictwo."

43. Kai Erikson, "Notes on Trauma and Community," in *Trauma: Explorations in Memory,* ed. Cathy Caruth (Baltimore: Johns Hopkins University Press, 1995), 183–200.

44. Susan J. Brison, "Trauma Narratives and the Remaking of the Self," in *Acts of Memory: Cultural Recall in the Present,* ed. Mieke Bal, Jonathan Crewe, and Leo Spitzer (Hanover, N.H.: University Press of New England, 1999), 39–55, 40.

45. Cathy Caruth, *Unclaimed Experience: Trauma, Narrative, and History* (Baltimore: Johns Hopkins University Press, 1996), 91.

46. There are many forms of such dissociations. For instance, a recurring image in the testimonies of rape victims is floating under the ceiling and watching what is happening to them "from the outside."

47. Caruth, *Unclaimed Experience,* 91.

48. Such a dissociative structure lies at the foundation of trauma theory as formulated by Freud. In *Mourning and Melancholia* Freud gives an example of a survivor of a train accident who leaves the accident unharmed yet later suffers from its psychological repercussions.

49. Judith Herman, *Trauma and Recovery* (New York: Basic Books, 1992), 1–47.

50. Lawrence L. Langer, *Holocaust Testimonies: The Ruins of Memory* (New Haven, Conn.: Yale University Press, 1991), 175.

51. Caruth, *Unclaimed Experience,* 151.

52. The need to accommodate the variety of traumatic experiences is a frequent theme in trauma studies, to mention only Kali Tal, *Worlds of Hurt: Reading the Literatures of Trauma* (Cambridge, Eng.: Cambridge University Press, 1996). Almost all books by Dominick LaCapra call for a more historically differentiated understanding of trauma, e.g., *Writing History, Writing Trauma* (Baltimore: Johns Hopkins University Press, 2001); *History and Memory After Auschwitz* (Ithaca, N.Y.: Cornell University Press, 1998).

53. Many of the theorists of trauma (e.g., Judith Herman, Bessela A. van der Kolk, and Onno van der Hart) employ Pierre Janet's distinction between traumatic, narrative, and habitual memory.

54. Full sublation is a utopian dream against which LaCapra repeatedly warns us. Rather than approach the traumatic and the narrative as "either-or," it is much more productive to look at their dynamics and the residue that the traumatic leaves on the victim's life even if it is worked through in a functional sense, that is, if the victim is able to lead a "normal" life with a basic sense of control over it.

55. Another important issue in trauma studies is the need to accommodate a more nuanced ethical vocabulary that would allow us, for instance, to distinguish within the vocabulary of trauma between the victim, witness, the bystander, and so on.

56. *MWU* 19.

57. Caruth, *Trauma: Explorations in Memory,* 4–5.

58. Barańczak, *Język poetycki Mirona Białoszewskiego,* 129.

59. Małgorzata Czermińska, "Opowiedzieć powstanie, opowiedzieć zniszczenie," in *Literatura wobec wojny i okupacji,* ed. Michał Głowiński and Janusz Sławiński (Wrocław: Zakład Narodowy Imienia Ossolińskich, 1976), 269–90.

60. As remarked by Janusz Sławiński in his analysis of the poem in "Miron Białoszewski 'Leżenia,'" in *Genologia polska,* ed. Ewa Miodońska-Brooks, Adam Kulawik, and Marian Tatara (Warsaw: Państwowe Wydawnictwo Naukowe: 1983), 528. Many of Białoszewski's "genres" repeat this pattern, e.g., "walk-diary" ("spacerownik"), "ojcownik" ("father-diary"), etc.

61. Joanna Orska makes this suggestion when she compares the function of the *Memoir* to the function of the "herbary" which collects various herbs. The "herbary" is a collection which not only displays the specimens, but also directs our attention to the process of collecting. Similarly, "*Memoir*" points both to the result—memories—and the process of bringing them to light. Joanna Orska, "Życie jako happening: O artystyczności 'tajnego dziennika,'" in *Białoszewski przed dziennikiem*, Browarny and Poprawa, 97–115.

62. *MWU* 52.

63. *PPW* 46. Emphasis in original.

64. Białoszewski's privileging of speech over writing as the medium of presence and participation is different from Derrida's critique of the logocentric bias. The difference lies, partly, in Białoszewski's insistence on the communal aspect of literature as an act of participation. He adhered to the ethical principles of oral culture in his own frequent performances of his own texts.

65. Van Der Kolk and van der Hart claim, for instance, that traumatic returns, fragmentary but repetitive, have a cumulative function and allow the victim to "complete" the memory of the experience (Caruth, *Trauma: Explorations in Memory,* 176).

66. Or, literally, a "talked *Memoir*." Madeline Levine also favors a translation of "gadanie" as "talking" in her English rendering of the *Memoir,* although "chatting" would better render the informality of the word.

67. Polish critics (e.g., Małgorzata Czermińska, Stanisław Barańczak) have observed this use of a double narrator and have noted that the dominant one is "naive," uses the present tense, and seems unaware of how the uprising developed, while the second, "experienced," narrator (or meta-narrator) reminds the reader that the *Memoir* was written years after the events. Czermińska perceives the 23-year gap between the uprising and its account as crucial for the *Memoir*'s concept of time and genre. Although she does not employ theoretical distinctions between Białoszewski's modes of memory and thus does not quite accommodate the crucial delay between the event and its account, in her reflections she intuitively expresses what years later theorists would label as the structure of the traumatic experience.

68. *PPW* 5; *MWU* 19.

69. The verb "latać" colloquially signifies "to run around, to scurry, to dash, to flit" and is probably the most frequently used word in the text (as Levine notes, the word appears with different prefixes approximately 250 times in this

colloquial meaning [Levine's "Translator's Introduction" to the *Memoir,* 17]). Janion pays particular attention to the pervasive presence of "latać" and its semantic variants in order to demonstrate that Białoszewski's approach is phenomenological rather than empirical, as others have maintained. For Janion, the *Memoir* is about the phenomenology of motion, in which the frantic "flying" of civilians contrasts with the topos of the "heroic flight" ("bohaterski lot"; Janion, "Wojna i forma," 47).

70. *MWU* 5.

71. Taranienko, *Rozmowy z pisarzami,* 399.

72. Decades after the Holocaust, autobiographical works are still being written by its survivors (as well as the second and third generations), such as works by Ruth Kluger and Charlotte Delbo; in the Polish context, Michał Głowiński and Wilhelm Dichter, and so on. In a non-Holocaust context, Kurt Vonnegut's *Slaughterhouse Five* (1968), which incidentally is delayed by a similar period of time as Białoszewski's *Memoir,* also attests to an immediate desire to write about the traumatic event (in Vonnegut's case, the bombing of Dresden) but the impossibility of doing so until some two decades after the experience.

73. Marita Sturken, "Narratives of Recovery: Repressed Memory as Cultural Memory," in *Acts of Memory,* ed. Mieke Bal, Jonathan Crewe, and Leo Spitzer (Hanover, N.H.: University Press of New England, 1999), 231–49, 235.

74. Caruth, *Trauma: Explorations in Memory,* 152–53.

75. Białoszewski, "To, w czym się jest," in *Rozmowy z pisarzami,* by Zbigniew Taranienko (Warsaw: Wiedza Powszechna, 1986), 32.

76. Not being able to shake off the surplus of traumatic memory, its "toomuchness" can, as van der Kolk notes, cause the trauma victims to live in parallel realities. One reality is that of traumatic returns (e.g., flashbacks and nightmares); the other is their "real" life. See Bessela A. van der Kolk and Onno van der Hart, "The Intrusive Past: The Flexibility of Memory and the Engraving of Trauma," in *Trauma: Explorations in Memory,* ed. Cathy Caruth (Baltimore: Johns Hopkins University Press, 1995), 158–83, 177.

77. In the post-*Memoir* works, a sequential mode can be seen in the seriality of the small narrations. It is quite possible that this shift from writing poetry before the *Memoir* to writing episodic prose afterward was influenced by Białoszewski-the-survivor's memory pattern, which influenced his tendency toward sequentiality.

78. *MWU* 67.

79. *PPW* 64.

80. In a different context, the word "kupa" also means "poop." "Kupa konstrukcyjna" ("the pile of construction" or "the structural heap") is perhaps not an accidental synthesis of the abject and the literary to describe an organizing prin-

ciple of the *Memoir.* Indeed, the work constantly negotiates between the imperative to represent a wide range of somatic experiences in the event (including the scatalogical) and the demands of literary representation.

81. Caruth, *Trauma: Explorations in Memory,* 154. Emphasis in original. Indeed, much of the therapeutic effect of narrative is the disappearance of the incomprehensibility of the traumatic event. For trauma survivors, the disappearance of the event's incomprehensibility is often marked by ethical ambivalence. Healing signifies leaving the realm of the traumatic memory; maintaining such a memory allows one to continue to share the same realm as those who did not survive. As a Vietnam War veteran says, "I do not want to take drugs for my nightmares, because I must remain a memorial to my dead friends." Quoted in ibid., vii.

82. *MWU* 205.

83. *PPW* 228.

84. "Szamotanie pamięci," which I translated as "scuffle of memory" (but "shuffle of memory" would work as well) Madeline Levine translates as "the difficulty of remembering." Although overall this is what Białoszewski expresses, what is really at stake in the *Memoir* (and what presents an enormous challenge to any translator) is an inscription onto each of Białoszewski's linguistic and narrative choices of the dynamic and oppressive nature of memory.

85. *PPW* 241; *MWU* 217.

86. *MWU* 96.

87. *PPW* 98.

88. *MWU* 91–92.

89. *PPW* 93.

90. *MWU* 59–60.

91. *PPW* 55.

92. *MWU* 48–49.

93. *PPW* 41.

94. As Jonathan Shay observes, "the destruction of time"—that is, erasing the past and foreshortening the future—"is an inner survival skill" (quoted in Susan J. Brison, "Trauma Narratives and the Remaking of the Self," in *Acts of Memory,* ed. Bal, Crewe, and Spitzer, 43).

95. *PPW* 85.

96. *MWU* 52.

97. *PPW* 45–46.

98. This aspect of Białoszewski's work is discussed by many critics. Jacek Kopciński's discussion of the theatrical charge of Białoszewski's writing in *Gramatyka i mistyka* is particularly illuminating. Jacek Kopciński, *Gramatyka i mistyka: Wprowadzenie w teatralną osobność Mirona Białoszewskiego* (Warsaw: Instytut Badań Literackich, 1997).

99. Taranienko, *Rozmowy z pisarzami,* 399.

100. Janusz Wilhelmi, *Wstęp* [Preface], *Pamiętnik z powstania warszawskiego,* by Miron Białoszewski (Warsaw: Państwowy Instytut Wydawniczy, 1970), 5–7.

101. As in Jacek Trznadel, *Płomień obdarzony rozumem: Poezja w poezji i poza poezją* (Warsaw: Czytelnik, 1978).

102. The precision of this seemingly chaotic language is obvious the moment one tries to translate Białoszewski. The French translator of the *Memoir,* Erik Veaux, in his interview with Tadeusz Sobolewski, describes how struck he was by Białoszewski's control over his language (*Gazeta Wyborcza,* March 21, 2002, 10).

103. In reviewing the *Memoir,* Maciej Szybist ("Warszawskie powstanie nowego porządku," *Miesięcznik Literacki* 9 [1970]: 140) emphasizes the condensation of colloquial diction and the resulting effect of tension and release.

104. The ability of the oral communication to trigger such interiorization is described in, for instance, Walter J. Ong, *Orality and Literacy: The Technologizing of the Word* (London: Routledge, 2002), 31–77.

105. Taranienko, *Rozmowy z pisarzami,* 411.

106. Julia Kristeva, *Powers of Horror: An Essay on Abjection,* trans. Leon S. Roudiez (New York: Columbia University Press, 1982), 196–97.

107. *MWU* 125.

108. *PPW* 133.

109. For instance, "pac! pac! My z podniesionymi kołnierzami. Co za głupi instynkt? Skaczemy. Pac-pac! . . . Szszu-brzrzum. Osypy," *PPW* 78. ("Ping! Ping! We raise our collars. What kind of stupid instinct?! We jump. Ping! Ping! . . . Ssssshh-booom. Falling plaster," *MWU* 78–79).

110. *MWU* 69.

111. *MWU* 69–70.

112. *PPW* 67–68.

113. *MWU* 70.

114. *PPW* 68.

115. *MWU* 135.

116. *PPW* 144.

117. *PB* 10.

118. I refer to a playful metaphor in the beginning of *Hums, Lumps, Threads* (*Szumy, zlepy, ciągi,* 1976) through which the narrator comments on the truth-value of his stories (10).

119. *MWU* 159; *PPW* 173.

120. *PPW* 5; *MWU* 19.

121. *MWU* 143; *PPW* 154.

122. *MWU* 74; *PPW* 73.

123. *MWU* 35; *PPW* 25 ("Kojarzyło mi się to z różnościami. Z kotletami w

bułce i utytłanymi w czymś. Jeden pamiętam naprawdę z kością, jedną, wystającą. Reszta utytłana").

124. Piotr Sobolczyk, "Hermetyczne pornografie Białoszewkiego," 175.

125. Michel Foucault in his famous essay "What Is an Author?" talks about authorship as "the author-function." See Michel Foucault, *Language, Counter-Memory, Practice: Selected Essays and Interviews* (Ithaca, N.Y.: Cornell University Press, 1977), 113–38.

126. *MWU* 206.

127. *PPW* 228.

128. A more straightforward precluding one can see in the following passage preceded by the narrator restraining himself from discussing the Warsaw population's deliberations on "how to welcome the Soviets" ("jak witać Sowietów! Nie mam zamiaru wchodzić w dalsze roztrząsanie i tak wyjaśnionych już rzeczy. To zaznaczam. Bo konieczne. Radio angielskie też nas nieraz denerwowało," *PPW* 203).

CHAPTER 2

1. After the publication of the *Memoir* (1970), Białoszewski published *Donosy rzeczywistości* (1973; *Reporting Reality*), *Szumy, zlepy, ciągi* (1976; *Hums, Lumps, Threads*), *Poezje wybrane* (1976; *Selected Poems*), *Miron Białoszewski* (1977; in the series Polish Poets), *Zawał* (1977; *The Heart Attack*), *Wiersze* (1978; *Poems*), *Odczepić się* (1978; *Got Lost*), *Wiersze wybrane i dobrane* (1980; *Poems Selected and Matched*), *Rozkurz* (1980; *Dust*), and *Przepowiadanie sobie* (1981; *Foretelling to Yourself*). The following works appeared posthumously: *Stara proza. Nowe wiersze* (*Old Prose. New Poems*, 1984), *Oho* (*A-ha*, 1985), *Obmapywanie Europy, czyli dziennik okrętowy. AAAmeryka. Ostatnie wiersze* (*Mapping Europe or a Ship's Log. AAAmeryka. Last Poems*, 1988), *Konstancin* (*Konstancin*, 1991), *Chamowo* (*Chamowo*, 2009), and *Tajny dziennik* (2012).

2. *PB* 10.

3. "Białoszewski już nie tylko lingwista i eksperymentator, ale jednocześnie wielki i odkrywczy realista—zaczyna się nieco później [that is, from the *Memoir* on], w roku 1973." Barańczak, "Rzeczywistość Białoszewskiego," in *PB* 9.

4. Głowiński, in *PB* 146.

5. Głowiński, in *PB* 148, 150–51.

6. Głowiński, in *PB* 149.

7. These traumatic stitches can also be viewed as a form of "points de capiton" (literally: "upholstery buttons" or "quilting stitches") which, according to Lacan, become the points where, in the constant movement of the signifying chain, the meaning is "pinned down"—the signifier momentarily pins down the signified. These quilting stitches ensure basic psychic survival by stopping a proliferation of constantly slipping signifiers. Traumatic moments, which invade Bia-

łoszewski's everyday, could be viewed, paradoxically, as the anchoring points in his constant movement of an open-ended everyday.

8. Michał Głowiński, comparing small narrations to *fait divers*, reminds us (by referring to Roland Barthes's statements on the structure of *fait divers*) that genre-wise *fait divers* are characterized by ambivalence; they oscillate between the rational and irrational, the comprehensible and the incomprehensible. See Głowiński, "Małe narracje Mirona Białoszewskiego," 319–38. This ambivalence is also important for Maria Janion's interpretation of Białoszewski's *Memoir* in "Wojna i forma."

9. Barańczak also mentions as a major difference the *Memoir*'s more coherent narration as opposed to the lapses of the small narrations. *PB* 11.

10. This utilization of poetic techniques in the *Memoir*'s orality and diction has been discussed by several critics (e.g., Maria Janion, Małgorzata Czermińska, and Stanisław Barańczak) and has become a commonplace assumption in Białoszewski's scholarship.

11. To mention only Helena Zaworska, Jarosław Fazan, Jacek Kopciński, and Adrian Gleń.

12. Jarosław Fazan, *Ale ja nie Bóg: Kontemplacja i teatr w dziele Mirona Białoszewskiego* (Cracow: Universitas, 1998), 23.

13. The motif of a return to the womb has been noticed from nearly the beginning of Białoszewski scholarship. See Barańczak, *Język poetycki Mirona Białoszewskiego*, 169.

14. Helena Zaworska, "Dom," *Twórczość* 10 (1970): 98–99.

15. Fazan, *Ale ja nie Bóg*, 15–16.

16. In order to convey the interpenetrability of context and contextualized, Culler coins the phrase "framing the sign" (Jonathan Culler, *Framing the Sign: Criticism and Its Institutions* [Oxford: Basil Blackwell, 1988], ix).

17. *O* 7.

18. *MWU* 100; *PPW* 104.

19. On the anticipation of reliable conclusions, see Paul Ricoeur, *Time and Narrative*, trans. Kathleen Blamey and David Pellauer (Chicago: University of Chicago Press, 1988).

20. Sobolewska also presents the view that Białoszewski "never lost a childlike sense of safety and belonging and a childlike astonishment and awareness of the magic of existence, in which both people and things participate with equal right." See Sobolewska, *Maksymalnie udana egzystencja.*

21. *R* 130.

22. *SZC* 295–96.

23. *SZC* 214.

24. "Przez jedno mgnienie powstanie. Podwórko po bombardowaniu. Rozłupki, dechy, słońce. Te ulice, Hoże, Wilcze" (*SZC* 233).

25. *SZC* 269.

26. Such potential is perhaps another modality of the "phantasmatic" nature (to use Maria Janion's expression) of Białoszewski's writing.

27. *SZC* 269.

28. The goal of healing ("working through") is to disrupt the otherness and self-contained nature of the traumatic and to assimilate it into the victim's life experiences. This assimilation presupposes that the traumatic is anchored, that is, it acquires the kind of temporality that allows its narration. Being able to place the traumatic into the broader context of his or her life allows the victim to disrupt the traumatic's somatic returns, transform it into a narrative memory, and ultimately merge it with other aspects and memories of the victim's life.

29. *SZC* 229.

30. *SZC* 229.

31. *K* 161–62.

32. The episode of throwing an old pair of pajamas onto an overgrown trash heap reveals another theme of Białoszewski's everyday, namely, a fascination with discarded objects. The function of the trash heap in Białoszewski's work—another form of liminality—merits its own book-length study. Białoszewski's narrator sees them as places where the human microhistories become visible. Nature's invasion of the trash heap—covering it with grass—transforms the discarded into a residual form of life.

33. *K* 172–73.

34. *K* 174.

35. *K* 178.

36. Michał Głowiński, *Gry powieściowe: Szkice z teorii i historii form narracyjnych* (Warsaw: Państwowy Instytut Wydawniczy, 1973), 338.

37. Jacques Derrida, *The Truth in Painting*, trans. Geoff Bennington and Ian McLeod (Chicago: University of Chicago Press, 1987), 9.

38. To paraphrase Bernstein's idea of sideshadowing. Michael André Bernstein, *Foregone Conclusions: Against Apocalyptic History* (Berkeley: University of California Press, 1994).

39. There is a sense of ethical impulse in this side-gazing where Białoszewski's narrator does not violate the "privacy" of someone's death with his gaze. Such side-gazing is also an important aspect of the *Memoir* in which even in the reality permeated by death, an individual death and an individual dead body—except perhaps for the exhumation scene—are not described.

40. In the Lacanian vocabulary, voice belongs to the Real, which Lacan understood as the traumatic. The concepts of the Real and Symbolic present productive reference points to interpret voice and side-gazing in Białoszewski, but I do not introduce them to my discussion because Lacan approaches the Real on the level of ontology, while I am interested in historically conditioned traumatization.

41. *SZC* 179–80.

42. Frank Kermode, *The Sense of an Ending: Studies in the Theory of Fiction* (1966; Oxford: Oxford University Press, 2000), 47.

43. Ibid.

44. Ibid., 48. Kermode was influenced in his understanding of *chronos* and *kairos* by the theologians Oscar Cullman (1950, *Christ and Time*) and John Marsh (1952, *The Fullness of Time*). As Kermode emphasizes, neither Greek nor Hebrew carries the antithesis between *chronos* and *kairos*—Hebrew has no word for *chronos* and thus does not provide the distinction between the plain duration of *chronos* and the concentrated time of *kairos* (47–48). It is interesting to note, however, that, although it was never juxtaposed with *chronos*, for the Greeks *kairos* was an important concept. It meant "opportunity" and was often used in rhetoric to designate the right moment of speech. Gorgias (c. 485–c. 380 B.C.E.), "the father of sophistry" renowned in the ancient world for his art of persuasion, taught "kairou chronou techne" (the art of knowing the right time).

45. Blanchot, *Infinite Conversation*, 242. Thus, for Blanchot, the everyday is radically atheist and the Lord's Prayer "secretly impious: give us our daily bread, give us to live according to the daily existence that leaves no place for a relation between Creator and creature"; ibid., 245.

46. Ibid., 242.

47. One of the most moving passages in the small narrations that illustrates the persistence of voice in traumatic memory is the story of Nanka (Białoszewski's aunt, who appears as a character in many episodes of the small narrations) being haunted by the voice of an old German woman whom she met on her way back to Warsaw after the war. In Nanka's memory, the old woman becomes identified with her voice. Białoszewski relates the story in *Rozkurz*:

> Nanka came back in May, after the war, with her people, on foot and with carts; on the way she passed other groups, assorted vehicles with big sacks. . . . It was hot. A hallucinatory sound or howl, increasingly like a human voice, grew louder in Nanka's ears, until they passed a village house that was calling with this voice. Nanka ran into the house. Empty. Nothing but a paralyzed old woman on a chair calling out:
> —Trinken! Trinken!
> Nanka grabbed a jug and rushed to the well. The well was dry. Nanka ran back with the empty jug, the old woman moaning:
> —Trinken.
> Nanka looks around, she doesn't know what to do, people from her group are moving farther and farther away. What will she do without them? She runs after them. In despair. After her runs that desperate:
> —Trinken . . . Trinken.
> Running after her to the end of her life.

> Nanka wracała w maju, po wojnie, ze swoimi na piechotę i z wózkami, po drodze mijała inne grupy, przeróżne pojazdy z tobołami. . . . Był upał. Nance w uszach zaczęło rosnąć jakieś omamienie czy skowyczenie, coraz więcej upodabniało się do ludzkiego głosu, aż mijali dom wiejski wołający tym głosem. Nanka wpadła do tego domku. Pustego. Tylko sparaliżowana staruszka na krześle wołała:
> —Trinken! Trinken!
> Nanka złapała za dzbanek, poleciała do studni. Studnia sucha. Nanka wpada z pustym dzbankiem do chałupy, staruszka jęczy:
> —Trinken.
> Nanka rozgląda się, nie wie, co robić, tamci z jej grupy odchodzą już coraz dalej. Co ona zrobi bez nich? Wylatuje za nimi. Zrozpaczona. Goni ją ropaczliwe:
> —Trinken . . . Trinken.
> Goniło ją to do końca życia. (*R* 24)

In Lacanian terms, we could read this voice as a *petit objet a* which manifests the Other's desire. Here the desire straightforwardly assumes the form of thirst, and Nanka's inability to fulfill this desire only strengthens the haunting presence of this disembodied howl. A voice that haunts the narrator is presented in the *Memoir,* when the terrified voice of Swen's mother calling Miron's name "runs after" the narrator (*PPW* 105–6).

48. So well attested by such critics as Sławiński, Barańczak, and Fazan.

49. Henri Lefebvre, "The Everyday and Everydayness," in *Everyday Life,* ed. Alice Kaplan and Kristin Ross (New Haven, Conn.: Yale University Press, 1987), 7–12, 11.

50. "Baśka," in *Małe i większe prozy opublikowane po roku 1980, Utwory zebrane,* 9:9–11. Miron Białoszewski, "Baśka" in *Małe i większe prozy opublikowane po roku 1980,* Utwory zebrane 9:9 (Warsaw: Państwowy Instytut Wydawniczy, 2000) 9.

51. Michel de Certeau, *The Practice of Everyday Life,* trans. Steven Rendell (Berkeley: University of California Press, 1988), 194.

52. *SZC* 172–73.

53. As Adam Zagajewski points out in his review of *Hums, Lumps, Threads,* Białoszewski's narrator lives according to seasonal changes. Adam Zagajewski, "W Warszawie jak na wsi," *Znak* 11–12 (1977): 1448–57.

54. Ryszard Nycz, "'Szare eminencje zachwytu': Miejsce epifanii w poetyce Mirona Białoszewskiego," in *PB* 189–90.

55. This quality of Nycz's approach to epiphany was noticed by Joanna Orska. "Życie jako happening," in *Białoszewski przed dziennikiem.*

56. Nycz claims that Białoszewski's epiphanies manifest "the truth about human existence as defined by the radical experience of temporality." He uses

the long episode "Raj" from *SZC* to exemplify his argument. Although I agree in general, I think it is important to qualify Białoszewski's treatment of temporal radicality. Nycz, "Szare eminencje zachwytu," 189.

57. Krzysztof Ziarek, who analyzes the representation of the everyday in Białoszewski's poetry, interprets this astonishment as a challenge to some tenets of the avant-garde: its elitist attitude, super-experimental aesthetics, group ideology, and utopian social vision. Krzysztof Ziarek, "How to Write the Everyday in Eastern Europe: Miron Białoszewski's 'Minor Poetry,'" in *The Historicity of Experience: Modernity, the Avant-Garde, and the Event* (Evanston, Ill.: Northwestern University Press, 2001), 241.

58. Blanchot, *Infinite Conversation,* 241.

59. Lefebvre, "The Everyday and Everydayness," 9.

60. As Lefebvre calls the everyday in Blanchot, *Infinite Conversation,* 240.

61. Blanchot, *Infinite Conversation,* 239.

62. This is what the narrator notices in the headlights of a bus traveling a country road in Konstancin (*K* 162).

63. Lefebvre, "The Everyday and Everydayness," 10.

64. Blanchot, *Infinite Conversation,* 238.

65. Ludwig Wittgenstein, *Philosophical Investigations,* 3rd ed., trans. G. E. M. Anscombe (Oxford: Blackwell, 2001), para. 129.

CHAPTER 3

1. Michał Witkowski, *Lubiewo* (Cracow: Korporacja ha!art, 2005), 178–79. *Lubiewo* has had five editions since it was first published in 2005. Every edition was considerably modified with new additions and cuts. The passage from Białoszewski's *Donosy rzeczywistości* appeared in the first edition, but was not included in subsequent ones. William Martin's English translation of *Lubiewo* published as *Lovetown* (2010) did not include a passage from Białoszewski. See also Miron Białoszewski, *Donosy rzeczywistości* (Warsaw: Państwowy Instytut Wydawniczy, 1998), 99.

2. "Lubiewo jest o świecie przekształcającym się z pedalstwa w gejostwo." Paweł Dunin Wąsowicz, "Oldskulowe pikiety," *Lampa* 1 (2005): 69.

3. For Warkocki, the publication of *Lubiewo* actually defines the "second emancipatory moment" for Polish literature. He points out the novels published at the turn of the 1980s and 1990s (e.g., Jerzy Nasierowski's *Seks, zbrodnia i kara,* Ewa Schilling's *Lustra,* Marcin Krzeszowiec's *Ból istnienia*) which, although not conceptualized this way in critical reception, could have been perceived as emancipatory. See Warkocki, *Homo niewiadomo: Polska proza wobec odmienności* (Warsaw: Wydawnictwo Sic, 2007), 35.

4. I am paraphrasing here Andy Medhurst's picturesque definition of camp.

See "Camp" in *Lesbian and Gay Studies: A Critical Introduction*, ed. Andy Medhurst and Sally R. Munt (London: Cassell, 1997), 276.

5. Warkocki proposes a new term, "homo niewiadomo," for reasons of its familiarity and semantic flexibility. As with the English "queer" and Polish "pedał," "homo niewiadomo" is a label of exclusion and, hence, can be re-signified. See Warkocki, *Homo niewiadomo*, 12.

6. A similar problem is evident even with more basic vocabulary which does not involve re-signification like "queer." For instance, the English term "gender" has several translations into Polish such as "płeć kulturowa/społeczna," "płciowość," or, rarely, "rodzaj." Contrary to how the term has been used in "gender studies," however, the Polish translations suggest a conjunction of "gender" with "sex" (or "sexuality"). Therefore, Polish critics often use the English term and adapt it to the morphology of the Polish language as in the term "krytyka genderowa" ("gender criticism"). This is a working solution in the language of criticism, but it indicates a larger problem with conceptualizing different social realities in the lingua franca of international theory.

An interesting assessment of how the vocabulary of gender and sexuality has been culturally and literally translated in Poland can be found in Joanna Mizielińska, *Płeć, ciało, seksualność: Od feminizmu do teorii queer* (Cracow: Universitas, 2006).

7. Witkowski, *Lubiewo*, 133–34.

8. Not only does Witkowski refuse to subdue the shocking quality of his characters' sexual practices, but he also further disturbs the reader by making Russian soldiers stationed in Poland the most desired sexual objects for Polish queens. The Polish-Russian aspect of the plot, feeding on anti-Russian sentiment, seems to be employed to further antagonize the hetero-normative reader.

9. This coming out, which assumed various public forms, from street demonstrations to pop magazines to academic publications and discussions, contextualizes the reception of the novel and provides the reader with tools to trace manifestations of homosexuality in cultural production.

10. David Halperin, *Saint Foucault* (New York: Oxford University Press, 1995), 62.

11. Janet R. Jakobsen, "Queer Is? Queer Does?: Normativity and the Problem of Resistance," *GLQ: A Journal of Gay and Lesbian Studies* 4 (1998): 516.

12. Sullivan aptly paraphrases Jakobsen: "It may be more productive to think of queer as a verb (a set of actions), rather than as a noun (an identity, or even a nameable positionality formed in and through the practice of particular actions)." Nikki Sullivan, *A Critical Introduction to Queer Theory* (New York: New York University Press, 2003), 50.

13. The concept of sylleptic subjectivity was introduced to Polish scholarship on Białoszewski by Ryszard Nycz and discussed in a recent study on Białoszewski by Elżbieta Winiecka, *Białoszewski sylleptyczny* (Poznań: Wydawnictwo

"Poznańskie Studia Polonistyczne," 2006). Almost all readings of Białoszewski include some aspects of the autobiographical approach, to mention only works by Głowiński, Sławiński, Barańczak, or Małgorzata Czermińska's *Trójkąt autobiograficzny* (Cracow: Universitas, 2000).

14. I am thinking here mainly about influential essays by Piotr Sobolczyk ("Hermetyczne pornografie Mirona Białoszewskiego" and "Homobiografia: Miron Białoszewski"), who analyzes the patterns of Białoszewski's homosexual self-disclosure as well as the mode of encoding homosexual desire from his early modernist poetry to the later writing.

15. As manifested in Wojciech Browarny and Adam Poprawa, eds., *Białoszewski przed dziennikiem* (*Białoszewski Before Diary*) (Cracow: Universitas, 2010).

16. Białoszewski is not the only author Witkowski quotes. He also incorporates passages from the novel *Adam Grywałd* (1936) by Tadeusz Breza.

17. Warkocki, *Homo niewiadomo,* 196.

18. "Odkrywa właściwy czy konkretny kształt semantyczny tego, co w swoim maskującym i poetyko niepowtarzalnym stylu opisywał wielokrotnie Miron Białoszewski . . .—siermiężną rzeczywistość peerelowskiego świata homoseksualnego." Marian Bielecki, "Wyjście z szafy," in *Białoszewski przed dziennikiem,* 13.

19. Ritz, *Nić w labiryncie pożądania,* 61.

20. Richard Dryer, "Believing in Fairies: The Author and the Homosexual," in *Inside/Out: Lesbian Theories, Gay Theories,* ed. Diana Fuss (New York: Routledge, 1991), 187.

21. Ibid., 187.

22. As stated by Tadeusz Sobolewski in his conversation with Olgierd Wołyński. See "Plac Dąbrowskiego" in *Miron: Wspomnienia o poecie,* ed. Hanna Kirchner, 202.

23. To refer again to Stanisław Rosiek's apt expression ("'Białoszewski' był zarazem bytem cielesnym i bytem słownym"). "Pamiętnik z półgrobu," in *PB* 132.

24. Piotr Sobolczyk in "Homobiografia: Miron Białoszewski" re-creates a chronology of Białoszewski's experience of homophobia.

25. According to Paweł Kurpios, some 11,000 files have been gathered. See "Poszukiwani, poszukiwane: Geje i lesbijki a rzeczywistość PRL," conference paper, www.dk.uni.wroc.pl/texty/prl_02.pdf.

26. For the treatment of homosexuality by the Communist government, see, for example, Krzysztof Boczkowski, *Homoseksualizm* (Cracow: Inter Esse, 2003); Barbara Pietkiewicz, "Gorzki fiolet," *Polityka* 8 (1981); Tadeusz Gorgol, "Homoseksualizm a opinia," *Życie literackie* 18 (1974); John Stanley, "Constructing a Narrative: The History of Homosexuality in Poland," in *New Social Movements and Sexuality: Conference Papers 2004,* ed. Melinda Chateauvert (Sofia: Bilitis Resources Center, 2006); "Opinie o homoseksualizmie: Tolerancja czy potępienie?" Komunikat z badań CBOS (Warsaw, 1988).

27. One can think of the second wave of feminism and its various attempts to create "l'écriture feminine" (to mention only the iconic *Les Guérillères* by Monique Wittig [1969]), whose stylistic and thematic idiosyncrasies were to counter the mainstream patriarchal narrative.

28. Dryer, "Believing in Fairies," 187.

29. However, such a sensationalistic reading also has an important place in the trajectory of criticism. I can sympathize with Piotr Sobolczyk's impulse in "Hermetyczne pornografie Białoszewskiego" to read some passages from Białoszewski in the context of, for instance, anal sex. Such reading is a backlash against the decades of silent treatment of Białoszewski's homosexuality in his criticism. It is necessary, but once done it needs to be transcended.

30. This is why we have the leitmotif of a narrator deliberating over various modes of representing a homosexual minority and the pressure for political correctness from an audience that wants a sympathetic novel about "well-educated, middle-class gays."

31. I refer here to Piotr Sobolczyk's expression "rozmyta podmiotowość." Sobolczyk, "Hermetyczne pornografie," 175.

32. Kaja Silverman, *Male Subjectivity at the Margins* (New York: Routledge, 1992).

33. The word "baba" (plural "baby") is polyvalent in Polish. For some situations in which camaraderie is involved, "gal" could be used as an English equivalent. The colloquial carelessness of the original may also be translated as "dame" for slang expressions, although "dame" may sound a bit archaic to the English ear. "Lady" or "girl" works well in forms of address when "baba" is used in a friendly, even intimate, and yet jokingly affectionate way. In pejorative or condescending contexts vis-à-vis women (which in the small narrations tend to involve the character of Le.), "broad" probably works best. Interestingly enough, Białoszewski usually does not employ this expression (or its popular diminutive—"babka") to describe young women whose equivalent in English would be "chick," "babe," or "doll." I thank Christopher Caes for these translatorial suggestions.

34. *SZC* 10.

35. As German Ritz succinctly put it, "Białoszewski's works prove unequivocally that the private can function without the confessional. The private means basically a 'non-discursive' mode of approaching reality." Ritz, *Nić w labiryncie pożądania*, 61.

36. Winiecka's statement about Białoszewski's poetry works equally well in relation to his prose. *Białoszewski sylleptyczny*, 231.

37. "Która inscenizuje swoje słowa, buduje na poły realny, na poły zmistyfikowany (lecz natychmiast włączany w obraz artystycznej osobości poety) obraz 'Mirona Białoszewskiego.'" Ibid.

38. "The writer has counterfeited his autobiographical pact, in which the

reader is to pay less attention to 'withdrawn' subjectivity. As a result, even if the reader catches Białoszewski doing something 'strange' or vulgar, the writer can always cite his blurred subjectivity and the prerogatives of reality" ("Pisarz sfingowal swój pakt autobiograficzny, w którym odbiorca ma zwracać mniejszą uwagę na wycofaną podmiotowość; w rezultacie, jeśli czytelnik przyłapie Białoszewskiego na czymś 'dziwnym', wulgarnym to Białoszewski może się wykręcić rozmytą podmiotowoscią, dyktatem rzeczywistości"). Sobolczyk, "Hermetyczne pornografie Bialoszewkiego," 175.

39. Ritz, *Nić w labiryncie pożądania,* 60.

40. What I find interesting in Sobolczyk's approach is his hinting at the possibility of maliciousness in Białoszewski's encoding of homosexuality, thus breaking up the "gentle" image of the writer.

41. The nonexistence of a mode of reading that would allow the homosexual to resurface is what Warkocki points out in response to the paradox of Ritz's claim that Polish literature is simultaneously permeated with homosexuality and that it hides homosexuality. See Warkocki, *Homo niewiadomo*, 184–96.

42. Butler introduced the notion of performativity in *Gender Troubles: Feminism and the Subversion of Identity* (New York: Routledge, 1990), and developed the concept in *Bodies That Matter: On the Discursive Limits of Sex* (New York: Routledge 1993).

43. The plot of the story became a point of departure for a range of fascinating analyses, to mention only the interpretations by Jacques Lacan, Jacques Derrida, and Slavoj Žižek. See Jacques Lacan, *Écrits* (Paris: Éditions du Seuil, 1966); and Žižek, *Looking Awry.* The story is also used by Błażej Warkocki to discuss the optics of knowing and not knowing in *Homo niewiadomo.*

44. Žižek, *Looking Awry,* 11–12.

45. "Wpadli i zaczęli szukać. Kogoś. Bo takie nieotwieranie. Ale kto myślał, że milicja. Potem szukali w pawlaczach, pod materacem. Nie wiadomo po co. Chyba dla zwyczaju. U Le. w saloniku wpili się oczami w damskie pończochy, znalezione w Paryżu. Le. miał je wysłać wieczorem do siostry, oglądał i zastanawiał się, jak jej jedna grubsza noga zmieści się w tej cieniutkiej pończosze. I tak zostało od wieczora do rana. Potem samochodem. Na Wilczą. Okazało się, że był na nas anonim. Rozstaliśmy się z milicją bardzo dobrze. Le.—bo słyszałem go przez ścianę—lekko i głośno mówił. Było parę rozmów. A że wiadomo było, i nam, i panom, tym od nas, że cała sprawa nie dotyczy nas, dopisywały nam humory. Le. deklamował cały fałat Balladyny, aż troszeczkę tego pana tym przestraszył." *DR* 102.

46. *DR* 103.

47. The expressions "chłop" (guy, chap, fellow) and "baba" (gal, dame, girl) are consistently employed in the small narrations as indiscriminate forms of address. Although "baby" on their own can be "perhaps the most interesting beings in the world," the gender binary expressed in the vocabulary of "baba" and

"chłop" and their rural connotations ("chłop" and "baba" trigger associations with peasantry) strip both genders of their complexities and suggest that regardless of the class, age, or educational status of men and women, all male–female relationships are the same. Neither the narrator nor Le. dwell on the psychological complexities of heterosexual relationships. For instance, the process of looking for a mate (as in the narrator's father's search for his second wife) validates the simplest social standards; a sought-after woman needs to be a "good wife and homemaker" ("On sam [ojciec] myślał o dobrej żonie, gospodyni," *SZC* 117–18). Although some stories about a tumultuous relationship between the narrator's father and his mistress, Zocha, suggest sexual attraction and passion, nothing is ever spelled out. Białoszewski's pattern is not to provide us with any coordinates that would grant specificity to heterosexual relationships.

48. As I mentioned before, the readings that celebrate Białoszewski's moments of disclosure (such as Sobolczyk's interpretations) clearly have their limitations, but they also mark a welcome shift in Białoszewski criticism. Their detective dimension is an understandable response to traditional criticism that barred the topic of Białoszewski's homosexuality.

49. *PPW* 112, *MWU* 107.

50. *PPW* 97, *MWU* 95.

51. I agree with Kanabrodzki's analogy between the uprising's position in the empirical and memorial sphere and the position of Miss Żenia's salon in the poetic. See Mateusz Kanabrodzki, *Kapłan i fryzjer: Żywioł materialno-cielesny w utworach Georga Buchnera, Witolda Gombrowicza, Mirona Białoszewskiego, Helmuta Kajzera* (Gdańsk: Słowo/obraz terytoria, 2004), 179.

52. Eve Kosofsky Sedgwick, *Epistemology of the Closet* (Berkeley: University of California Press, 1990), 8. The very notion of heterosexual desire in its cultural manifestations is a socially constructed, "naturalized" aftereffect of the performance of heterosexual subjectivity.

53. Silverman, *Male Subjectivity at the Margins*, 342.

54. Jacek Kopciński, "Stare klabzdry na wojnie," *Teksty drugie* 1 (1995): 73–74.

55. *SZC* 306.

56. Wojciech Browarny, "Babszczyzna Mirona Białoszewskiego," in *Białoszewski przed dziennikiem*, 40.

57. I would contend that Browarny's reflections can be applied to Białoszewski's published works as well.

58. I would extend Browarny's remarks on the "generic" character of Białoszewski's descriptions of men and say that they tend to emphasize men's "cultural" features rather than bodily qualities.

59. "Gdyby podmiot Białoszewskiego pragnął innego ciała lub poddawał je idealizacji, nie mógłby uniknąć opozycji 'ja'—obiekt. 'Baby' pozwalają jej uniknąć. Nie są przedmiotem percepcji erotycznej czy estetycznej, ale pozostając

zdecydowanie ucieleśnione, istnieją w tekście także jako postaci władające zaimkiem 'ja.' Kompozycja notatek dziennika, niehierarchiczna i wielogłosowa, gwarantuje im podwójny status, którego nie mają mężczyźni—kulturowo przywiązani do swojej podmiotowości, a przy tym cieleśnie odrealnieni i wizualnie ascetyczni (rzadziej postrzegani jako ciała szczególnie nacechowane)." Browarny, *Białoszewski przed dziennikiem,* 51.

60. Ibid., 50.

61. The *Memoir* gives us some glimpses of women soldiers, but they are represented as part of the male world—their position and function overrides their femininity.

62. "W czasach wojny zawsze jest nawrót do matriarchatu. A jeszcze ta wojna. A jeszcze to zejście w dół, pod Warszawę (w to mrowisko schronowe), to powstanie. To był nawrót—wybuch. Matriarchatu. Piwnicznego? Jaskiniowego? Co za różnica. Kupy ludzi. Rządzą matki. Siedzenie pod ziemią. Kryj się! Nie wychylaj się! Niebezpieczeństwo śmiertelne. Wciąż." *PPW* 93.

"In times of war, it seems, there is always a return to matriarchy. And especially during that war. That uprising. Particularly with that descent underground, under Warsaw (into the anthill of the shelters). The outbreak of the Uprising was a turning point. For matriarchy. Of the cellars? The caves? What's the difference? Masses of people. The mothers rule. Sitting underground. Hide! Don't crawl out! Mortal dangers. All the time." *MWU* 92.

63. *MWU* 82. ". . . Mama Swena. Kręciła te zacierki. Jak wszystkie kobiety. Bez przerwy. Albo różańce. To i to drobione. Podobna technika." *PPW* 84.

64. "Nasz pośpiech udzielił się i reszcie. Szczególnie Matce i Ciotce. Czyli dwom matkom." *PPW* 140. "Our haste was communicated to the others too. Especially to Swen's mother and Aunt Uff. Or rather, to the two mothers." *MWU* 131.

65. "Dokładane treści: Fragmenty nie publikowanego dziennika Mirona Białoszewskiego (1975–1976)." *Gazeta Wyborcza* 220 (1997): 16.

66. *DR* 111.

67. *DR* 26.

68. At the same time, Le. is also the character who rearticulates basic social standards. It is Le. who usually showers the narrator and other characters with his unsolicited advice about relationships. When, for instance, a female friend of the narrator complains about quarreling with her husband, Le. says, "Teresa, co ty narzekasz. Dobrego masz chłopa," ("Teresa, why are you complaining. You have a good man [*chłop*]"). What exactly constitutes a "good man" we do not know, as we do not know anything specific about the relationship between Teresa and her husband.

69. For instance, in the episode "Poznańska," when the narrator describes the life of the building we find a description of an old heterosexual couple, which

makes a direct reference to sexuality, but what is important for the narrator is the very fact of confessing the secret by the "grandma" and her response to her husband's demands and not the content of the demand as such:

> Babka zwierzyła się Żeni, że stary chce, żeby ona z nogami w górze, a gdzie ona, stara, reumatyzm. No i ją zostawił, i Poznańską z podwórkiem. I zniknął w świecie, tym lepszym, nieprzyzwoitym, z figurami. *SZC* 125
>
> The grandma confessed to Żenia that her old man wants her to do it with her legs up in the air, but she's too old for that, with her arthritis. So he left her and Poznańska Street with the courtyard. And he disappeared in the world, the better one, the indecent one, the one with acrobatics.

70. *SZC* 125–26.

71. The theme of the safe and fragile home as connected to the experience of the war and especially the Warsaw Uprising is explored by Helena Zaworska in "Dom," *Twórczość* 10 (1970): 98–99.

72. Wojciech Browarny, in response to my statement about the interchangeability of gender (Joanna Niżyńska, "'Znaleziony list' Mirona Białoszewskiego: Próba lektury 'małych narracji' w perspektywie teorii queer," in *(Nie)obecność: Pominięcia i przemilczenia w narracjach XX wieku,* ed. Hanna Gosk and Bożena Karwowska. [Warsaw, 2008], 272–91), makes a caveat that interchangeability of gender does not mean gender erasure. I agree with Browarny's statement that Białoszewski "embodies" women, that is, describes their body; however, these descriptions are not eroticized. Browarny, "'Babszczyzna' Mirona Białoszewskiego," 44.

73. Only two characters seem to differ in their speech patterns and thus are not exchangeable: Le. and Lu., modeled after Leszek Soliński and Ludwik Hering, respectively.

74. "I asked Włodek—'get undressed and crawl under the covers.' He says to me, offended, 'What? You wanna turn me into a fag?' So I tell him, 'you'll be sorry—I'm in the zone tonight'" ("Prosiłem Włodka": "rozbierz się i wleź do łóżka." To on na to oburzony "Co ty, lalę ze mnie chcesz zrobić?" Ja go proszę i mówię "bo będziesz żałował, jestem w afekcie.") "Russin we wnęce" ("Russin's nook"), in *DR* 122.

75. *AAA* 232.

76. *AAA* 257–59.

77. The intertextuality of *AAAmerica* and the diary is addressed by Marian Bielecki in "Wyjście z szafy" in *Białoszewski przed dziennikiem,* Browarny and Poprawa, 11–26.

78. *AAA* 236–37.

79. The exchange is even more politically potent and double-coded in light

of the fact that the acquaintance asking the question is characterized as someone "who emigrated from Poland in sixty-eight. He was a boy then and now, he's saying, they want to make him a professor here, but he keeps resisting" (*AAA* 236).

80. I am referring to Kosofsky-Sedgwick's example, in which she describes a conversation between two longtime friends during which a homosexual man "comes out" to a heterosexual female friend. What is important is the performative aspect of this "coming out" and not a "real" knowledge. Kosofsky-Sedgwick, *Epistemology of the Closet*, 4.

81. David Levin's transposition of the difference between truth as "correctness" and truth as "unconcealment" into phenomenology, specifically in terms of the visual experience, might be useful here:

> Statements require "correct" vision. Truth as correctness requires a "correct" gaze: a gaze correctly positioned, correctly focused, correctly pointed. The most extreme case of vision would thus be the stare. The style of vision that I would associate with the hermeneutical discourse of poetizing, and with truth as aletheia, is exemplified by the playful gaze, gently relaxed, calm, centered by virtue of its openness to experience, its delight to being surprised, decentered, drawn into the invisible.

See David Levin, *The Opening of Vision: Nihilism and the Postmodern Situation* (New York: Routledge, 1988), 438.

82. "Temu wrażeniu trudno się oprzeć—Lubiewo to książka, na jaką zabrakło odwagi i Gombrowiczowi, i Białoszewskiemu." Andrzej Skrendo, "Miejsce ujawnienia," *Pogranicza* 1 (2005): 11–16.

83. To use Diana Fuss's expression. See "Inside/Out" in *Inside/Out: Lesbian Theories, Gay Theories*, ed. Diana Fuss (New York: Routledge, 1991), 15.

84. Ibid.

EPILOGUE

1. Miron Białoszewski, *Tajny dziennik* (Cracow: Znak), 2012.

2. I am thinking here particularly about Piotr Sobolczyk's stimulating accounts of Białoszewski's "homobiography" and his reading of homosexual themes in Białoszewski's early poetry, already mentioned in chapter 3. Sobolczyk, "Homobiografia: Miron Białoszewski"; and "Hermetyczne pornografie Białoszewskiego." Marian Bielecki's article from *Białoszewski przed dziennikiem* follows in Sobolczyk's footsteps.

3. I thank Ofer Dynes for stimulating conversation on the topic.

4. I'm thinking here particularly of the edited volume *Białoszewski przed dziennikiem* (2010).

5. Catherine Gallagher and Stephen Greenblatt, *Practicing New Historicism* (Chicago: University of Chicago Press, 2000), 26.

6. On a gender-related note, it is also worth mentioning that although statistically the greatest losses among the military participants of the uprising were suffered by the couriers/messenger girls (*łączniczki*) they were the last military group to receive their own monument.

7. Emmanuel Levinas, *Otherwise Than Being, or Beyond Essence,* trans. Alphonso Lingis (Pittsburgh: Duquesne University Press, 1998), 15.

8. Sobolczyk persuasively presented homosexual disclosures in the *Memoir* in "Homobiografia: Miron Białoszewski."

9. Saul Friedlander, "Trauma, Transference and 'Working Through,'" *History and Memory* 4 (1992): 39–55.

10. Ibid.

11. *PPW* 201–2; *MWU* 184. Białoszewski uses the low colloquial term "wychodek" to designate the public bathroom in Skaryszewski Park. Unfortunately, it is hard to find a single word in English that captures his slang expression with the idea of a public facility in an urban environment. Levine's "outhouse" sounds too rural and implies a level of detail that doesn't seem appropriate for the public toilet that Białoszewski describes. Other words such as "john," "privy," "latrine," and "lavatory" also cannot be used in this context (although "john" seems the closest), and neither can the too formal "restroom." I choose to translate "wychodek" simply as "bathroom" since in American English the expression "public bathrooms" is used to describe facilities in parks.

12. I take this information from Sobolczyk's "Homobiografia: Miron Białoszewski," 18. Sobolczyk signals a possible interpretation of the wall of the bathroom as a metaphor of the narrator's scarred psyche.

13. Walter Benjamin, *Illuminations,* trans. Harry Zohn (New York: Schocken Books, 1969), 261.

14. David M. Halperin, *How to Do the History of Homosexuality* (Chicago: University of Chicago Press, 2002), 17–18.

15. Gallagher and Greenblatt, *Practicing New Historicism,* 45.

16. Kosofsky-Sedgwick, *Epistemology* 3.

Bibliography

Adamson, Jane, Richard Freadman, and David Parker. *Renegotiating Ethics in Literature, Philosophy, and Theory*. Cambridge, Eng.: Cambridge University Press, 1998.

Adkins, Lisa, and Vicki Merchant, eds *Sexualizing the Social: Power and Organization of Sexuality*. New York: St. Martin's, 1996.

Adorno, Theodor. *Aesthetic Theory*. Ed. Gretel Adorno and Rolf Tiedemann. Trans. Robert Hullot-Kentor. Theory and History of Literature 88. Minneapolis: University of Minnesota Press, 1997.

Agamben, Giorgio. *Homo Sacer: Sovereign Power and Bare Life*. Trans. Daniel Heller-Roazen. Stanford, Calif.: Stanford University Press, 1998.

———. *Remnants of Auschwitz: The Witness and the Archive*. Trans. Daniel Heller-Roazen. New York: Zone Books, 1999.

Alexander, Jeffrey, Ron Eyerman, Bernard Giesen, et al., eds *Cultural Trauma and Collective Identity*. Berkeley University of California Press, 2004.

Almeida, Rochelle. *The Politics of Mourning: Grief Management in Cross-Cultural Fiction*. Madison, N.J.: Fairleigh Dickinson University Press, 2004.

Anderson, Benedict. *Imagined Communities: Reflections on the Origin and Spread of Nationalism*. London: Verso, 2006.

Anderson, Linda. *Autobiography*. London: Routledge, 2001.

Auerbach, Eric. *Mimesis: The Presentation of Reality in Western Literature*. Trans. Willard R. Trask. Princeton, N.J.: Princeton University Press, 1991.

Badiou, Alain. *Being and Event*. Trans. Oliver Feltham. London: Continuum, 2005.

———. *Manifesto for Philosophy*. Trans. Norman Madarasz. Albany: State University of New York Press, 1999.

Baer, Monika, and Marzena Lizurej, eds. *Z odmiennej perspektywy: Studia queer w Polsce*. Wrocław: Oficyna wydawnicza "Arboretum," 2007.

Bakhtin, Mikhail. *The Dialogic Imagination: Four Essays by M. M. Bakhtin*. Trans. Caryl Emerson and Michael Holquist. Austin: University of Texas Press, 1981.

———. *Speech Genres and Other Late Essays.* Ed. Caryl Emerson and Michael Holquist. Trans. Vern W. McGee. Austin: University of Texas Press, 1986.

Bal, Mieke. *Narratology: Introduction to the Theory of Narrative.* 2nd ed. Toronto: University of Toronto Press, 1985.

Bal, Mieke, Jonathan Crewe, and Leo Spitzer, eds. *Acts of Memory: Cultural Recall in the Present.* Hanover, N.H.: University Press of New England, 1999.

Balcerzan, Edward. *Przez znaki: Granice autonomii sztuki poetyckiej na materiale polskiej poezji współczesnej.* Poznań: Wydawnictwo Poznańskie, 1972.

Baran, Józef. *Autor! Autor! Rozmowy z ludźmi pióra i palety.* Warsaw: Ludowa Spółdzielnia Wydawnicza, 1985.

Barańczak, Stanisław. "Człowiek bezbronny." In *Literatura wobec wojny i okupacji,* ed. Michał Głowiński and Janusz Sławiński. Wrocław: Zakład Narodowy Imienia Ossolińskich, 1976.

———. *Etyka i poetyka: Szkice 1970–78.* Biblioteka "Kultury" 303. Paris: Instytut Literacki, 1979.

———. *Język poetycki Mirona Białoszewskiego.* Z dziejów form artystycznych w literaturze polskiej 41. Wrocław: Zakład Narodowy Imienia Ossolińskich, 1974.

———. *Nieufni i zadufani: Romantyzm i klasycyzm w młodej poezji lat sześćdziesiątych.* Wrocław: Ossolineum, 1971.

———. *"'Patyk' Mirona Białoszewskiego": Nowela, opowiadanie, gawęda,* ed. K. Bartoszyński, Maria Jasińska-Wojtkowska, and Stefan Sawicki. Warsaw: Państwowe Wydawnictwo Naukowe, 1974.

———. *Przed i po: Szkice o poezji krajowej przełomu lat siedemdziesiątych i osiemdziesiątych.* London: Aneks, 1988.

Baranowska, Małgorzata. *Prywatna historia poezji.* Warsaw: Wydawnictwo Sic!, 1999.

Barbusse, Henri. *Under Fire.* Trans. Fitzwater Wray. London: J.M. Dent, 1933.

Bartoszewski, Władysław. *Powstanie warszawskie.* Warsaw: Świat Książki, 2009.

———. *1859 dni Warszawy.* 1974. Cracow: Znak, 2008.

Bauer, Zbigniew. "Powrót czy ucieczka: W stronę prozy." *Poezja* 2 (1976): 46–57.

Bauman, Zygmunt. *Life in Fragments: Essays in Postmodern Morality.* London: Basil Blackwell, 1995.

———. *Modernity and the Holocaust.* Ithaca, N.Y.: Cornell University Press, 1989.

———. *Postmodern Ethics.* London: Basil Blackwell, 1993.

Barthes, Roland. *The Preparation of the Novel: Lecture Courses and Seminars at the Collège de France.* Trans. Kate Briggs. New York: Columbia University Press, 2011.

———.*Writing Degree Zero.* Trans. Annette Lavers and Colin Smith. London: J. Cape, 1984.

Basiuk, Tomek, "Queerowanie po polsku." *Furia Pierwsza* 7 (2000).

Benjamin, Walter. *Illuminations*. Trans Harry Zohn. Ed. Hannah Arendt. New York: Schocken Books, 1986.

Bernasconi, Robert, and Simon Critchley, eds. *Re-Reading Levinas*. Bloomington: Indiana University Press, 1991.

Bernstein, Michael André. *Foregone Conclusions: Against Apocalyptic History*. Berkeley: University of California Press, 1994.

Białoszewski, Miron. *Było i było*. Warsaw: Państwowy Instytut Wydawniczy, 1965.

———. *Chamowo*. Warsaw: Państwowy Instytut Wydawniczy, 2009.

———. *Donosy rzeczywistości*. Warsaw: Państwowy Instytut Wydawniczy, 1973.

———. *Konstancin*. Warsaw: Państwowy Instytut Wydawniczy, 1991.

———. "Listy do Eumenid." *Teksty drugie* 6 (1991): 83–137.

———. "Listy Mirona Białoszewskiego do Józefa Barana." *Pismo* 6 (1984): 4–14.

———. *A Memoir of the Warsaw Uprising*. Trans. and ed. Madeline Levine. Evanston, Ill.: Northwestern University Press, 1977.

———. *Miron Białoszewski*. Poeci Polscy. Warsaw: Czytelnik, 1977.

———. "Mój wiersz." *Odra* 8 (1982): 21–22.

———. *Mylne wzruszenia*. Warsaw: Państwowy Instytut Wydawniczy, 1961.

———. "Nieznana proza z teki pośmiertnej." *Tygodnik Powszechny*, February 10, 1985, 8.

———. *Obmapywanie Europy, czyli dziennik okrętowy: AAAmeryka: Ostatnie wiersze*. Warsaw: Państwowy Instytut Wydawniczy, 1988.

———. *Obroty rzeczy*. Warsaw: Państwowy Instytut Wydawniczy, 1956.

———. *Odczepić się*. Warsaw: Państwowy Instytut Wydawniczy, 1978.

———. *Oho*. Warsaw: Państwowy Instytut Wydawniczy, 1985.

———. "O tym Mickiewiczu jak go mówię." In *Debiuty poetyckie 1944–1960*, ed. Jacek Kajtoch and Jerzy Skórnicki, 291–300. Warsaw: Iskry, 1972.

———. *Pamiętnik z powstania warszawskiego*. Warsaw: Państwowy Instytut Wydawniczy, 1970.

———. *Poezje wybrane*. Warsaw: Ludowa Spółdzielnia Wydawnicza, 1976.

———. *Przepowiadanie sobie*. Warsaw: Państwowy Instytut Wydawniczy, 1981.

———. *Rachunek zachciankowy*. Warsaw: Państwowy Instytut Wydawniczy, 1959.

———. *The Revolution of Things: Selected Poems*. Trans. Andrzej Busza and Bogdan Czaykowski. Washington: Charioteer, 1974.

———. *Rozkurz*. Warsaw: Państwowy Instytut Wydawniczy, 1980.

———. "Rozmowa z Leszkiem Elektorowiczem" ("Interview with Leszek Elektorowicz"). *Życie Literackie* 32 (1958): 3–6.

———. *Stara proza: Nowe wiersze*. Warsaw: Czytelnik, 1984.

———. *Szumy, zlepy, ciągi*. Warsaw: Państwowy Instytut Wydawniczy, 1976.

———. *Tajny dziennik*. Cracow: Znak, 2012.

———. *Teatr Osobny: 1955–1963*. Warsaw: Państwowy Instytut Wydawniczy, 1971.

———. "To, w czym się jest: Rozmowa Anny Trznadel-Szczepanek z Miro-

nem Białoszewskim w dniu 2 II 1983" ("Interview with Anna Trznadel-Szczepanek"). *Twórczość* 9 (1983): 29–38.
———. *Trzydzieści lat wierszy*. Kolekcja Polskiej Literatury Współczesnej. Warsaw: Państwowy Instytut Wydawniczy, 1982.
———. *Wiersze*. Biblioteka Poetów. Warsaw: Państwowy Instytut Wydawniczy, 1978.
———. *Wiersze wybrane i dobrane*. Warsaw: Czytelnik, 1980.
———. "Wstęp" ("Introduction"). *Poezje wybrane*, by Białoszewski. Warsaw: Ludowa Spółdzielnia Wydawnicza, 1976.
———. *Zawał*. Warsaw: Państwowy Instytut Wydawniczy, 1977.
Fragments from Miron Białoszewski's *Dziennik* (*Diary*) before the publication of the full text in February 2012:
———. "Dokładane treści: Druga część fragmentów 'tajnego dziennika' Mirona Białoszewskiego, który zostanie wydany w 2010 roku." *Gazeta Wyborcza* 226 (1997): 16–17.
———. "Dokładane treści (fragmenty dziennika) (1977). *Kwartalnik Artystyczny* 1 (2003): 10–22.
———. "Dokładane treści: Fragmenty nie publikowanego dziennika Mirona Białoszewskiego (1975–1976)." *Gazeta Wyborcza* 220 (1997): 16–18.
———. "Dziennik: Pogorszenie (1982)." *Kwartalnik Artystyczny* 1 (2008): 7–13.
———. "Dziennik—Pogorszenie (fragmenty) (1982)." *Gazeta Wyborcza* 180 (2002): 12.
———. "Festiwal poezji w Skopje (fragment dziennika) (1978)." *Odra* 9 (2009): 40–41.
———. "Fragment dziennika (rok 1975)." *Arkadia* 19–20 (2006): 7–8.
———. "Fragment książki: Dzienniki 1975–1983 (1977)." http://www.polityka.pl/fragment-ksiazki-dzienniki-1975–1983/Lead33,1342,301887,18/.
———. "Fragmenty dziennika amerykańskiego (1982)." *Zeszyty Literackie* 2 (2009): 34–37.
———. "Joga, Konopnicka, Mickiewicz: Fragment z dziennika, 1977." *Odra* 9 (2004): 58–63.
———. "Nadawanie (fragment dziennika Obory 1978)." *Odra* 11 (2007): 53–55.
———. "Obory: Fragment Dziennika (1977)." *Odra* 9 (2005): 36–40.
———. "Pogorszenie (fragment dziennika) (1982)." *Arkadia* 13–14 (2003): 48–51.
———. "Przyjazd papież (fragment dziennika) (1979)." *Odra* 9 (2006): 62–64.
———. "Śmierć Mamy: Fragment dziennika (1980)." *Odra* 1 (2003): 64–70.
———. "Wieczór autorski (fragment dziennika) (1976)." *Odra* 9 (2008): 64–65.
Bidney, Martin. *Patterns of Epiphany: From Wordsworth to Tolstoy, Pater, and Barrett Browning*. Carbondale: Southern Illinois University Press, 1997.
Bielecki, Marian. "Wyjście z szafy." In *Białoszewski przed dziennikiem*, ed. Wojciech Browarny and Adam Poprawa, 11–26. Cracow: Universitas, 2010.

Blair, George A. *Energeia and Entelecheia: "Act" in Aristotle.* Ottawa: University of Ottawa Press, 1992.

Blanchot, Maurice. "Everyday Speech." In *Everyday Life,* ed. Alice Kaplan and Kristin Ross, 7–12. New Haven, Conn.: Yale University Press, 1987.

———. *The Infinite Conversation.* Trans. and foreword Susan Hanson. Theory and History of Literature 82. Minneapolis: University of Minnesota Press, 1993.

———. *The Space of Literature.* Trans. Ann Smock. Lincoln: University of Nebraska Press, 1982.

———. *The Work of Fire.* Trans. Charlotte Mandell. Stanford, Calif.: Stanford University Press, 1995.

———. *The Writing of the Disaster.* Trans. Ann Smock. Lincoln: University of Nebraska Press, 1995.

Blatterer, Harry, Pauline Johnson, and Maria R. Raukus, eds. *Modern Privacy: Shifting Boundaries, New Forms.* New York: Palgrave Macmillan, 2010.

Błoński, Jan. *Zmiana warty.* Warsaw: Państwowy Instytut Wydawniczy, 1961.

Boczkowski, Krzysztof. *Homoseksualizm.* Cracow: Inter Esse, 2003.

Bolecki, Włodzimierz, and Erazm Kuźma. *Literatura wobec niewyrażalnego.* Z dziejów form artystycznych w literaturze polskiej 79. Warsaw: Instytut Badań Literackich Polskiej Akademii Nauk, 1998.

Bolton, Jonathan. "Everyday Epiphanies: Power, Language, and Stories in Czech and Russian Autobiography of the 1970s." Diss. University of Michigan, 2001.

Borkowska, Grażyna. "Pędy, rytmy: Jeszcze o Białoszewskim." *Teksty drugie* 5 (1995).

Boym, Svetlana. *Common Places: Mythologies of Everyday Life in Russia.* Cambridge, Mass.: Harvard University Press, 1994.

Brison, Susan J. "Trauma Narratives and the Remaking of the Self." In *Acts of Memory: Cultural Recall in the Present,* ed. Mieke Bal, Jonathan Crewe, and Leo Spitzer, 39–55. Hanover, N.H.: University Press of New England, 1999.

Browarny, Wojciech, and Adam Poprawa. *Białoszewski przed Dziennikiem.* Cracow: Universitas, 2010.

Bruns, Gerald. *Heidegger's Estrangements: Language, Truth, and Poetry in the Later Writings.* New Haven, Conn.: Yale University Press, 1989.

———. *Hermeneutics Ancient and Modern.* New Haven, Conn.: Yale University Press, 1992.

———. *Inventions: Writing, Textuality, and Understanding in Literary History.* New Haven, Conn.: Yale University Press, 1982.

———. *Maurice Blanchot: The Refusal of Philosophy.* Baltimore: Johns Hopkins University Press, 1997.

———. *Modern Poetry and the Idea of Language: A Critical and Historical Study.* New Haven, Conn.: Yale University Press, 1974.

———. "Poethics: John Cage and Stanley Cavell at the Crossroads of Ethical Theory." In *John Cage: Composed in America,* ed. Marjorie Perloff and Charles Junkerman, 206–25. Chicago: University of Chicago Press, 1994.

———. *Tragic Thoughts at the End of Philosophy: Language, Literature, and Ethical Theory.* Evanston, Ill.: Northwestern University Press, 1999.

Brzozowski, Jacek, ed. *O wierszach Mirona Białoszewskiego.* Łódź: Oficyna Bibliofilów, 1993.

Buber, Martin. *I and Thou.* Trans. Walter Kaufmann. New York: Touchstone Book—Simon and Schuster, 1996.

Buczkowski, Leopold. *Czarny potok.* Warsaw: Pax, 1954.

Budick, Sanford, and Wolfgang Iser, eds. *Languages of the Unsayable: The Play of Negativity in Literature and Literary Theory.* Stanford, Calif.: Stanford University Press, 1987.

Bullock, Alan. *Hitler and Stalin: Parallel Lives.* London: Fontana, 1998.

Burkot, Stanisław. *Miron Białoszewski.* Warsaw: Wydawnictwo Szkolne i Pedagogiczne, 1992.

Butler, Judith. *Bodies That Matter: On the Discursive Limits of "Sex."* New York: Routledge, 1993.

———. *Gender Trouble: Feminism and the Subversion of Identity.* 1999. New York: Routledge, 2006.

———. *Precarious Life: The Powers of Mourning and Violence.* London: Verso, 2006.

Cadava, Eduardo, Peter Connor, and Jean-Luc Nancy, eds. *Who Comes After the Subject?* London: Routledge, 1991.

Cameron, Deborah, and Don Kulick. *Language and Sexuality.* Cambridge, Eng.: Cambridge University Press, 2003.

Cameron, Sharon. *Lyric Time: Dickinson and the Limits of Genre.* 1979. Baltimore: Johns Hopkins University Press, 1981.

Carpenter, Belinda J. *Re-Thinking Prostitution: Feminism, Sex, and the Self.* New York: Peter Lang, 2000.

Carpenter, Bogdana. *The Poetic Avant-Garde in Poland 1918–1939.* Publications on Russia and Eastern Europe of the School of International Studies, University of Washington. Seattle: University of Washington, 1983.

Caruth, Cathy. "An Interview with Robert Jay Lifton." In Caruth, *Trauma: Explorations in Memory,* 128–51.

———. "Introduction." In Caruth, *Trauma: Explorations in Memory,* 3–13.

———, ed. *Trauma: Explorations in Memory.* Baltimore: Johns Hopkins University Press, 1995.

———. *Unclaimed Experience: Trauma, Narrative, and History.* Baltimore: Johns Hopkins University Press, 1996.

Cascardi, Anthony J., ed. *Literature and the Question of Philosophy.* Baltimore: Johns Hopkins University Press, 1987.

Cassirer, Ernst. *The Philosophy of Symbolic Forms.* 3 vols. 1955. Trans. Ralph Manheim. New Haven, Conn.: Yale University Press, 1977.

Cavell, Stanley. *The Claim of Reason: Wittgenstein, Scepticism, Morality, and Tragedy.* New York: Oxford University Press, 1999.

———. *In Quest of the Ordinary: Lines of Skepticism and Romanticism.* Chicago: University of Chicago Press, 1988.

———. *Must We Mean What We Say?* Cambridge, Eng.: Cambridge University Press, 1998.

———. *The Senses of Walden: An Expanded Edition.* Chicago: University of Chicago Press, 1992.

———."Something out of the Ordinary." *Proceedings and Addresses of the American Philosophical Association* 71, no. 2 (1997): 23–37.

———. *This New Yet Unapproachable America: Lectures After Emerson After Wittgenstein.* Albuquerque, N.M.: Living Batch, 1989.

Chappell, V. C., ed. *Ordinary Language: Essays in Philosophical Method.* Contemporary Perspectives in Philosophy Series. Englewood Cliffs, N.J.: Prentice-Hall, 1964.

Chatman, Seymour. *Story and Discourse: Narrative Structure in Fiction and Film.* Ithaca, N.Y.: Cornell University Press, 1980.

Ciechanowski, Jan. *The Warsaw Rising of 1944.* London: Cambridge University Press, 1974.

Cleto, Fabio. *Camp: Queer Aesthetics and the Performing Subject: A Reader.* Ann Arbor: University of Michigan Press, 1999.

Cockburn, David, ed. *Human Beings.* Cambridge, Eng.: Cambridge University Press, 1991.

Cohn, Dorrit. *Transparent Minds: Narrative Modes for Presenting Consciousness in Fiction.* Princeton, N.J.: Princeton University Press, 1983.

Critchley, Stanley. *The Ethics of Deconstruction: Derrida and Levinas.* Edinburgh: Edinburgh University Press, 1992.

———. *Very Little . . . Almost Nothing: Death, Philosophy, Literature.* London: Routledge, 1997.

Cruz-Malave, Arnaldo, and Martin F. Manalansan IV. *Queer Globalizations.* New York: New York University Press, 2002.

Cudak, Romuald. *Czytając Białoszewskiego.* Katowice: "Śląsk," 1999.

Culbertson, Roberta. "Embodied Memory, Transcendence, and Telling: Recounting Trauma, Re-Establishing the Self." *New Literary History* 26 (1995): 169–95.

Culler, Jonathan. *Framing the Sign: Criticism and Its Institutions.* Oxford: Basil Blackwell, 1988.

———. *The Pursuit of Signs: Semiotics, Literature, Deconstruction.* London: Routledge and Kegan Paul, 1981.

Czapliński, Przemysław. *Wzniosłe tęsknoty: Nostalgie w prozie lat dziewięćdziesiątych.* Cracow: Wydawnictwo Literackie, 2001.

Czapliński, Przemysław, and Piotr Śliwiński. *Literatura polska 1976–1998: Przewodnik po prozie i poezji.* Cracow: Wydawnictwo Literackie, 1999.

Czarnecka, Ewa [Renata Gorczyńska]. *Podróżny świata: Rozmowy z Czesławem Miłoszem: Komentarze.* Cracow: Wydawnictwo Literackie, 1992.

Czermińska, Małgorzata. *Autobiograficzny Trójkąt: Świadectwo, wyznanie i wyzwanie.* Cracow: Universitas, 2000.

———. "Opowiedzieć powstanie, opowiedzieć zniszczenie: O *Pamiętniku* Mirona Białoszewskiego." In *Literatura wobec wojny i okupacji,* ed. Michał Głowiński and Janusz Sławiński, 269–90. Wrocław: Zakład Narodowy Imienia Ossolińskich, 1976.

Dallery, Arleen B., and Charles E. Scott, eds. *The Question of the Other: Essays in Contemporary Continental Philosophy.* Selected Studies in Phenomenology and Existential Philosophy 15. Albany: State University of New York Press, 1989.

Dan-Bruzda, Stanisław. "*Obroty rzeczy* Mirona Białoszewskiego." *Pamiętnik Literacki* 4 (1961): 468.

Davies, Norman. *Rising '44: The Battle for Warsaw.* London: Macmillan, 2003.

Dąbrowska, Maria. *Szkice o Conradzie.* Warsaw: Czytelnik, 1974.

Debord, Guy. *The Society of the Spectacle.* New York: Zone Books, 1994.

de Certeau, Michel. *The Practice of Everyday Life.* Trans. Steven Rendell. Berkeley: University of California Press, 1988.

de Man, Paul. *Aesthetic Ideology.* Ed. Andrzej Warminski. Theory and History of Literature 65. Minneapolis: University of Minnesota Press, 1996.

———. *Allegories of Reading: Figural Language in Rousseau, Nietzsche, Rilke, and Proust.* New Haven, Conn.: Yale University Press, 1979.

Derrida, Jacques. *Adieu to Emmanuel Levinas.* Trans. Pascale-Anne Brault and Michael Naas. Stanford, Calif.: Stanford University Press, 1999.

———. *The Ear of the Other: Otobiography, Transference, Translation.* Trans. Peggy Kamuf. Ed. Christie McDonald. Lincoln: University of Nebraska Press, 1988.

———. *Speech and Phenomena and Other Essays on Husserl's Theory of Signs.* 1973. Trans. David B. Allison. Evanston, Ill.: Northwestern University Press, 1989.

———. *The Truth in Painting.* Trans. Geoff Bennington and Ian McLeod. Chicago: University of Chicago Press, 1987.

———. *Writing and Difference.* Trans. Alan Bass. Chicago: University of Chicago Press, 1978.

Dryer, Richard. "Believing in Fairies: The Author and the Homosexual." In *Inside/Out: Lesbian Theories, Gay Theories,* ed. Diana Fuss. New York: Routledge, 1991.

———. *The Culture of Queers.* New York: Routledge, 2001.

Dunin-Wąsowicz, Paweł, Jarosław Klejnocki, and Krzysztof Varga, eds. *Macie swoich poetów: Liryka polska urodzona po 1960r., wypisy*. Warsaw: Lampa i Iskra Boża, 1997.

Dybciak, Krzysztof. "Filozofia 'małoznaczącości.'" Review of *Rozkurz*, by Miron Białoszewski. *Pismo* 4 (1981): 121–25.

Edensor, Tim. *National Identitity, Popular Culture and Everyday Life*. Oxford: Berg, 2002.

Erickson, Kai. "Notes on Trauma and Community." In *Trauma: Explorations in Memory*, ed. Cathy Caruth, 183–200. Baltimore: Johns Hopkins University Press, 1995.

Fazan, Jarosław. *Ale ja nie Bóg: Kontemplacja i teatr w dziele Mirona Białoszewskiego*. Cracow: Universitas, 1998.

Felman, Shoshana. *Literature and Psychoanalysis: The Question of Reading, Otherwise*. Baltimore: Johns Hopkins University Press, 1982.

———. "On Reading Poetry: Reflections on the Limits and Possibilities of Psychoanalytical Approaches." In *The Purloined Letter: Lacan, Derrida and Psychoanalytic Reading*, ed. John P. Muller and William J. Richardson, 133–56. Baltimore: Johns Hopkins University Press, 1988

Felman, Shoshana, and Dori Laub. *Testimony: Crises of Witnessing in Literature, Psychoanalysis, and History*. New York: Routledge, 1992.

Ficowski, Jerzy. "Trafunek zaściankowy." *Nowa Kultura* 10 (1959).

Fink, Bruce. *The Lacanian Subject: Between Language and Jouissance*. Princeton, N.J.: Princeton University Press, 1995.

Foster, Hal. *The Return of the Real: Avant-Garde at the End of the Century*. Cambridge, Mass.: MIT Press, 1996.

Foucault, Michel. *Discipline and Punish: The Birth of the Prison*. Trans. Alan Sheridan. New York: Vintage, 1979.

———. *Language, Counter-Memory, Practice: Selected Essays and Interviews*. Ed. Donald F. Bouchard. Trans. Donald F. Bouchard and Sherry Simon. Ithaca, N.Y.: Cornell University Press, 1977.

———. *The History of Sexuality*. Trans. Robert Hurley. New York: Pantheon Books, 1978.

Freud, Sigmund. *The Complete Psychological Works of Sigmund Freud*. Trans. and ed. James Strachey. New York: Vintage, 2001.

Friedlander, Saul. "Trauma, Transference and 'Working Through.'" *History and Memory* 4 (1992): 39–55.

Fuss, Diana, ed. *Inside/Out: Lesbian Theories, Gay Theories*. New York: Routledge, 1991.

Gadamer, Hans-Georg. "The Hermeneutics of Suspicion." In *Hermeneutics: Questions and Prospects*, ed. Gary Shapiro and Alan Sica. Amherst: University of Massachusetts Press, 1984.

———. *Truth and Method*. 2nd ed. Trans. Joel Weinsheimer and Donald G. Marshall. New York: Crossroad, 1989.

Gal, Susan. "A Semiotics of the Public/Private Distinction." *Differences: A Journal of Feminist Cultural Studies* 13, no. 1 (2002): 77–95.

Gallagher, Catherine, and Stephen Greenblatt. *Practicing New Historicism*. Chicago: University of Chicago Press, 2000.

Garwolińska-Błaszczykowa, Krystyna. "Między Dworkową a Widok." In *Miron: Wspomnienia o poecie,* ed. Hanna Kirchner, 121–27. Warsaw: Tenten, 1996.

Gasché, Rodolphe. "Postmodernism and Rationality." *Journal of Philosophy* 74 (1988): 528–38.

Gasset, José Ortega y. *The Dehumanization of Art and Other Essays on Art, Culture, and Literature.* 1948. Princeton, N.J.: Princeton University Press, 1968.

Gebauer, Gunter, and Christoph Wulf. *Mimesis: Culture, Art, Society.* Trans. Don Reneau. Berkeley: University of California Press, 1995.

Gibbs, Robert. *Why Ethics? Signs of Responsibilities.* Princeton, N.J.: Princeton University Press, 2000.

Gleń, Adrian. *W tej latarni: Pózna twórczość Mirona Białoszewskiego w perspektywie hermeneutycznej.* Opole: Uniwersytet Opolski, 2004.

Głowiński, Michał. *Kręgi obcości: Opowieść autobiograficzna.* Cracow: Wydawnictwo Literackie, 2010.

———. "Małe narracje M. Białoszewskiego." In *Gry powieściowe: Szkice z teorii i historii form narracyjnych.* Warsaw: Państwowy Instytut Wydawniczy, 1973.

———. "Niezwykłe zwykłe." Interview with Janusz Majcherek. *Teatr* 5 (1993): 5–7.

———. *Nowomowa po polsku.* Warsaw: PEN, 1991.

Głowiński, Michał, and Zdzisław Łapiński, eds. *Pisanie Białoszewskiego.* Warsaw: Instytut Badań Literackich, 1993.

Głowiński, Michał, and Janusz Sławiński, eds. *Literatura wobec wojny i okupacji.* Z dziejów form artystycznych w literaturze polskiej 43. Wrocław: Zakład Narodowy Imienia Ossolińskich, 1976.

Goffman, Erving. *The Presentation of Self in Everyday Life.* 1959. London: Penguin Books, 1990.

Gołąb, Mariusz. *Język i rzeczywistość w twórczości Białoszewskiego.* Łódź: Wydawnictwo Uniwersytetu Łódzkiego, 2001.

Goodman, Nelson. *Languages of Art: An Approach to a Theory of Symbols.* Indianapolis, Ind.: Hackett, 1976.

———. *Ways of Worldmaking.* Indianapolis, Ind.: Hackett, 1978.

Gorgol, Tadeusz. "Homoseksualizm a opinia." *Życie literackie* 18 (1974).

Graff, Agnieszka. *Rykoszetem: Rzecz o płci, seksualności i narodzie.* Warsaw: WAB, 2008.

Halbwachs, Maurice. *The Collective Memory.* New York: Harper and Row, 1980.

Halliday, Michael. *An Introduction to Functional Grammar.* 2nd ed. London: E. Arnold, 1994.

Halperin, David. *How to Do the History of Homosexuality.* Chicago: University of Chicago Press, 2002.

Handelman, Susan A. *Fragments of Redemption: Jewish Thought and Literary Theory in Benjamin, Scholem, and Levinas.* Jewish Literature and Culture. Bloomington: Indiana University Press, 1991.

Hanson, Joanna K. M. *The Civilian Population and the Warsaw Uprising of 1944.* Cambridge, Eng.: Cambridge University Press, 1982.

Hartman, Geoffrey, ed. *Holocaust Remembrance: The Shapes of Memory.* Cambridge, Mass.: Blackwell, 1994.

Hassan, Ihab. *The Dismemberment of Orpheus: Toward a Postmodern Literature.* New York: Oxford University Press, 1971.

Hauerwas, Stanley, and Alasdair MacIntyre. *Revisions: Changing Perspectives in Moral Philosophy.* Notre Dame, Ind.: University of Notre Dame Press, 1983.

Heidegger, Martin. *Being and Time.* Trans. John Macquarrie and Edward Robinson. New York: Harper and Row, 1975.

———. *Introduction to Metaphysics.* Trans. Ralph Manheim. Garden City, N.Y.: Doubleday, 1961.

———. *On the Way to Language.* Trans. Peter Hertz. New York: Harper and Row, 1971.

———. *Poetry, Language, Thought.* Trans. Albert Hofstadter. New York: Harper and Row, 1971.

Herman, Judith. *Trauma and Recovery.* New York: Basic Books, 1992.

Highmore, Ben. *Everyday Life and Cultural Theory: An Introduction.* London: Routledge, 2002.

Honet, Roman, and Mariusz Czyżowski. *Antologia nowej poezji polskiej 1990–1999.* Cracow: Wydawnictwo Zielona Sowa, 2001.

Iwasiów, Inga. "Alexis, czyli gdzie jest kobiecość." *Pogranicza* 1 (2005): 27–31.

Jakobson, Roman, and Morris Halle. *Fundamentals of Language.* The Hague: Martinus Nijhoff, 1956.

Jameson, Frederic. *The Prison-House of Language: A Critical Account of Structuralism and Russian Formalism.* Princeton, N.J.: Princeton University Press, 1972.

Janion, Maria. *Odnawianie znaczeń.* Cracow: Wydawnictwo Literackie, 1980.

———. *Płacz generała: Eseje o wojnie.* Warsaw: Wydawnictwo Sic!, 1998.

———. *Projekt krytyki fantazmatycznej.* Warsaw: Wydawnictwo PEN, 1991.

———. "Wojna i forma." In *Literatura wobec wojny i okupacji,* ed. Michał Głowiński and Janusz Sławiński, 187–267. Wrocław: Zakład Narodowy Imienia Ossolińskich, 1976.

Jarosiński, Zbigniew. *Literatura lat 1945–1975.* Mała Historia Literatury Polskiej. Warsaw: Wydawnictwo Naukowe PWN, 1997.

———. "Powstanie warszawskie w powojennej literaturze pięknej." In *Powstanie warszawskie w historiografii i literaturze 1944–1994,* ed. Zygmunt Mańkowski and Jerzy Święch, 195–208. Lublin: Wydawnictwo Uniwersytetu Marii Curii-Skłodowskiej, 1996.

Jarzębowski, Zbigniew. "Piszę tę ciotowską księgę . . ." *Pogranicza* 1 (2005): 19–22.

Jaworski, Adam. *The Power of Silence: Social and Pragmatic Perspectives.* Newbury Park, Calif.: Sage, 1993.

Jay, Martin. *Downcast Eyes: The Denigration of Vision in Twentieth-Century French Thought.* Berkeley: University of California Press, 1994.

Jefferson, Anne. *Biography and the Question of Literature in France.* Oxford: Oxford University Press, 2007.

Jonas, Hans. *The Phenomenon of Life: Toward a Philosophical Biology.* 1966. Chicago: University of Chicago Press, 1982.

Jost, Walter, and Michael Hyde. *Rhetoric and Hermeneutics in Our Time: A Reader.* New Haven, Conn.: Yale University Press, 1997.

Kanabrodzki, Mateusz. *Kapłan i fryzjer: Żywioł materialno-cielesny w utworach Georga Buchnera, Witolda Gombrowicza, Mirona Białoszewskiego, Helmuta Kajzera.* Gdańsk: Słowo/obraz terytoria, 2004.

Kant, Immanuel. *Critique of Judgement.* Trans. J. H. Bernard. New York: Hafner, 1953.

Kaplan, Alice, and Kristin Ross. *Everyday Life.* Yale French Studies 73. New Haven, Conn.: Yale University Press, 1987.

Kermode, Frank. *The Sense of an Ending: Studies in the Theory of Fiction.* 1966. Oxford: Oxford University Press, 2000.

Kirchner, Hanna, ed. *Miron: Wspomnienia o poecie.* Warsaw: Tenten, 1996.

———. "O Mironie, o Ludwiku." In *Miron: Wspomnienia o poecie,* ed. Kirchner, 275–303.

Kochanowski, Jacek. *Fantazmat zróżnicowany: Socjologiczne studium przemian tożsamości gejów.* Cracow: Universitas, 2004.

Kopciński, Jacek. *Gramatyka i mistyka: Wprowadzenie w teatralną osobność Mirona Białoszewskiego.* Warsaw: Instytut Badań Literackich, 1997.

———. "Stare klabzdry na wojnie." *Teksty drugie* 1 (1995).

———. "Teatr z makaty." In *Pisanie Białoszewskiego,* ed. Michał Głowiński and Zdzisław Łapiński, 251. Warsaw: Instytut Badań Literackich, 1993.

Krall, Hanna. *Subtenant: To Outwit God.* Evanston, Ill.: Northwestern University Press, 1992.

Kristeva, Julia. *Powers of Horror: An Essay on Abjection.* Trans. Leon S. Roudiez. New York: Columbia University Press, 1982.

Krupiński, Piotr. "Legenda romantyczna i cioty." *Pogranicza* 1 (2005): 22–27.

———. "Within the Microcosm of 'The Talking Cure.'" In *Interpreting Lacan,* trans. Thomas Gora and Margaret Wailer. New Haven, Conn.: Yale University Press, 1983.

Kulpa, Robert, and Joanna Mizielińska, eds. *De-Centering Western Sexualities: Central and Eastern European Perspectives*. Burlington, Vt.: Ashgate, 2011.

Kurpios, Paweł. "Poszukiwani, poszukiwane: Geje i lesbijki a rzeczywistość PRL." www.dk.uni.wroc.pl/texty/prl_02.pdf.

Kwiatkowski, Jerzy. "Abulia i liturgia." In *Klucze do wyobraźni: Szkice o poetach współczesnych.* Warsaw: Państwowy Instytut Wydawniczy, 1964.

Lacan, Jacques. *Écrits: A Selection.* Trans. Alan Sheridan. New York: W.W. Norton, 1977.

———. *The Ethics of Psychoanalysis.* Trans. D. Porter. New York: Norton, 1992.

———. *The Four Fundamental Concepts of Psycho-Analysis.* Ed. Jacques-Alain Miller. Trans. Alan Sheridan. London: Hogarth, 1977.

LaCapra, Dominick. *History and Memory After Auschwitz.* Ithaca, N.Y.: Cornell University Press, 1998.

———. *History in Transit: Experience, Identity, Critical Theory.* Ithaca, N.Y.: Cornell University Press, 2004.

———. *Representing the Holocaust: History, Theory, Trauma.* Ithaca, N.Y.: Cornell University Press, 1996.

———. *Writing History, Writing Trauma.* Baltimore: Johns Hopkins University Press, 2001.

Lacoue-Labarthe, Philippe, and Jean-Luc Nancy. *The Literary Absolute: The Theory of Literature in German Romanticism.* Trans. Philip Barnard and Cheryl Lester. Albany: State University of New York Press, 1988.

Lamarque, Peter, and Stein Haugom Olsen. *Truth, Fiction, and Literature: A Philosophical Perspective.* Oxford: Clarendon, 1996.

Langer, Lawrence L., ed. *Art from the Ashes: A Holocaust Anthology.* Oxford: Oxford University Press, 1995.

———. *Holocaust Testimonies: The Ruins of Memory.* New Haven, Conn.: Yale University Press, 1991.

Langer, Susan. *Feeling and Form.* New York: Scribner, 1953.

Laub, Dori, and Nanette C. Auerhahn. "Failed Empathy—A Central Theme in the Survivor's Holocaust Experience." *Psychoanalytic Psychology* 6 (1989): 377–400.

Lefebvre, Henri. *Critique of Everyday Life.* Trans. John Moore. London: Verso, 2008.

———. "The Everyday and Everydayness." In *Everyday Life,* ed. Alice Kaplan and Kristin Ross, 7–12. New Haven, Conn.: Yale University Press, 1987.

———. *Everyday Life in the Modern World.* Trans. Sacha Rabinovitch. New Brunswick: Transaction, 1999.

Lejeune, Philippe. *On Autobiography.* Trans. Katherine Leary. Minneapolis: University of Minnesota Press, 1989.

Levi, Primo. "Shame." In *Art from the Ashes: A Holocaust Anthology*, ed. Lawrence L. Langer, 108–20. Oxford: Oxford University Press, 1995.

Levin, David M. *The Opening of Vision: Nihilism and the Postmodern Situation*. New York: Routledge, 1988.

Levinas, Emmanuel. *Collected Philosophical Papers*. Trans. Alphonso Lingis. Pittsburgh: Duquesne University Press, 1998.

———. *Existence and Existents*. Trans. Alphonso Lingis. The Hague: Martinus Nijhoff, 1978.

———. *Otherwise Than Being, or Beyond Essence*. Trans. Alphonso Lingis. Pittsburgh: Duquesne University Press, 1998.

———. *Proper Names*. Trans. Michael B. Smith. Stanford, Calif.: Stanford University Press, 1996.

———. *Totality and Infinity*. Trans. Alphonso Lingis. Pittsburgh: Duquesne University Press, 1964.

Levine, Michael. *Writing Through Repression: Literature, Censorship, Psychoanalysis*. Baltimore: Johns Hopkins University Press, 1994.

Leys, Ruth. *Trauma: A Genealogy*. Chicago: University of Chicago Press, 2000.

Lipski, Jan Józef. *Szkice o poezji*. Paris: Instytut Literacki, 1987.

Lobeck, Anne. *Ellipses: Functional Heads, Licensing*. Oxford: Oxford University Press, 1995.

Lotman, Jurij. *The Structure of the Artistic Text*. Trans. Gail Lenhoff and Ronald Vroon. Michigan Slavic Contributions 7. Ann Arbor: University of Michigan Press, 1977.

———. *Universe of the Mind: A Semiotic Theory of Culture*. Trans. Ann Shukman. Bloomington: Indiana University Press, 1990.

Łubieński, Tomasz. *Ani tryumf ani zgon: Szkice o powstaniu warszawskim*. Warsaw: Wydawnictwo Nowy Świat, 2004.

———. *Bić się czy nie bić? O polskich powstaniach*. 1978. Warsaw: Świat Książki, 1997.

Łukasiewicz, Jacek. "Białoszewski." In Łukasiewicz, *Rytm, czyli powinność: Szkice o książkach i ludziach po roku 1980*. Wrocław: Towarzystwo Przyjaciół Polonistyki Wrocławskej, 1993.

Lukaszuk-Piekara, Małgorzata. *"Niby-ja": O poezji Białoszewskiego*. Lublin: Wydawnictwo Katolickiego Uniwersytetu Lubelskiego, 1997.

Madajczyk, Czesław, ed. *Ludność cywilna w powstaniu warszawskim*. Warsaw: Państwowy Instytut Wydawniczy, 1974.

Madejski, Jerzy. "Żorżeta, przegięcie, literatura." *Pogranicza* 1 (2005): 7–11.

Magliola, Robert R. *Phenomenology in Literature: An Introduction*. West Lafayette, Ind.: Purdue University Press, 1977.

Majcherek, Janusz. "Widok z mostu na M.B. (z Królikiem w tle)." *Teatr* 5 (1993): 19–20.

Mandelker, Amy, ed. *Bakhtin in Contexts: Across the Disciplines.* Evanston, Ill.: Northwestern University Press, 1995.

Mańkowski, Zygmunt, and Jerzy Święch, eds. *Powstanie warszawskie w historiografii i literaturze 1944–1994.* Lublin: Wydawnictwo Marii Curie-Skłodowskiej, 1996.

Marcus, Greil. *Lipstick Traces: A Secret History of the Twentieth Century.* Cambridge, Mass.: Harvard University Press, 1989.

Medhurst, Andy. "Camp." In *Lesbian and Gay Studies: A Critical Introduction,* ed. Andy Medhurst and Sally R. Munt. London: Cassell, 1997.

Merleau-Ponty, Maurice. *The Visible and the Invisible.* Trans. Alphonso Lingis. Ed. Claude Lefort. Evanston, Ill.: Northwestern University Press, 1968.

Meyer, Moe. *The Politics and Poetics of Camp.* New York: Routledge, 1993.

Miłosz, Czesław. "Postscriptum." *Teksty drugie* 5/6 (1990): 163–76.

———. "Przeciw poezji niezrozumiałej." *Teksty drugie* 5/6 (1990): 151–62.

———. *The Witness of Poetry.* Cambridge, Mass.: Harvard University Press, 1983.

Mitosek, Zofia. *Mimesis: Zjawisko i problem.* Warsaw: Wydawnictwo Naukowe PWN, 1997.

Mizielińska, Joanna. *Ciało, płeć, seksualność: Od feminizmu do teorii queer.* Cracow: Universitas, 2006.

Moran, Joe. *Reading the Everyday.* London: Routledge, 2005.

Morson, Gary Saul. *Narrative and Freedom: The Shadows of Time.* New Haven, Conn.: Yale University Press, 1994.

Morson, Gary Saul, and Caryl Emerson. *Mikhail Bakhtin: Creation of a Prosaics.* Stanford, Calif.: Stanford University Press, 1990.

Mosse, George. *Nationalism and Sexuality: Respectability and Abnormal Sexuality in Modern Europe.* New York: H. Fertig, 1985.

Muller, John P., and William J. Richardson, eds. *The Purloined Poe: Lacan, Derrida & Psychoanalytic Reading.* Baltimore: Johns Hopkins University Press, 1988.

Murdoch, Iris. "Against Dryness: A Polemical Sketch." In *Revisions: Changing Perspectives in Moral Philosophy,* ed. Stanley Hauerwas and Alasdair MacIntyre, 43–49. Notre Dame, Ind.: University of Notre Dame Press, 1983.

Nagel, Thomas. *The View from Nowhere.* Oxford: Oxford University Press, 1986.

Nichols, Ashton. *The Poetics of Epiphany: Nineteenth-Century Origins of the Modern Literary Moment.* Tuscaloosa: University of Alabama Press, 1987.

Niżyńska, Joanna. "'Znaleziony list' Mirona Białoszewskiego: Próba lektury 'małych narracji' w perspektywie teorii queer." In *(Nie)obecność: Pominięcia i przemilczenia w narracjach XX wieku,* ed. Hanna Gosk and Bożena Karwowska, 272–91. Warsaw: Dom Wydawniczy Elipsa, 2008.

Nofikow, Ewa. *Metafizyczne gospodarstwo Mirona.* Białystok: Towarzystwo im. Adama Mickiewicza, 2003.

Nussbaum, Martha C. *The Fragility of Goodness: Love and Ethics in Greek Tragedy and Philosophy.* Cambridge, Eng.: Cambridge University Press, 1986.

———. *Love's Knowledge: Essays on Philosophy and Literature.* New York: Oxford University Press, 1990.

Nycz, Ryszard. *Język modernizmu: Prolegomena historycznoliterackie.* Wrocław: Fundacja na Rzecz Nauki Polskiej, 1997.

———. *Literatura jako trop rzeczywistości: Poetyka epifanii w nowoczesnej literaturze polskiej.* Cracow: Universitas, 2001.

———. *Sylwy współczesne.* Cracow: Universitas, 1996.

———. "Szare eminencje zachwytu: Miejsce epifanii w poetyce Mirona Białoszewskiego." In *Pisanie Białoszewskiego,* ed. Michał Głowiński and Zdzisław Łapiński, 179–91. Warsaw: Instytut Badań Literackich, 1993.

Ochs, Elinor, and Lisa Capps. *Living Narrative: Creating Lives in Everyday Storytelling.* Cambridge, Mass.: Harvard University Press, 2001.

Ong, Walter J. *Orality and Literacy: The Technologizing of the Word.* 1982. London: Routledge, 2002.

Opinie o homoseksualizmie: Tolerancja czy potępienie? Komunikat z badań CBOS. Warsaw, 1988.

Orska, Joanna, "Życie jako happening: O artystyczności 'tajnego dziennika." In *Białoszewski przed dziennikiem,* by Wojciech Browarny and Adam Poprawa, 97–117. Cracow: Universitas, 2010.

Osęka, Andrzej. "Nie wydrukują mi żadnego wiersza." In *Miron: Wspomnienia o poecie,* ed. Hanna Kirchner, 137–39. Warsaw: Tenten, 1996.

Patočka, Jan. *Heretical Essays in the Philosophy of History.* Trans. Erazim Kohák. Ed. James Dodd. Chicago: Open Court, 1996.

Pawelec, Dariusz. "Wojna, stan wojenny, ironia, kabaret, Białoszewski . . ." In *Znajomym gościncem: Prace ofiarowane Ireneuszowi Opackiemu,* by Tadeusz Sławek. Katowice: Universytet Śląski, 1993.

Pecora, Vincent P. *Self and Form in Modern Narrative.* Baltimore: Johns Hopkins University Press, 1989.

Perloff, Marjorie. "Poetry and the Common Life." *Sulfur* 12 (1984): 160–64.

———. *Radical Artifice: Writing Poetry in the Age of Media.* Chicago: University of Chicago Press, 1991.

———. *Wittgenstein's Ladder: Poetic Language and the Strangeness of the Ordinary.* Chicago: University of Chicago Press, 1990.

Pietkiewicz, Barbara. "Gorzki fiolet." *Polityka* 8 (1981).

Pilichowski, Czesław. "Grabież i niszczenie Warszawy." In *Powstanie warszawskie: Sesja w 40 rocznicę.* Warsaw: Główna Komisja Badania Zbrodni Hitlerowskich w Polsce, 1987.

Płachecki, Marian. "Obie barwy samotności." Review of *Przepowiadanie sobie,* by Miron Białoszewski. *Twórczość* 9 (1981): 114–19.

Płonowska-Ziarek, Ewa, ed. *Gombrowicz's Grimaces: Modernism, Gender, Nationality.* Albany: State University of New York Press, 1998.

Poezja 2 (1976), special edition.

Poezja 12 (1985), special edition.

Powstanie warszawskie w literaturze pięknej: Bibliografia selektywna. Leszno: Wojewódzka Biblioteka Publiczna, 1994.

Powstanie warszawskie z perspektywy półwiecza: Studia i materiały z sesji naukowej na Zamku Królewskim w Warszawie, 14–15 czerwca 1994. Warsaw: Polska Akademia Nauk, 1995.

Pratt, Mary Louise. *Towards a Speech Act Theory of Literary Discourse.* Bloomington: Indiana University Press, 1977.

Prószyński, Stanisław. "Poezja, teatr, muzyka." In *Miron: Wspomnienia o poecie*, ed. Hanna Kirchner, 21–59. Warsaw: Tenten, 1996.

Przyboś, Julian. "Nowy poeta." In *Linia i gwar: Szkice.* Cracow: Wydawnictwo Literackie, 1959.

———. "Z powodu *Było i było* Mirona Białoszewskiego." *Poezja* 3 (1966).

Putnam, Hilary. "Literature, Science and Reflection." *New Literary History* 7 (1975–76).

———. "Taking Rules Seriously—A Response to Martha Nussbaum." *New Literary History* 15 (1983).

Rapaport, Herman. *Between the Sign and the Gaze.* Ithaca, N.Y.: Cornell University Press, 1994.

Reinfeld, Linda. *Language Poetry: Writing as Rescue.* Baton Rouge: Louisiana State University Press, 1992.

Ricoeur, Paul. *The Conflict of Interpretations: Essays in Hermeneutics.* Ed. Don Ihde. Evanston, Ill.: Northwestern University Press, 1974

———. *Freud and Philosophy: An Essay on Interpretation.* Trans. Denis Savage. New Haven, Conn.: Yale University Press, 1970.

———. *Hermeneutics and the Human Sciences.* Trans. John B. Thompson. Cambridge, Eng.: Cambridge University Press, 1981.

———. *Interpretation Theory: Discourse and the Surplus of Meaning.* Fort Worth: Texas Christian University Press, 1976.

———. *Oneself as Another.* Trans. Kathleen Blamey. Chicago: University of Chicago Press, 1992.

———. *Time and Narrative.* Trans. Kathleen Blamey and David Pellauer. Chicago: University of Chicago Press, 1988.

Rijksbaron, Albert. *Aristotle, Verb Meaning and Functional Grammar: Towards a New Typology of States of Affairs. With an Appendix on Aristotle's Distinction Between Kinesis and Energeia.* Amsterdam: J.C. Gieben, 1989.

Ritz, German. *Nić w labiryncie pożądania: Gender i płeć w literaturze polskiej od romantyzmu do postmodernizmu.* Trans. Bronisław Drąg, Andrzej Kopacki, and Małgorzata Łukasiewicz. Warsaw: Wiedza Powszechna, 2002.

Rosiek, Stanisław. "Pamiętnik z półgrobu." In *Pisanie Białoszewskiego,* ed. Michał Głowiński and Zdzisław Łapiński, 130–44. Warsaw: Instytut Badań Literackich, 1993.

Rothberg, Michael. *Traumatic Realism: The Demands of Holocaust Representation.* Minneapolis: University of Minnesota Press, 2000.

Rutkowski, Krzysztof. *Ani było ani jest.* Warsaw: Czytelnik, 1984.

———. *Przeciw (w) literaturze: Esej o "poezji czynnej" Mirona Białoszewskiego i Edwarda Stachury.* Bydgosz: Pomorze, 1987.

———. "Wielogłosowość wypowiedzi Białoszewskiego." *Twórczość* 9 (1983): 39–55.

Rzewuska, Elżbieta. "Panie profesor u Białoszewskiego: Listy do Eumenid." In *Lustra historii: Rozprawy i eseje ofiarowane Profesor Marii Żmigrodzkiej z okazji pięćdziesięciolecia pracy naukowej,* ed. Maria Kalinowska and Elżbieta Kiślak, 207–13. Warsaw: Instytut Badań Literackich, 1998.

Sandauer, Artur. *Białoszewski.* Trans. Adam Czerniawski. Warsaw: Authors Agency and "Czytelnik," 1979.

———. "Poezja rupieci: Rzecz o M. Białoszewskim." In *Poeci czterech pokoleń.* Cracow: Wydawnictwo Literackie, 1977.

———. *Samobójstwo Mitrydatesa.* Warsaw: Czytelnik, 1968.

Sandoval, Chela. *Methodology of the Oppressed.* Minneapolis: University of Minnesota Press, 2000.

Santner, Eric. *On the Psychotheology of Everyday Life: Reflections on Freud and Rosenzweig.* Chicago: University of Chicago Press, 2001.

———. *Stranded Objects: Mourning, Memory and Film in Postwar Germany.* Ithaca, N.Y.: Cornell University Press, 1990.

Schmidtz, David. *Rational Choice and Moral Agency.* Princeton, N.J.: Princeton University Press, 1995.

Schor, Naomi, and Elizabeth Weed. *Feminism Meets Queer Theory.* Bloomington: Indiana University Press, 1997.

Schweder, Richard A. "Anthropology's Romantic Rebellion Against the Enlightenment, or, There's More to Thinking Than Reason and Evidence." In *Culture Theory: Essays on Mind, Self, and Emotion,* ed. Richard A. Schweder et al. Cambridge, Eng.: Cambridge University Press, 1984.

Ścibor-Rylski, Aleksander. *Pierścionek z końskiego włosia.* Warsaw: Fundacja Kultura, 1991.

Scott, Joan W. "Experience." In *Feminists Theorize the Political,* ed. Judith Butler and Joan W. Scott, 22–40. New York: Routledge, 1992.

Sedgwick, Eve Kosofsky. *Epistemology of the Closet.* Berkeley: University of California Press, 1990.

Shapiro, Gary, and Alan Sica. *Hermeneutics: Questions and Prospects.* Amherst: University of Massachusetts Press, 1984.

Shetley, Vernon. *After the Death of Poetry: Poet and Audience in Contemporary America.* Durham, N.C.: Duke University Press, 1993.

Silverman, Kaja. *Male Subjectivity at the Margins.* New York: Routledge, 1992.

Skrendo, Andrzej. "Miejsce ujawnienia." *Pogranicza* 1 (2005): 11–16.

Sławiński, Janusz. "Białoszewski: Sukces wycofania się." Introduction to *Miron Białoszewski, Wiersze.* Warsaw: Państwowy Instytut Wydawniczy, 1976.

———. "Miron Białoszewski: 'Ballada od rymu.'" In *Liryka polska: Interpretacje,* ed. Jan Prokop and Janusz Sławiński, 498–511. Cracow: Wydawnictwo Literackie, 1971.

———. "Miron Białoszewski 'Leżenia.'" In *Genologia polska,* ed. Ewa Miodońska-Brooks, Adam Kulawik, and Marian Tatara, 523–35. Warsaw: Państwowe Wydawnictwo Naukowe: 1983.

———. *Teksty i teksty.* Warsaw: Wydawnictwo PEN, 1990.

Śmieja, Wojciech. "Była, jest, będzie? Polska literatura homoseksualna i gejowska. Próba zarysu." *Pogranicza* 1 (2005): 31–42.

Śnieżko, Dariusz. "*Lubiewo* czyli projekt eposu pedalskiego." *Pogranicza* 1 (2005): 16–19.

Sobolczyk, Piotr. "Hermetyczne pornografie Białoszewskiego." *Teksty drugie* 6 (2006): 165–81.

———. "Homobiografia: Miron Białoszewski." *Pogranicza* 6 (2008): 15–32.

Sobolewska, Anna. "Lepienie widoku z domysłu." In *Pisanie Białoszewskiego,* ed. Michał Głowiński and Zdzisław Łapiński, 114–29. Warsaw: Instytut Badań Literackich, 1993.

———. "Maksymalnie udana egzystencja: Miron Białoszewski." In *Sporne postaci polskiej literatury współczesnej,* ed. Alina Brodzka, 103–33. Warsaw: Instytut Badań Literackich, 1994.

———. *Maksymalnie udana egzystencja: Szkice o życiu i twórczości Mirona Białoszewskiego.* Warsaw: Instytut Badań Literackich, 1997.

———. *Mistyka dnia powszedniego.* Warszawa: Open, 1992.

Sobolewska, Anna, and Tadeusz Sobolewski. Interview with Janusz Majcherek. "Nie mogę kołysać się razem ze wszystkimi." *Teatr* 5 (1993): 10–14.

Sobolewski, Tadeusz. *Dziecko Peerelu: Esej, dziennik.* Warsaw: Wydawnictwo Sic!, 2000.

———. "Interview." *Gazeta Wyborcza.* March 21, 2002, 10.

———. "Mirona Białoszewskiego 'Listy do Eumenid.'" *Teksty drugie* 6 (1991): 137–42.

———. "Szaman." *Odra* 9 (1984): 51–56.

———. "Zaczarowany dywan Mirona Białoszewskiego." *Tygodnik powszechny* July 18, 1993, 1, 9.

Sontag, Susan. "Notes on 'Camp.'" In *Against Interpretation and Other Essays,* 275–93. New York: Picador, 2001.

Stańczakowa, Jadwiga. *Dziennik we dwoje.* 2 vols. Warsaw: Wydawnictwo Borgis, 1992–94.

Stanley, John. "Constructing a Narrative: The History of Homosexuality in Poland." In *New Social Movements and Sexuality: Conference Papers 2004,* ed. Melinda Chateauvert. Sofia: Bilitis Resources Center, 2006.

Stefanowska, Zofia. "Białoszewskiego *Pamiętnik z powstania warszawskiego.*" *Teksty* 4 (1973).

Steiner, Jean-Francois. *Warszawa 1944.* Trans. Maria Kłyszewska. Warsaw: Wydawnictwo Krąg, 1991.

Strauss, Walter A. *Descent and Return: The Orphic Theme in Modern Literature.* Cambridge, Mass.: Harvard University Press, 1971.

Sturken, Marita. "Narratives of Recovery: Repressed Memory as Cultural Memory." In *Acts of Memory: Cultural Recall in the Present,* ed. Mieke Bal, Jonathan Crewe, and Leo Spitzer, 231–49. Hanover, N.H.: University Press of New England, 1999.

Sullivan, Nikki. *A Critical Introduction to Queer Theory.* New York: New York University Press, 2003.

Świech, Jerzy. *Literatura polska w latach II wojny światowej.* Warsaw: Wydawnictwo Naukowe PWN, 1997.

Świrek, Anna. *Z gatunkiem czy bez . . . O twórczości Mirona Białoszewskiego.* Zielona Góra: Wydawnictwo Wyższej Szkoły Pedagogicznej, 1997.

Sypniewski, Zbyszek, and Błażej Warkocki. *Homofobia po polsku.* Warsaw: Wydawnictwo Sic, 2004.

Sztompka, Piotr. *The Trauma of Post-Communism.* Cambridge, Mass.: Minda de Gunzburg Center for European Studies, Harvard University, 1999.

———. *The Space of Everyday Life.* Cracow: Judaica Foundation, 2009.

Szybist, Maciej. "Warszawskie powstanie nowego porządku." *Miesięcznik Literacki* 9 (1970): 139–41.

Tal, Kali. *Worlds of Hurt: Reading the Literatures of Trauma.* Cambridge, Eng.: Cambridge University Press, 1996.

Taranienko, Zbigniew. *Rozmowy z pisarzami.* Warsaw: Wiedza Powszechna, 1986.

Taylor, Charles. *The Ethics of Authenticity.* Cambridge, Mass.: Harvard University Press, 1991.

———. *Human Agency and Language.* 1985. Cambridge, Eng.: Cambridge University Press, 1999.

———. *Sources of the Self: The Making of Modern Identity.* Cambridge, Mass.: Harvard University Press, 1989.

Tigges, Wim, ed. *Moments of Moment: Aspects of the Literary Epiphany.* Amsterdam: Rodopi B.V., 1999.

Tolstoy, Leo. "Why Do Men Stupefy Themselves?" Trans. Aylmer Maude. In *Leo Tolstoy: Selected Essays,* 185–203. New York: Random House, 1964.

Trznadel, Jacek. *Płomień obdarzony rozumem: Poezja w poezji i poza poezją.* Warsaw: Czytelnik, 1978.

Twórczość 9 (1983), special issue.

Van Alphen, Ernst. "Symptoms of Discursivity: Experience, Memory, and Trauma." In *Acts of Memory: Cultural Recall in the Present*, ed. Mieke Bal, Jonathan Crewe, and Leo Spitzer, 24–39. Hanover, N.H.: University Press of New England, 1999.

Van der Kolk, Bessela A., and Onno Van der Hart. "The Intrusive Past: The Flexibility of Memory and the Engraving of Trauma." In *Trauma: Explorations in Memory*, ed. Cathy Caruth, 158–83. Baltimore: Johns Hopkins University Press, 1995.

Vattimo, Gianni. *The Adventure of Difference: Philosophy After Nietzsche and Heidegger.* Trans. Cyprian Blamires and Thomas Harrison. Baltimore: Johns Hopkins University Press, 1993.

———. *The End of Modernity: Nihilism and Hermeneutics in Postmodern Culture.* Trans. Jon R. Snyder. Baltimore: Johns Hopkins University Press, 1988.

Veaux, Erik. "Pamiętnik po francusku" (interview with Tadeusz Sobolewski). *Gazeta Wyborcza,* March 21, 2002, 10.

Wańkowicz, Melchior. *Ziele na kraterze.* Warsaw: Pax, 1957.

Warkocki, Błażej. *Homo niewiadomo: Polska proza wobec odmienności.* Warsaw: Wydawnictwo Sic, 2007.

Weed, Elizabeth, and Naomi Schor, eds. *Feminism Meets Queer Theory*. Bloomington: Indiana University Press, 1997.

Wilhelmi, Janusz. "Wstęp" [Preface]. *Pamiętnik z powstania warszawskiego.* By Miron Białoszewski, 5–7. Warsaw: Państwowy Instytut Wydawniczy, 1970.

Williams, Bernard. *Ethics and the Limits of Philosophy.* Cambridge, Mass.: Harvard University Press, 1985.

Winch, Peter. *Ehics and Action.* London: Routledge and Kegan Paul, 1972.

Winiecka, Elżbieta. *Białoszewski sylleptyczny.* Poznań: "Wydawnictwo Poznańskie Studia Polonistyczne," 2006.

Wiśniewski, Jerzy. *Białoszewski i muzyka.* Lódź: Wydawnictwo Uniwersytetu Lódzkiego, 2004.

Witkowski, Michał. *Lubiewo.* Cracow: Korporacja ha!art, 2005.

Wittgenstein, Ludwig. *Philosophical Investigations.* 1953. 3rd ed. Trans. G. E. M. Anscombe. Oxford: Blackwell, 2001.

Wolosky, Shira. *Language Mysticism: The Negative Way of Language in Eliot, Beckett, and Celan.* Stanford, Calif.: Stanford University Press, 1995.

Wołyński, Olgierd. "Plac Dąbrowskiego: Rozmawiał Tadeusz Sobolewski." In *Miron: Wspomnienia o poecie,* ed. Hanna Kirchner, 189–203. Warsaw: Tenten, 1996.

Wyka, Kazimierz. *Rzecz wyobraźni.* Warsaw: Państwowy Instytut Wydawniczy, 1959.

Wyschograd, Edith. *Emmanuel Levinas: The Problem of Ethical Metaphysics.* The Hague: Nijhoff, 1974.

Zagajewski, Adam. "W Warszawie jak na wsi." *Znak* 11–12 (1977): 1448–57.

Zaleski, Marek. *Formy pamięci: O przedstawianiu przeszłości w polskiej literaturze współczesnej.* Warsaw: Instytut Badań Literackich, 1996.

Zawodny, Janusz. *Nothing but Honour: The Story of the Warsaw Uprising 1944.* Stanford, Calif.: Hoover Institution, 1978.

———. *Uczestnicy i świadkowie powstania warszawskiego: wywiady.* Warsaw: Wydawnictwo Naukowe PWN, 1994.

Zaworska, Helena. "Dom." *Twórczość* 10 (1970): 98–99.

———. "Wszystko jest ciekawe." *Twórczość* 9 (1983): 56–63.

Zayath Baker, Dorothy. *Mythic Masks in Self-Reflexive Poetry: A Study of Pan and Orpheus.* Chapel Hill: University of North Carolina Press, 1986.

Ziarek, Krzysztof. "How to Write the Everyday in Eastern Europe: Miron Białoszewski's 'Minor Poetry.'" In *The Historicity of Experience: Modernity, the Avant-Garde, and the Event,* 225–62. Evanston, Ill.: Northwestern University Press, 2001.

Zielińska, Marta. "Białoszewski i zapachy." In *Lustra historii: Rozprawy i eseje ofiarowane Profesor Marii Żmigrodzkiej z okazji pięćdziesięciolecia pracy naukowej,* ed. Maria Kalinowska and Elżbieta Kiślak, 191–206. Warsaw: Instytut Badań Literackich, 1998.

———. *Warszawa—Dziwne miasto.* Warsaw: Instytut Badań Literackich, 1995.

Zieniewicz, Andrzej. *Małe iluminacje: Formy prozatorskie Mirona Białoszewskiego.* Warsaw: Państwowy Instytut Wydawniczy, 1989.

Žižek, Slavoj. *Looking Awry: An Introduction to Jacques Lacan Through Popular Culture.* 1991. Cambridge, Mass.: MIT Press, 2000.

———. *The Sublime Object of Ideology.* London: Verso, 1989.

Żukrowski, Wojciech. "Lotna." In *Z wrześniowych dni: antologia opowiadań o wojnie 1939 roku,* ed. W. Maciąg, 13–41. Poznań: Wydawnictwo Poznańskie, 1969.

———. "Mironek w powstaniu." *Nowe ksiażki* 19 (1970): 1191–94.

Index